# On Latinidad

UNIVERSITY PRESS OF FLORIDA

Florida A&M University, Tallahassee
Florida Atlantic University, Boca Raton
Florida Gulf Coast University, Ft. Myers
Florida International University, Miami
Florida State University, Tallahassee
New College of Florida, Sarasota
University of Central Florida, Orlando
University of Florida, Gainesville
University of North Florida, Jacksonville
University of South Florida, Tampa
University of West Florida, Pensacola

# On Latinidad

## U.S. Latino Literature and the Construction of Ethnicity

Marta Caminero-Santangelo

University Press of Florida
Gainesville/Tallahassee/Tampa/Boca Raton/Pensacola
Orlando/Miami/Jacksonville/Ft. Myers/Sarasota

Copyright 2007 by Marta Caminero-Santangelo
Printed in the United States of America on acid-free paper
All rights reserved

14  13  12  11  10  09     6  5  4  3  2  1

First cloth printing, 2007
First paperback printing, 2009

Library of Congress Cataloging-in-Publication Data:
Caminero-Santangelo, Marta, 1966–
On Latinidad: U.S. Latino literature and the construction of ethnicity / Marta Caminero-Santangelo.
p. cm.
Includes bibliographical references and index.
ISBN 978-0-8130-3083-8 (cloth)
ISBN 978-0-8130-3448-5 (paper)
1. American literature—Hispanic American authors—History and criticism. 2. Hispanic Americans—Ethnic identity. 3. Hispanic Americans in literature. I. Title.
PS153.H56C36  2007
810.9'868073—dc22

The University Press of Florida is the scholarly publishing agency for the State University System of Florida, comprising Florida A&M University, Florida Atlantic University, Florida Gulf Coast University, Florida International University, Florida State University, New College of Florida, University of Central Florida, University of Florida, University of North Florida, University of South Florida, and University of West Florida.

University Press of Florida
15 Northwest 15th Street
Gainesville, FL 32611-2079
www.upf.com

The author gratefully acknowledges permission to reproduce excerpts from the following sources:

From *Memory Mambo* by Achy Obejas, copyright 1996 by Achy Obejas. Used by permission of Cleis Press.

From *Bless Me, Ultima* by Rudolfo Anaya, copyright 1974 by Rudolfo Anaya. Published in hardcover and mass-market paperback by Warner Books, Inc., 1994; originally published by TQS Publications. Reprinted by permission of Susan Bergholz Literary Services, New York. All rights reserved.

From *In the Time of the Butterflies* by Julia Alvarez, copyright 1994 by Julia Alvarez. Published by Plume, an imprint of Penguin Group (USA) and originally in hardcover by Algonquin Books of Chapel Hill. Reprinted by permission of Susan Bergholz Literary Services, New York. All rights reserved.

From ¡*Yo!* copyright 1997 by Julia Alvarez. Published by Plume, an imprint of Penguin Group (USA). Originally published by Algonquin Books of Chapel Hill. Reprinted by permission of Susan Bergholz Literary Services, New York. All rights reserved.

From *Monkey Hunting* by Cristina García, copyright 2003 by Cristina García. Used by permission of Alfred A. Knopf, a division of Random House, Inc.

From *Down These Mean Streets* by Piri Thomas, copyright 1967 by Piri Thomas. Copyright renewed 1995 by Piri Thomas. Used by permission of Alfred A. Knopf, a division of Random House, Inc.

From *So Far from God: A Novel* by Ana Castillo, copyright 1993 by Ana Castillo. Used by permission of W. W. Norton & Company, Inc.

From *Days of Awe* by Achy Obejas, copyright 2001 by Achy Obejas. Used by permission of Ballantine Books, a division of Random House, Inc.

From *Mother Tongue* by Demetria Martínez, copyright 1994 by Demetria Martínez. Used by permission of Ballantine Books, a division of Random House, Inc.

From *Latino Crossings* by Nicholas De Genova and Ana Y. Ramos-Zayas, copyright 2003 by Nicholas De Genova and Ana Y. Ramos-Zayas. Reproduced by permission of Routledge/Taylor & Francis Group, LLC.

From *The Dirty Girls Social Club* by Alisa Valdés-Rodríguez, copyright 2003 by Alisa Valdés-Rodríguez and reprinted by permission of St. Martin's Press, LLC.

From "The Latin Deli: An Ars Poetica" by Judith Ortiz Cofer, copyright 1992 by Arte Público Press. Reprinted with permission of the publisher.

From "Margarita Engle, Cuban American Conservatism and the Construction of (Left) U.S. Latino/a Ethnicity" by Taylor & Francis Group, copyright 2002. Published by *LIT: Literature Interpretation Theory* and reproduced by permission of Taylor & Francis Group, LLC., http//www.taylorandfrancis.com.

In memory of my beloved mother,
Rosario Caminero

# Contents

Acknowledgments ix

Introduction: Who Are We? 1

**Part One: Race and Ethnicity**

1. "Jasón's Indian": Mexican Americans and the Denial of Indigenous Ethnicity in Rudolfo Anaya's *Bless Me, Ultima* 39

2. "Puerto Rican Negro": Defining Race in Piri Thomas's *Down These Mean Streets* 51

**Part Two: Complicating the Origins**

3. Speaking for Others: Problems of Representation in the Writing of Julia Alvarez 73

4. Complicating *Cubanidad*: Novels of Achy Obejas and Cristina García 93

**Part Three: Difference and the Possibilities of Panethnicity**

5. "The Pleas of the Desperate": Magical Realism, *Latinidad*, and (or) Collective Agency in Ana Castillo's *So Far from God* 139

6. Dirty Girls, German Shepherds, and Puerto Rican *Independentistas*: "The Latino Imaginary" and the Case of Cuba 161

7. Imagining Identity/Seeing Difference: Demetria Martínez's *Mother Tongue* 196

Conclusion: The Shifting Nature of *Latinidad* 213

Notes 221

Works Cited 265

Index 285

# Acknowledgments

I would like to gratefully acknowledge the College of Liberal Arts and Sciences at the University of Kansas, which funded this project through a sabbatical leave in Spring 2005. This investigation was also supported by the University of Kansas General Research Fund, allocation numbers 2301138, 2301527, and 2301105.

Earlier versions of some chapters of this book appeared originally in various journals. An earlier version of the chapter on Ana Castillo appeared in *Tulsa Studies in Women's Literature* 24.1 (Spring 2005). An earlier version of the chapter on Rudolfo Anaya was published by Heldref Publications in *Critique* 45.2 (Winter 2004). An earlier version of the chapter on Piri Thomas originally appeared in *MELUS* 29.2 (Summer 2004). An earlier version of the chapter on Julia Alvarez was published in *Antípodas: Journal of Hispanic Studies of Australia and New Zealand* 10 (1998). In addition, my discussion of Margarita Engle in chapter six was originally part of a larger article that appeared in *LIT: Literature / Interpretation / Theory* 13.4 (October–December 2002); and small passages of my article "Contesting the Boundaries of 'Exile' Latino/a Literature," from *World Literature Today* 74.3 (Summer 2000), have been reproduced in revised form in chapters three and six, as well as in my introduction. I thank all the editors for permission to include this material here.

Various colleagues lent their generous support, in ways small and large. I thank Maryemma Graham and Doreen Fowler, my colleagues at the University of Kansas, as well as John Carlos Rowe, my former mentor from University of California, Irvine, for their support, encouragement, and efforts on my behalf. Jean Wyatt read several sections of the manuscript and devoted untold amounts of time to a virtual stranger. John Monberg was an amazing internet resource, digging up a wealth of valuable information about Latino demographics that I would never have found on my own. Debra Castillo, one of the readers for the University Press of Florida, provided many helpful suggestions for an earlier version of this manuscript; the project is much the better for her thorough critique. I also thank Delia Poey for her warm and enthusiastic support of the project. Amy Gorelick, my editor at University Press of Florida, was miraculously prompt, efficient, and level-headed. I frequently consulted my friend Dan Waterman, at the University of Alabama Press, during the submission process; he gave me wonderful advice and patiently put up with all my questions.

My sincere gratitude goes to my friends at KU, Anna Neill, Giselle Anatol, Yo Jackson, Katie Conrad, and Laura Hines, for keeping me sane with occasional "girls' nights" (no shop talk allowed), and to Sarah Thailing, my dear friend far from home. Maggie Carpenter and Matt Lewis, as well as Jack and Kathy Healy, were our good friends in Lawrence for several years; their company and comfort is sorely missed. Jen Sachs and Laura Kincade also continue to send their care and concern across the miles. My deep appreciation, as well, goes to Beth and Gerry Santangelo. As always, my love to my family: my sister, Mary Ann Cucuzza, and her husband, Keith; my father, Rafael Caminero (a.k.a. "St. Joseph"); and my brother, Ralph Caminero. No one is complete without their family, friends, or history.

Most important, I thank my husband, Byron, for his indispensable feedback on some of my chapters (not to mention the help with composing persuasive letters and e-mails), as well as for putting up with me through stressful times and never faltering in his faith in me. My thanks and love, also, to my two children, Gabriel and Nicola, for bringing me such joy.

My mother, Rosario Caminero, was instrumental in advancing Latino Studies at Millersville University in Pennsylvania until her death in 2006. I follow in her footsteps.

# Introduction

## Who Are We?

Earl Shorris's hefty tome *Latinos: A Biography of the People* (1992) begins with a telling anecdote. Shorris, in his ethnographer persona, asks one of his subjects, Margarita Avila, "If you were writing this book, what would you want it to say?" Avila responds, "Just tell them who we are and that we are not all alike." Shorris interprets Avila's comments as a statement about the differences that divide Latinos, noting that he has heard the same sentiment expressed countless times by interviewees across the country.

But those differences are more profound, perhaps, than even Shorris perceives. In his prologue (entitled "The Name of the People"), Shorris expresses an interest in nomenclature, terminology—he wants to pin Avila down about how he should refer to the group: "Before I could begin, there was a word to be chosen, a name to be given to the noun represented by 'we.'" But when he asks Avila who "we," is, she responds, "Mejicanos." When he prods, "Yes, but there is a larger group"—still apparently assuming that it was this larger entity that Avila originally referred to when she said "we are not all alike"— Avila insists (and resists), "We are Mejicanos" (xv). Shorris then recounts a litany of resistance:

> "Hispanic?" I asked.
> "Mejicano," she said. [. . .]
> "Hispano, Latino, Latin, Spanish, Spanish-speaking."
> "Mejicano," she said. (xvi)

Of course, Shorris understands Avila's point; she is rejecting any umbrella term. And yet, he never lets go of the assumption that there *is* a "set of people"(xvi) named by such a term, or that this is the "we" Avila originally referred to when she said "we are not all alike." The idea that Avila might have been commenting on what Suzanne Oboler calls "the heterogeneity of the Mexican-American population" (68),[1] rather than on the diversity of "Latinos"—that is, that she might have been talking only about "Mejicanos" all along—does not seem to occur to him.

The story is a vivid enactment, in brief, of the ways in which the *category* "Latino" (or "Hispanic") has, at least at times, been applied from outside while adamantly rejected from within. Avila *refuses* to acknowledge any "we" outside of "Mejicanos"; anyone else, in her construction, is "them" (as in, "Tell them ..."). Suzanne Oboler's interviews with people of Latin American origin, in her 1995 study *Ethnic Labels, Latino Lives*, confirms this sense of umbrella terms such as "Hispanic" or "Latino" being "imposed by Americans" (155). When respondents were asked about how they might identify Latin Americans in the United States who were of national origins different from their own, one Latin American immigrant replied, "If I introduce you to someone I would say 'This is my friend, she's from Peru.' Or else, I'd say, 'She's South American, or Peruvian.'" Another responded, "I always call people according to their country: a Salvadorean, an Uruguayan, an Argentinean" (153).[2] As happened with Shorris, this response prompted further questioning:

> *But not a Hispanic?*
> Soledad: No, I identify them according to their country.
> Why wouldn't you say they're Hispanic?
> Soledad: Well, it just doesn't sound right to me. [. . .] [W]e're not just a lump [. . .]—because even though we may use the same language, our cultures are different and we have to think about what we're going to say to each other. [. . .] Many of the things we might say in Spanish [are] offensive to one person, funny to another. Another thing is the food. . . . For example, we have to learn to eat what [Central Americans] eat. (153–54)

On the basis of *cultural difference* (not, as so many commentators seem to insist, a "common culture"), indicated by the differences in "ethnic markers" such as food and language usage, Oboler's interviewees repudiate the use among themselves of an umbrella term. Oboler notes that they are engaged "in the process of defining the group's internal boundaries" (153), but what is striking is that the sense of "group" as Oboler is using it is simply not present at all.

The question of whether a single, identifiable "Latino" identity exists has been asked, in various ways and under a multitude of rubrics, by an increasing number of scholars. And that is a welcome development, certainly, since the state of affairs prior to the deliberate asking of the question was generally simply to assume from the outside—along with U.S. popular culture and the census—that "Latinos" were, in fact, a group and proceed from there.[3]

The critical insight, by now a commonplace, that ethnicity is a "social construct" has gone a significant way toward modifying and complicating this assumption. As Nicholas De Genova and Ana Y. Ramos-Zayas put it, "there is no automatic or inevitable necessity to the emergence of a shared sense of Latino identity, as indeed there are never any natural or self-evident positive grounds for *any* identity. Identities must be *produced* through social relations and struggle" (21). Werner Sollors, one of the leading early theorists of ethnicity in relation to literature, has drawn (in *The Invention of Ethnicity*, 1989) on Benedict Anderson's writings to call attention to the premise that ethnicities, like nations, are "imagined communities" rather than peoples connected by any essential, natural, or unchanging relations. What connects these communities is a set of "collective fictions" that, far from being themselves stable, are "intensely debated" and "continually reinvented" (xi). This is where literature comes in, for, as Sollors argues elsewhere, literature and its study play a crucial role in generating a sense of ethnicity based on contrast ("X writes like an X, not like a Y") and also "help to create the illusion of a group's 'natural' existence from 'time immemorial'" ("Ethnicity" 290).

Stephen Cornell and Douglas Hartmann, grappling in *Ethnicity and Race* (1998) with the question of how to define ethnicity in a way that accounts for its power as an idea as well as its "constructed" nature, have invoked German sociologist Max Weber's contention that it is based on "a subjective belief in [...] common descent" (Weber 389, qtd. in Cornell and Hartmann 16), as well as Richard A. Schermerhorn's criteria that "[e]thnic groups are self-conscious populations; they see themselves as distinct" (19) and that, more than "actual cultural distinctiveness" (19), they share "a cultural focus on one or more symbolic elements defined as the epitome of their peoplehood" (12, qtd. in Cornell and Hartmann 19). Cornell and Hartmann go on to clarify that "[t]o say that ethnicity is subjective is not to say that it is unaffected by what others say or do. Indeed, outsiders' conceptions of us may be a major influence leading to our own self-consciousness as an ethnic population. Others may assign to us an ethnic identity, but what they establish by doing so is an ethnic category. It is our own claim to that identity that makes us an ethnic group" (20). It is arguable that the origins of "Hispanic" ethnicity in the United States lie at least as much in outsider perception of a singular group (e.g., "They all speak Spanish") as in the group's own perception of "groupness."

Much has been made of the fact that the U.S. Census Bureau introduced "Hispanic" as a classification in the 1980 census,[4] a possible example of Cornell and Hartmann's point that ethnic group identity can *originate* in "outsiders' conceptions of us," though it is only when the group itself takes on that identification as its own that it becomes an ethnic group. Rubén Rumbaut conveys precisely this dynamic when he writes that "Hispanic" is "a label developed and legitimized by the state, diffused in daily and institutional practice, and finally internalized" ("Making" 19). The force of outsider perception is also what Oboler suggests through the title of her book's first chapter: "Hispanics? That's What *They* Call Us." As one Puerto Rican mainland respondent interviewed by Oboler puts it, "White people have a name for everybody else. [...] I mean, Puerto Ricans never call each other Hispanic. [...] When they ["white people"] said Hispanics, that's just a group of people that they've just put together that speaks Spanish. . . . They just count all Latin people in one bunch" (155).

Most savvy commentators now disavow (at least explicitly) the notion of an essential Latino identity—after all, by now we know that even gender and national identities are not "essential" (there is no defining female "soul" or inherent American "spirit")—even though those same commentators often follow up by sneaking in suspiciously "essentialist"-sounding statements about Latino identity through the back door, in the guise of comments on "Latino culture."[5] But that does not mean that Latino identity "doesn't exist," for, as is frequently pointed out, social constructs still exist and can exert a strong force. Perhaps a better question would be, Is there such a thing as a collective, *panethnic* Latino identity—one that Latinos themselves generally recognize? For, as Felix Padilla has persuasively argued, there is a world of difference between exhibiting ethnic consciousness as a Mexican American or Puerto Rican and doing so as a Latino or Hispanic; the latter implies a sense of relations between and among Latino groups (2). Or is the category really little more than a label "assigned," in Cornell and Hartmann's terminology, by "outsiders" rather than a real way in which so-called Latinos understand themselves?

At first glance, the 2000 census gives some indication that perhaps Latinos are identifying panethnically in greater numbers. The census finds that the number of people writing in the word "Hispanic," as opposed to a specific national origin that had not been already named in the previous options, increased, from 6.4 percent of the total responding Hispanic population (in 1990) to 15.7 percent. Write-ins of the category "Latino" also increased from a mere 1,577 (or 0 percent) to 1.2 percent (Cresce et al., table 2). As Matt A. Barreto notes, some Latino organizations, such as the National Council of La Raza (NCLR) and the League of United Latin American Citizens (LULAC), have postulated that "the increase in the 'other' category may be primarily due to a growing pan-Hispanic identity" (46).

Elizabeth Martin cautions, however, that while "[i]t might be tempting to conclude that a decline in reporting of detailed groups [i.e., of specific national origin] was due to Hispanics' changing self-identifications over the past decade" (i.e., to an increasing identification with a general "Hispanic" or "Latino" category over a nation-specific category), "the change can be attributed [instead] to a change in the design of the mail questionnaire" (591). In 1990 the "write-in" option included examples of national origin such as "Argentinean, Colombian, Dominican, Nicaraguan, Salvadoran, Spaniard, and so on" (1990 census); in 2000 the examples were left out. The "other" option thus read simply "Yes, other Spanish/Hispanic/Latino—*Print group*." As Martin points out, this wording is "vague" and "may have been interpreted by some respondents as a request to indicate which of the three terms they preferred" (590).

The 2002 National Survey of Latinos conducted by the Pew Hispanic Center reveals that 85 percent of Latinos questioned believe that "Hispanics from different countries [...] [a]ll have separate and distinct cultures," while only 14 percent believe they "[s]hare one Hispanic/Latino culture" (chart 9); the 2004 National Survey finds 51 percent of registered Latinos believing that "Latinos from different countries" are "not working together politically," while only 43 percent say they are "working together to achieve common political goals" (chart 28). (While the findings from the 2002 Survey were similar on this question, the 2006 National Survey, by contrast, finds that 58 percent of Latinos, a new majority, feels that Latinos "are working together to achieve common political goals"—a result possibly attributable to Latinos' sense of discriminatory backlash from the immigration policy debates and to the pro-immigrant marches earlier in 2006 [Suro and Escobar i, 11].)

If a collective sense of self is constructed through "collective fictions" (Sollors's term) and "symbolic elements" which come to stand as "the epitome of their peoplehood" (Schermerhorn's), then it is quite telling that Puerto Ricans on the mainland and Chicano/as—the two groups most often connected to each other in scholarship on Latinos in the United States[6]—have historically derived their sense of peoplehood, and their political energy, from *different* myths and symbols. As Suzanne Oboler writes of the Chicano movement of the 1960s, "Chicanos grounded their version of Mexican Americans' 'colonized' history in the mythical space and time of 'Aztlán' [...] the name for the legendary northern Mexican lands to which all Chicanos would one day return" (66). The movement rallied around and was energized by this "nationalist narrative of [...] a legendary and heroic Aztec past" (66). Puerto Ricans who were becoming politically active during the same period were also adopting "a strong cultural nationalist rationale" (57), but were imagining a *different* "nation" and set of nationalist symbols. Instead of Aztlán, the Virgin of Guadalupe, and the Aztec eagle,[7] Puerto Ricans who were becoming "increasingly aware of the implications of their island's status [...] renamed the island Borinquen, and many began to self-identify as Boricuas in an effort to return to its pre-Columbian indigenous Taino roots" (57).

While the dynamics were quite similar, the *stories* were different. De Genova and Ramos-Zayas have written, in their fascinating study *Latino Crossings* (2003), about more recent symbolic struggles between Puerto Ricans and other Latino groups, especially Mexicans, in Chicago:

> In response to the perceived "threat" posed by an increasing Mexican and Central American influx into the Humboldt Park neighborhood—traditionally marked as "Puerto Rican," and indeed, symbolically central as "the" Puerto Rican barrio—grassroots activists launched strenuous

campaigns during the 1990s to discourage Puerto Rican residents from moving out of the barrio. Local businesses and ambulatory vendors selling Puerto Rican–identified goods worked alongside of grassroots activists to enforce physical and symbolic "boundaries" that were intended to maintain the "Puerto Rican"-ness of the neighborhood, by deploying nationalist and even separatist Puerto Rican symbols (such as a campaigning to install a statue of renowned nationalist leader Pedro Albizu Campos) [. . .]. The simultaneous perceived onslaught of "encroachments" by gentrifying whites, displaced poor Blacks, and other poor Latinos, especially Mexican migrants, produced a sense of alarm that Puerto Ricans were being "squeezed out." (53)

If a sense of peoplehood is deployed largely through symbols, it is striking that the most prominent symbols in the arsenal of U.S. Latino history have so often been nationally specific, rather than panethnic, in nature.

As a loud chorus of commentators have observed, it is difficult indeed to pinpoint what exactly might link people of Chicano/a, Puerto Rican, Cuban, Dominican, and Central/South American descent into a single, and singular, collective ethnicity labeled "Latino" or "Hispanic." While, as Debra Castillo notes in *Redreaming America* (2005), the questions "Who is a Latino/a?" and "Who or what defines 'real' *latinidad*?" have been asked (and answered) with sometimes increasing urgency and stridency, often invoking "identitarian claims" (*Redreaming* 10–11), there is a growing scholarly tendency to reject the category altogether, at least insofar as it could be said to refer to an "identity." Earl Shorris simply maintains that "there are no Latinos, only diverse peoples struggling to remain who they are" (12) (yet his book is paradoxically entitled *Latinos: A Biography of the People*). Invoking the common association of ethnicity with kinship and family (as Cornell and Hartmann have written, "Ethnicity is family writ very large indeed" [20])—Marcelo M. Suárez-Orozco and Mariela M. Páez, in the introduction to their nuanced and sophisticated volume *Latinos: Remaking America* (2002), note that "the tired and facile 'Latinos-are-a-big-family' glosses over the contradictions, tensions, and fissures—around class, race, and color—that often separate them. [. . .] Bluntly, what does an English-speaking third-generation upper-status white Cuban American in Florida have in common with a Maya-speaking recent immigrant from Guatemala?" (3). (Debra Castillo adds, "[H]ow about a Jew from Argentina?" [*Redreaming* 11].) Silvio Torres-Saillant agrees, deriding the popular construct of U.S. Hispanics as *"una sola familia"* (a single family; 445) and insisting that "[t]he claim that Latinos constitute one big happy family conceals the tensions, inequities, and injustices in our midst, contributing to a conceptual ambience that legitimizes the absence of black and Indian faces and voices from Latino fora. The operating logic seems to be that, because everyone in our polychromatic community is really the same, everyone is inherently represented even when only one color continues to peer out at us from the tube" (444).

Commenting particularly on "Latino" cultural production, Guillermo Gómez-Peña argues that "[t]erms like Hispanic, Latino [...] are inaccurate and loaded with ideological implications. They create false categories [...]. There is no such thing as 'Latino art' or 'Hispanic art.' There are hundreds of types of Latino-American-derived art in the United States. Each is aesthetically, socially, and politically specific" (46, 48). Oboler, whose focus is precisely the meaning and impact of labels, insists that the term "Hispanic obscures rather than clarifies" issues of group identity with regard to a highly diverse population of peoples of Latin American origin (2).

One of the most eloquent and passionate critics of any umbrella term, Martha Gimenez, denies the validity of any "label" flat out. As early as 1989 Gimenez insisted that "the label [...] only creates an artificial population; i.e., a statistical construct formed by aggregates of people who differ greatly in terms of national origin, language, race, time of arrival in the United States, culture, minority status [...], social class, and socioeconomic status" ("Latino/'Hispanic'" 559).[8] Elaborating at length on the meaninglessness of the term for public policy, social scientists, health professionals, and so on, Gimenez reviews research about birth rates, fertility rates, and median ages for "Hispanics" (treated collectively) and points out that such statistics tell us absolutely nothing, because the figures for the various national-origin Hispanic groups differ widely.

Her observations still hold true. According to the National Campaign to Prevent Teen Pregnancy (NCPTP), "Since 1995, Latina teens have had the highest teen birth rate among the major racial/ethnic groups in the United States" ("Fact Sheet: Latinos" 2); it cites a statistic of 82.3 per 1,000 in 2003 ("Fact Sheet: Latinos" 2), compared to 63.8 per 1,000 for African Americans, the next highest group ("Fact Sheet: Black" 2). The report goes on to state, however, that the rate for Mexican Americans was 93.2 (in 2003); for Puerto Ricans, by contrast, it was 60.8, and for "other" national-origin Latino groups (again grouped together), it was 60.4 ("Fact Sheet: Latinos" 2–3).[9] It is important, then, to note that, if Puerto Ricans (for example) were taken separately, their rate would *not* be the highest of any ethnic group in 2003; this happens only when they are grouped in with Mexican Americans, whose rate is over 30 per 1,000 higher.[10] The report also cites that 76.2 percent of teenaged Latina mothers who gave birth in 2003 were unmarried. But this figure, too, conceals substantial differences: "Mexican-American teen mothers [...] were least likely to give birth out-of-wedlock [...] (69.4%), followed by Cuban-American teen mothers (72.5%) [while] [t]he highest percent nonmarital was among teens of

Puerto Rican descent (87.7%)" ("Latinos" 3)[11]—in other words, a difference of almost 20 percent between the least- and most-likely groups.

Similarly, the results of the 2000 census tell us that only 56 percent of Latinos aged twenty-five or older are high school graduates, while a mere 11 percent are college graduates (compared to 83 percent high school graduates and 25 percent college graduates nationwide) (U.S. Dept. of Health and Human Services, *Mental Health* 131). Yet again this figure masks significant disparities: for Cuban Americans over 25 the figure is 70 percent who have graduated from high school, compared to 64 percent of Puerto Ricans and 50 percent of Mexican Americans; the figures for college are roughly 25 percent for Cuban Americans, compared to 11 percent for Puerto Ricans and 7 percent for Mexican Americans (*Mental Health* 132). In another example, the Census Bureau reports that the median age of Hispanics in 2000 was 25.8, but this figure encompasses a range from 24.3 years for Mexican Americans to 40.1 years for those of Cuban origin (U.S. Census Bureau, "Hispanic Heritage"). Given such differences among national groups, what can lumping them together and taking an average possibly tell us that the breakout statistics do not? Does the aggregate statistic, rather, obscure pertinent information?[12]

With somewhat more ambivalence than Gimenez, Juan Flores, in his provocative *From Bomba to Hip-Hop* (2000), is highly critical of the use of the catchall categories when they are used to refer to a single homogeneous group, without adequate attention to "structural variations in the placement [within a U.S. context] of the different national groups relative to hierarchies of power and attendant histories of racialization" (203).[13] The experience of upper- and middle-class Cuban exiles, welcomed with open arms into the United States as immigrants (until the Clinton administration) and given substantial government aid, is quite different, for example, from that of poverty-stricken Puerto Rican "immigrants" in New York (not immigrants at all, since all Puerto Ricans are U.S. citizens), which is different in turn from that of Mexican Americans in the Southwest, who frequently recount fear of or problems with "la migra" even when they are citizens.[14] The INS, now renamed U.S. Citizenship and Immigration Services (USCIS), is repeatedly portrayed by Chicano/a authors as assuming that Mexican Americans who cannot immediately produce proof of identity are "illegal." In contrast, since all Puerto Ricans are U.S. citizens who can therefore enter the country freely, they do not face this particular threat; De Genova and Ramos-Zayas, as well as Michael Jones-Correa, have argued quite powerfully that such differences in citizenship status have created marked divisions between Puerto Ricans and other groups.[15] A dominant U.S. culture's racial perceptions of the different groups, and consequently their historical and even current treatment, also vary: Cuban exiles have generally been perceived as "white"; Mexican Americans are perceived as part of the (nonexistent) "Hispanic" race (i.e., they are "brown"); Puerto Ricans have frequently been perceived as (close to) "black," as countless social scientists comparing Puerto Ricans to African Americans demonstrate.[16]

Commenting on the interests and perceptions of "Latinos" themselves, Geoffrey Fox writes that U.S. Hispanics include "some 25 million people who don't know or care much about one [an]other, don't think or talk alike, and have not until recently thought of themselves as having any common interests" (22). As if to prove Fox's point, most prominent examples of Latino/a literature virtually do not address the differences—or even the relationships—between the various Latino/a groups at all. Sandra Cisneros, Rudolfo Anaya, and Ana Castillo write about Mexican Americans. Cristina García and Oscar Hijuelos write about Cubans.[17] Julia Alvarez and Junot Díaz write about Dominicans. Esmeralda Santiago, Judith Ortiz Cofer, and Piri Thomas write about Puerto Ricans. And so on. Interactions between characters from the author's own ethnic group and other "Latino" groups have been represented infrequently or not at all. (Literary critics have generally followed suit by dealing with the separate ethnicities separately, even in critical texts that wrap them together under the broader umbrella term "Hispanic" or "Latino" in the title.) And while some novels have, at the very least, raised the looming specter of cultural "authenticity" by writing about Latino groups other than their own (examples include *In Search of Bernabé* [1993], a novel about the civil war in El Salvador, written by Graciela Limón, a Chicana; *The Infinite Plan* [1993], which in part depicts a Mexican American community in Los Angeles, by Isabel Allende, a Chilean immigrant and prominent Latin American author; *Send My Roots Rain* [1991], again about Chicanos, by Ibis Gómez-Vega, a Cuban American; *The Love Queen of the Amazon* [1992], set in Peru, by Chicana Cecile Pineda), these texts have not foregrounded the groups' interrelations, connections, or differences among the groups—leading readers either to assume that the authors, being "Latino" themselves, are writing from a standpoint of cultural "authority" or, conversely, that they are simply doing what writers do all the time: inventing worlds of fiction unrelated to their own experience.[18] Prominent Chicana writer Gloria Anzaldúa, in her groundbreaking classic *Borderlands/La Frontera* (1987), seems to suggest that umbrella terms such as "Latino" or "Hispanic" undermine a specific, politicized Chicano/a community: "We call ourselves Hispanic or Spanish-American or Latin American or Latin when linking ourselves to other Spanish-speaking peoples of the Western hemisphere and when copping out" (62). Cuban American author Gustavo Pérez Firmat puts the case in its perhaps most extreme form: "Latino is a statistical fiction, a figment of the imagination of ethnic ideologues, ad executives and salsa singers. [. . .] [T]o me, Latino is an empty concept. Latino doesn't have a culture, a language, a place of origin" (qtd. in Alvarez Borland 150). In *Cincuenta lecciones de exilio y desexilio*, Pérez Firmat insists on being Cuban rather than Hispanic and adds, "Si me dicen *Latino*, respondo, la tuya" (If they say to me *Latino*, I respond, up yours; 108). Pérez Firmat suggests that "Latino" is not essence but invention and implies that—despite the occasional sellout "salsa singer"—it is not an invention participated in by the community itself (a "collective fiction") but one imposed from the outside and to which he takes offense.

Of course, it is more than just offensive "ad executives and salsa singers"— or even official government forms and mainstream media—that have participated in the construction of a group category now known as "Latino." The academic publishing industry, to name just one other example, has for years now been producing anthologies under the rubric of "Latino/a literature," and college courses under this title abound. Yet, as Karen Christian has noted in *Show and Tell* (1997), until quite recently most literary scholarship did not follow suit: "A survey of U.S. Latina/o literary criticism indicates that the prevailing tendency has been to regard Chicana/o, Nuyorican, and U.S. Cuban literatures as distinct cultural phenomena. The most recent comprehensive scholarly studies continue this trend" (4).[19] (George J. Sánchez has made the same argument about historical monographs and articles.)

Alternatively, even some studies employing the "panethnic" label pay scant attention to the implications of its use. Ellen McCracken's *New Latina Narrative* (1999), still one of only a few full-length literary treatments of Latino *or* Latina literature as a panethnic grouping, briefly raises the issue of the label's "homogenizing" effects (4–5) but quickly goes on to assert the "difficulty of placing writers into discrete national categories" (5), and then drops the subject. Another study, Paul Allatson's *Latino Dreams* (2002), justifies the "overarching" category of his title by noting that his "aim is to set up a cumulative dialogue between disparate experiences and understandings of 'America,' the locus for a range of myths and discourses of belonging"—a rationale which leaves open the question of what the internal coherency of the group might be. In yet a third, *Reading U.S. Latina Writers* (2003), Alvina E. Quintana defends the "'Latina' designation [. . .] as a strategic intervention aimed at highlighting some of the cultural and political similarities that emerge when individuals living in the United States are identified by the mainstream press under a 'Hispanic' label" (3). For Quintana the difference between "Latina" and "Hispanic" is, shall we say, essential: she argues that, "[a]lthough the terms 'Hispanic' and 'Latino' both make reference to categories of difference, it is only the latter that allows for a recognition of the cultural hybridization created by the European fusion with Indigenous, Asian, or African peoples" (3–4), a rather far-fetched claim—given that "Latino" certainly does not refer etymologically to any of these peoples any more than "Hispanic" does—which goes unelaborated. "Latinas," for Quintana, are implicitly connected by their hybrid cultural and racial backgrounds (an argument I will return to shortly) as well as by some "cultural and political similarities" that emerge (but were not originally present) as a result of their homogenization as "Hispanic" within U.S. culture. "Hispanic," as an imposed term, apparently erases differences, while "Latina" offers an intervention into this homogenizing dynamic, presumably by allowing for its scrutiny. Yet Quintana's subsequent comments on hybridization would seem to replicate the homogenizing tendency by subsuming various cultural and racial hybridizations unproblematically (and without scrutiny) under the "Latino" category.

Fatima Mujčinović's *Postmodern Cross-Culturalism and Politicization in U.S. Latina Literature* (2004) explains her use of the umbrella term for practical reasons: "it would be hard to use specific terms [. . .] when referring to the entire range of the ethnic grouping"; she adds that it "serves my argument for a more [. . .] unified conception of Latino/a literary production" (169 n. 1). She justifies this argument on the basis of a shared marginality that—once again—ignores some significant differences in the nature of the "experience of oppression" among different groups (6). For Mujčinović, the collision between originary culture and Anglo-American culture "exposes the incompatibility and contradictions of different cultural signifiers" (8); but the cultural signifiers among different Latino-origin groups are assumed to be roughly the same, or at least certainly compatible (7).

William Luis's monograph *Dance between Two Cultures* (1997) presents a similar argument: Luis comments on "differences in development" and "varying political and economic conditions" among Caribbean Spanish-speaking nations, then goes on to say that, "[w]hen Hispanics migrate to the United States, native differences are reinforced and others are created. They speak a 'foreign' language many do not understand, and because of barriers in communication and widespread attitudes toward foreigners, stereotypes are created" (xiii). Though Luis discusses differences among Caribbean countries, the "native differences" exacerbated by migration to the United States can apparently only be Anglo-Hispanic differences, while inter-Caribbean differences are erased or forgotten. (As we will see in my discussion of Achy Obejas's *Memory Mambo*, however, the U.S. context can in fact magnify inter-Caribbean conflicts between Cubans and Puerto Ricans.)

For Luis, as for Mujčinović, Latinos are bound together by their marginality within U.S. culture: "for many Anglo-Americans, [. . .] Hispanics, whether born in the United States or abroad, from privileged or low socioeconomic classes, economic or political exiles, black or white, are grouped into a single category and viewed as foreigners." But Luis goes on to argue that, "[r]egardless of the differences among them, Latinos share *the same* marginal experience in the United States" (xiv; emphasis added). Such glib generalizations overlook sometimes substantial differences in the ways that groups have been treated in the United States. Consider again De Genova and Ramos-Zayas's arguments about how U.S. citizenship has created an experience of marginalization for Puerto Ricans that is qualitatively *different* (not "the same") from that of Mexican immigrants; Cuban immigrants were, for decades, offered a degree of federal aid unbeknownst to other groups. Indeed, as María Cristina García documents in *Havana U.S.A.* (1996), Cuban exiles in Florida in the early 1960s received more federal assistance than was available for Miami's non-Cuban U.S. citizens (28–29, 41). By contrast, Central American political refugees in the 1980s were often not only not provided aid, but denied asylum altogether.

Other scholars who have attempted to answer the questions "Who are Latinos?" and "What is Latino/a literature?" (or perhaps more simply, "Why consider these texts together?") have frequently generalized about "cultural resistance and/or protest" and a "Third world stance" (Rivero, "Hispanic" 187, 183), about a "timeless struggle for social justice" (Ray Gonzalez xiii–xiv), about "a working-class identity and aesthetic" (Kanellos, *Hispanic* 4), or about a "Latino imaginary" pitted against "ongoing oppression" and directed toward justice, civil rights, and sovereignty (Flores, *From Bomba* 199–200). The prevailing assumption in much of the history of Latino/a literary scholarship has seemed to be that Latino/a literature will generally—perhaps even essentially, by definition—advance a progressive ideology. When actual Latino/a literary texts turn out not to fit the mold, critics may decide not to "count" them as "real" Latino/a literature.[20] Or they might try to force them into the mold.[21] Or—perhaps more commonly—differences in the artistic production of the different Latino/a groups (including, sometimes, political and ideological differences) may simply be glossed over, ignored.

Ray Gonzalez, in his introduction to *Currents from the Dancing River* (1994), demonstrates the powerful impulse to construct a unified Latino/a identity that elides significant group distinctions by asserting, amazingly, that, "[a]lthough cultural differences remain between Mexican Americans, Puerto Ricans in the United States, and Cuban Americans, Latino writers *are coming together in a cohesive* [. . .] *whole*" (xiii–xiv; emphasis added).

At the opposite end, prominent performance artist and cultural critic Guillermo Gómez-Peña insists that there is no single, or even dominant, ideology discernable in "Latino art," distinguishing even between Latinos that most people would group together, at least in terms of their cultural production: "California Chicanos and Nuyorricans [*sic*] inhabit different cultural landscapes. [. . .] Right-wing Cubanos from Miami are unconditional adversaries of leftist South American exiles. The cultural expressions of Central American and Mexican migrant workers differ drastically from those of the Latino intelligentsia in the universities, ad infinitum" (48).

*The Chronicles of Panchita Villa and Other Guerrilleras* (2005), by Tey Diana Rebolledo, who could accurately be called a "foremother" of Chicana literary criticism (it was she and Eliana Rivero who edited the canon-shaping anthology *Infinite Divisions* in 1993, which Rebolledo followed with a critical book on Chicana writers, *Women Singing in the Snow*, in 1995), is remarkably refreshing in that it does not claim any fundamental, underlying similarity for her grouping of both Mexican American and other Latina writers, despite the fact that her selection thus admittedly "disrupts what might be a more coherent focus on just Chicana writers" (7). Rather, Rebolledo states quite simply, "[I]n this collection I wanted to include essays on writers who have influenced me, molded me, and impressed me over the years" (7). This principle of selection is related to two wonderful anecdotes Rebolledo tells about hearing stories told to her by others that were actually taken from her own life, eliciting from her the reaction, "Hey, that's MY story!" (9).

Rebolledo's reflections here get at an undeniable phenomenon: in teaching classes on U.S. Latino/a literature, I (and others) frequently hear Latino/a students describe feeling some sort of identification with the stories that they read, despite the authors' ethnic backgrounds not always being the students' own. It is intriguing to mull over why, and under what circumstances, this feeling of "Hey, that's MY story!" might be generated without necessarily jumping from there to claims of fundamentally similar cultures or experiences among all Latino groups. (I will return to this point near the end of this chapter and again in the Conclusion.)

Despite the continuing and often un-self-reflective use of the umbrella term "Latino" as a singular category, much scholarship that directly addresses the panethnic implications of this label has made it much less easy to generalize about common culture, common political orientation, or even common experiences of marginalization within the United States. At the very least, this scholarship openly acknowledges the differences (in culture of origin, in racial and class demographics, and even in "official" treatment by the U.S. government) among the various Latino groups that threaten to make the term all but meaningless. (Scholars such as Marcelo Suárez-Orozco and Mariela Páez, Suzanne Oboler, Juan Flores, and Earl Shorris, for example, all vehemently decry the "homogenizing" of the various groups through an unthinking assumption of a singular identity.) At best, this scholarship also searches for alternative means of understanding a "Latino" collective identity that is not based in reductive essentialisms about language or culture.

For instance, scholars have forcefully challenged a long intellectual tradition of constructing *latinidad* in terms of a racial and cultural hybridity, as Quintana does—and as José Martí did in his landmark essay "Nuestra América." Amaryll Chanady describes how "the hybrid nature of the newly developing societies in the New World and the heterogeneous influences they received [came to be] considered as constitutive of its [Latin American] identity. Terms such as Martí's 'mestizo America,' José María Arguedas's 'Indo-America,' Angel Rama's 'transculture,' and Ventura García Calderón's 'Indo-Afro-Sino-Ibero-America' [. . .] indicate an attempt to conceive of Latin American culture as hybrid" (xxxii–xxxiii; Ortega 86 qtd. in Chanady).[22] "To this day," José Piedra reminds us, "Hispanic unity is celebrated among Spanish-Americans as Día de la Raza ('Day of [the?] Race') on the date of Columbus's first landing" (285; brackets in original). As Cornell and Hartmann explain, "Ethnic ties are blood ties" (16); ethnicity presupposes a belief in common descent.[23]

Yet—even setting aside for a moment the understanding that race is always a social construct, with no scientific validity (more on this in Chapter 2)—the idea of a single Hispanic race makes no sense, given the presence of people of indigenous, European, and African origin in Latin America. (It would make as much sense to say that there is a U.S. "race.") As Shorris puts it, "there is no Hispanic or Latino race. The spectrum of races is the American [that is, U.S.] spectrum, although the proportions are different" (151). For one thing, of course, the Hispanic-race-as-melting-pot construction, in its most extreme form, ignores the *continuing* existence of indigenous or African-descent populations in Latin America. (Not *everyone* identifies as "mestizo" or "mulatto.") For another, not all historical manifestations of syncretism are the same; the mixture of peoples and cultures looks very different in the Caribbean, where the indigenous peoples were decimated and large numbers of African slaves imported to sugar plantations, from how it looks in Mexico, Guatemala, or El Salvador, where the influence of the indigenous presence is much more obvious. And, needless to say, the indigenous peoples in different geographical spaces were themselves different peoples.[24]

Another persistent line of argument now being more rigorously challenged is that Latinos are connected by their "mother tongue"; here Spanish itself is the bond that makes of the various groups a single "family."[25] "Speaking Spanish," John A. García writes in *Latino Politics in America* (2003), "is still a fairly universal experience for most Latinos" (40). Perhaps recognizing the problem of asserting that Spanish is "universal," but only for "most," García falls back on the metaphor of family: "While not totally analogous, variations in character, lifestyle, personality, and so on, [. . .] can be found within most families" (22). The implication is that, like diverging members of a family, Latinos need not all speak Spanish to be connected; but this only begs the question of what, then, initially connects them.

Yet the notion of Spanish as the basis for a common culture, too, is being increasingly and resoundingly repudiated by other scholars. Tackling the topic of panethnic (or at least interethnic) *latinidad* in a U.S. context as early as 1985, Felix Padilla avoided terminology that suggested a *preexisting* group identity by referring to the Mexican and Puerto Rican populations under discussion as "Spanish-speaking" rather than as "Latino" or "Hispanic" (see, e.g., 16ff). In the conclusion of his study, Padilla—gesturing briefly toward the possibility of English-dominant, second- or third-generation Latinos (151)—switches briefly to the term "Spanish-surname" (148). As De Genova and Ramos-Zayas have commented, "prior administrative/demographic categories [such] as 'Spanish-surname' and 'Spanish-speaking' [...] inevitably failed to adequately encompass the anomalies of U.S.-born English-speaking Latinos, or Latinos with non-Spanish surnames" (19)—"anomalies" that have only increased in number since the mid-eighties.[26] Oboler, likewise commenting on the use of a common language as a justification for the panethnic grouping "Latino," notes that an increasing number of Latinos do not fit this characterization (xvi). Most recently, a 2004 study by the Pew Hispanic Center revealed that 25 percent of U.S. Latinos—including both citizens and noncitizens—speak primarily English ("2004 National Survey" 13); and this statistic does not include the additional 29 percent who are bilingual.[27] If, as Shorris puts it, "third or fourth generation Latinos who live in suburbs of Minneapolis or Atlanta have no more reason to know Spanish than Polish-Americans need to know Polish" (181–82), then what makes them "Latinos" at all (rather than simply being, say, Mexican American, the accurate analogy to Polish American)? As Chanady has reminded us, furthermore, even in the context of Latin American studies the paradigm of the Spanish language as a unifying element has come under fire: "the restriction of the concept of 'Latin American literature' to cultural productions written in European languages [...] necessarily entails the marginalization of autochthonous and popular literary traditions" (xxxiii–xxxiv).[28]

Even among those who do speak Spanish, however, its deployment as a common denominator apparently runs up against problems. It is worth recalling here that a majority of Latinos do not see themselves as sharing a common culture, regardless of the potential commonality of Spanish (Suro and Escobar 10), as one person snipes, "[t]hat's like saying that White Americans and Black South Africans are the same people because they both speak English" (Alderete). In *Latino Crossings*, which revisits Felix Padilla's earlier theme of the possibility of panethnic *latinidad* among Mexicans and Puerto Ricans in Chicago, De Genova and Ramos-Zayas note that "Spanish language was not a natural or automatic source of mutual recognition or Latino unity [for their interview subjects] and frequently became a source of further division. [...] Thus, even language—the one element commonly presumed to supply a basis for Latino-identified unity between the two groups—often served instead as a forcefully divisive basis for racializing their divergent identities as 'Mexican' or 'Puerto Rican'" (29).

Suárez-Orozco and Páez also acknowledge this difficulty; even while pointing out that Latinos statistically retain Spanish language use for longer than any other ethnic group, they add that "the language of Latinos in the United States presents a complicated picture. [. . .] [S]pecific words, folk sayings, and accents often produce different meanings and values within the different Latino communities. Language varieties act as a way of signifying subethnic identifications and marking subgroup identities" (8). For example, as Ana Celia Zentella elaborates, "Colombians in New York City [. . .] think very highly of Colombian Spanish and very little of Caribbean Spanish [. . .]. Linguistic differences as simple as the presence or absence of an /s/ at the end of a syllable can become identified with superiority or inferiority" (324).

There is plenty of anecdotal evidence to suggest that the "common" Spanish language can lead to a sense of cultural difference as often as of commonality. In an intriguing autobiographical essay, Berta Esperanza Hernández-Truyol—writing about her experience arriving in Albuquerque to teach at the University of New Mexico—represents herself as buying into the illusion of a common Hispanic culture: though she is Cuban, the Mexican-infused culture of Albuquerque "felt like home, the familiar Spanish influence, the rice and beans, the sunlight and the bright clothing" (28). In a subsequent hilarious vignette, Hernández-Truyol describes her search for food on her first night:

> I went into the only place I found open and ordered a tortilla, a plain tortilla. There, I was so happy, I could even order food in Spanish. The waitress looked at me kind of funny and asked, simply, "Are you sure all you want is a tortilla?" "Yes," I said. "Plain?" she asked. "Yes," I said, "it's late." So with a shrug of the shoulders she disappeared and promptly returned and put this plate in front of me. Sitting on the plate was this flat thing, white, warm, soft. My turn to ask, "And what is this?" "Your order, ma'am." And we stared at each other. I ate this thing, although I did not quite know how I was supposed to do that. I got funny looks when I went at it with fork and knife. (25)

Hernández-Truyol was, of course, thinking of what is now referred to in the United States as a *"Spanish* tortilla" (or "frittata")—that is, a sort of firm omelette with potatoes and onions baked into the egg mixture. She uses her anecdote to comment self-reflexively on the assumption of "home" and "common culture" ("Hey, that's MY story!") that even Latinos/as in the United States can participate in, and on the cultural gaps filled in by these assumptions. As she writes, "Here we were dealing with the same word: tortilla, and the same language: Spanish. Yet our different cultures give the word different meanings" (25). A common language, then, is in and of itself no guarantor of common culture for the various Latino ethnic groups.

As for religion—another cultural element frequently cited as part of Latino "common culture"[29]—while we can certainly acknowledge that the widespread influence of Catholicism has heavily impacted Latin American cultures, we should also keep in mind that the home-grown versions of Catholicism in Mexico and other Central American countries, heavily shaped by the indigenous spiritual beliefs and practices that preceded it, looks strikingly different from the home-grown versions in Caribbean nations, where the main syncretism was with beliefs imported from Africa and preserved by the slave populations. Juan Gonzalez, in his smart and comprehensive *Harvest of Empire* (2000), tells the story of getting a phone call from a Puerto Rican in East Harlem complaining about the Mexicans "taking over our church." The caller continued, "And the first thing they [the Mexicans] want to do [. . .] is put the statue of the Virgen de Guadalupe in the front of the church! [. . .] I told them, 'That's your Virgin, not ours'" (xvi–xvii). And if only about three-fourths of U.S. Latinos are Catholic at all (see Mosher et al. 376), do we still "count"?

Despite these substantial difficulties, nonetheless, several scholars are unwilling to do away entirely with the concept of a panethnic group identity. For one thing—and this is quite a persuasive argument—the category "Latino" allows scholarship at its best to be *more* nuanced about particular trajectories and dynamics by comparing and contrasting the various Latino groups. Suárez-Orozco and Páez, for example, make an excellent case that a fuller understanding of the phenomenon of transnationalism among immigrant Latino populations is achieved by comparing the trajectories of different Latino immigrant groups. Puerto Ricans and Dominicans, in particular, have been cited as having strong transnational ties, including periodic returns, a degree of political involvement in the homeland, and financial remittances to relatives and friends there. In contrast, Mexican immigration to the United States seems to be undergoing a trend away from transnational behaviors and toward a more "permanent" status within the United States (6–7). As Suárez-Orozco and Páez ask, "Will Dominicans, over time and across generations, follow the Mexican pattern? Or will they adopt the Puerto Rican version of transnationalism, which by some indicators has intensified rather than decreased over time?" (7). Only a panethnic framework of study allows scholars to ask such questions in this particular way. (Indeed, such an argument is the guiding principle of this book, which is precisely about how, and to what degree, writers of *differing* national origins have grappled with transnational and panethnic categories.)

Of course, such arguments assert less the "groupness" of Latinos than they do the usefulness of the category for other reasons. But scholars—Suárez-Orozco and Páez included—are also increasingly making use of more sophisticated arguments for asserting certain important commonalities that might go some way toward explaining a sense of Latino peoplehood. Historically, Flores asserts, "it is possible to find a common thread in the intricate 'Latino' weave, or at least a framework in which to interpret the [...] Latino presence in some more encompassing way" (*From Bomba* 145). Flores is adamant that any analysis of the panethnic category "Latino" must be undertaken within a broader view of the "larger international context, Latin America" (*From Bomba* 151). Latin Americans themselves have, for over a century, been engaged in the construction of a continental, panethnic identity: "The sense and practice of a 'Latino/Hispanic' unity across national lines [...] go way back, as does the recognized need for names to designate such tactical or enduring common ground" (*From Bomba* 148). Flores grounds this unity in the pan-national movement toward independence from Spain, making frequent references to José Martí's "Nuestra América" as a prominent historical example of the construction, in a Latin American continental context, of a panethnic identity. Further, Flores points out, these efforts took place on U.S. soil as well as within Latin America itself (*From Bomba* 148).

Agustín Laó-Montes, in his introduction to *Mambo Montage* (2001), concurs that Latinization—helpfully defined as an "overall process of production of *discourses* of latinidad" (4; emphasis added)—can be traced to national struggles for independence against Spain, as well as to resistance to U.S. domination in the region (6). As Chanady points out in a similar vein, the central contrast of Martí's "Nuestra América," "'Our [mestizo and Hispanic] America,' as opposed to the 'Other' America—the United States [...] must be situated within a strategy of resistance to U.S. hegemony, and related to the desire to constitute a specific Latin American identity as opposed to the United States, as well as to that of Spain" (Chanady xv; bracketed phrase in original). And as Oboler reminds us, the 1823 Monroe Doctrine, which declared that any European efforts to control the independent nations of the Western Hemisphere would be viewed by the United States as hostile, and which was largely aimed at preventing Spain from reasserting its power over its former colonies (as well as the 1904 Roosevelt Corollary, which asserted that the United States *did* have the right to intervene in Latin American nations), effectively constructed all of Latin America, from the point of view of the United States at least, as a single entity (4). Latin American unity, or a sense of continental peoplehood, has thus been instrumentally useful as a strategy of resistance: "Bolívar's dream [of a unified Latin America] has been continually (though selectively) invoked for over a hundred and fifty years to express solidarity in the face of outsiders. First as a revolutionary sentiment, then as an anti-imperialist slogan, the idea of an indivisible Latin America has been useful in Latin Americans' dealing with foreigners" (Jones-Correa, *Between Two Nations* 118).

This idea potentially gains even greater currency for U.S. Latinos when, as a multitude of scholars insist, current and past Latin American migration to the United States is understood to be a direct function of U.S. domination.[30] In this argument, it is the history of U.S. intervention in the various Latin American nations, as well as its current position within a global economy that (for example) exploits cheap labor abroad, which provides the "weave" of common experience (although within that weave differences inevitably emerge, such as the degree of direct intervention or of economic dependency). As Suárez-Orozco and Páez put it, "We are here because you were there" (18).

It may be noted, of course, that the specific nature of U.S. relations with any given nation determines that the character of immigration has taken substantially different forms. Poor Mexicans seeking better economic opportunities, especially in the wake of the North American Free Trade Agreement,[31] cannot be expected to share a "common" sensibility with the first wave of upper- and upper-middle-class Cuban exiles, many of whom were already used to having extensive business dealings with companies in the United States that controlled much of Cuba's economy.[32] But this divergence might, finally, be read through the lens of a general "common" history (U.S. economic domination) to which the various actors will respond differently. As Chanady glosses (and translates) Antonio Cornejo Polar's discussion of Latin American literatures, it is helpful to think in terms of a "paradigm of 'contradictory totality,' in which a 'single historical process' affects diverse [...] groups in different ways" (Cornejo Polar 128, qtd. in Chanady xxxiv). After all, analogously, any national history is shared by all of a country's citizens, although different constituencies among those citizens will respond to that history differently, based on their positioning within it. (This understanding allows us to conceive of the category "Latino" in a way which does not presuppose a particular ideological or political perspective.)

Oboler, however, diverges from the notion that the source of Latino identity can be found in the historical legacies of Spanish colonialism and U.S. domination, pointing out that the possibility of a transnational *latinidad* is "a debate that Latin American intellectuals have themselves waged since the nineteenth century" (17). Further, the question of a unified identity—which even Latin Americans have never agreed on—is still profoundly unresolved in the U.S. context (Oboler xiv). "Latino" is not the extension into the United States of a formerly stable "Latin American" identity. That identity has always been contested. (Here Laó-Montes's distinction between the multiplication of discourses [Latinization] and the category of identity [*latinidad*] is particularly helpful, because it allows us to conceive of the two things separately. The production of discourses may certainly be instrumental in constructing what eventually becomes internalized as an identity category, but their existence need not imply that the identity already exists in a stable form.)

Further, since collective identities are inevitably constructs, we cannot simply assume that a particular collective identity called into being in a given set of historical circumstances will then become fixed and remain unchanged over time. A common history is not enough for a collective identity. (The "common history" of European colonization—and miscegenation—followed by U.S. intervention has certainly not been enough to give Haiti and the Dominican Republic, which even share the same island, a common identity. Rather, historically they have seen themselves in opposition, calling on a history that emphasizes their differences.) Here we do well to remember—whatever the lingering power of Simón Bolívar's dream—that only a distinct minority of U.S. Latinos actually believe they share one culture (Suro and Escobar 10).

A study by Michael Jones-Correa and David Leal also presents some interesting findings in this regard; the authors found that the most significant predictor of whether someone Latino was likely to choose a panethnic label was whether she or he was a first- , second- , or third-generation immigrant.[33] That is, the further removed from the moment of immigration, the *more* likely the person was to use a term such as "Latino" or "Hispanic" to refer to himself/herself (224). The authors' conclusion is that "panethnic identification is, in fact, being constructed in the United States, not being brought fully formed by Latin American immigration" (229). Or, as Suárez-Orozco and Páez put it, "Latinos are made in the USA" (4).

One problem with the notion of a panethnic identity, from a Latin American perspective, is that national identity has always trumped continental identity in the home countries. Thus, as Jones-Correa explains, "Latin American immigrants' ethnic identities are shaped not just by the choices they make in the United States, but also by the weight of identity choices made in the past. Previous constructions of identity have a kind of inertia to them; they become the raw materials for ethnic choices and ethnic politics in the United States. The continuity of previous constructions of identity explains, in part, the difficulties in forming political coalitions among Hispanics of various national origins in the United States" (*Between Two Nations* 122). But the latent possibility of identifying as Latin American and of conceiving of a "common" continental history vis-à-vis both Spain and the United States—also a "previous construction of identity," even if not the primary one—can nonetheless be given new life under the right (or, perhaps, the wrong) set of circumstances within the United States. Chanady elaborates: "The *reactualization* of the past (as appropriation, invention, fictionalization, and institutionalization), [. . .] has always been an essential element of the constitution of cultural identity" (xxix; emphasis added). The past, that is to say, under certain circumstances is called into the service of the present. In Cornell and Hartmann's explanation of ethnicity (drawing on Schermerhorn), they suggest that "the common history a group claims" can be understood as one of several "symbolic elements that may be viewed as emblematic of peoplehood," but that "these claims need not be founded in fact" to be symbolically powerful (19). In explaining ethnic self-consciousness, the *invocation* of a common history (real or imagined) is more important than the factual existence of shared historical circumstances.[34] Ethnicity, like nation, is narration. If, as Flores puts it, a collective Latino identity is "always provisional and subject to reexamination" (*From Bomba* 164), then we must look at the particular "provisions" within the more recent context that would continue to call such an identity into being.[35]

The most common view among scholars who take this approach is that ethnicity, and in particular Latino panethnicity, is "instrumental," invoked to address pressing political, economic, and other disparities. The argument goes that the new U.S. context does, indeed, tend to homogenize the various groups and thus generates experiences that are similar across at least several of the various Latino groups. (In its most nuanced forms, this argument takes account of subgroup differences, especially when one group—most often Cubans—does not fit the general "profile" as well as the others. Thus the argument, at its best, focuses more on common "themes" that span several groups and are therefore properly panethnic than on giving the entire panethnic label coherence.) Felix Padilla was one of the earliest proponents of this view, insisting that "the expression of Latino ethnic-conscious behavior is *situationally* specific, crystallized under certain circumstances of inequality experience shared by more than one Spanish-speaking group at a point in time" (61). It is the experience of analogous inequalities—as well as U.S. policies and programs such as "civil rights laws, equal employment opportunities, and affirmative action" (F. Padilla 8)—that has spurred a strategic sense of "connectedness" among Latinos at certain times.

Elaborations on the particular types of structural inequalities experienced across national subgroups are many. John A. García cites educational attainment (25, 43), as well as "lower levels of family income, and corresponding higher rates of family poverty" (49), as "common ground" that places Latinos across various subgroups "at risk in terms of quality of life (e.g., housing conditions, educational isolation, limited employment opportunities, economic segregation, and vulnerability to violent crime)" (49). "Quite alarming," as Suárez-Orozco and Páez point out, "are the recent findings of the Harvard Civil Rights project, which established that Latino children are now facing the most intense segregation [. . .] of any ethnic and racial group in the United States" (28). Shorris is eloquent on the topic of poor education and its creation of diminished opportunities for working-class Latinos, particularly those who do not speak English as a first language: "a child who speaks only Spanish and is not allowed to develop his conceptual abilities in his own language while he learns to speak another will fall behind his peers. After the first failure, the next comes easily; the pattern develops so quickly that a child in the third or second or even the first grade may be lost to despair" (225). Shorris makes a compelling case that the educational problems for Latinos lie not with bilingual education—which others have claimed is responsible for holding Spanish speakers back—but with the poverty of many school systems in which bilingual programs are in place.

A related issue, as numerous scholars have pointed out, is the racialization of Latinos in the U.S. context (Suárez-Orozco and Páez 3). Noting that, officially, the "Hispanic" question on the U.S. Census is not about race but about ethnicity, De Genova and Ramos-Zayas argue that, "[n]evertheless, this hegemonic 'ethnic' distinction instituted by the U.S. state has been [...] widely treated as a racial condition all the same," since it designates Hispanics as a "'minority' population analogous to African Americans" and is used in determining "the allocation of affirmative action entitlements" (16). Quite strikingly, Clara E. Rodríguez, in *Changing Race* (2000), discusses a 1993 proposal to amend the U.S. Census form for 2000 that "called for the elimination of the 'Hispanic' identifier and the addition of a 'Hispanic' race category to the race question" (159). Rodríguez notes that the proposal (notably *not* advanced by any Hispanic constituency) would, of course, have changed the "Hispanic" classification from an ethnic one, "in which Hispanics could be of any race," to a racial one, in which by implication "all Hispanics were one race" (159). The proposal did not pass, but Rodríguez records that this is not the first time such a proposal has been made (161). As Suárez-Orozco and Páez comment, "it is abundantly clear that in the context of the workings of the state apparatus, the subgroup labels are generally quite secondary to the panethnic construct" (6).

Here is an example of a label imposed from above that may well be influencing a people's own perception of itself, at least in part. Asked to identify *racially* in the 2000 census,[36] an amazing 47.4 percent of Latinos declined to identify themselves in the standard racial categories offered by the census form and instead volunteered some other term, usually a panethnic one such as "Latino" or "Hispanic"—that is, they constructed their own racial category (Logan 1, 3).[37] That is to say, our encounter with U.S. dominant culture, which sees us similarly, has made us one. This may well be partly the assumption of a strategic or instrumental identity; in the face of common treatment by dominant U.S. culture, crystallized by the assignation of an umbrella label such as

"Hispanic," people of Latin American descent may well require the assumption of a group identity which provides strength in numbers. On the other hand, that group identity might more simply be an internalization of dominant racial ideology in the United States. Martha Gimenez, for one, argues that these labels can be seen as "forms of ideological interpellation which, under certain material conditions, are likely to produce 'Hispanic' or Latino subjects" ("Latino Politics" 178). As Jones-Correa and Leal have observed, "an identity may be constructed (by the state or by the individual within the parameters set by the state) without being instrumental" (239). Indeed, Silvio Torres-Saillant has argued powerfully that a notion of seamless and unified *hispanidad* is one constructed and sold by Spanish-language media such as Univisión and Telemundo; in this sense such an identity might be "instrumental" for the amassing of corporate profits rather than for political goals of the communities themselves (444–48). Nonetheless, needless to say, daily exposure to such messages must surely have some effect on the people whom they address. Considered in these contexts, panethnicity need not be understood only as a manifestation of "instrumental" resistance to hegemonic control; it might be precisely the opposite: "It is ironic [. . .] that in the United States the anti-imperial tradition of *el sueño de Bolívar* [Bolívar's dream] is invoked to reinforce a state-defined Hispanic identity" (Jones-Correa, *Between Two Nations* 119)

Further, shared experiences of educational disadvantage, poverty, and racialization are not, in and of themselves, enough to generate a sense of common peoplehood. For common experiences to be *experienced* as "in common," Latino groups—it has been frequently argued—need to be in close enough contact with one another, geographically speaking, that they can perceive the similarities. Juan Gonzalez makes a case for "the emergence during the last several decades of a rich new Latino identity on U.S. soil" precisely along these lines (187), observing that, "[f]rom what was at first largely a Mexican American population in the Southwest and a Puerto Rican enclave in New York City, the different Hispanic groups have undergone, and continue to undergo, cultural amalgamation among themselves—through intermarriage, through shared knowledge of one another's music, food, and traditions, through common language, through a common experience of combating anti-Hispanic prejudice and being shunted into the same de facto segregated neighborhoods" (187).

The "space" where this "momentous pan-Latinization" (Flores, *From Bomba* 142) has occurred is, needless to say, an urban one, since it is to urban centers such as New York, Los Angeles, Chicago, and Miami that the latest waves of Latino immigrants have flocked. This newest influx means that the Latino groups do interact in close proximity to one another and, often, build organizations around particular points of shared interest that span national-origin identities. As John A. García writes, "The coexistence of native-born and 'immigrant' living in the same or proximate neighborhoods, familial social networks, and common work environments and business interactions provide a regular basis for cultural exchanges and experiences. These interactions can reinforce cultural expressions and values" (41). The importance of close and regular contact over time cannot be underestimated as an important factor in community building, as Jean Wyatt argues in *Risking Difference* (188–90). At the level of the city, then, a notion of panethnic, Latin American–origin identities may indeed begin to make sense. In the view of Juan Flores, the realities of lived experience for Puerto Ricans in New York summon up, of necessity, some concept of *latinidad*—a useful category for referring to their enmeshed relationships with other Latino groups (*From Bomba* 142).

Approaching the notion of an emerging Latino community from another angle, some linguists—in a new take on the old notion of a "common language"—were engaged in a study that compared pronoun use (in Spanish) by various Latino groups in New York City; the study's goal, as reported in a December 2002 article in the *New York Times*, was to determine whether, in New York and other U.S. cities, the different linguistic traits of the various groups were coming together, thereby suggesting a new panethnic collectivity in formation (Scott). As Katherine Sugg comments, the immigrants being studied "demonstrate the persistence of national identifications in Latino communities. And yet the linguists' study and its guiding questions also suggest a perceived 'convergence' of these groups into a new Latino identity and community in the United States" (228). The linguists, that is, are engaged in a project of "tracing the linguistic origin point of a US-based *latinidad*" (228). Ana Celia Zentella, one of the linguists involved in the study, writes that Spanish usage in the United States changes to reflect its new context:

> Technology produces many *anglicismos* ("anglicisms"), such as *la compyuta/computadora* ("the computer"), *bipéame* ("beep me"), and *tu emilio* ("your e-mail") [. . .]. Other borrowings reflect the daily lives of most workers: *el bos/la bosa* ("the boss," male/female), *fultaim/partaim/overtaim* ("full-time/part-time/overtime"), *el cheque* ("the paycheck," "the restaurant bill"), *los biles* ("the bills"), and *trobol* ("trouble"). Most linguistic loans are shared across the country—for example, *chirona* ("cheater") is heard on the playgrounds of Los Angeles and New York City (329).

These comments suggest the intriguing possibility that, existing side by side with linguistic habits that mark and distinguish separate national-origin communities, a new "made in the U.S.A." Spanish signals an emerging panethnic exchange.

This evolving sense of panethnic Latino communities—or at least panethnic contact—in U.S. cities is born out in some examples of literary production in the last two decades. In *The Forbidden Stories of Marta Veneranda* (1997; trans. 2001), a marvelous volume of short stories by Cuban exile Sonia Rivera-Valdés, Cubans and Puerto Ricans in New York are matter-of-factly married to each other. Working-class Puerto Ricans make brief appearances among the Cuban exiles in the New York of Cuban American writers Cristina García (*Dreaming in Cuban*, 1992) and Oscar Hijuelos (*The Mambo Kings Play Songs of Love*, 1989), as well as in the Chicago of Carlos Eire (*Waiting for Snow in Havana*, 2003). In the poem that opens Puerto Rican author Judith Ortiz Cofer's collection of autobiographical vignettes, stories, poems, and essays set largely in Paterson, New Jersey, *The Latin Deli* (1993)—whose title itself suggests a more collective sensibility, even though most of the stories feature primarily Puerto Rican "Latins"—the owner of the deli spends her days

> listening to the Puerto Ricans complain
> that it would be cheaper to fly to San Juan
> than to buy a pound of Bustelo coffee here,
> and to Cubans perfecting their speech
> of a "glorious return" to Havana—where no one
> has been allowed to die and nothing to change until then;
> to Mexicans who pass through, talking lyrically
> of *dólares* to be made in El Norte.(3)

In the Chicago of Achy Obejas's collection *We Came All The Way from Cuba So You Could Dress Like This?* (1994), a Mexican American and a Puerto Rican are friends in the story "Forever"; a Mexican American marries a Mexican immigrant to give him citizenship in "The Spouse"; and an unspecified Latino and his Anglo boyfriend banter about the "Latin fascination with baseball" and the "Latin inferiority complex" (60) in "Above All, a Family Man." In the title story, as well as in Obejas's subsequent two novels (*Memory Mambo* [1996] and *Days of Awe* [2001]), the Cuban narrators also find themselves in Chicago, much like Obejas herself.

In Héctor Tobar's *The Tattooed Soldier*, a mail service, El Pulgarcito Express ("The Little Thumb"), caters to Central American immigrants of varying national origins in Los Angeles, promising (but failing) to send their letters and packages safely home. A homeless Guatemalan immigrant wanders the streets of Los Angeles with his Mexican friend; when he has trouble speaking English, the narrator comments, "Los Angeles was the problem. In Los Angeles, Antonio could spend days and weeks speaking only his native tongue, breathing, cooking, laughing, and embarrassing himself with all sorts of people in Spanish" (3).

In a twist on the notion of urban center as Latino contact zone, in Guatemalan American writer Francisco Goldman's *The Ordinary Seaman* (1997), men of varying Central American origin (Honduran, Nicaraguan, Guatemalan) come to the United States to serve as crew for a ship under Panamanian registry docked at the Brooklyn waterfront (a strange, liminal contact zone floating in the margins of the urban center of New York), then find themselves stranded and abandoned aboard the ship. Eventually, one of the crewmen, Esteban, ventures off the ship into New York, where he encounters a Cuban beauty salon owner, a Mexican manicurist, a Dominican waitress, a Colombian factory owner, and several other Central Americans of diverse origin. As with Tobar's Los Angeles, we are told, "It's true, you can live in Nueva York [...] and never have to speak English to anyone but telephone operators and bill collectors" (246). (In Part Three, I discuss at greater length some works which pay sustained attention to the points of difference and tension among various national-origin Latino groups.) Perhaps it is fair to say that, as the conditions emerge in the United States for a collective Latino identity, we can begin to observe more "narration" of that identity in Latino literature. But it is nevertheless still striking how very tentative that particular form of narration seems to be.

Jean Wyatt has argued that any construction of multicultural community—and surely, at this point we can recognize that the "Latino community" at best must be conceived in this way—carries risks, for communities, by the very nature of their narratives of "community," strive for

> a collective form of identification. If cultural pluralism is an aim of multicultural community—and by pluralism I mean not just a principle of inclusiveness but an organizing principle that would give equal voice to all and enable the full expression of diversity and dissension—then identification poses a threat to pluralism. For identification, at both individual and community levels, tends toward an assimilation of difference to the same. The desire for identification moves the subject toward an illusory unity of self and other that erases difference and threatens the perception of the other as other. ("Toward Cross-race Dialogue" 880)

Wyatt's comments add a cautionary note to the "Hey, that's MY story!" reaction. We can see her warning borne out in Michael Jones-Correa's discussion, in *Between Two Nations*, of tensions between Puerto Ricans and other Latino groups in New York City: "For the past several years, [...] there has been a

'*Somos Uno*' ('We're All One') conference held in New York to set a statewide Latino political agenda. Every year there are complaints from non–Puerto Ricans. One Colombian complained to me that 'everything was about Puerto Ricans and Puerto Rican problems. Why do they call it *Somos Uno* if they are not going to include everyone?'" (116). Here we can see how efforts on the part of Latinos to imagine themselves as a single community come up against precisely the sort of problems that Wyatt predicts; identification as "one" occludes the equal expression of distinct voices, as Puerto Ricans "present themselves as the spokespersons for Latinos in the city" (116).

Even narratives of panethnicity offered by Latinos themselves do not necessarily reflect a true sense of consensus or collectivity, however instrumental they may be. De Genova and Ramos-Zayas add a further caveat to the notion of urban space as Latino contact zone, citing "robust evidence of significant divisions between" national-origin groups in Chicago and remarking that "this has tended to be especially so precisely in some of the predicaments where they found themselves in greatest proximity" (55). Close contact might result in a greater sense of panethnicity or at least of "instrumental" deployment of the category; but it can also result in confrontation, antagonism, and even alienation.

Indeed, as Jones-Correa and Leal's important 1996 study, "Becoming 'Hispanic,'" suggests, *neither* a view of "common culture" *nor* a view of instrumental, strategic ethnicity is enough to explain the use of the panethnic label among Latinos themselves. (As Jones-Correa has subsequently noted, a purely instrumental view of ethnicity cannot account for the persisting power within a U.S. context of national-origin identities, and the predominance of these over a panethnic identification, which would surely seem to have more instrumental value [*Between Two Nations* 116]). Jones-Correa and Leal's study revisits data first compiled in 1989–90 for the Latino National Political Survey. The original study would seem at first glance to suggest a relative absence of panethnic identity among respondents, most of whom preferred to identify by national origin (217). Jones-Correa and Leal found, however, that, when respondents "gave more than one answer to the question asking for their ethnic identification" (220), the number of respondents identifying either primarily or secondarily using a panethnic term went up. "Panethnic identification jumps from the 14% who used these identifiers as their primary identification to the 41.7% who used panethnic identifiers at some time" (220). While these figures are now of course dated, it is worth pointing out that a similar dynamic still seems to hold true, indeed, perhaps even more so today. For example, in the 2002 National Survey of Latinos by the Pew Hispanic Center, while only 24 percent of respondents chose "Latino" or "Hispanic" as their primary term of identification, this number went up to 81 percent when they were asked if they had *ever* described themselves using such a panethnic term (charts 4 and 5).

Jones-Correa and Leal argue that common culture cannot by itself account for panethnic identification, because "identifying panethnically does not have a *very pronounced* effect on how respondents perceive cultural commonalties" (230; emphasis added). They go on to explain: "The effect, when it occurs, is not among those who believe that these cultures are very similar"—these were notably a distinct minority, ranging from 14.65 percent to 18.45 percent, in *every* category of identification—

> but, rather, among those who believe that they are somewhat similar. For instance, [...] 65% of those who expressed a primary preference for panethnic identification (along with other identification choices) thought that all Hispanics in the United States shared a somewhat similar culture, versus 59% who expressed any preference at all for panethnic identification and 49% who expressed no such preference at all. The difference that panethnicity makes is at the margin; people are somewhat more likely to think that there is a shared Hispanic culture if they choose or prefer a panethnic label. (230)

I would revise this statement as follows: people are somewhat more likely to think that the different Hispanic cultures are *somewhat similar* (which is not the same thing as a single "shared culture")—if they identify panethnically.[38] For Jones-Correa and Leal, the difference in sense of cultural similarities between those who did *not* identify panethnically (49 percent) and those who did (up to 65 percent) is not enough to explain choosing to identify as "Latino" or "Hispanic"; almost half of those who *do not* identify panethnically still feel the cultures are somewhat similar, for one thing, and there is only a 16 percent increase for respondents with a much stronger panethnic identification.[39] Presumably, if the sense of "common culture" were the key to Latino identity, one would see a much smaller percentage of the nonpanethnics feeling this way, and a significantly greater proportion of the panethnics doing so.

Given the current state of scholarship, this is perhaps no great surprise; more intriguingly, however, Jones-Correa and Leal come up with similar findings with regard to political commonalities among the various groups: "The findings go in the right direction but are not significant" (230). For instance, a total of 35.48 percent of respondents who did not identify panethnically said that the political concerns of Mexicans and Cubans were "Somewhat Similar" or "Very Similar" compared to 47.69 percent of those who identified primarily with a panethnic label (but also identified with other labels). As we can see, use of a panethnic label such as "Latino" or "Hispanic" corresponded with a greater likelihood of seeing some political commonalities, but if common politics were the basis for panethnic identity, one would expect to see a lower number from those who *do not* identify as panethnic and a much higher one (surely a majority, at least) among those who do. When comparing Puerto Rican and Cuban concerns, the differences were even less notable: 48.44 percent of the nonpanethnics thought the concerns of these groups were somewhat or very similar, versus only 56.81 percent of those who identified primarily as panethnic (along with other secondary labels) (232).

As I have already discussed, by contrast, the most significant predictor of whether someone was likely to choose a panethnic label was whether she or he was a first- , second- , or third-generation immigrant. On the other hand, the authors reject the notion that panethnicity is instrumental or cultural in nature, since the results on each of these questions do not point to a definitive explanation of the panethnic label. The authors conclude that "[p]eople who choose a panethnic identifier seem to do so in general, regardless of the specific circumstances and apart from any strategic considerations. Nor is it [panethnicity] a feeling of solidarity with the political interests of other Latin American–origin groups" (239–41). In other words, we know that succeeding generations are more likely to identify as panethnic, but we do not know why.

The answer, perhaps, could be found in an earlier statement that is somewhat buried in the article—having to do with what the respondents themselves listed as their understandings of the panethnic label(s). As the authors note, the respondents listed *various* ways of understanding this label, including geographical, cultural, or political commonalities. What this suggests is the possibility that no *one* understanding of the term might be sufficient to explain people's *various* identifications with it. I would offer, then, that this study suggests the intriguing possibility that Latino identity may indeed be even more "elastic" than the authors themselves recognize (Jones-Correa and Leal 220). People may well have *varying* reasons for employing the term (when they do), ranging from a simple acceptance of the census categorization whereby individual national identities also "count" as Latino, to a belief in cultural similarities (that may have become more pronounced in a U.S. culture where the dominant language is English and Spanish-speakers are a minority who often face language-based discrimination), to an awareness of common historical dynamics (activated or energized for a variety of reasons by the U.S. context), to a growing sense that within U.S. society certain structural inequalities create similar political concerns for Latino groups under certain circumstances, to an "instrumental" conviction that such political concerns can be better addressed in larger numbers. As Debra Castillo puts it, "Strategic choices, internalized constraints, and historical and cultural factors *all* affect the degree to which individuals reinforce or resist identity claims made on their behalf" (*Redreaming America* 8; emphasis added). None of these factors is enough to explain Latino identity in isolation; taken together, they provide a range of ways in which people can understand being "Latino." Put another way, these findings might confirm the plethora of explanations for *latinidad* that a multitude of scholars and commentators, from a wide variety of disciplinary fields, have offered. It perhaps goes without saying that *each* of these scholars is engaged in the construction of "Latino" ethnicity. The narratives that construct the boundaries of a collective group of people known as "Latino" continue to be told in competing and sometimes contradictory ways. Alternatively, as Castillo's comment implicitly suggests, certain counternarratives can continue to pose serious obstacles to a sense of *latinidad*, even when a belief in cultural, political, or historical convergences might be present.

\* \* \*

As early as 1989 Werner Sollors was lamenting that, "by and large, [literary] studies tend less to set out to explore [ethnicity's] construction than to take it for granted as a relatively fixed or, at least, a known and self-evident category" (*Invention* xiii).[40] Elaborating on this complaint elsewhere, Sollors writes, "the notion has gained dominance that a 'people' is held together by a subliminal culture of fairy tales, songs, and folk beliefs [. . .]. As a result of this legacy 'ethnicity' as a term for literary study largely evokes the accumulation of cultural bits that demonstrate the original creativity, emotive cohesion, and temporal depth of a particular collectivity" ("Ethnicity" 290). (Largely, this approach to ethnic literature has treated signs of cultural difference in terms of their resistance to a dominant, mainstream U.S. culture bent on assimilation.) Sollors calls on literary criticism to ask, instead, "What is the active contribution literature makes, as a productive force, to the emergence and maintenance of communities [. . .] and of ethnic distinctions?" (*Invention* xiv). And he is less interested in the "cultural bits" than in the ways that ethnic literature might imagine the boundary lines of ethnic groupings. Sollors adopts "Fredrik Barth's thesis that ethnicity rests on the *boundary*, not on the 'cultural stuff that it encloses'" ("Ethnicity" 299), and points out that "Barth's theory can easily accommodate the observation that ethnic groups in the United States have relatively little cultural differentiation, that the cultural *content* of ethnicity is largely interchangeable [. . .] . From such a perspective, contrastive strategies—naming and name-calling among them—become the most important thing about ethnicity" (*Beyond Ethnicity* 28).[41]

Of course, Sollors's claim about the "largely interchangeable" nature of cultural content can surely be taken as exaggerated. A Cuban American who practices Santería *is* participating in a different culture from that of a Mexican

American who prays to the Virgin of Guadalupe. Nevertheless, shifting attention from the content of ethnicity to the construction of its boundaries can highlight issues of inclusion and exclusion. What kinds of boundary-drawing maneuvers would allow the two people in my example above to get included in the same "ethnicity"? For that matter, what kind of boundary-drawing maneuvers would mean that the Mexican American in my example (let us assume now, for the sake of argument, that he is a light-skinned New Mexican) might not see a person of fully indigenous Mexican ancestry as part of his own "ethnicity" (despite the cultural "commonality" derived from centuries of syncretic Catholic/indigenous practices), or that the (again hypothetically, "white") Cuban American might not see a black Cuban as part of hers?

Karen Christian's *Show and Tell* is the first critical study of Latino/a literature, as a panethnic category, to give serious attention to the *construction* of Latino ethnicity, not only by those outside the ethnic "group" but by those within it. Her particular focus in literary analysis, however, is on the cultural content that gets marked as ethnic and its performance in particular literary texts. Christian is interested in the ways that individual characters "perform" *cubanidad* or *chicanismo*, in what texts do with "cultural markers" such as "the images of the Chicano migrant worker" and "the Latin Lover" as "symbols of Latina/o 'essence' in the American popular imagination" (16), and in the ways in which novels can undermine the illusion of authentic ethnicity that is generated by such performances.

In this project, however, I am more interested in looking at the *boundaries* of ethnicity: how they are narratively drawn; how they have fluctuated; who—in terms of race, national origin, citizenship (United States versus country of origin)—gets included and who gets excluded; and the like. My focus is on stories of collective identity (those "collective fictions" Sollors names), which are inevitably battle lines of sorts, designating an "us" and a "them," but which, as we will see in the texts that follow, can shift and be redrawn to suit particular sociohistorical contexts. Who gets to be "us" and who gets to be "them" are questions under constant debate and revision in literature.

I have chosen (after all my laborious dissection of it) to accept the category "Latino" and use it, without assuming any more fundamental connections between the various groups but in acknowledgment of the fact that a sense of a larger group identity has tentatively been constructed—often by popular culture—in the United States. Since the category "Latino" or "Hispanic" has acquired very real meaning and power in U.S. public discourse, inevitably, those named by the category must therefore engage with it somehow. Calling Cuban Americans, Mexican Americans, Puerto Rican mainlanders, and Dominican Americans (to name just a few groups) "Latino" allows me a certain easy (if dangerous) shorthand; but, more important, it also gives me the tools for discussing how the various groups engage with dominant-culture conceptions of themselves, as well as with each other. Sometimes—but not always, or even frequently—that engagement does indeed come to look something like a forged sense of peoplehood.

My main concerns in this book revolve around the question of how Latino/a narratives represent (or do not represent) various collectivities implicit in the social construction of "Latinoness," which forges an identity that makes of very different people a single group. This study asks how and when Latino/a literary texts imagine points of identity among specific ethnic "Latino" groups (e.g., Cubans, Mexicans), as well as between Latino/as and overlapping groups (e.g., indigenous peoples, African Americans), and when, indeed, such texts highlight the differences or fissures among groups that have come to constitute Latinoness. How do these texts respond to the homogenizing tendency on the part of mainstream U.S. culture to erase significant historical, cultural, and economic differences among Latino/a groups under the general heading of "Latino" or "Hispanic"? How do they respond to the equally pervasive assumptions that U.S. Latino/as are essentially connected to their countries and cultures of origin? And how do the works treat supposedly self-evident differences between Latino/as and other groups, such as African Americans or American Indians? How in general do these texts insert themselves into the politics of identity and difference that form such a central part of ethnic studies in academia today? Finally, what strains emerge when texts do, indeed, investigate the possibility of a panethnic "Latino" identity or solidarity?

This is a book about a particular set of issues and theoretical concerns rather than a comprehensive overview of Latino literature. Indeed, the latter becomes increasingly impossible; as the field of writers and texts expands exponentially every year, an overview of "Latino literature" in general becomes just as unimaginable as an overview of "American literature." This project, then, does not pretend to coverage. Rather, I am interested in texts which foreground, in particularly vivid and intriguing ways, the problematic nature of panethnic, transracial, transnational, and even transclass identities. For the sake of providing some coherence to the project I have chosen to limit myself to Latino/a narrative in the succeeding chapters—primarily fiction, although some fiction is, to a greater or lesser degree, autobiographically based, and one memoir, Piri Thomas's *Down These Mean Streets*, is inevitably to some degree fictionalized. Needless to say, addressing the issue of an imagined panethnic Latino/a identity requires that I examine texts from several national-origin groups; a focus on a single group would simply not permit an adequate exploration into the sorts of *cross*-group transactions and imaginings that intrigue me. Nonetheless, since many Latino/a writers have understood themselves primarily in terms of a more specific ethnicity of national origin, at times my discussion focuses on a collective identity imagined in those more specific terms; such texts nevertheless inevitably question and poke at group boundaries and present various cross-racial, cross-class, and transnational (i.e., U.S. *and* country-of-origin) notions of collective identity. In these texts I examine how the authors might recognize differences between themselves and "Others" (in terms of race, geography/citizenship, or class) and yet reach across those boundaries to pull the Others in. But I also turn, in Part Three, to how the authors deal more explicitly with the panethnic "Latino" category: how they question it, challenge it, appropriate it, and, at times, hope to reimagine it along more productive lines.

Part One, "Race and Ethnicity," includes two chapters on texts which attempt to understand an ethnic identity racially, in terms of its "overlap" with Native Americans (in Rudolfo Anaya's *Bless Me Ultima*) or African Americans (in Piri Thomas's *Down These Mean Streets*). Taken together, the two chapters illustrate the disparate ways in which Latino writers of different ethnic groups (Chicano vs. Puerto Rican) have imagined collective group identities based in part on suppressed racial identities. Looking at these two significantly earlier and now "classic" works of Latino literature, from the two central groups that constituted the main "Hispanic" population in the United States until the influx of Cubans began in 1959, allows us to see not only how each author imagined a collective identity—redrawing a boundary line to include a racial group that had historically been understood as *distinct* from Hispanics—but also how each author *did not* imagine collective identity. Coalitions of Mexican Americans and Puerto Ricans in Chicago in the 1970s notwithstanding (see Felix Padilla), it is notable how absent each group is in the writing of the other. The Anaya-Thomas pairing, in other words, illustrates how very little pan-Latino identity was registering in the most prominent writing of the two largest Latino groups during this period.

Part Two, "Complicating the Origins," deals with authors who, I argue, challenge dominant narratives about ethnic identity and its connection to the nation of origin, rendering that "nation" itself panethnic and/or transnational. In her novels ¡*Yo!* and *In the Time of the Butterflies*, Julia Alvarez explores her assumed cultural authority as an ethnic (and upper-class "white") Dominican American to represent Dominican nationals, especially those of the lower classes and of African heritage. *Monkey Hunting* by Cristina García and *Days of Awe* by Achy Obejas both significantly challenge the dominant Cuban exile narrative of homogeneous white and Catholic Cubanness—largely accepted and even disseminated in mainstream U.S. media—to explore prior forms of Cuban hybridity and the ways in which they fit with, or rub against, the narration of the Cuban nation. Once again, notions of panethnic Latino/a identity are strangely absent from all of the works explored in this section, although they each imagine transnational and transracial (and thus "panethnic") identities in other forms.

Part Three, "Difference and the Possibilities of Panethnicity," addresses head-on this book's most vexing issue: the forms by which texts address, implicitly or explicitly, the panethnic construct "Latino," and the ways they negotiate differences among groups of diverse national origin that get elided under that category. In Chapter 5, I argue that Ana Castillo, in her novel *So Far from God*, challenges the ubiquitous critical ascription of magical realism to texts by Latinos/as and the presumed connection that this implies between Chicano/a writers and the Latin American Boom. In Castillo's text, which is centrally concerned with the theme of collective agency, magical realism actually becomes figured as a threat to empowered collectivity, rather than being a signifier of it; the implication is that assumed, essential, and even magical connections (to each other, to nature, to Latin American origins, etc.) undermine real efforts at solidarity and agency building. In Chapter 6, I address the sometimes uneasy fit that Cuban Americans have historically had with the imagined "Latino" collective and the ways in which various Cuban American writers—including Cristina García, Achy Obejas, Margarita Engle, Elías Miguel Muñoz, Alisa Valdes-Rodriguez, and Ana Menéndez—have attempted, explicitly or, as in Engle's case, more implicitly, to address and negotiate a relationship between Cuban Americans and a panethnic Latino whole.[42] In Chapter 7, I discuss Demetria Martínez's novel *Mother Tongue*, which tropes on the primordial category of a common language as cultural unifier in order to disrupt the assumption of an essential Latino identity. Having done so, however, the novel substitutes a vision of a U.S. Latino/a identity based not on essential sameness but on a carefully forged political solidarity.

Juan Flores has written that it is useful to distinguish between an "analytic" approach to Latinos, which always is predicated on "the need to break down, to identify not the sum total but the constituent parts" and which recognizes "the evident diversity of Latino groups and experiences" (*From Bomba* 195), and what he calls "the Latino imaginary," a "conceptual space of pan-group aggregation" in which the separate members imagine their relationship to the larger whole (199, 198). It is, of course, this imagining that I take as the subject of my book.

But the "Latino imaginary" is not one, but many. The various authors I explore understand their membership within a larger "ethnic" whole in different ways and sketch figurative lines to delineate the imagined membership of that whole. In almost all cases, those lines are tentatively drawn, with the understanding that group memberships overlap and fluctuate—that groups come together into (as Ray Gonzalez puts it) a "cohesive whole," and that groups also disassemble, dissipate. The relationship of literature to group formation is nothing so straightforward as a simple affirmation of an essentialist identity, as Sollors once seemed to suggest.[43] By engaging critically with the cultural production of Latino writers, we can begin to understand the multitude of ways in which people of Latin American heritage have answered the question, "Who Are We?"

# Part One

# Race and Ethnicity

# 1

# "Jasón's Indian"

## Mexican Americans and the Denial of Indigenous Ethnicity in Rudolfo Anaya's *Bless Me, Ultima*

The critical and pedagogical problem posed by Rudolfo Anaya's *Bless Me, Ultima* is that, while it is regarded as a classic of Chicano/Latino literature and even of ethnic American literature generally,[1] the narrative is driven by personal identity issues which do not seem connected to the larger issues of collective identity at the heart of the Chicano movement of the 1960s and early 1970s—a movement which largely strove to construct and celebrate an ethnic identity based on *mestizaje*, hybridity, and the recovery of an indigenous past. The struggle of the novel's young protagonist, Antonio (or "Tony") Márez, to negotiate a dual inheritance, the elements of which seem incompatible if not mutually exclusive, may call to mind Gloria Anzaldúa's well-known description of the mestiza who also negotiates apparently incompatible aspects of identity: "The new *mestiza* copes by developing a tolerance for contradictions, a tolerance for ambiguity. She learns to be an Indian in Mexican culture, to be Mexican from an Anglo point of view. She learns to juggle cultures. She has a plural personality" (79). But, unlike Anzaldúa's new mestiza, who is, conceptually, fully a product of the Chicano movement's antagonism toward hegemonic Anglo culture and of its valorization of indigenous heritage, Anaya's representation of identity conflict appears highly personal—a family matter without larger implications for Chicanos.[2] Antonio's father's side of the family, the Márez clan, is associated with the freedom of the vaquero who roams the expansive llano; the Lunas, his mother's family, are linked with the more stable life of farming. The conflict for Antonio is whether he will become a vaquero, following in the footsteps of the Márez men, or a farmer like his Luna uncles—or even a priest, his fervently Catholic mother's dearest wish.

These alternatives seem strikingly disconnected from the issues that provided a rallying cry for the Chicano movement and that generated an empowering, collective sense of self for Chicanos. As Genaro M. Padilla, looking back on the body of critical reaction to the novel, observed in 1989, "Many critics objected to *Bless Me, Ultima* (1972) on the grounds that it seemed non-referential even though it was set in a definable historical moment in a New Mexican village";[3] there was simply no obvious connection to "the social contexts of the novel" (128).[4] There are no struggles in *Bless Me, Ultima*—as there are in the much earlier Mexican American bildungsroman *Pocho* (1959) by José Antonio Villarreal—with issues of assimilation and integration versus cultural preservation, no obvious or foregrounded "Anglo" influences trying to Americanize Antonio at the expense of his Mexican roots. Passing references to Antonio's education in the English language and the "old people [who] did not accept the new language" (180), or to his discomfort when he brings a lunch of tortillas to school and is mocked by children with "sandwiches [. . .] made of bread" (58), seem tangential—perhaps even irrelevant—to the core identity conflict of the novel. As Juan Bruce-Novoa decisively states, "Antonio is not torn between an Anglo and a Chicano world, but between two ways of being Chicano" (183); and given that the term "Chicano" connotes a self-conscious, politicized, collective Mexican American identity, even that description seems inaccurate. Growing up some two decades before the Chicano movement, Tony is absolutely unaware of being a "Chicano," much less torn between different modes of *chicanismo*. And even if we understand Bruce-Novoa to be referring more simply to colliding strains of Mexican American heritage (e.g., Spanish and indigenous) which Antonio, much like Anzaldúa's "New Mestiza," must negotiate, it is hard to see how the particular familial choices that are constructed for Tony (plain or valley, cowboy or priest, etc.) might serve this kind of "referential" capacity.[5]

Perhaps in response to the implied censure of the novel for not being "Chicano enough" (Cantú 13), some critics have focused on its ostensibly ethnic "content"—those elements of *Ultima* which serve as "ethnic markers," including bilingualism and code-switching as well as "folklore" or "pagan" figures like La Llorona and the golden carp.[6] Indeed, it is by now a critical commonplace in Anaya scholarship that *Bless Me, Ultima* "draws deeply on Native American mythology" (Kanoza 160).[7] Such readings, however, are generally more concerned with the "influence" or traces of indigenous thought and belief systems than they are with the ways in which *Ultima*'s storyline might comment on (much less construct) an indigenous Chicano ethnic identity. Indeed, critics have persistently ignored the significance of the characters' strange and glaring lack of recognition of any Indian ancestry, as well as the even stranger ways in which the term "Indian" signifies in the novel when it does appear. Yet a third strain of criticism sidesteps the question of ethnicity by approaching the novel in terms of either "universal" or specifically Western structures and influences.[8] Thus the thorny question of just what, if anything, the novel has to say about ethnicity and the matter of being Chicano continues to be elided.

I suggest that the novel actually *does* have much to say about Chicano/a ethnicity, but that recognizing (or, more accurately, *re*-recognizing) that this subject is by no means overt is a first and crucial step in interpreting the novel's commentary. Beneath the fairly straightforward plot of Antonio's family-based identity conflict, there indeed lies a submerged subtext concerning Mexican American collective, mestizo identity. But the *obscuring* of this subtext is thematically significant and has for too long been overlooked. In this chapter I argue that Anaya, in his classic Chicano novel, is actually concerned with portraying an earlier moment of New Mexican history (prior, that is, to the rise of the Chicano movement of the 1960s), when New Mexicans of Mexican heritage were engaged in a project of constructing ethnicity by claiming whiteness and Spanish descent. (After all, it is surely significant that *Bless Me, Ultima* is set not during the '60s or '70s but during World War II.) Historically, New Mexicans, despite being largely mestizo, excluded "Indians" as irreparably Other from their conception of themselves (their notion of "We"). The novel suggestively invokes the cultural pressures that propelled this denial of Indian heritage, and it structurally mirrors these pressures by suppressing issues of Native American heritage so that they are masked by the father versus mother conflict and need to be unearthed by readers.[9] By representing an earlier construct of ethnicity while pointing toward the historical revaluation of indigenous heritage that became central to the Chicano movement, Anaya gives us (whether intentionally or not) a clear window into the fluid and changing construction of ethnic boundaries.

Perhaps the easiest way into the ethnic content of the text is not through Antonio's familial identity conflict, but, rather, through his religious struggles. As countless scholars have already noted, Antonio weighs the Catholic Church against the golden carp, a "pagan" god vaguely associated with indigenous beliefs. Of course, one of the "lessons" that Tony must learn on the road to maturity in this bildungsroman is that elements of Catholicism and "paganism" can be combined to form a new, hybrid religion. He rejects the colonialist imposition of Catholic conversion onto "pagans," mimed in the scene in which the other children demand that Florence, a nonbeliever, confess his sins and submit to the Catholic faith:

> "Give him a penance! Make him ask for forgiveness for those terrible things he said about God!" Agnes insisted. [. . .]
> "Make his penance hard," Rita leered.
> "Make him kneel and we'll all beat him," Ernie suggested.
> "Yeah, beat him!" Bones said wildly.
> "Stone him!"
> "Beat him!"
> "Kill him!"
> They circled around me and advanced on Florence, their eyes flashing

with the thought of the punishment they would impose on the non-believer. [. . .]

"Give him the Indian torture!" someone shouted.

"Yeah, the Indian torture!" they chanted. (213–14)

The scene's historical parallel is, of course, the efforts by Spanish colonizers to force conversion of the indigenous peoples of New Mexico. (The phrase "Indian torture" is wonderfully ambiguous; though the children no doubt believe that "Indian torture" is torture administered *by* Indians, their own acts serve as a reminder and distant echo of torture exacted *upon* Indians.) Antonio rejects the dogmatic imposition of religious adherence, as a result of which Florence later tells him, "You could never be their priest" (215). Instead, by the end of the novel, Antonio opts for religious hybridity; he discovers that he can take "God and the golden carp[,] and make something new" (247).

But what Antonio fails utterly to recognize is that the sort of religious syncretism he envisions as a solution to his dilemma has *already taken place*; a hybrid religion is a reality for Mexicans and Mexican Americans, who routinely incorporate aspects of belief systems inherited from Native American ancestors into the Catholicism imposed by the Spanish conquerors. In one of Antonio's dream sequences, the more obviously ethnic religious conflict is linked to the familial conflict as he begs, "Oh please tell me which is the water that runs through my veins," and his parents give opposing responses:

> It is the sweet water of the moon, my mother crooned softly, it is the water the Church chooses to make holy and place in its font. It is the water of your baptism.
> 
> Lies, lies, my father laughed, through your body runs [. . .] the water that binds you to the pagan god of Cico, the golden carp! (120)

While the mother demands allegiance to Catholic rites in the dream, "pagan" beliefs such as faith in the golden carp are here associated with the father. Later in the novel, Antonio's father, Gabriel, expresses preference for an Indian burial ceremony over a Catholic burial in a casket (233), and Antonio tells us that it is from his father (along with Ultima) that he has learned an appreciation of the interconnectedness of "man" with the "noble expanse of land and air and pure, white sky" (228)—a lesson surely meant to be inflected by Native American spirituality.

Yet the Márez family—the story insists more than once—is descended from conquistadors, who would more logically be associated with Spanish Catholicism. And although Antonio's mother battles his father on Catholic versus pagan grounds in Antonio's highly symbolic dream, in actuality she holds Ultima, a *curandera*, in the highest regard and actually *asks* for her help in the matter of the curse on Antonio's uncle. That is, for Antonio's mother, Catholicism and Ultima's "pagan" form of spirituality are not incompatible—however Antonio might represent her to himself in his dream. What Antonio constructs as a simple either/or dichotomy is already infinitely more complicated, with each supposed "side" itself a hybrid, contradictory construction, bearing the traces of a creative syncretism that was part of the history of colonial New Mexico:

> Because the Indians were deeply religious anyway, they followed many Christian teachings perfectly. [. . .] Only one God was placed before them, but the many Christian saints, and especially the [Virgen] de Guadalupe, found ready acceptance by a people accustomed to a pantheon. Baptism, rituals, ceremonies, prayers, fasting, confessions, heaven, hell, and purgatory were not new concepts to the Indians and were thus easily adopted. [. . .] When possible, missionaries incorporated Indian practices to teach Catholic dogma. [. . .] For example, in pre-Columbian times towns honored a patron deity with a processional. The clerics staged the affair on the already established day but replaced Indian idols with Christian saints; thus, a mixed Indian-Spanish ceremony evolved. (Vigil 71–72)

Of course, it has already been widely acknowledged that the "synthesis" Ultima advocates as a solution to Antonio's struggles points precisely toward the (already achieved) historical solution of syncretism and hybridity. But what has gone virtually without commentary, yet is surely significant, is that Anaya represents this hybridity as *obscured*—so repressed that Antonio does not see it, understands each of his dual heritages as "pure" and nonoverlapping, and "discovers" hybridity as though it were a new solution.

Particularly problematic, as I have been hinting, is the fact that *nowhere* is Indian heritage explicitly mentioned as a part of Antonio's conflicted identity. Yet, as Roberto Cantú notes, Antonio's "conflictive genealogy [is] generally understood to be Spanish and Indian" (40). We can only speculate that such a tacit understanding might come from readers' presumptions about Chicana/o literature generally or about Anaya specifically; it certainly does not come from the text.[10] Antonio's father's family, as I have observed, identifies its ancestors exclusively as conquistadors, and his mother, meanwhile, also describes hers as "colonizers"—although Mexican, in her case, rather than Spanish: "They were the first colonizers of the Llano Estacado. It was the Lunas who carried the charter from the Mexican government to settle the valley" (52).

It is certainly not the Lunas' Indian or even mestizo heritage that is emphasized through this history. Mexican land grant policy after independence from Spain in 1821 was "to increase the size of land grants to individuals or groups who would settle on the dangerous frontiers, to enclose enclaves of [. . .] Indian nomads, and to drive others of them beyond the edge of a moving occupance line" (Cline 17). The centralist Mexican government that took control in 1836, likewise, did not "recognize native rights to Mexican public lands; so far as they had a view at all, the government officials shared a developing Mexican opinion, current to the Mexican Revolution of 1910, that Indians were a drag on progress and the sooner they disappeared, the better for the nation" (Cline 18). In other words, the Mexicans who colonized New Mexico saw themselves as distinct from and in opposition to the Indians (despite their own mestizo inheritance), much as the Spanish had before them.[11]

That sense of Indians as fully Other is surely what is intimated in Gabriel's reaction to his children's use of slang words like "gosh" and "okay": "What good does an education do them [if] they only learn to speak like Indians[?]" (54). The father's response is remarkable for the way in which it displaces Anglo influence, identifying the "foreignness" of the words instead as "Indian" (perhaps a less-threatening alternative to Gabriel than the pressing forces of assimilation into dominant Anglo culture). All this suggests the degree to which, far from being represented as one of the competing aspects in Antonio's conflictive genealogy, Indian heritage is actually so obscured that the characters understand "Indian" as "alien."

Even Ultima, generally understood by critics as deeply in touch with indigenous spirituality (from Ultima, for example, Antonio learns that "even the plants had a spirit, and before I dug she made me speak to the plant and tell it why we pulled it from its home in the earth" [39]), apparently does not acknowledge a common ancestry with Indians. Antonio explains that Ultima "spoke to me of the common herbs and medicines we shared with the Indians of the Rio del Norte. She spoke of the ancient medicines of other tribes, the Aztecas, Mayas, and even of those in the old, old country, the Moors. But I did not listen, I was thinking of my brothers" (42). The most intriguing aspect of this passage is its constructed distance between Native peoples and a distinct, collective We. The suggestion is that Mexican Americans (We) share herbs and medicines with those of native cultures, rather than having drawn their knowledge precisely from those cultures. In other words, the passage, distressingly, seems to imply that even Ultima, connected as she is to Indian spirituality, fails to recognize a common heritage with Indians—until one realizes that Ultima's words are reported through Antonio, who is so uninterested in the whole issue of any resemblance to Indians that he "did not listen" (and so is perhaps hearing Ultima only incompletely). Antonio views Ultima's lesson about "ancient" tribes as absolutely tangential to his central concerns.

If Antonio's identity crisis is in fact meant to represent the tensions of being of both Spanish and Native American heritage, why did Anaya not make his Indian ancestry more explicit? I suggest that Anaya supplies the cue for interpreting this silence in his brief but mysterious anecdote about "Jasón's Indian":

> He was the only Indian of the town, and he talked only to Jasón. Jasón's father had forbidden Jasón to talk to the Indian, he had beaten him, he had tried in every way to keep Jasón from the Indian.
> But Jasón persisted. (10)

Jasón's Indian raises several critical questions. Given that the novel is set in Guadalupe, a New Mexican town inhabited largely by Mexican Americans (who are, of course, predominantly mestizo), why does the narrative so strongly assert irreconcilable and absolute ethnic *difference* here ("the only Indian of the town")? And why is Jasón's father trying so vehemently—indeed, so violently—to keep Jasón from the Indian?[12] And what is the critical significance of Jasón's persistence—never mentioned again in the novel—in talking to the Indian? In virtually the only critical discussion to date of this enigmatic passage in *Bless Me, Ultima* (yet a discussion which ignores the possible implications for Chicano mestizo identity), Roberto Cantú observes that, although it is said that the Indian speaks only to Jasón, it turns out, contradictorily, that the Indian speaks to quite a few characters besides Jasón. Cantú poses the additional question, "Why does Antonio affirm that the Indian talks 'only to Jasón' [. . .] when obviously that is not the truth?" (17).[13]

As one of the two moments in the text where Native American presence is made explicit (the other has to do with the curse laid on the ghosts of three murdered Indians), this apparently tangential and inconsequential passage actually reveals much. For one thing, it underscores how the Mexican Americans of Guadalupe (and, for that matter, of Las Pasturas, where the Márez family is from) have buried any memory of possible Indian ancestry. They do not see themselves as Indian—even in part—so Jasón's Indian is regarded as the "only Indian of the town." (Perhaps we hear again in this passage the echoes of Mexican land grant policy toward "Indians," viewed in terms quite separate and distinct from "Mexicans.") The anecdote of Jasón's Indian, in other words, dramatizes the deeply-entrenched denial of that ancestry by Mexican Americans prior to the Chicano movement (such that even a character like Ultima, powerfully informed by Indian spirituality, does not explicitly insist on a common heritage).

But this denial is hardly unproblematic; the force necessary to maintain it is suggested by Jasón's father, who beats Jasón in an effort to "keep [him] from the Indian." Only through a violent act of repression, it is suggested, can the connection of Mexican Americans to their Indian ancestry (symbolized here by Jasón's intense desire to communicate with the Indian) stay buried. And as Cantú observes, the text elsewhere implies that Jasón's Indian *does* talk to others in the town as well, specifically to pass on information about the golden carp, the pagan god presented as an alternative to Catholicism (17)—perhaps suggesting metaphorically that, through such oral transmission, fragments of Indian belief systems persist, despite denial and repression.

In their essay "Return to Aztlán," Guillermo Lux and Maurilio E. Vigil review the powerful pressures toward assimilation against which the Chicano movement reacted. A significant aspect of such pressures involved precisely the denial of Native American heritage—an attitude originating out of the "colonial tradition of being pro-White (Spanish or other European) and anti-Indian" (96) and given an additional dimension for Mexican Americans, who had to "struggle to overcome pernicious, cruel and misleading stereotypes which have been created by Anglo society through motion pictures and other mass media. [ . . . ] [T]he Indian [ . . . ] has been cast as savage, mean, and treacherous. [ . . . ] [N]ot only was the Mexican American impelled to shed his Mexican-ness [ . . . ], but *he has not been able even to begin to consider his Indian origins*" (94; emphasis added). (Here Lux and Vigil echo Armando B. Rendón's *Chicano Manifesto*, which declared in the year before *Bless Me, Ultima* first appeared in print, "We have hardly begun to investigate the fathomless inheritance that is ours from our Indian forbears" [280].) While denial of Native American heritage has historically been an aspect of Mexican culture as well,[14] Lux and Vigil point out that strong pressures in the United States to assimilate into an Anglo model created additional, culturally specific, forces acting on Mexican Americans to deny Native American heritage. Indeed, while "[i]n Mexico of the 1930s, during the presidency of Lázaro Cárdenas, the Indian origin of the Mexican people was accepted with pride" (94), differing political and cultural conditions ensured that an analogous cultural shift among Mexican Americans would have to wait until the Chicano movement.

Suzanne Oboler elaborates on this topic with regard to "the elites of New Mexico," who, in the late nineteenth century, "increasingly began to refer to themselves as Hispanos [ . . . ] specifically as a response to the American social and racial context. [ . . . ] [I]n adopting the term Hispano they were emphasizing not their racially miscegenated, mestizo origins, but rather their specific class-based descent from the original 'pure-blooded' Spanish conquistadores who settled in New Mexico" (25).[15] Earl Shorris observes that this particular construction of ethnicity had concrete material and political benefits for New Mexicans, who, by insisting that they were of exclusively Spanish ancestry, "were able to elect Hispanos to local and state office, and even the U.S. Senate, long before other Latinos could get past gerrymandering, ward politics, and 'at-large' elections. [ . . . ] In many parts of New Mexico only an Anglo or an Hispano could get a haircut in a public barbershop before World War II; Mexicans had to go to a Mexican barber or have their hair cut at home" (167). (Needless to say, such a construction of ethnic identity presented an immediate, preemptive barrier to notions of a panethnic *latinidad* that would include, for instance, darker-skinned Puerto Ricans.) As Lux and Vigil put it, "For the person who may not physiologically appear distinctive or different it is relatively easy to pass for white. For the distinctive person, the mestizo, the recourse must be '*my family descended from the conquistadores; we are Hispanos, Spanish*'" (97; emphasis added)[16]—a claim that cannot help but remind us of Antonio's father, who is drawn to beliefs that the novel labels "pagan" yet insists that "the Márez [. . .] were conquistadors" (25). But as Shorris sardonically comments, "The case against racial purity is simple and incontrovertible; there were no female *conquistadores* and no recorded cases of parthenogenesis" (167).

It is important to note that, while Antonio clearly knows about his conquistador ancestors—that is, he knows, in this sense, about his "past"—news of an even more distant past causes him quite a bit of anxiety. Early in the novel Ultima attempts to give Antonio a history lesson: "'Long ago,' she would smile, 'long before you were a dream, long before the train came to Las Pasturas, before the Lunas came to their valley, before the great Coronado built his bridge—' Then her voice would trail off and my thoughts would be lost in the labyrinth of a time and history I did not know" (40).

Interestingly, although (as I have suggested) not even Ultima fully claims the indigenous ancestry of Mexican Americans—notwithstanding her practice of indigenous spirituality—she nevertheless takes on the role of *historical* mentor for Antonio, hinting at a past of which he is ignorant. Antonio hears a bit more about his history from the people of Las Pasturas who come to Guadalupe for supplies:

> [A]lways the talk would return to stories of the old days. [. . .] The first pioneers there were sheepherders. Then they imported herds of cattle from Mexico and became vaqueros. [. . .] They were the first cowboys in a wild and desolate land which they took from the Indians.
>
> Then the railroad came. The barbed wire came. The songs, the corridos became sad, and the meeting of the people from Texas with my forefathers was full of blood, murder, and tragedy. The people were uprooted. They looked around one day and found themselves closed in. The freedom of land and sky they had known was gone. Those people could not live without freedom and so they packed up and moved west. They became migrants. (125)

What is fascinating about this history is what Antonio does *not* learn from it. The stories the people from Las Pasturas tell is about the history of their confrontation with Anglos, who take their land and thus circumscribe their freedom. Yet the vaqueros themselves, the stories almost inadvertently reveal, took the land from the Indians, thus circumscribing *their* freedom. There is a historical lesson embedded in the stories about the parallels between Anglo and Spanish/Mexican colonization, but neither the people of Las Pasturas nor Antonio hear that lesson. The taking of "their" land is belabored as a tragedy; the taking of the land from the Indians is mentioned only in passing, as a sort of "background" to the *real* story. On the other hand, Anaya, writing from the context of the Chicano movement, with its renewed awareness of the history of colonization and the violence done to indigenous peoples, is quite surely aware of, and intends, the historical lesson that his characters fail to apprehend.

This particular history surfaces again later in the novel, when Ultima is called to remove a curse plaguing the Téllez household. Explaining the curse's origins, Ultima narrates: "A long time ago, [. . .] the llano of the Agua Negra was the land of the Comanche Indians. Then the comancheros came, then the Mexican with his flocks—many years ago three Comanche Indians raided the flocks of one man, and this man was the grandfather of Téllez. Téllez gathered the other Mexicans around him and they hanged the three Indians. They left the bodies strung on a tree; they did not bury them according to their custom. Consequently, the three souls were left to wander on that ranch" (227). In the condensed historical narrative that opens this passage, the Indians are semantically supplanted first by the comancheros—traders from Spanish settlements who exchanged goods with Comanche camps (G. Anderson 231)—and then by the "Mexican with his flocks," suggesting a gradual ceding of the land. Once again, the history of land-takeover seems to be told almost in passing, as "background"; but here, the background is more intimately connected to the main thrust of the story (the origins of the curse). The violence inflicted on the Comanche Indians is quite vividly metaphorized in the brutal hanging by Téllez's ancestor and is not justified within the text by the Indians' raid, which is itself only an outcome of their land loss to Mexicans. (The central focus in the passage is the violence and desecration of the hanging and improper burial, rather than the criminality of the raid.)

Interestingly, the Indians who "haunt" Téllez's household are specifically identified in the novel as Comanche rather than Aztec or Mayan. (That is, they do not share an obvious genealogy with the Mexicans who killed them.) As Lux and Vigil point out, the Comanches were enemies of Mexicans who were descended from Aztecs. Comanches were viewed as "indios bárbaros" (barbaric Indians); this identification provided ideological sanction of the cooperation of Mexican mestizos with Anglo settlers in their campaigns against the "indios bárbaros" (95).

Ultimately, of course, the Anglos did not draw fine distinctions between different native peoples: the "only good Indian was a dead Indian" (Lux and Vigil 95). Thus the Mexican identification of Comanches as "barbarians" became a factor in the suppression of Mexican "Indianness." Teresa McKenna observes that Alurista, one of the major early literary figures of the Chicano movement, "helped define and foster the notion of 'Amerindia,' which connotes the unification of all Indian peoples into one creative, political, and social force" (16). One aspect of the Chicano movement, then, was to reject the divisions and antagonisms among different indigenous peoples which had aided in their conquest and continuing suppression in the first place, and to draw instead a larger and more inclusive—one might say a panethnic—group boundary. It is notable that, although the spirits of the Indians are now wreaking havoc on the Téllez family (hot skillets and coffee pots fly in the air and burn them; rocks rain on their rooftop), Anaya takes great pains to shift responsibility for the "evil" from the Indians to the wicked Trementina sisters (the central antagonists and villains throughout the novel), who have placed a curse on them. The Comanche Indians of Anaya's text are not (counter to eighteenth- and nineteenth-century representations of them) barbaric or savage; they are simply responding to a threat to their way of life.

And, because they have been unjustly killed and improperly buried, they will not stay dead—they return to haunt their killers. As Kathleen Brogan writes regarding ghostly "hauntings" in ethnic literature, "To be haunted in this literature is to know, viscerally, how specific cultural memories that seem to have disappeared in fact refuse to be buried and still shape the present, in desirable and in troubling ways" (16). Read in connection with the anecdote about Jasón's Indian, the scene of the three Indian spirits begins to take on a larger symbolic significance, along the lines of the "return of the repressed." Though the town continues to want to deny, suppress, and repress its Indianness, that Indianness will not stay dead; Jasón, for one, returns to rediscover it. Incidents of "cultural haunting," Brogan tells us, "figure prominently [in ethnic literature] wherever people must reconceive a fragmented, partially obliterated history, looking to a newly imagined past to redefine themselves for the future" (29).[17]

Anaya's novel, published at the height of the Chicano movement, is engaged in precisely such an endeavor; it provides the submerged pieces of a "fragmented, partially obliterated history" which must be constructed into the "newly imagined past" of a panethnic indigenous identity (one which included several different and distinct—even antagonistic—indigenous peoples under the concept of "Amerindian"). It is this imagined pan-Indian past that came to redefine the Chicano/a group identity. In other words, *Bless Me, Ultima* fully participates in the imaginative project of the Chicano movement: to lay the groundwork for an understanding of Chicanos/as as a "people."

Consequently, to be sure, it is arguable that Anaya's novel shares the larger essentialism that often characterized the movement. As Michael Hames-García explains, the push toward cultural nationalism in the '60s and early '70s "often resulted in an injunction for Chicano artists to find artistic and liberatory truth in highly idealized visions of an authentic indigenous past. [...] [Images of an] essential (masculine) 'Indianness' represented the essence of Chicano identity" (466). But while Anaya certainly offers a renewed exploration of indigenous identity as a possible grounds for Chicano/a identity, it is also certainly the case that what is dramatized in *Bless Me, Ultima* is the process by which identity—including ethnic identity—is a social construct that is continually being *re*-constructed. Indigenous identity has *no part* in the characters' understanding of their ethnic identity in the novel, despite the possibilities of biological/genealogical ties, suggesting that what has determined their ethnic reality is the pressure of specific social forces. From this point, it is no great leap to the observation that even the cultural nationalist "essentialism" which would privilege indigenous identity was a response to a particular social situation. The history of native peoples subjected to dual conquests (by Spain and the United States) rendered indigenousness a powerful symbol and rallying point for a movement that grounded its struggles for economic and social justice in an oppositional (rather than an assimilationist) stance.

In this way we can read, behind a boy's ostensibly personal and highly individual bildungsroman of negotiation between his mother and his father, a complicated story of the recovery project instrumental in constructing a collective Chicano consciousness. And, just as Antonio's development to maturity is not complete by the novel's end, so also the process of identity (re)construction is an ongoing process, rather than fully accomplished at the novel's conclusion. As Antonio comments, quite obliquely, after he has heard the story of the Indians, "And there is also the dark, mystical past, I thought, the past of the people who lived here and left their traces in the magic that crops out today" (229). Antonio is now paying more attention to a particular past that he has neglected before (for example, when he "did not listen" to Ultima's lesson about what "We" share with Indian peoples); and he seems to feel less lost in and threatened by "the labyrinth of a time and history I did not know." An explicit connection of "the people who lived here" to Antonio himself has yet to be made, but at least he is now watching for their "traces."

# 2

# "Puerto Rican Negro"

## Defining Race in Piri Thomas's *Down These Mean Streets*

In *Latino Crossings,* Nicholas De Genova and Ana Y. Ramos-Zayas recount a joke "that was circulating among Mexican migrants in Chicago in the spring of 1997":

> It is the time of the Mexican Revolution, and Pancho Villa's army has just captured an invading U.S. regiment; addressing his lieutenants, Pancho Villa gives the order: "Take all the Americans [*americanos*]—shoot them, kill them; the Blacks [*morenos*] and Puerto Ricans—just let them go." The lieutenants are confused and dismayed: "What?! What are you saying?!? But why??" Coolly, Pancho Villa replies, "Don't waste the bullets—they'll all just die of hunger—because here, there's no welfare." (76)

Although hegemonic U.S. culture generally assumes that Latinos see themselves as a single group—or at least as having very strong ties among the subgroups—De Genova and Ramos-Zayas maintain that very often Puerto Ricans and Mexicans (at least in Chicago) have seen themselves in opposition and even marked antagonism to each other. As they note, "the inequalities generated through the politics of citizenship"—for instance, Puerto Ricans' access to "welfare" programs that were not available to Mexican immigrant noncitizens—"became particularly salient for Mexicans' and Puerto Ricans' understandings of the differences between one another, as groups, in ways that ultimately came to be quite forcefully racialized" (27).

These racialized identities, of course, have a history in U.S. colonizing efforts and attendant policies toward Mexico and Puerto Rico. As De Genova and Ramos-Zayas recount of historical debates about the possible colonization of Mexico by the United States, "the position that finally prevailed against the proposition to colonize all of Mexico was that articulated by Michigan senator Lewis Cass, who declared, 'We do not want the people of Mexico, either as citizens or subjects. All we want is a portion of territory, which they nominally hold, generally uninhabited, or, where inhabited at all, sparsely so, and with a population, which would soon recede [by which he meant Indians], or identify itself with ours [by which he meant those who could be considered whites]'"

(12; Horsman 241, qtd. in De Genova 12; bracketed phrases in original). The hegemonic U.S. perspective routinely considered Mexicans to be largely "'savage' or 'barbarous' Indians" (De Genova and Ramos-Zayas 13). By contrast, "Puerto Rico [. . .] was widely characterized as being populated by a 'hybrid' people produced principally from the racial mixing of Spaniards and Africans, a significant portion of whom, furthermore, were considered to be simply Black" (De Genova and Ramos-Zayas 14). We can see the Mexican American acceptance and revision of this racial construction in the joke that opens this chapter, in which Puerto Ricans are dramatically opposed to Mexicans (by the Mexicans) and linked, instead, to blacks.[1] In De Genova and Ramos-Zayas's findings, "Mexicans and Puerto Ricans viewed themselves as racially distinct from one another" (27), rather than as the "same" people.

Piri Thomas's classic Puerto Rican autobiography *Down These Mean Streets* (1967), published five years before Anaya's *Bless Me, Ultima*, shares with that Chicano novel the theme of racial denial. Like Antonio in *Ultima*, the protagonist of *Mean Streets* (whom I will call "Piri" to distinguish him from the author, "Thomas") must learn the "lessons" of racial identity suppressed by his family and its narrated myths of origin, no doubt in a defensive move against precisely the racial construction outlined above. In their place, he comes to embrace a construction of Puerto Rican racial identity that acknowledges a common "peoplehood" with African Americans. (In this respect, Thomas's writing can also be grouped with that of Nuyorican poets of the 1960s and 1970s such as Felipe Luciano and Miguel Algarín, who—as William Luis points out—thematized "the important African component of Puerto Rican culture, race, and identity" [68].) Yet this perceived commonality based on racial identity, arguably, also appears in many ways to be racially essentialist (as the Chicano celebration of "*raza*" can also seem to be in retrospect).

William Luis, in his discussion of *Down These Mean Streets*, has noted that the Young Lords Party's 13-Point Program and Platform, which appeared in the late sixties, included an insistence on Puerto Rican solidarity with Chicanos, based on experiences of common marginalization:

> We Want Self-Determination for All Latinos. Our Latin Brothers and Sisters, inside and outside the united states [sic], are oppressed by amerikkkan business. The Chicano people built the Southwest, and we support their right to control their lives and their land. The people of Santo Domingo continue to fight against gringo domination and its puppet generals. The armed liberation struggles in Latin America are part of the war of Latinos against imperialism. Que viva La Raza! (Young Lords Party and Abramson, qtd. in Luis 279)

Other accounts, however, would suggest that Puerto Rican and Chicano/a solidarity under a "Latino" rubric, in the late sixties and early seventies, was shaky at best, and that a panethnic Latino or Hispanic identity was perhaps as much a concept imposed from without as generated from within. De Genova and Ramos-Zayas intriguingly assert that, in 1969 (that is, in the same period as the publication of Anaya's and Thomas's landmark texts *and* the Young Lords' platform),

> U.S. president Richard Nixon's proclamation of a "National Hispanic Heritage Week" served to conflate the different historical experiences of Mexicans and Puerto Ricans at the precise juncture when Mexicans (especially those born or raised in the U.S. who had increasingly come to assert a specifically nonmigrant identity as "Chicanos") and Puerto Ricans were each engaged in increasingly militant and often nationalist acts of cultural affirmation *as distinct groups* with particular histories of subjugation and resistance, and were emphasizing their specific (and potentially divergent) political demands. (17; emphasis in original)

By setting *Mean Streets* and *Ultima*, published in such close proximity, next to each other, we can see some dramatic differences between the racial/ethnic constructs that these authors were attempting to reimagine and the ways that they reimagined them. For, in Anaya's novel, indigenousness is the shameful identity that has been suppressed and must be reintegrated into a Chicano identity, while in Thomas's memoir, indigenousness is the excuse given in family stories to avoid a more difficult identification—with blackness. Needless to say, while Anaya strives to extend the boundaries of who "we" are to include Indians, nowhere do Puerto Ricans (much less African Americans) appear in his imagined landscape of an expanded collective identity. Likewise, while Piri moves from a defensive belief that African Americans and Puerto Ricans are two separate, distinct groups to a growing conviction that the circles encompassing each group overlap, he does not register Mexican Americans in even his reimagined sense of self. Arguably, this silence suggests the degree to which the concept of a panethnic "Hispanic" or "Latino" identity that binds Chicanos and Nuyoricans was without compelling force for both Anaya and Thomas, concerned as they both were with the issue of transracial imagined communities.

* * *

In a crucial scene in *Down These Mean Streets*, almost exactly at the halfway mark of the text, a character named Gerald Andrew West describes himself as "so blended racially that I find it hard to give myself to any [. . .] one of the blends" (174). This description would seem to fit perfectly with much more recent, resistant, accounts of racial and ethnic identity. Once again, as with my discussion of *Bless Me, Ultima*, Gloria Anzaldúa's image of inhabiting the "borderlands" among racial, ethnic, national, and sexual categories comes to mind: the "new *mestiza* [. . .] learns to be an Indian in Mexican culture, to be Mexican from an Anglo point of view" (79). Gerald's self-representation, like Anzaldúa's, seems—within a contemporary, poststructural critical context in which stable, fixed, and singular notions of identity have been challenged and debunked—to powerfully suggest subversion of socially constructed and all-too-limiting racial categories that, in truth, have little meaning in biology. Indeed, it is surely this scene, among others, that has triggered the critical view that, "years before the concepts 'hybridity,' 'heterogeneity,' and 'difference' gained academic and social repute," Thomas was engaged in a "bold attempt to undermine the black/white categories of U.S. racialization" (M. Sánchez 44).[2] As it turns out, however, Gerald is a highly unlikable character whose rejection of racial paradigms is wholly predicated on his desire to "make the next step to white" (177), as he himself admits. In his need to claim racial privilege, Gerald is an echo of Piri himself, who has been struggling all along with precisely such an impulse. Thus Gerald, whose understanding of race seems more "radical," is actually a deeply conservative character.

While Thomas's autobiography certainly points toward the instability of racial categories, it ultimately relies less on notions of hybridity and heterogeneity than on what Gayatri Spivak might call a strategic essentialism that often reproduces the language of racial polarities. That is to say, it implies that race can be useful in constructing a group identity that is based in a sense of solidarity. As Antonia Darder and Rodolfo D. Torres have noted, the concept of "race" in the 1960s provided Latinos with "a discursively powerful category of struggle and resistance upon which to build in-group identity and cross group solidarity with African Americans" (9).[3] Taken as a whole, *Mean Streets* suggests that notions of race are radical or conservative depending on the circumstances of their deployment, rather than on their "inherent" challenge to dominant ideology. In this respect, *Down These Mean Streets* resonates with more recent currents in theoretical discussions of race and racial discourse, to which I now, briefly, wish to turn.

\* \* \*

Gerald Andrew West would, no doubt, have embraced and celebrated news that race was, scientifically speaking, an illegitimate category. This news was still treated as startling (that is, as "news") when Henry Louis Gates observed in the mid-1980s that "[r]ace, as a meaningful criterion within the biological sciences, has long been recognized to be a fiction" (4). As Gates's statement implies, this "news" had in fact been around for a while, although when Gates edited the two issues of *Critical Inquiry* (1985–86) that became the groundbreaking volume *"Race," Writing, and Difference* (1986), he still felt the need to assert in his introduction the lack of biological grounding for any idea of "race" and to signal this fact through the use of quotation marks around the word "race" in the title of the volume. Anthony Appiah, another prominent contributor to the volume, was apparently even more anxious about the degree to which this "long [...] recognized" fact was indeed recognized, in the academic community and elsewhere. Declaring at the outset that "[e]very reputable biologist will agree that human genetic variability between the populations of Africa or Europe or Asia is not much greater than that within those populations" ("Uncompleted Argument" 21), Appiah was at pains to point out that by 1911, with the publication of the August issue of *Crisis*, the outlines of this scientific conclusion were already publicized ("Uncompleted Argument" 30). Yet, he commented, "it is my experience that the biological evidence about race is not sufficiently known and appreciated" ("Uncompleted Argument" 22).

Surely Appiah's anxiety was not misplaced. In 1995, almost a decade after the publication of *"Race," Writing, and Difference*, *Newsweek* ran an article on the scientific (non)basis for racial categorizations under the subheading "Surprising new lessons from the controversial science of race" (Begley 67). "Even with racial mixing," the first paragraph runs, "the existence of primary races is as obvious as the existence of primary colors." "Or is it?" the second paragraph begins, in what was clearly meant to be a jarring lead-in to the "surprising new" information about race, namely, that it does not exist (Begley 67). At about the same time, *Time* magazine covered the publication of a new book, *The History and Geography of Human Genes*, in an article whose subhead reads, "A landmark global study flattens *The Bell Curve*, proving that racial differences are only skin deep" (see Cavalli-Sforza, Menozzi, and Riazza). The bottom line, the article notes, is that "the whole concept of race becomes meaningless at the genetic level" (Subramanian 54). Clearly, for mainstream popular culture, the idea that race is not biology was still "surprising" news.

If the notion of race as a scientific fiction has become a given for academics, however, we still cannot seem to agree on what to do with this information. For Appiah, it was (in 1986) apparently quite a concern that W.E.B. Du Bois was never able to fully escape a biological conception of race, despite his "life's work" being devoted to challenging the underpinnings of racial and racist thought in America ("Uncompleted Argument" 36). More recently, Paul Gilroy argues in *Against Race* (2000) that race is a "tainted logic" (15), suggesting that any concept of race as biology is politically suspect and contaminates all efforts toward a truly liberatory radical politics.[4] More strident voices push this position toward its extreme conclusion, arguing that, if race does not exist, we ought not to continue discussing it.[5]

In turn, the latter approach has faced its detractors. Houston Baker, in the same volume as Appiah's essay, critiques the latter on the grounds that it is "instructive but, ultimately, unhelpful in a world where New York cab drivers scarcely ever think of mitochondria before refusing to pick me up" (385). The risk of such arguments, Baker points out, lies in their possible effects

> at a time when a violent reinforcement and retrenchment of whitemale hegemony dictates the dismantling of quotas meant to repair damages done by old (and scientifically sanctioned) differentiations, of revolutionary initiatives (such as women's and black studies) predicated upon accepted and championed differences, and of federal support systems grounded on policies that forthrightly acknowledge manifest (and scientifically sanctioned) racial differences. The scenario they seem to endorse reads as follows: when science apologizes and says there is no such thing, all talk of "race" must cease. (385)

In *Crossing the Line* (2000), Gayle Wald echoes Baker's concern, noting with dismay "the emergence of arguments seeking to appropriate anti-essentialist racial critique to question the social relevance of race" (9); the fear is that "radical" arguments (if ninety-year-old arguments about the lack of a scientific basis for race can be called "radical") are being deployed for "conservative" purposes. Wald shares with Baker a concern about the *pragmatic political effects* of arguments about race that, to some degree, supersedes concern with their scientific (not to say "political") "correctness."[6] Wald and Baker want us to consider *effects* and *ends* before judging the "means" to be illegitimate because they are somehow tainted by racial thinking.[7] A "tainted" argument and "tainted" politics do not necessarily go hand in hand, just as the spouting of arguments about the nonexistence (and therefore insignificance) of race is no guarantor of radical or liberatory politics.

In the debate over "race," then, a vocal collection of voices underscores the importance of taking into account the context within which, and purposes for which, racial discourse is deployed. Wald seeks to replace an overly simplistic condemnation of tainted ideology with a focus on pragmatics in studying how "subjects appropriate 'race,' a discourse they do not control, for their own needs, wishes, and interests" (10); she calls on critics and readers to take account of "the necessity of constructing our choices and our agency out of the material of racial discourse itself" (10), including, presumably, the *popular* (rather than the more narrowly disseminated scientific) discourses on race, which remain, by and large, grounded in unconsidered assumptions of biology. Gilroy, in an argument that otherwise urges moving toward "a deliberate renunciation of race" (12), seems to concur with Wald in her concern for strategies undertaken within a circumscribed context:

> [P]eople who have been subordinated by race-thinking and its distinctive social structures [. . .] have for centuries employed the concepts and categories of their rulers, owners, and persecutors to resist the destiny that "race" has allocated to them and to dissent from the lowly value it placed upon their lives. Under the most difficult of conditions and from imperfect materials that they surely would not have selected if they had been able to choose, these oppressed groups have built complex traditions of politics, ethics, identity, and culture. [. . .] For many racialized populations, "race" and the hard-won, oppositional identities it supports are not to be lightly or prematurely given up. (12)

As Gilroy suggests, the "imperfect materials" of (biologically-tinged) understandings of race—the master's tools—have, historically, occasionally been put to use in dismantling the master's house. ("Dismantling" is surely an overstatement, but they have, at the very least, broken a window or two.) We can give them up only if, and when, we have found more effective tools.

\* \* \*

The long-standing and more recent attacks on biological understandings of race, and the subsequent arguments about the status of racially inflected arguments, provide an especially useful frame of reference for an analysis of racial discourse in Piri Thomas's autobiography, *Down These Mean Streets*. Thomas's exploration of Puerto Rican racial identity, which is now commonly understood to be predominantly derived from the dual Spanish and African heritage, depicts a climate in which racial and ethnic politics encourage Puerto Ricans living within the continental United States to identify themselves against African Americans, to erect an imaginary boundary between "us" and "them" as a means of establishing a slightly higher position on a hierarchy determined by fine degrees of social marginalization. Certainly, however, the denial of a racial connection between Puerto Rican blacks and African Americans seems to refute any sort of biological understanding of race. The text explores several possible definitions of race: as rooted in biology, in social perception, or in self-definition. It both challenges and, at times, strategically appropriates dominant social understandings of race. In the process, it raises interesting questions about the context in which any given definition of racial or ethnic identity is adopted.

The autobiography's structure is loosely that of a bildungsroman, in which Thomas's young protagonist Piri struggles to come to terms with his own racial and ethnic identity and to accept and embrace his "blackness." In his undeveloped or immature phase (that is, in the early portion of the bildungsroman, when he still has everything to learn), Piri consistently rebuts essentialist biological explanations of race, rejecting the idea that race is a stable, natural category based on biology. Yet his repeated refusal to accept that biology reveals race (as signaled by physical characteristics) is obviously motivated by the desire to "defend" himself from "accusations" of blackness, despite his dark skin and kinky hair. Consider, for example, the following confrontation with two Italian boys:

> "Hey, you," he said. "What nationality are ya?"
> 
> I looked at him and wondered which nationality to pick. And one of his friends said, "Ah, Rocky, he's black enuff to be a nigger. Ain't that what you is, kid?"
> 
> My voice was almost shy in its anger. "I'm Puerto Rican," I said. "I was born here." I wanted to shout it, but it came out like a whisper. (24)

In response to the question about nationality, Piri struggles with context; should he assert his status as an American citizen (and one, furthermore, born on the mainland) against the possible accusation of foreignness, or should he assert his sense of Puerto Rican peoplehood in the face of Italian ethnic pride? The choice becomes moot, however, when he is confronted in the next question with the possibility of being black, where blackness would seem to preempt, as a category, the possibility of any (other) nationality.

Implicit in this exchange is the intimate *connection* of race with nationality that is inextricable from the history of the evolving concept of race.[8] In Ivan Hannaford's massive *Race: The History of an Idea in the West* (1996), he identifies early (pre-) manifestations of modern conceptions of race in a search for national origins, as in Francis Tregian's poetic urgings that the English "learn thy name, thy *race*, thy offspring" and Richard Verstegan's claim that "Englishmen are descended of German *race*, and were heeretofore generaly [*sic*] called Saxons" (180; emphasis in original). But in the logic of emerging European nationalisms which gave rise to the concept of race as we know it today, blackness and nationalism were mutually exclusive. To be "black," "negro," or "negroid" (a "race" identified geographically with the entire continent of Africa) was to have absolutely no part in the origins of a European nation, if indeed it did not imply being of an entirely separate species.[9] Thus, in response to an accurately perceived challenge to his ability to claim *any* nationality (for the slur "nigger" renders the whole question of nationality moot in the minds of the Italian boys), Piri scrambles defensively to assert any and all possible "nationalisms":

"I'm Puerto Rican [. . .]. I was born here." To have a national identity will, by the logic of race, mean that he is not black.

The underlying assumption of the Italian boys, needless to say, is that whatever Piri is, he is not "American." As De Genova and Ramos-Zayas write of the "joke" which opens this chapter, "Notably, African Americans are perceived to be separate, distinct, and, indeed, excluded from the category 'Americans'— exposing the fact that 'American' comes to connote whiteness. [. . .] Neither for African Americans nor for Puerto Ricans does birthright U.S. citizenship secure the status of 'American'-ness, which constitutes a national identity that is understood, in itself, to be intrinsically racialized—as white" (77). It is precisely because Piri is aware of the ways in which African Americans and Puerto Ricans share certain structural analogies within a U.S. context that he actively struggles to disassociate these categories from each other—to draw distinct and nonoverlapping boundaries.

Scenes of such defensiveness repeat themselves insistently in the first half of the text with an accumulative weight that suggests the enormity of pressures contributing to the construction of Piri's racial/ethnic identity. It is clear that the retrospective Thomas is critiquing these early impulses on Piri's part to deny that he is black. In each case, Piri's responses are obviously meant to establish social *difference* from African Americans, with the assumption that such difference of necessity grants a certain privilege.[10] After playing a game of "dozens" with an African American friend, in which Piri asserts, "I'm a Porty Rican," and his friend Brew responds, "Ah only sees another Negro in fron' of me" (121), Piri becomes for the first time self-conscious about the implications of using either remark in a "game of insults" (121): "What the hell was I trying to put down? Was I trying to tell Brew that I'm better than he is 'cause he's only black and I'm a Puerto Rican darkskin? Like his people copped trees on a white man's whim, and who ever heard of Puerto Ricans getting hung like that?" (122). Insistence on Puerto-Ricanness, in these contexts, is not nationalistic or ethnic pride but an assertion of privilege ("I'm better than he is") in a complicated racial hierarchy. As Roberto Rodriguez-Morazzani has powerfully asserted, one of the ways that "Puerto Ricans have negotiated the racialization process [. . .] is by deployment of a national identity in an effort to escape identification as black or as non-white. The identification as Puerto Rican first [that is, of a cultural identification over a racial one] is not itself racially neutral" (151).[11] Piri's insistence on being Puerto Rican is, furthermore, clearly a self-protective denial of shared experience with African Americans in a U.S. context; if he is not black, he assumes, he need not fear being lynched.[12]

Even after his moment of self-consciousness, however, Piri continues to insist that he is not African American and that therefore the hardships of African Americans are not his own:

> "Yeah, Brew," I said, "it must be tough on you Negroes."
> "Wha' yuh mean, us Negroes? Ain't yuh includin' yourself? Hell, you ain't but a couple shades lighter'n me, and even if yuh was even lighter'n that, you'd still be a Negro."
> I felt my chest get tighter and tighter. I said, "I ain't no damn Negro and I ain't no paddy. I'm Puerto Rican."
> "You think that means anything to them James Crow paddies?" Brew said coolly. (123)

Against Piri's insistence on difference, Brew posits both biological and social definitions of race. On the one hand, the physical "sign" of Piri's dark skin seems to speak for itself and to be sufficient cause to make Piri "Negro." On the other, and simultaneously, Brew seems to be aware on some level that it is *social* definitions, or how the "sign" of dark skin is "read" under the social system of Jim Crow segregation, that make Piri black; he is black because whites say he is. In Du Bois's words, "the black man is a person who must ride 'Jim Crow' in Georgia" (qtd. in Appiah, "Uncompleted Argument" 33). Both biological and social means of defining race will later be appropriated by Piri.

In terms of the autobiography's bildungsroman structure, the first step in Piri's development of a presumably more enlightened identity is that he must reject the privilege that comes with the assertion of racial difference; within the structure of the autobiography, he learns to modify his vocabulary so that, in place of the dichotomy "Puerto Ricans and Negroes," he speaks of "Puerto Rican Negroes" and "American Negroes" (125, 173). Interestingly, however, Piri's transformation is based on the "realization" that his family has "black blood." In a heated argument with his brother José, who insists on asserting his whiteness through physical features such as white skin, "almost blond" hair, blue eyes, a straight nose, and lips that "are not like a baboon's ass" (144), Piri insists on his own blood relationship to his white-looking brother and on the resulting conclusion that his brother, too, is black, no matter how "white" he looks on the "outside" (145). When José invokes the family myth of origins, claiming that Piri's darker skin comes from their father's "Indian" blood, Piri challenges him: "What kinda Indian? Caribe? Or maybe Borinquén? Say, José, didn't you know the Negro made the scene in Puerto Rico way back? And when the Spanish spies ran outta Indian coolies, they brought them big blacks from you know where. Poppa's got moyeto blood. I got it. Sis got it. James got it. And, mah deah brudder, you-all got it!" (145). In the polarized racial dichotomy of white/black, "Indian blood" gets "read," at least by Piri's brother, as a defense against blackness. (In contrast, as we have seen, in *Bless Me, Ultima* it is the Indian blood itself that is vigorously suppressed in family and community myths of origin.) As a first step toward repudiating white privilege and constructing a sense of solidarity with African Americans, Piri rejects the comforting excuse of "Indian blood" for the insistence on "moyeto," or black, blood,[13] but in so doing, he relies on the very notion of race as biology and the one-drop rule that are the foundations of the racial structure of American society. In other words, he bases his argument on the grounds of biological essentialism, which will connect him to African Americans. Ironically, then, biological essentialism (the dominant American understanding of race) is used to establish a sense of racial solidarity, in a process quite similar to that which Appiah observes (and critiques) in the writings of W.E.B. Du Bois.[14]

In contrast, Thomas's autobiography also offers radical images of racial instability and nonessentialism, yet seems to imply that they are not always the most effective strategy for challenging the American racial system, perhaps because they allow Piri too much "wiggle room" for the assertion of difference from, and consequent privilege over, African Americans. In another example of racial defensiveness, Piri explains his identity to a white girl who is surprised to learn that he is Puerto Rican because he "talk[s] English very well":

> "I told you I was born in Harlem. That's why I ain't got no Spanish accent."
> 
> "No-o, your accent is more like Jerry's."
> 
> *What's she tryin' to put down*? I wondered. Jerry was the colored kid who recently had moved to Bayshore.
> 
> "Yeah, I know Jerry [. . .]. I know Jerry is colored and I know I got his accent. Most of us in Harlem steal from each other's language or style or stick of living." (83–84)

Against the hinted "accusation" that he is African American like Jerry, Piri defends himself by presenting a radical image of identity as *constructed*, a product of borrowing and cross-pollination. As Rodriguez-Morazzani has observed, "While it is traditional to think of different groups as hermetically sealed, social interaction includes exchange, borrowing, and transformation. [. . .] The social position of African Americans and Puerto Ricans resulted in a sociocultural and ideopolitical complex of exchanges and transformations not easily reduced to their individual parts" (145). In the aftermath of such cross-pollination, external "signs" such as accent or language or lifestyle are no longer accurate indicators of a stable, essential identity. Yet Piri in no way recognizes the implications of this model in terms of its potential challenge to dominant notions of identity as "blood" or of the intriguing possibility it suggests of a group identity that is strategically constructed rather than essentially determined. Instead, he uses the severing of identity markers from "essential" identity to "defend" himself from the "accusation" of being black; he might *look* and *sound* like a black friend from Harlem, but he insists *he* is not black. Indeed, his use of the metaphor of theft (they "steal from each other") suggests that his Harlem accent still, properly, belongs to African Americans.

Similarly, although the text brings up the important culturally based distinction between African Americans and Puerto Ricans, that distinction is also shown to be potentially dangerous if used to draw a boundary line that reinscribes racial hierarchy. The possibility of defining group identity based on culture, rather than on biology, is raised by Alayce, an African American friend of Brew's. In response to Brew's claim that Piri's "skin makes him a member of the black man's race an' hit don't make no difference he can talk that Porty Rican Talk," Alayce responds, "But honey, [...] Porto Ricans act different from us. They got different ways of dancin' an' cookin', like a different culture or something" (159). Alayce, it may be argued, is "onto" Appiah's observation that race "works as an attempt at a metonym for culture; and it does so only at the price of biologizing what *is* culture" (36; emphasis in original). Yet although Brew's understanding of identity is more essentialist than Alayce's, which grounds notions of race in a shared culture rather than in "blood," Alayce's cultural sensitivity, as it turns out in this context, simply translates into yet another means of preserving the existing racial hierarchy: "Ah've met a whole lot of dark Porto Ricans, an' I ain't met one yet who wants to be a Negro. An' I don't blame 'em. I mean, like anything's better'n being a li'l ole darkie" (159). Just as biological essentialism is used strategically by Piri to repudiate white privilege and establish solidarity with African Americans, so more flexible postmodern and postcolonial understandings of identity are sometimes used by both Piri and Alayce to reaffirm rigid racial hierarchies. No understanding of race or racial difference, this text suggests, is inherently conservative or inherently resistant; all meanings are contextual.

While Thomas's text insistently reverts to biological understandings of race, it also, simultaneously, exposes race as a social construct that is, at best, only loosely anchored to physical "markers." Mixed in liberally with Piri's assertions about his family's "black blood" are suggestions that "proof" of blackness is in white reactions. He tells his father, "If you're really so sure you're white, come on down South with Brew and me and see where you're really at" (151). Piri's words echo those of Brew, who earlier had countered Piri's distinction between Puerto Rican and black with the question, "You think that means anything to them James Crow paddies?" (123). Piri's identity as a black man is confirmed when he actually does go to the South and is kicked out of a restaurant on the grounds that he is a "nigra" (185–86).[15] In these instances, it is social perception, rather than biology, that defines race; Piri is apparently black because white southerners say he is. Such moments point to the social construction of race and thus undermine the essentialist biological explanations that have underpinned American social structures.

Interestingly, however, the moment when biological essentialism is most undermined in the text as an explanation of race is also the most ambiguous in terms of its politics. In protest against a "two-tone South" that recognizes only the dichotomous opposition of white and black, Piri decides that he wants to "fuck a white woman in Texas" (187). In this scene he uses the system of social perception of race against itself; he goes to a brothel and poses as a Puerto Rican who can speak no English, playing with socially defined distinctions which do, indeed, "read" dark-skinned Puerto Rican "foreigners" differently from African Americans. As the clerk at the brothel explains, "Well, you know, we got all kinds of people coming in, all kinds of foreigners, and Spanish people who come from Argentina and Colombia and Peru and Cuba, and that's all right, but we got to keep these damn niggers down" (188).

Briefly here, Piri's use of Spanish signals what might be read as a panethnic Latino identity—one connected by Spain as the European homeland and therefore, implicitly, by whiteness. To use language as a "deciding" factor in the determination of race, as the clerk does here, seems counterintuitive to any notion of race as biology (if race is biology, then, logically, it should make no difference whether Piri is descended from African slaves brought to Puerto Rico or to the U.S. mainland), although observations about language differences have been a key component in the history of the developing concept of race, as Ivan Hannaford notes (181, 227, 243).

The clerk, however, is blissfully unaware of past "theories" of race linking biology with language; rather, he is acting on a form of historical "amnesia" whereby he conveniently "forgets" the historical dispersal of African peoples to lands colonized by the Spanish, as well as by the English. He is speaking, instead, out of a much more recent racially-defined context, in which white privilege in the United States has been maintained through the continued suppression of political advances for the black population ("we got to keep these damn niggers down").[16] In this immediate context, only *American* blacks pose a threat to American whites; thus only American blacks count as "niggers." As Ian López puts it, "Context is the social setting in which races are recognized, constructed, and contested" (11). This scene is, I might add, an ironic reversal on the earlier exchange with the two Italian boys, in which to be black is *not* to be "American"; in this scene, *only* if Piri is "American" is he black. Here, again, the text shows how social concepts of race as based on biology are actually quite fluid, contextually specific, and unconnected to biological explanations.

Piri's "revenge" against the racial system in the United States is to have sex with the prostitute and only afterwards declare to her in perfect English that she has just slept with "a black man" (189); the narrator describes the "look of horror" on the prostitute's face as she "realizes" his race, and her resulting miscegenation, a realization based not on any change in physical characteristics or even on the revelation of "secret" biological information (as in Faulkner's *Light in August* or *Absalom, Absalom!*) but on Piri's use of a different language, which would seem to have nothing to do with race.[17] In this instance, Piri exploits bizarre and illogical social codes which categorize him *racially* in one way if he speaks only Spanish but in another if he speaks English; but the *use* of this subversive understanding of race is to "fuck a white woman." As Marta Sánchez writes, Piri "displays the inherent instability of the racial binary, proving that its boundaries are indeed fluid and permeable" (51); yet, at the same time, "Piri's ability to see beyond binary racial oppositions is undermined by his commitment to sexual and gender hierarchies" (53–54). That is to say, Piri's willful disruption of the stability of racial categories serves the purpose here of *affirming* his male power and of enacting aggression within a dichotomous gender relation. The deployment of notions of race as fluid, unstable, or constructed is thus in no way a guarantee of liberatory ideological representation more generally.

The incident with the prostitute also brings up the issue of race as defined by *self*-identification, since the narrator's race changes in the prostitute's eyes the moment he self-identifies as black rather than Puerto Rican.[18] But elsewhere, self-identification is clearly problematic as a determinant of race, since it opens up the very possibility for denial based on privilege that Piri and his family enact at the beginning of the text.

This understanding of race is reviewed again with the introduction of Gerald Andrew West, with whom I began this discussion. Gerald claims to be "only one-eighth colored" (173) and insists on the right to determine for himself which race he will belong to: "It's true I don't look like a true Caucasian, but neither do I look like a true Negro. So I ask you, if a white man can be a Negro if he has some Negro blood in him, why can't a Negro be a white man if he has white blood in him? I will say that you hit it on the head when you insinuated that I was trying to be a Puerto Rican so I could make the next step to white. You're right! I feel white, Mr. Johnson; I look white; I think white; therefore I *am* white" (176–77). Gerald's understanding of race once again challenges dominant ideology in the form of the one-drop rule and its implicit reliance on the illusion of biological definitions of race; further, it opposes the concept of social construction, in which the dominant society holds the power to define race, with the possibility of self-definition. Indeed, as I noted at the opening of this chapter, Gerald's "radical" understandings of race seem to invite celebratory responses from critics, who tend to overlook the fact that he undermines dominant racial definitions for clearly conservative purposes.[19] Gerald, like the earlier Piri, is motivated by his own desire to assert privilege and distance from African Americans.

Gerald's function is to hold a mirror up to Piri of his own unlikable racism, a fact which Piri dimly recognizes: "I was thinking that Gerald had problems something like mine. Except that he was a Negro trying to make Puerto Rican and I was a Puerto Rican trying to make Negro" (177). This is perhaps Piri's most ambiguous statement about race. On the one hand, he clearly perceives and wishes to distance himself from Gerald's motivations for "passing"; thus he posits an "exception" to the similarity he spots between them. By this midpoint in the text, after all, Piri is identifying himself as a "Puerto Rican Negro" (173), even in the face of Gerald's seeming insistence that Hispanic ethnicity exempts one from classification as black. On the other hand, to claim to be "trying to make Negro" still suggests the difficulty Piri is having with racial categories as they apply to him. In what sense, the scene forces us to ask, could Piri be "trying to make Negro" but not really *be* "Negro"? One could of course argue that, since "black" is not a scientific racial category, Piri is not "really" black in any meaningful sense. But in that sense, Brew is no more a "Negro" than Piri; nor is Gerald. Is Piri not, on some level, suggesting that he is "better" than Gerald, not because Gerald is still trying to claim racial privilege and Piri no longer is, but because Piri is not *really* a "Negro" and Gerald (in Piri's eyes) "really" is? To the degree that race *does* exist as a social construct, and to the degree that Piri *is* identified as "black" by dominant American culture, he cannot be said to be "trying to make" black; the thrust of Thomas's autobiography is that Piri must accept that he *is* black—that his Puerto Rican heritage offers him no escape clause from this.[20]

It is Piri's continuing investment in racial *status* that the bildungsroman structure of the text suggests he must move beyond. As he says to Brew shortly after the encounter with Gerald Andrew West, "I ain't got rid of that fuckin' status that I got brought up on" (180). Piri is starting to recognize the motivations for racial identifications such as his much earlier insistence to Brew that "I ain't no damn Negro [. . .] . I'm Puerto Rican" (123). In the early stages of his development of what we might term "racial consciousness," as we have seen, he sounds much like Gerald, assuming as he does that being "Puerto Rican" exempts him from being "Negro." Indeed, his journey south with Brew is his deliberate effort to move past his own embrace of privilege, by confronting head-on the way in which he is constructed by dominant American racial ideology, which is at its most intense (although not different in substance) in the American South. As the journey begins, Piri starts to sit in the front of a bus, but Brew pulls him toward the back. When he asks why, Brew explains,

> "Once we all cross the Mason-Dixon line, all spades will commence to sit their asses in the ass of the bus. I thought it right good fo' yuh to git used to the idea from the jumps."
>
> I laughed and said, "Dig it." But in my mind I hadn't thought it was gonna apply to me. (166)

Piri's education consists in learning precisely how much it *does* apply to him.

The process is a gradual one. In Washington he notes that, indeed, the black people now sit in the back of the bus (166). In Norfolk, Virginia, he bridles when a white man calls him "boy" (168). In Mobile, Alabama, we can see how Piri still clings to racial privilege (even, notably, *after* the central scene with Gerald Andrew West) by entering a white restaurant although he is with Brew, who, as Piri knows, cannot enter: "On the way back to the ship I got hungry and walked into the first restaurant I saw. It was a white place. [. . .] Brew had warned me about going in, and I could see him through the plate-glass window, standing outside, waiting, with no expression on his black face, the only black face around. I was the alonest" (185). Again, the scene is highly ambiguous. Piri's entrance into the diner marks a willful insistence on a racial status different from that of Brew, who represents "the only black face around," including, presumably, Piri's own. He is the "alonest" because, although he is not white, he also does not see himself as black. But when the counterman refuses to wait on him, making it clear that, as Brew has insisted all along, he *is* black, Piri "smashe[s his fist] on the counter with all my Puerto Rican black man's strength" (186), once again embracing the *dual* identification as Puerto Rican and as black, rather than positing, as he does at other times, that the first rules out the second. As he summarizes the lesson he learns on his travels, "Wherever I went—France, Italy, South America, England—it was the same. It was like Brew said: any language you talk, if you're black, you're black" (191).[21] Piri increasingly responds to the perception that he is read as black by society with an acceptance of his status as black.

Such a dynamic is obviously troublesome. When Piri accedes to the supposed "fact" that he is black, because others have made this clear to him, is he simply, as Marta Sánchez writes, "accept[ing] the gaze of a social system that blackens him" (41)? While on one level such a reading is hard to avoid, it is notable that Piri's identity struggles are never framed in terms of acquiescing to dominant notions of race by succumbing to "blackness." What is textually foregrounded in Thomas's autobiography is not the issue of capitulation or resistance to racial ideology but the issue of claiming or rejecting racial privilege. Indeed, Piri's acceptance of "blackness" is positioned within the bildungsroman structure as a positive step toward what we might call "panethnic solidarity" (that is, between Afro-Caribbeans and African Americans), rather than a negative one indicating surrender to society. When, during his arrest after a botched robbery, Piri responds to a cop's slur of "black bastard" with the statement, "If you don't mind, I'm a Puerto Rican black bastard" (235), we are clearly meant to measure how far he has come from the days when he said to Brew, "I ain't no damn Negro" (123). "Puerto Rican" is now no longer used to defend him from the lower social status of blackness that is marked by the cop's linking of "black" with "bastard." His ethnicity is only an additional modifier of "black bastard"; it no longer serves as a qualifier *limiting* that blackness. Relying largely on what seem like essentialist categories, Piri now disavows racial privilege, while formerly he had used the fluctuating boundaries of the social construction of race to assert difference and distinction. This scene, less than one-third from the end of the book, for all practical purposes resolves this particular identity conflict.[22]

As I have suggested, Thomas's autobiography contains a sophisticated understanding of racial politics. The text suggests that an awareness of the social construction of race is, in and of itself, not resistant, any more than the acceptance of biological explanations of race is, in and of itself, conservative. In the text, all definitions of race call out to be judged contextually, in terms of the strategic purposes they serve.[23] Repeatedly, Thomas undermines essentialist biological notions of race, exposing the ways in which it is, rather, a socially constructed category only arbitrarily linked to ideas of "blood." Thus he does much to shake the foundations of racial thinking that, as we have seen, continue to persist in popular culture, despite the long-standing and more recent "evidence" of science.

Yet at the same time, Thomas's text suggests that nonessentialist understandings of race are no guarantee of political progressiveness, while strategic essentialism, it is implied, can be used effectively, even against more "radical" notions of race, to assert and construct a solidarity based on the exigencies of American life. *Down These Mean Streets* thus offers an interesting counterpoise to Gilroy's concern about the "tainted" discourse of race. The mean streets are a long way from the ivory towers of academe and are ill-informed about the discoveries that are made there. But that does not make them any less a site for subversion, even if such subversion deploys tainted categories. It turns out that, to play in the mean streets, you sometimes have to get dirty.

\* \* \*

Though Thomas's memoir never explicitly considers the notion of a panethnic *Latino* identity that would include, for example, both Puerto Ricans and

Mexican Americans—as I began this chapter by noting—it is suggestive nevertheless, by analogy, of the possibilities for such an identity. In concluding this chapter I would like to dwell for a moment on *Mean Streets'* implications for conceiving of a *latinidad* that it never, in fact, conceives of. For as Michael Jones-Correa and David L. Leal have noted, scholars increasingly reject, as "imperialistic at best," the idea of a common culture that binds Latinos together (215)—that is, as another form of tainted logic. And, indeed, it would seem crucial to the pursuit of knowledge to critically dismantle such inaccurate categories. Nonetheless, it is striking how useful they have, on occasion, been.

In *Latino Crossings*, De Genova and Ramos-Zayas criticize previous studies which postulated *latinidad* as "a kind of 'instrumental ethnicity,'" because in practice these studies continued "to either uphold essentialist assumptions about the presumed cultural 'content' that is contained by those malleable boundaries or to regard essentialist myths as inexorable and necessary" (20–21). Surely, one of the targets of their criticism here—which echoes quite powerfully the writings of Appiah and Gilroy in its concern about the lingering presence of essentialist categories of identity—is the 1985 study by Felix Padilla, *Latino Ethnic Consciousness*, which argues precisely for such an instrumentalist understanding of Latino identity, even while at times appearing to reinscribe the notion that a common language is one salient manifestation of a (preexisting) "common culture" that is then *mobilized* or deployed in coalition-building. What is striking when reading Padilla's book is how frequently respondents themselves—even when arguing quite transparently for the *instrumental* value of panethnic *latinidad*, rely on "essentialist myths" about "presumed cultural 'content.'" One of Padilla's respondents, for example, insists that "[t]he idea of Latinismo is *a very good strategy*," then goes on to complain about Puerto Ricans and Mexican Americans who "do not understand Latinismo. They do not know that we have *basically the same culture and needs*. And the only way to alleviate those problems and gain political respect is to work together as one group" (F. Padilla 73; emphasis added).

The discourse of instrumentality (strategy) and the discourse of primordiality (common, preexisting culture) are inextricable in this passage; indeed, the suggestion appears to be that groups have the "same needs" *because* they have the same culture (rather than, as Padilla argues, because of similar problems of poverty and discrimination).[24] Though the transparent, pressing concern for this respondent is to "alleviate problems," using *latinismo* as a "strategy" to gain political recognition, the strategy will clearly work only if Latinos first recognize themselves as a group. As Padilla comments, "the unique potential of Latinismo or Hispanismo for mobilizing Spanish-speaking people as a collective 'political force' must stem from its appeal to sentiments of 'common origin' [and] its ability to arouse emotions and loyalties founded on people's real or assumed ethnic ties" (148).

Here we can see quite clearly what De Genova and Ramos-Zayas have subsequently critiqued, that is, the notion that "essentialist myths [are] inexorable and necessary." Elsewhere in his study Padilla points out that some respondents relied on rhetoric that was far less dependent on primordial categories; and as we have seen in the Introduction, later findings suggest that a belief in "common culture" cannot account for a majority even of those who currently identify themselves with a panethnic label (Jones-Correa and Leal 230–31).[25] While it has become quite difficult, then, to argue that essentialist myths are inexorable and necessary to a panethnic identity—or even to panethnic political mobilization—it is surely not an overstatement to say that, in certain situations, they may continue to be useful, even if tainted. Nonetheless, if essentialist myths erase and ignore salient differences that need to be attended to, they become dangerous—as I will discuss in Chapter 7.

Needless to say, essentialist myths need not be exclusively panethnic ones; we have seen in the texts of Thomas and Anaya that they can be national (and racial) ones as well. In the following chapter, then, I turn to novels which—while still not explicitly invoking the panethnic category of *latinidad*—nevertheless seriously complicate and challenge essentialist myths regarding more group-specific ethnic identities.

Part Two

# Complicating the Origins

# 3

# Speaking for Others

## Problems of Representation in the Writing of Julia Alvarez

The rise of ethnic literary studies, including Latino/a studies, is predicated, it would seem, on the given that groups must be allowed to speak for themselves, to represent themselves. And at face value, this seems an absolutely indisputable claim. Nevertheless, it hides some pressing difficulties—for example, those invoked by the two senses of "representing." As outlined by Gayatri Spivak in "Can the Subaltern Speak?" "representation" has two quite distinct senses: "representation as 'speaking for,' as in politics, and representation as 're-presentation,' as in art or philosophy" (275). Spivak insists that the two meanings must be considered separately when discussing the dynamics of speaking *for* a particular group, for "[t]he complicity [of these separate meanings] can only be appreciated if they are not conflated by a sleight of word" (277).

The "complicity" Spivak wants to highlight, by emphasizing the separate meanings of "to represent," lies in the assumption that a "representative" of a particular group can accurately and successfully "re-present" (reproduce) the needs, desires, and interests of the entire group. To conflate the two meanings of "represent" (what Spivak calls "proxy" and "portrait" [276]) is to assume as a given that any representative of a group can fully, faithfully re-present the group to others; thus the serious problems or risks of re-presentation go unexplored when a representative (someone positioned to "speak for" the group) is doing the re-presenting.

Writers are often called on to "represent" their ethnic groups in the slippery sense about which Spivak warns: that of colliding both meanings of "represent." It is not simply that an ethnic writer is viewed as *a* "representative" of a particular culture (in the simple sense of speaking from within that culture to a larger audience that lies, in part, outside of it), but that she is assumed to be *representative* of that culture. Take, for example, the comment by a writer for *New York Magazine*, printed as a selling point on the 1983 Signet paperback cover of Toni Morrison's *Tar Baby*, which proclaims Morrison to be "the D. H. Lawrence of the black psyche." Every time we invoke phrases such as "the black psyche" or "the Latino/a experience," we reveal the presumption that this experience is fairly singular, homogeneous, and "knowable" by any representative, who can therefore "speak for" the group. Thus we are led to what Trinh T. Minh-ha has called the "automatic and arbitrary endowment of an insider with legitimized knowledge about her cultural heritage and environment": "An insider can speak with authority about her own culture, and she's referred to as the source of authority in this matter" (374). Representatives of a group, then, are assumed to have the "authority" to re-present the group accurately. The converse, of course, is that if you are not a "representative" (recognized proxy) of a particular group, then you cannot re-present it.

I have already discussed the deeply problematic assumption that a Latina/o from one national-origin group could in any sense be said to be "representative" of Latinos/as from another group—hence the fundamental problem with Latino/a panethnicity. Yet critics have often made such assumptions in practice. Roberto González Echevarría begins his essay on Julia Alvarez's second novel, *In the Time of the Butterflies*, by establishing what he sees as "the central concern of Hispanic writers in this country [the United States]": "the pains and pleasures of growing up in a culture and a language outside the mainstream." Based on this judgment of central experience for a (presumed) group, González Echevarría privileges Cristina García's *Dreaming in Cuban* and Julia Alvarez's first novel, *How the García Girls Lost Their Accents*; these novels are by recognized representatives of the Hispanic "group" who re-present that group accurately (according to González Echevarría) by writing about (his version of) U.S. Latino/a experience. In such an analysis, a Cuban American text and a Dominican American text are rendered fairly interchangeable, since both represent what has been designated as the essential Hispanic experience (linguistic and cultural marginality).

But the problem of representation arises in much more subtle and even unpredictable forms, as well. For instance, while González Echevarría seems not to have a problem placing Cuban Americans and Dominican Americans in the same group, he is apparently much more resistant to a transnational understanding of group identity which would include Dominican Americans and Dominican nationals. Julia Alvarez's *In the Time of the Butterflies* does not deal with the immigrant experience in the United States. Rather, this novel attempts to imaginatively re-create the stories of three sisters in the Dominican Republic who have become historical figures because of their efforts in the resistance movement against Rafael Leónidas Trujillo (dictator of the Dominican Republic from 1930 to 1961), for which they were killed. González Echevarría takes issue with the premise of *Butterflies*, suggesting that Alvarez writes "as if she needed to have her American self learn what it was really like in her native land, the Dominican Republic." Noting the metafictional figure in the narrative frame of *Butterflies* who is "a thinly disguised version of Ms. Alvarez, an Americanized Dominican woman who wants to write something about the

Mirabals and is looking for information," González Echevarría maintains that Alvarez lacks "the realization that the *gringa dominicana* would never really be able to understand the other woman [i.e., the surviving Mirabal sister whom she interviews in the Dominican Republic], much less translate her." In other words, González Echevarría seems to be saying to Alvarez, "Speak for yourself."[1]

As Diane Elam observes of rhetorical situations like these, "in being told to speak, you are really being told *not* to speak. [. . .] In this case, 'speak for yourself' is tantamount to a faintly polite way of saying 'shut up'" (231). As an author raised largely in the United States, Alvarez has lost the right/ability to "represent" (in the conflated sense of the word) Dominicans who stayed in the Dominican Republic. Implicit in González Echevarría's review is the assumption that there is an unproblematic, fairly homogeneous, group—U.S. Latinos/as —for which Alvarez can speak, and a similarly homogeneous group—Dominican nationals—for which she cannot. González Echevarría insists, furthermore, on recognition of difference between Dominican Americans and "third world" Dominicans, but other differences within each group, such as class or race, go unarticulated.

Much more typical, in the U.S. popular imaginary, than González Echevarría's assumption of insurmountable difference between Dominicans and U.S. Latinas/os is the perception that Latinos/as continue to be essentially connected to their countries of origin. As Dalia Kandiyoti puts it, "One aspect of Latino identities as disseminated in media discourses is their assumed inherent transnationality—the seamlessness of the Latino–Latin American connection" (422). The stereotypical and uninformed understanding of Latino culture in the United States is that it is a fairly well-preserved carryover from the country of origin and that Latinos are fairly authoritative representatives of that culture. Indeed, the racist and xenophobic exhortation to "go back where you came from"—no matter for how long the recipients of such comments have been in the United States—is undergirded by the presumption that Latinos' real homes and proper places are "there" rather than "here." Further, as Rubén Rumbaut has written, "a language of kinship and of home—'homeland,' patria, 'fatherland,' 'mother tongue,' 'blood ties,' a 'birth connection'—is often invoked [by immigrants themselves] to describe these attachments to an imagined common origin or ancestry" ("Severed" 44). Ilan Stavans writes, for instance, that Latinos are connected by an "umbilical cord [which] keeps us eternally tied" to our countries of origin (*Hispanic* 32).

This subjective rhetoric of intimate and biological connection is belied by objective measures of "transnationalism" even among first-generation immigrants. As Michael Jones-Correa has noted in *Between Two Nations*, for example, "[v]ery few Latin American immigrants are actively involved in the electoral politics of their home countries" (125). Immigrants, Jones-Correa argues, resist full political identification with their countries of origin as being "irreconcilable" with their present circumstances and their choice to reside in the United States (132). More markedly, Rumbaut's report on a ten-year longitudinal study of the children of immigrants notes that "the level of transnational attachments, both subjective and objective [. . .] is quite small[;] there is very little evidence that the kinds of attachments that are fundamental to pursuing a meaningful transnational project [. . .] are effectively sustained in the post-immigrant new second generation" ("Severed" 90–91).[2]

Silvio Torres-Saillant argues forcefully against the notion of the coextensiveness of U.S. Latino and Latin American identity, insisting that borders matter (436–37). In Alvarez's case, for example, the assumption of "seamlessness" obscures the ways in which her "first world" positioning gives her a particular *kind* of privilege unavailable to Dominicans. As a U.S. citizen, best-selling writer, and writer-in-residence at an American university in the Northeast, Alvarez is separated by far more than just miles from the Dominican Republic—even when, as recent book jackets attest, she "lives" there.[3] González Echevarría, as we can now see, stands at one end of a spectrum: Dominican Americans should not try to represent Dominicans. At the other end stands an equally problematic assumption: Dominican Americans are "essentially" connected to Dominicans.

Let us return to *In the Time of the Butterflies*, which González Echevarría condemns on the basis of insurmountable difference. (Alvarez could never understand a Dominican woman.) González Echevarría would apparently insist that the impossibility of "understanding much less translating" Dominicans renders any such effort futile if not downright imperialistic. But to reject his stance is neither to reaffirm that Alvarez has the authority as a Dominican American to speak for Dominicans (to widen the circumference of group identity which grants "authority" to speak), nor to claim that Alvarez is somehow able to imaginatively enter into, and represent, the subjectivity of Dominican women in some unproblematic, nonappropriative way. As Diane Elam (using Derrida's "Force of Law") forcefully asserts, "any attempt to do justice to the other, to speak of the condition of the other, necessarily involves appropriation of the other's discourse, involves, that is, a certain injustice." Yet Elam goes on to insist that "[t]he risk of speaking must still be taken, but it always remains a *risk*" (235). We might hypothesize that an early step in efforts toward cross-cultural understanding involves the effort to imaginatively engage in the experience of the "Other," such that the other is no longer viewed as an unintelligible, unreadable, or inscrutable category. Of course, the Other cannot be viewed "from the inside" in any real sense; no subject can ever escape his or her own limited subject position to "become" another. Yet, as Jean Wyatt puts it, "if one does not identify with the cultural other to some degree, does not make the conceptual leap to stand in her shoes, how can one be in a position to hear her point of view, to perceive things from her perspective?" ("Toward Cross-Race Dialogue" 880–81). An imaginative occupation of the Other's subject position (or something like what was once called "empathy"), with all its attendant problems and risks, is nevertheless potentially an initial stage in the process of coming to terms with, and taking ethical responsibility for, the conditions of others.[4]

Trinh T. Minh-ha, arguing along with Wyatt and Elam that "[a]wareness of the limits in which one works need not lead to [. . .] the narrow conclusion that it is impossible to understand anything about other peoples," goes on to explicate the position of a subject very much like Alvarez, writing both "inside" and "outside" the group identity "Dominican":

> The moment the insider steps out from the inside she's no longer a mere insider. She necessarily looks in from the outside while also looking out from the inside. Not quite the same, not quite the other, she stands in that undetermined threshold place where she constantly drifts in and out. Undercutting the inside/outside opposition [. . .] this inappropriate other or same [. . .] moves about with always at least two gestures: that of affirming "I am like you" while persisting in her difference[,] and that of reminding "I am different" while unsettling every definition of otherness arrived at" (374–75).

I would argue that, rather than treating the Dominican Other as a position for which she can speak with full authority, Alvarez continually risks speech about/for the Other while continuously resisting the guise of authority in her speech (whether the authority that comes with "identity" or the Western authority so often assumed when speaking about the Other).

As a writer, Alvarez is in fact quite aware of the difficulties of understanding differences, including those cultural differences which are a product of being Dominican American rather than Dominican, and she takes the problematics of cross-cultural understanding and translation (a project which inevitably involves "speaking for") explicitly as her subject matter. As González Echevarría observes, "*In the Time of the Butterflies* reads like the project the Americanized Dominican woman at the beginning of the novel [. . .] would have come up with after pondering the fate of the Mirabal sisters from her perspective as a teacher on a United States college campus today." And although he seems to think this a scathing criticism, it is clear that this is *precisely* the project of *In the Time of Butterflies*; the function of the "Americanized Dominican woman" in the novel is to investigate the problems of translation without abandoning the attempt.

The novel begins with an explicit reference to the imaginative perspective from which the stories of the Mirabal sisters will be re-created. Alvarez's persona is coming to interview the surviving sister for a book project about the Mirabals. The sister, Dedé, thinks to herself,

> The woman will never find the old house [. . .]. Not a *gringa dominicana* in a rented car with a road map asking for street names! Dedé had taken the call over at the little museum this morning.
>
> Could the woman please come over and talk to Dedé about the Mirabal sisters? She is originally from here but has lived many years in the States, for which she is sorry since her Spanish is not so good. The Mirabal sisters are not known there, for which she is also sorry for it is a crime that they should be forgotten. (3)

The barriers of language and of culture (Dedé must explain to the gringa that roads do not have names because "most of the *campesinos* around here can't read, so it wouldn't do us any good to put names on the roads" [4]) create an enormous distance and potential for misunderstanding; the interviewer stumbles haltingly in Spanish, "I am so compromised [. . .] by the openness of your warm manner" (4). Alvarez's mocking treatment of her persona in the novel suggests the degree to which she is aware of the distance between herself and her subject matter. She knows, that is to say, that she shares only the most tenuous and fragile group identity with the Dominican national. Yet her own effort at storytelling works to reconstruct that larger group identity and testifies to her continuing sense of responsibility and commitment to Dominicans "at home."

Even when the *gringa dominicana* drops out of narrative view, Alvarez insists on calling repeated, self-conscious attention to the political imperative of speaking for others and the impossibility of ever doing so accurately. Within the main narrative of the novel, the surviving sister, Dedé, serves as a figure through whom Alvarez continues to investigate issues of representation and authority. Dedé is besieged by interviewers and journalists asking about her sisters at the same time every year, so she has developed mechanical responses which are already a warped distortion of the truth—she speaks in a "fixed, monolithic language around interviewers and mythologizers of her sisters" (7). Though as the surviving sister Dedé is granted by her country the authority to speak for the others, she is poignantly aware of the false claims of such authority; she has survived precisely because she was *not* actively involved in the resistance against Trujillo, as her sisters were. But if the act of speaking for another is dangerous, it is also potentially life-giving. Dedé is hyperaware of her role as the remaining reporter of her sisters' lives, and she receives the interviewers and responds to their questions, however imperfect her answers might be. Dedé knows that it is through her efforts that the story of her sisters is preserved, passed on, and she worries that "she doesn't want to be the only one left to tell their story" (10), so she continues to tell it to others, despite the inevitable distortions.

A third figure within the novel who tells others' stories—along with Dedé and the *gringa dominicana*—is Fela, who claims that the dead sisters literally speak through her:

> Possessed by the spirits of the girls, can you imagine! People were coming from as far away as Barahona to talk "through" this ebony black sibyl with the Mirabal sisters. [. . .] It gives Dedé goose bumps when Minou says, "I talked to Mamá at Fela's today, and she said . . ."
>
> Dedé shakes her head, but she always listens to what the old woman has to say. (63–64)

What is particularly disconcerting about Fela's version of the voices of the Mirabal sisters is that she claims that they are unmediated by her own interference and reconstruction. (She is what Spivak might call "transparent" ["Can the Subaltern Speak?" 275].) Fela, in other words, claims to be able to completely escape the limitations of perspective.

Dedé's reconstructions for the American writer are repeatedly likened to Fela's more mystical imaginings (and, tracing the chain of speakers back to the *gringa dominicana* who looms in the background, we can assume that Alvarez is implicating herself in this commentary, as well):

> "I'll tell you what I remember [. . .]," Dedé offers, stroking the lap of her skirt dreamily. She takes a deep breath, just the way Minou describes Fela doing right before the sisters take over her body and use her old woman's voice to assign their errands. [. . .] Nonsense, so much nonsense the memory cooks up, mixing up facts, putting in a little of this and a little of that. She might as well hang out her shingle like Fela and pretend the girls are taking possession of her. Better them than the ghost of her own young self making up stories about the past! (66, 72)

The remainder of the novel is presented in the apparently unmediated "voices" of the dead sisters, speaking through Dedé as they would through Fela. Sections are named after the different sisters and narrated in alternating first-person points of view. The only disruption in the illusion of retrospective stories told by ghosts through their sister lies in the sections "narrated" by the youngest sister, María Teresa ("Mate"), which, because they are presented in the form of diary entries, create the impression of greater immediacy. (We are presumably reading what Mate actually wrote at different stages of her life, rather than hearing it retrospectively in a recalling which is always also a reconstruction and re-creation.)

Yet it is these diary entries, with their different quality of immediacy, which, ironically, begin to unravel the illusion of unmediated voice. As with the voices that speak through Fela, the danger is that we will mistake the diary for Mate's unmediated voice; to warn us against this mistake, moments in the diary call attention to its own artifice—its own impossibility. For example, in one entry, Mate notes that her sister Minerva scolds her about having abandoned her French studies, but "I decided to take English instead—as we are closer to the U.S.A. than France. [And then, in italics] *Hello, my name is Mary Mirabal. I speak a little English. Thank you very much*" (124). The italics that are meant to represent the change from Spanish to English remind us, as readers, that we have of course been reading English all along—this *cannot* be a verbatim transcription of Mate's diary; a "translator" has mediated between us and it. And, just in case we miss the point, the proximity of the Dominican Republic to the United States is invoked, to remind us that the real translator (the one "speaking for" the dead Mirabal sisters) is not Dedé but her alter ego, Alvarez herself.

In some sense, of course, both Dedé (within the novel) and Alvarez *are* speaking for themselves; both of their projects of storytelling are informed by a desire to understand their relationship to a group of which they both are and are not a part. A story about another, this novel suggests, is always also a story about the relation between self and Other. Interestingly, the violent distortions of history associated with Dedé's packaged story for the journalists and interviewers are linked to her hesitation to explore this connection: "she is setting up her life as if it were an exhibit labeled neatly for those who can read: THE SISTER WHO SURVIVED. [. . .] [U]sually they leave, satisfied, without asking the prickly questions that have left Dedé lost in her memories for weeks at a time, searching for the answer. Why [. . .] are you the one who survived?" (5). The meaning of Dedé's life is fully implicated in the lives of her sisters. To understand herself, then, she must tell herself a story in which she wills herself across difference to understand her sisters, so that she may understand the things that separated her from them in life—even while she reminds herself, in little ways, that she will never fully know the answer, because she can never really speak her sisters' voices. Similarly, Alvarez tells the story of the Mirabal sisters' resistance in a way which points toward the distance between their positions and that of Alvarez, who left the Dominican Republic as a child and grew up in the nearby United States—speaking English, not Spanish.

Of course, there are others in the text of *Butterflies* whose "subject positions" are even further from Alvarez's own than that of the Mirabal sisters, namely, the lower-class, uneducated, illegitimate daughters of Enrique Mirabal. While class differences are an issue in *García Girls* as well, *García Girls* seems to be the least self-conscious of Alvarez's novels to date in its treatment of the possibility of representing "others"; as David Mitchell notes, Alvarez takes on the first-person perspective of Chucha, the García family's maid, only to give us a problematically reductive portrait in which Chucha bears a disturbing resemblance to the "clichéd role of the loyal domestic slave [...] left to mourn her kind keepers" ("Immigration" 35). In *Butterflies*, the issue of class difference is revisited with a greater degree of acknowledgment of the ways in which such difference can be an obstacle to understanding (much less to collective national—or even transnational—identity). The Mirabal sisters must learn to swallow their "pride" in order to rely on their illegitimate sisters for help in the struggle against Trujillo; the theme of coalition across class difference is repeated in the prison scenes, where Mate must overcome her initial revulsion toward the lower-class prisoners who share her cell.

Interestingly, Alvarez never attempts in this novel to speak from the "voice" of a lower-class Dominican (or even to create the illusion of such speech), suggesting an increased attention to the difficulties of bridging class division; we view the poorer illegitimate daughters of Enrique Mirabal only through the eyes of their privileged sisters, who must learn to overcome prejudice but perhaps can never fully escape their upper-class perspectives.

Indeed, it is arguable that there are other ways—in addition to class and Americanized first world identity—in which Alvarez, in *Butterflies*, cannot fully escape her perspective. It is surely worth noting that, for all her attention to the divisions that impede understanding, Alvarez does not substantially take up the subject of a different transnational divide: the Haitian-Dominican conflict. During the Trujillo regime, this conflict had serious ramifications for a specific group of oppressed peoples within the Dominican Republic: those of Haitian descent.[5]

In *Americas* (1992), Peter Winn explains, "In most of the Americas, new nations forged a sense of their identity in opposition to the European colonial power from which they had separated. In the Dominican Republic, a national identity was created in opposition to Haiti: the independence day they celebrate is not their separation from Spain in 1865 but their liberation from twenty-two years of Haitian occupation in 1844" (287–88). Haiti had a history, Winn explains, of importing much larger numbers of African slaves than did the Dominican Republic in order to fuel a plantation economy; this would be a key factor in the construction of a Dominican national identity "defined in opposition to Haiti: If Haiti was black, African, and Voodooist, then the Dominican Republic would be white, Spanish, and Catholic" (288).

The history of what Ernesto Sagás terms "antihaitianismo" was not new to Trujillo's regime; rather, "[a]ntihaitianismo ideology is the manifestation of the *long-term evolution* of racial prejudices, the selective interpretation of historical facts, and the creation of a nationalist Dominican" collective identity (Sagás 21; emphasis added).[6] But it reached its nadir in 1937, with the massacre of thousands of Haitians—figures range from twelve thousand to thirty-five thousand—on the Dominican side of the border (Wucker 50–51; López-Calvo 12).[7] The massacre has been linked by scholars with the stirring up of racist fears about the "'Africanization' of the border" among Dominicans (López-Calvo 13; see also Winn 290). Sagás argues forcefully, however, that "[t]he Trujillo regime and its intellectuals did not invent antihaitianismo; it already was an integral part of Dominican culture. What the Trujillo regime did was to take antihaitianismo to new intellectual heights and convert it into a state-sponsored ideology" (46).

It is striking that, while Alvarez is very concerned to depict the evils of Trujillo's totalitarian regime in *Butterflies*, she gives virtually no attention to the broader issues of national identity and its aggressions which were a central aspect of the regime's repressive functions. Indeed, in *Butterflies* the racial issues implicit in Dominican nationalism, which rendered Dominican society complicit in the Haitian massacre, are largely suppressed. We can discern the outlines of this contrast in the single mention of the Haitian massacre in Alvarez's novel—a fact striking in itself, since the story narrated by the most "political" sister, Minerva, begins in 1938, only a year after the massacre. Yet Minerva does not mention the massacre, either at this point in her narrative or later; instead, the reference is put in the mouth of the sister named Patria (meaning "homeland"), almost ten years later, in 1946. Patria and Minerva look at side-by-side pictures of Jesus and Trujillo; Minerva scorns both figures, and Patria (who is represented as the more "religious" sister) narrates, "That moment, I understood her hatred. My family had not been personally hurt by Trujillo, just as before losing my baby, Jesus had not taken anything away from me. But others had been suffering great losses. There were the Perozos, not a man left in that family. And Martínez Reyna and his wife murdered in their bed, and thousands of Haitians massacred at the border, making the river, they say, still run red—¡*Ay, Dios santo!*" (53).

This passage is quite striking for its conflating of things that would seem to be of both different nature and different scope. The "disappearance" and murder of members of particular Dominican families, as a result of political oppression and silencing, are—while horrible in their own right—not parallel (in terms of causes or sheer numbers) to the nationalist killing, amounting to ethnic cleansing, of virtually an entire population within the borders of the Dominican Republic. One might argue, however, that since family is a dominant metaphor for, and way of understanding, ethnicity (Cornell and Hartmann 20), this represents a parallel structure for Patria—Haitians are simply another "family" that is separate and distinct from the Dominican "family." Also notable in the scene is the focus of culpability on the singular figure of Trujillo. Just as Jesus is ultimately seen as the giver and taker of life, whatever individual circumstances might have literally caused death, so Trujillo is the sole individual responsible for both the political oppression and the massacre of Haitians (whoever did the actual killing).

Patria's focus on Trujillo as the sole source of oppression is supported by the novel as a whole. Making the case for the horrors of Trujillo's regime, Alvarez depicts his crimes as political killings combined with lascivious womanizing (and perhaps rape). In this narrative, responsibility is contained, limited; while, clearly, those who commit the killings and tortures are also guilty, the only national culpability is silence, as Dedé thinks at the novel's end: "People [. . .] kept their mouths shut when a little peep from everyone would have been a chorus the world couldn't have ignored" (317). Even the racial issues that, as Michele Wucker notes in *Why the Cocks Fight* (1999), drove Trujillo to lighten his complexion with pancake makeup in order to fit into the national narrative of Dominican whiteness (51) are reduced in *Butterflies* to his own personal whimsy—a vanity on a par with his collection of medals (Alvarez 95–96). In this sense, Alvarez's narrative can be read as *itself* a nationalist narrative, not only because she seeks to reimagine the "nation" (for example, along feminist lines),[8] but because the issues of nation-building that are so closely linked to the Haitian massacre are retold as the evils of an individual, though very powerful, man. (After all, "Patria" condemns the massacre.) As Dedé says at the end of the novel, trying to explain her need to tell her dead sisters' stories, "we were a broken people [. . .] and we needed a story to understand what had happened to us" (313). But the story—the collective fiction—that Alvarez tells through Dedé is one which in many ways exonerates the Dominican nation.

Indeed, a look at Alvarez's earlier novel, *How the García Girls Lost Their Accents*, suggests how the anti-Haitian construction of the Dominican nation is at times inadvertently reified in her narrative. The latter section of this backwards and multiple bildungsroman—the part of the novel set in the Dominican Republic during the García girls' childhood—also mentions the Haitian massacre: "It was the night of the massacre when Trujillo had decreed that all black Haitians on our side of the island would be executed by law. There's a river the bodies were finally thrown into that supposedly still runs red to this day, fifty years later"—that is, by rough calculation, in 1987 (218).

Chucha the maid, who survived the massacre, sought refuge with the de la Torre family and has been with them ever since. The introductory description of Chucha is as follows: "there was this old lady, Chucha, who [. . .] had this face like someone had wrung it out after washing it to try to get some of the black out. I mean, Chucha was super wrinkled and Haitian blue-black, not Dominican *café-con-leche* black. She was real Haitian too and that's why she couldn't say certain words like the word for parsley" (218). Two prominent symbolic identifiers used to distinguish between Dominicans and Haitians, race and language, are invoked in the description of Chucha: she is a *particular* kind of black ("blue-black," or dark skinned, that is, Haitian as opposed to Dominican); likewise, because she's "real Haitian" she can't say "parsley." This detail is itself a reference to the Haitian massacre; the pronunciation of the word "parsley" was the "test" given to Haitians to supposedly distinguish them accurately from Dominicans. As Wucker recounts,

> For Haitians [. . .]—in the streets or in the fields—the soldiers applied a simple test. They would accost any person with dark skin. Holding up sprigs of parsley, Trujillo's men would query their prospective victims: "*¿Cómo se llama ésto?*" What is this thing called? The terrified victim's fate lay in the pronunciation of the answer. Haitians, whose Kreyol uses a wide, flat *r*, find it difficult to pronounce the trilled *r* in the Spanish word for parsley, *perejil*. If the word came out as the Haitian *pe'sil* [. . .], the victim was condemned to die. (49)

Intriguingly, as Ana Celia Zentella has noted about Dominicans in the United States, "Dominicans, who are predominantly mulattoes, may hold on to Spanish more than other [U.S. Latino] groups because Spanish serves to identify them as non-Haitian in the Dominican Republic and as non–African American in the United States" (326)[9]—once again suggesting the pervasiveness of this collective construction of national identity, in which language and race are linked. Arguably, of course, the use of race and language as "keys" to national identity in the Alvarez passage cited above is that of the narrating García girls—and perhaps more broadly of upper-class Dominican society as a whole—rather than Alvarez's own; she is simply representing mimetically the culture of which she writes. But within the novel, these identifiers are not significantly challenged.[10]

In the only other mention of Haitianness in *García Girls*, the description of another maid, the "one-eyed" Pila, the signifiers are again reinscribed: "She had splashes of pinkish white all up and down her dark brown arms and legs. The face itself had been spared: it was uniformly brown [. . .]. She was Haitian, though obviously, only half. The light-skinned Dominican maids feared her, for Haiti was synonymous with voodoo" (279). Once again, the light-skinned are the Dominicans, while the "dark brown" maid is Haitian and therefore irredeemably "Other." The intriguing comment that she is "obviously, only half" Haitian is left without explication; what is "obvious" about this? If we read the obviousness in the mottling of her dark-brown skin with "pinkish white"—if, in the eyes of the young Yolanda, the pinkish white skin makes Pila obviously only *half* Haitian—then perhaps we can read the passage as poking fun at the absolutist equation of Haitianness with dark-skinned blackness (so that splotches of light skin obviously mean some other nationality), and as beginning in this way to unravel the strict construction of Dominicanness with whiteness.

Yet these correlations are not significantly undermined; much less is their collective force, and collective threat, exposed. That is, the text makes no particular link between the Haitian massacre, from which Chucha escaped, and the García girls' blithe equation of her blackness with her Haitianness, or the light-skinned maids' equation of Haitianness with fearful voodoo. The underlying causes—or at least the necessary preconditions—of the massacre, however, may well have been rooted in precisely such equations, which Dominican nationalist discourse on Haitians reproduced and reified. (In this alternative historical narrative, which takes account of the peculiar form of Dominican nationalism, Trujillo's orders *alone* do not hold sufficient explanatory power, whereas in both *García Girls* and *Butterflies* they are made to bear the burden of historical explanation by themselves.) For a fictional narrative of the massacre which *does* substantially thematize the complicity of Dominican society, we need to turn, tellingly, to a novel by a Haitian American: *The Farming of Bones* (1998), by Edwidge Danticat.[11] This contrast underscores, yet again, the fraught terrain of speaking for others—the inevitable blind spots, gaps, and silences—which Alvarez, to her credit, nevertheless refuses to shy away from.[12]

Though Alvarez's third novel, *¡Yo!* does not fill in this particular gap, it does take as its central theme the dangers of speaking for/representing others. The novel foregrounds the possibility that telling the story of another robs that Other of control over her own story—that is, of how she will represent herself. The prologue of *¡Yo!* introduces this theme through the resentment of the fictional sisters of Yolanda García, the main character and author-figure from *How the García Girls Lost Their Accents*, because Yolanda has written a novel loosely based on the events of their lives. (The self-conscious analogy to Alvarez's own novel *García Girls* is obvious.) As one of the sisters makes explicit in the opening paragraph of *¡Yo!* the issue is *control* ("[She is] talking about our family like everyone is some made-up character she can do with as she wants" [3]), suggesting that the act of representation of another might inevitably exercise a degree of power over that Other.

The project of the novel is apparently to "compensate" for this imbalance in textual control by having other characters from Yolanda's life tell their own stories about "Yo." The novel's title, referring overtly to Yolanda as the absent center around which this novel is constructed (unlike in *García Girls*, Yolanda's own voice is never heard in this novel except through the narration of others), is also the Spanish word for "I," suggesting the various subjects who will now, within the postulated world of the text, get to "speak for themselves." But the word "Yo" printed on a book jacket above the words "Julia Alvarez" cannot fail also to invoke the presence of Alvarez herself as author, emphasizing that all of these characters (like all the characters of *García Girls*) are her creations, described through her perspective. While the fictional characters offended by Yolanda's textual control can "take the mic" within the fictional world of *¡Yo!* this in no way corrects the problem of *Alvarez's* representation of others, and the potential violence of that representation. In this metafictional manner, Alvarez highlights once again her own presence as re-presenter, undermining the textual illusion of what Spivak might call "transparency" (i.e., the characters speak, "through" Alvarez, for themselves, in an unmediated way).

Alvarez extends the implications of this self-referential opening to the problems involved in representing the "less privileged" in two of the subsequent vignettes that constitute *¡Yo!*: "The Maid's Daughter" and "The Stranger." In "The Maid's Daughter," the narrator, Sarita, comes as a girl to the United States from the Dominican Republic in order to be with her mother, who is the García family's maid. Intriguingly, then, Sarita would seem to share an obvious group identity with Yolanda, who also came to the United States as a girl (just as, for González Echevarría, Alvarez and Cristina García share a group identity by virtue of being Latina immigrants). But Alvarez actually radically undermines even the more narrow group identity posited by a specifically Dominican immigration by emphasizing the ways in which class differences cut through this group. From the beginning, the García sisters—and particularly Yolanda—foster the illusion that Sarita is their "little sister" (56); but Sarita remains vividly aware of the class differences between them: "[Mamá] had spent her whole life working for the de la Torres [Mrs. García's family], and it showed. If you stood them side by side—Mrs. García with her pale skin kept moist with expensive creams and her hair fixed up in the beauty parlor every week; Mamá with her unraveling gray bun and maid's uniform and mouth still waiting for the winning lottery ticket to get replacement teeth—why Mamá looked ten years older than Mrs. García, though they were both the same age, forty-three" (66). Economic differences are not merely manifested through an unequal share of material possessions, but, rather, are engraved in the flesh itself, an inextricable part of identity. This understanding on Sarita's part makes her skeptical of the García girls' claims that they regard her as "family" (despite the ostensibly unimportant differences of class which separate them): "those girls treated me like a combination of favorite doll, baby sister, and goodwill project" (57).

Claims of kinship, of course, cannot fail to remind us of the ethnic ties which inevitably invoke them. As Stephen Cornell and Douglas Hartmann have insisted, ethnicity always involves a "claim to kinship, broadly defined" (19); "[e]thnic ties are blood ties" (16). Not only is dominant U.S. culture overwhelmingly likely to see Sarita and the García girls as "related" by virtue of their ethnicity, despite class differences, but Yolanda herself sees ethnicity as a close and intimate connection that overrides class. (More on this shortly.) Yet the physical differences occasioned by class seem to dismantle what might have been perceived racial similarities (which Cornell and Hartmann note may be one of the "potential bases of this belief in common descent" [17]).

While the privileged García girls repeatedly profess that Sarita is, so to speak, "one of us," Sarita knows better. Well-intentioned expressions of "familial" love by Yolanda, like a "dedication" of a school report to "Sarita y Primitiva, parte de mi familia" (part of my family), are rewritten by Sarita in her head to express her own resistance to such claims, which she knows are false: "I knew exactly what I wanted to do with that dedication. I wanted to write it over, using Mamá's rightful name. More than once, I had tried to get my mother to go back to her real name, María Trinidad. But Mamá refused. The de la Torres had given her that nickname when she was a young wild girl just hired out of the campo. 'I'm used to it now, m'ija'" (65–66). While Yolanda's dedication means to express her sense that the maid and her daughter are "parte de mi familia," and therefore regarded as "same" rather than "other," her wording reveals the extent to which class both determines and then occludes her vision: she has given the maid the name "Primitive" (Primitiva).

The crux of the story lies in this tug-of-war over representation. Yolanda wishes to write a "report" about Sarita for school: "What she proposed to do was observe my acculturation—I'd never heard of such a thing—as a way of understanding her own immigrant experience" (62). Once again, Yolanda convinces herself of identity while Sarita understands difference. Yolanda's report about Sarita is meant to be "a way of understanding" herself, but what Sarita feels is the way in which this report will be an attempt to capture and fix her: "I still felt as if something had been stolen from me. Later, in an anthropology course I took in college, we read about how certain primitive (how I hate that word!) tribes won't allow themselves to be photographed because they feel their spirits have been taken from them. Well, that's the way I felt. Those pages were [...] a part of me" (66). Like Yolanda's sisters, Sarita feels a lack of control over the way in which she will be represented. It is not *what* Yolanda writes about her that is at stake—it is not, that is, the accuracy of the representation ("Everything was set down more or less straight" [66]); rather, it is the simple fact that, in her textual representation of Sarita, Yolanda (like the "anthropologists" Sarita reads about in college) renders her an object of study. Sarita cannot speak, as a subject, out of the pages of Yolanda's report. Thus Sarita steals the report—an act of resistance in response to her sense that she is not in control of the text which represents her.

In "The Stranger" the dangers of theft through representation are even more pronounced, since in this story the inaccuracy of the text *is* an issue. Consuelo, an illiterate Dominican woman, receives a letter from her daughter Ruth (who has immigrated to the United States) seeking Consuelo's advice: the Puerto Rican man she married in order to obtain legal-resident status is now refusing to grant her a divorce. (In this "guest appearance" in the text by a Puerto Rican, it is worth noting that Alvarez again emphasizes difference over similarity: the Puerto Rican has advantages of citizenship that the Dominican immigrant lacks.) In a dream, the answer to her daughter's plea comes to Consuelo: "Consuelo was speaking wonderful words that flowed out of her mouth as if language were a stream filled with silver fish flashing in the water. Everything she said was so wise that Consuelo wept in her own dream to hear herself speak such true words" (99). But when she wakes up, she cannot remember the words from her dream. Nevertheless, she seeks the assistance of the American woman Yolanda—on a visit "home" to the Dominican Republic—to transcribe her words in a letter to her daughter.

The resulting scene enacts, at multiple levels, the struggle between Consuelo and Yolanda for control over the text of the letter. Consuelo begins: "*'My dear daughter Ruth* [. . .] *I have received your letter and in my dream came these words which this good lady is helping me to write down here with all due respect to el Gran Poder de Dios and gratitude to la Virgencita without whose aid nothing can be done.*' It was just as it had been in her dream: the words came tumbling from her tongue!" (105–6). But Yolanda responds that "[i]t's not a sentence [ . . .] Let's say one thing at a time, okay?" (106), immediately moving beyond her role as transcriber to one of editor imposing a standard of order and correctness on Consuelo's words. When Consuelo dictates the message that her daughter must respect the "holy vow" of marriage and that "he will stop beating you if you do not provoke him" (106), Yolanda flatly refuses to transcribe Consuelo's words:

> "I'm sorry. I can't write that. [. . .] If I were you, I definitely would not advise her to stay with a man who abuses her [. . .] but, I mean, you write what you want."
>
> But Consuelo did not know how to write. [. . .] "You have reason," she said to the lady. "Let us say so to my Ruth."
>
> She had meant for the lady's words to be added to the ones that had already been written. But the lady crumbled the sheet in her hand and commenced a new letter. [. . .]
>
> "*My dear Ruth,*" the lady began, "*I have thought long and hard about what you have written to me.* Does that sound all right?" The lady looked up.

"Sí, Señora." Consuelo sat back in the soft chair. This indeed was a better start. [...]
"*A man who strikes a woman does not deserve to be with her,*" the lady wrote. (107–9)

By the end of this struggle over who will control representation, Consuelo's words have been literally obliterated under the pressure of Yolanda's authorial efforts.

The battle over textual control is further complicated by a series of ever-more-troubling questions, begged by the story's structure, which explore the problematics of representation. For the story surely represents Consuelo as unable to "speak for herself" in the sense that, by speaking in a manner which perpetuates gendered violence, she fails to accurately represent her own interests. But if we believe that Yolanda's advice to Consuelo's daughter is "correct" (or alternatively, if the text suggests that Yolanda's advice is correct) while Consuelo's advice is "wrong," are we then (is the text then) implicitly granting legitimacy to the position that Yolanda is *right* to wrest authorial control from Consuelo (that Yolanda, as first world, liberated, and educated American woman, can speak *for* her when she cannot speak for herself)?[13] The episode is even more disturbing, given that, when Consuelo was advising Ruth to stay with her husband, she "felt the words she was speaking were not the wonderful words of the dream" (107), while, when Yolanda wrote her own letter without input from Consuelo, Consuelo "could feel her dream rising to the surface of her memory. And it seemed to her that these were the very words she had spoken" (109). The text, in other words, opens itself up to the reading that Consuelo "authenticates" Yolanda's representation and appropriation through her sense that Yolanda's words are actually her own.

I would argue that, at a deeper level, the story works against such an interpretation, precisely by emphasizing the violence of Yolanda's appropriative act—for example, at the very moment where Yolanda substitutes, rather than supplements, Consuelo's words with her own, thus moving from textual manipulation or distortion to *destruction* of Consuelo's "text": "[Consuelo] had meant for the lady's words to be added to the ones that had already been written. But the lady crumbled the sheet in her hand and commenced a new letter" (108). Indeed, Consuelo's doubt about her own words being the inspirational words spoken in her dream, and her sense that in fact those words are Yolanda's rather than hers, suggests the almost violent force of Yolanda's will (ironically, since Yolanda's vigorous stance here is *against* violence), which discredits Consuelo's perspective even while attempting to represent it faithfully. (In other words, the story suggests the possibility that Consuelo discredits her own perspective because Yolanda does.) In "translating" Consuelo's words into writing, Yolanda does inevitable violence to them. I would argue, then, that the text does not work to endorse Yolanda's forceful appropriation of Consuelo's text (although it does not allow us simply to condemn Yolanda either, as I discuss below).

Nevertheless, the disturbing elements of the text (those elements which suggest the violence *of* the story, rather than the violence *within* it) are not fully eliminated by such a reading. We as readers cannot fail to be troubled by Consuelo's "endorsement" of Yolanda's substitution (which points beyond Yolanda's violence to Alvarez's, as the represener of a lower-class Dominican woman). Alvarez refuses to let herself off the hook by inscribing into the text a simple critique of Yolanda's textual violence; that violence is, indeed, arguably reproduced by Alvarez, who "represents" Consuelo as endorsing Yolanda's words. Stories such as "The Maid's Daughter" and "The Stranger" insist on the impossibility of representing the "Other"—in this case, the lower-class Dominicans—*without* doing violence. Indeed, we can see these stories not simply as attempts to "represent" or "understand" the lower class but, more significantly, as explorations of the class differences which render Alvarez's own position (as an American-raised, college-educated, upper-middle-class author) so precarious. Like Dedé's stories (in *In the Time of the Butterflies*) about her sisters, which are a means of grappling with her difference from them (they became politicized; she did not), Alvarez's fiction about "others" turns out to be in large part an exploration of the relationship of her own position vis-à-vis those others. The stories, in other words, call attention to the differences between Dominicans and U.S. Latinas (thus complicating the transnational model), as well as between privileged members of the upper- and upper-middle class and the working class who so often serve them.

And yet, in an ongoing project that *also* challenges the notion of unbridgeable difference, what is revealed is that the effort at understanding continues despite the obvious dangers—dangers which are neither preempted by empathetic identification (Yolanda "cares" about the working classes) nor vindicated by "ends" (Yolanda's letter contains better advice) nor even ameliorated by self-consciousness about the dangers (Yolanda herself is highly self-conscious of the dangers of appropriation). While Yolanda's representation efforts are marked by violence, the refusal to represent could be read as an abdication of responsibility, what Linda Martín Alcoff calls a "'retreat' response [. . .] in which a privileged person takes no responsibility whatsoever for her society" (106–7). It is clear, of course, that Alvarez is still trying to understand Dominican society as in some sense "hers," at least to the degree that she must continue to take responsibility for it, even from a distance. As she writes in the concluding pages of her fourth novel, *In the Name of Salomé* (2000), "It's continuing to struggle to create the country we dream of that makes a patria" (352). Alvarez's writings may sometimes be set in the United States but they invariably dream of the Dominican Republic.

In this sense Alvarez is indeed participating in a larger phenomenon of transnationalism: as Suárez-Orozco and Páez point out, "Dominican immigrants have developed political, economic and cultural adaptations that involve high levels of transnationalism. They remit large sums of money to their homeland, they remain substantially engaged in political processes there, and they return periodically with their children to nourish social and cultural ties" (6). We might connect Alvarez's decision to run a coffee plantation in the Dominican Republic to this larger cultural-economic phenomenon. In the afterword to *A Cafecito Story* (2001), a novella by Alvarez, her husband, Bill Eichner, explains the evolution of the coffee plantation:

> We met a group of farmers [in the Dominican Republic] trying to organize themselves around growing and finding markets for their organic, shade-grown coffee. We sensed that they were battling an agribusiness trend toward growing coffee in full sun, for better short-term yields, while deforesting the mountains and poisoning the rivers with pesticide and chemical fertilizers. We praised their efforts. They asked, would we like to join their struggle and buy some land before it was grabbed up by the big technified coffee plantations? Julia and I looked at each other [. . .] and said, why not? (40).

What is interesting about this particular depiction of transnationalism, however, is its emphasis on work and solidarity across lines of clear difference rather than on a presumed seamlessness of identity.

It is these lines of difference that Alvarez's work is increasingly attuned to, and her commitment to writing about them can surely be read as an expression of solidarity. By insisting on Yolanda's violence despite both her own best intentions and Consuelo's ultimate approval and agreement, Alvarez highlights the violence that attaches to *any* attempt to represent others (including those others that a mainstream U.S. culture might view as seamlessly connected to Alvarez herself, and as part of her own "group"). Nevertheless, Alvarez persists in her efforts. As Elam puts it,

> Responsibility to the other is excessive, although it is not simply paralyzing. Trying to do justice to the other, trying not to appropriate the other's discourse, is an unresolvable epistemological bind—which still does not mean that we stop trying to be just. Rather, the significance of this predicament lies in an *ethical* [. . .] recognition that there is no guilt-free speech. Injustice and appropriation are part of the violence of language;

language can never be completely just, although we can continue to try to make it more so. (235)

If Alvarez's first representation of lower-class servants, Chucha from *García Girls*, enacts a particularly striking form of violence (Alvarez writes Chucha's first-person narrative—a narrative which creates the illusion that the working-class, Haitian maid "speaks for herself"—as one which "constructs" her only in terms of her employers), it is to Alvarez's credit that she returns to such representations in her third novel, in an attempt to make her language more just. Her self-consciousness does not mean innocence; while the acknowledgment that the servants in *¡Yo!* have lives of their own, never touched or even understood by their employers, is now clearly made (in stories like "The Maid's Daughter" and "The Caretakers"), other forms of violence continue to exist. Nonetheless, we can understand Alvarez's writing, at its best, as an expression of solidarity with those whose subject positions she represents, across lines of difference she acknowledges. As Kandiyoti has written, "notions of solidarity [...] based *primarily* on ideas of transethnic similarity may lead to [...] oppression, mutual misunderstanding and failure." Alternatively, "the recognition of unequal power relations [...] provide[s] a firmer ground for solidarity," allowing us "to continue imagining various forms and possibilities of mutual care and support in the contact zones of the Americas" (444). That is to say, when we (like Alvarez) recognize and explore difference, we can begin to imagine community.

# 4

## Complicating *Cubanidad*

### Novels of Achy Obejas and Cristina García

I have to admit to experiencing a degree of mild surprise when I discovered, in the summer of 2004, during my first visit to Havana, that the Cuban capital has a Chinatown. Apparently, though it is now reduced to virtually a single street, Havana's "Barrio Chino" was once "the largest Chinese outpost in Latin America" (Bauzá). Yet the existence of Cuban Chinese was not part of the narrative I received of Cuba as a child of first-wave Cuban exiles—those who left Cuba in the years immediately following Castro's 1959 revolution. So, though I should have guessed some Chinese influence on the culture—my parents called me "mi china" as a term of endearment, even though we are not of Chinese descent—I did not. (As testament to my surprise, a full-color 8×10 photograph of the entrance to Havana's Chinatown now hangs on my office door. I am fond of playing guessing games with my students. "What is that a picture of?" I ask. "Uh . . . Chinatown?" "Yes, but *where*?")

My own anecdotal experience of surprise at Chinese Cubans suggests something broader, I believe, about the dominant Cuban exile narrative of *cubanidad*—Cubanness. Very recently, U.S. Latino/a literature has begun to directly address, and challenge, that element of surprise. In his exile memoir of Cuba, *Waiting for Snow in Havana* (2003), Carlos Eire mentions visiting Chinatown as a young child and immediately adds, "Yes, Havana had a Chinatown, and a Chinese cemetery too. Lots of Chinese had somehow ended up in Havana, and some were named Felipe" (59).[1] In a similar tone, but with reference to Jewish Cubans, Alisa Valdes-Rodriguez's incisive Cuban narrator, Lauren, in *The Dirty Girls Social Club* (2003), snaps to her readers, "[Y]es, we Latinas come in 'Jew', too—shame on *you* for being surprised" (11–12). Of course, such literary quips are in part a challenge to uninformed, mainstream "American" stereotypes about Cubans. But they also, I would suggest, speak to the ways that the Cuban "nation" has been predominantly constructed by Cuban exiles themselves.

\* \* \*

The nation, Homi Bhabha writes in his introduction to *Nation and Narration* (1990), is an "idea whose cultural compulsion lies in the impossible unity of the nation as a symbolic force" (1). We might unpack his statement: the "compulsion" is toward a symbolic "unity," even though the *fact* of that unity is "impossible." David Mitchell glosses Bhabha, in a reading of Cristina García's first and best-known novel, *Dreaming in Cuban* (1992): the "notion of national identity is [. . .] an imaginative fortress constructed as the protective outpost of individual and collective belonging that defines and confirms its authenticity by its interminable exclusions" ("National Families" 51). What happens to the construction of national identity, already defined by exclusion, when it is driven by the nostalgia of the Cuban exile community? For, as María de los Angeles Torres has written, "the first group of postrevolution émigrés turned nostalgia into a principle of constructing community" ("Encuentros" 214).

The most common speculation is that nostalgia generates a static notion of national identity, as if it were preserved in amber: "Cuban exile culture became frozen in a version of the past, turning into *la cultura conjelada* (the frozen culture)" (M. Torres, "Encuentros" 214). Thus American-published cookbooks on Cuban food, for example, include recipes for *picadillo* (a ground-beef hash) and *ropa vieja* (made with shredded beef)—even though, as I have discovered on two trips to Cuba, beef of any sort is now virtually impossible to come by, except for privileged tourists. These meals are not representative of a currently existing Cuban culture, in other words, but of an imagined Cuban *past* (needless to say, of a certain class of people) projected to represent a timeless "Cuba." Kate McCullough says that "exile presupposes a relationship to a lost physical place or land that comes to embody the temporal zone of the past" (580); in this explanation, the lost physical place (Cuba) actually "embodies" or represents *something else*—a temporal "past" that may be missed for a variety of reasons, only some of which might have to do directly with the national idea of "Cuba."[2]

"Cuba" thus becomes a loaded metaphor, more figurative than factual. As Salman Rushdie has famously written of exiles' efforts to reconstruct their point of origin, "we will not be capable of reclaiming precisely the thing that was lost; [. . .] we will, in short, create fictions, [. . .] imaginary homelands" (10). We might hypothesize, of course, that the shape and texture of those fictions will be affected as much by the exile's present situation as by his or her past. "It may be argued," Rushdie notes, "that the past is a country from which we have all emigrated, that its loss is part of our common humanity"; but for the exile, the past is also marked by the "physical fact of discontinuity, *of his present being in a different place from his past*, of his being 'elsewhere'" (12; emphasis added). The exile's narrative, in other words, is always already transnational in its production, although the "look" of that narrative is so often strikingly monocultural, mononational.

The present place, that is to say, shapes the imaginary past, even if that shaping is obscured or glossed over by an apparently detached narrative of pastness. For Cuban exiles in the United States, nostalgic imaginings of a Cuban past are inevitably informed by how the community wants to "imagine" itself and represent itself to mainstream U.S. culture, its "elsewhere." In this chapter, I wish to examine two Cuban American novels, *Monkey Hunting* (2003) by Cristina García and *Days of Awe* (2001) by Achy Obejas, against the backdrop of Cuban exile narratives that have posited a singular, white, and Catholic national identity for Cuba. The novels of García and Obejas challenge this vision of national unity by narrating a prerevolutionary Cuban nation that was already multiethnic, multiracial, and irretrievably conflicted and divided from within: a panethnic nation that (like the current panethnic Latino community in the United States) did not cohere. (That narratives of cultural hybridity may themselves do nothing to disrupt nationalist myths and their oppressive functions is a further complication implicit in García's and Obejas's texts.)

It is surely no great leap to suggest that, in the context of the 1960s struggle over civil rights, immigrant Cubans arriving in the United States had particular incentive, in their new, "present," location, to represent themselves to their host country as *white*. Cuban exiles have had a history of preferential treatment by the U.S. government since 1959 (Lisandro Pérez 261; M. C. García 28–29)—and that history is as tied to the racial demographics of this group as it is to their function as a symbol of the failures of communism: "until the Mariel exodus of 1980, most Cuban immigrants derived from upper- and middle-class sectors, [and] were predominantly white or white identifying" (Allatson 188).[3] Indeed, race and anticommunism were intimately related in the group's self-representation; as Pedro Pérez Sarduy and Jean Stubbs have written, "the slogan 'neither Black nor Red' formed part of a white backlash against major redistributive measures in the early revolutionary years. Even before socialism had been proclaimed, racism and anti-communism were being equated" (9). That is to say, the "anticommunism" of the Cubans who became exiles was intricately connected to a self-presentation, both in Cuba and, later, in the United States, as racially white. The image of Cuba, and especially of Havana, advanced by the first-wave Cuban exile community is, likewise, most often a white one: of *quinceañera* parties with white-looking debutantes in white dresses and equally "white" wedding portraits.[4] Havana, in its former glory, was ostensibly a white city, modeled after the European metropolis.

The success of this self-representation was palpable.[5] Articles in the U.S. news media in the 1960s that touted the Cuban immigrant success story frequently reinforced the notion that Cubans were white. One article appearing in *Business Week* in 1966, entitled "Cuba's New Refugees Get Jobs Fast," notes that "few if any complaints are heard from Negro leaders, who at first feared the new influx would rob their people of work" (69). The obvious implication is that Cubans were *not* "Negroes"—that the two categories were mutually exclusive. Another article, in *Fortune*, "Those Amazing Cuban Emigres" by Tom Alexander, is accompanied by several photographs of Cuban immigrants at work—all of them strikingly white-looking (144–49). In an analysis of "the social and political construction of the Cuban success story" (Croucher 105) touted by such articles, Sheila L. Croucher notes that, "[r]elated to [. . .] the tales of a 'Cuban economic miracle,' is a portrayal of Cubans in the United States as 'white,' like the majority host society, as opposed to 'black,' like the African American minority" (107).[6] Benigno E. Aguirre, writing in 1976 (that is, prior to the 1980 Mariel boatlift, which brought much larger numbers of black Cubans to the United States), acknowledged the existence of "Cuban Negroes" among the exile population but suggested that they did not share "a feeling of ethnic identification" with the other exiles and experienced a "moral isolation [. . .] from the exile community" (115). That is to say, the majority exile community generally did not represent itself, and was not perceived, as a racially "mixed" community in the 1960s; rather, black (and other nonwhite) Cubans simply fell off the radar in terms of the picture of Cubanness presented to mainstream U.S. culture.

This representation continues today: the Pew Hispanic Center's 2004 report on Latinos and race notes that 89.7 percent of naturalized Cuban citizens, and 83.5 percent of noncitizens, identify as white (Tafoya 7).[7] María de los Angeles Torres attributes this choice to the fact that "Cubans still use home country referents to define their cultural identity, and indeed those who choose white were probably considered white in Cuba" (*In the Land* 222 n. 1). The Pew Hispanic Center, however, offers another possibility: "For both the native and the foreign born [in the United States], feelings of inclusion and civic engagement [. . .] can be related to race. [. . .] [T]he consequences of identifying as white vary from place to place" (Tafoya 8, 13).[8]

Speaking of Latin American immigrants in general, Michael Jones-Correa elaborates on the significance of identifying as white specifically in a U.S. context:

> [I]t makes sense instrumentally that, confronted with a rigid color line defined by the [U.S.] state, on one side of which lies the likelihood of discrimination and prejudice, Latin American immigrants choose to avoid self-identifying as black. There is probably little *objective* difference between some of those Hispanics identifying as "black" and those

who were listed as white or "Spanish race" by the Census Bureau. The difference is not in skin color, but in the choice of identity. (*Between Two Nations* 120)

It is, at the least, intriguing to speculate on the degree to which U.S. reception might have exerted—and continues to exert—an additional pressure on Cuban immigrants to claim whiteness for themselves if they can.[9]

Part of the persistence of this representation can be attributed to the distancing maneuvers of the first-wave exile community from subsequent waves. As James and Judith Olson note, when the Mariel boatlift in 1980 brought much larger numbers of Afro-Cuban immigrants to the United States than had previously been seen, "the 'Marielitos' were not welcomed with open arms by American society in general *or even by the Cuban-American community*. This time the press coverage of their arrival in the United States [was] different" (81; emphasis added). And they suggest, remarkably, that perhaps the most important reason for that difference in reception was race (84).[10] Croucher reports of the Mariel incident that "[t]he established Cubans in Miami became some of the harshest critics of the new arrivals, fearing that the 'Marielitos' would tarnish their hard-earned reputation [. . .]. One Cuban American city official stated: 'Mariel destroyed the image of Cubans in the United States and, in passing, destroyed the image of Miami itself for tourism. The marielitos are mostly black and mulattoes of a color that I never saw or believed existed in Cuba'" (57; Portes and Stepick, 21, qtd. in Croucher).[11]

In the latter Cuban American speaker's fascinating rhetorical sleight of hand, the darker Cubans are somehow suggested to be fraudulent; they never "existed in Cuba." The image of white Cubanness is thus projected backward, onto the home country itself. And while the Mariel boatlift in 1980 and the waves of *balseros* in the 1990s visibly complicated the racial demographics of the exile population,[12] to the degree that cultural or racial hybridity has since been recognized, it is the syncretism of African and Spanish elements that has drawn attention.[13] It is perhaps unnecessary to say that other minority segments of the Cuban and Cuban exile population, and other forms of cultural hybridity, have remained all but invisible to the mainstream.

As I have been suggesting, the nostalgic idealizing of a past as point of origin tends to represent the Cuban nation as a singular unity disrupted only by the revolution, which is depicted as the unique cause of the "diaspora." María de los Angeles Torres summarizes this narrative trend: "Paradise had been lost forever to the 'forces of evil'" ("Encuentros" 214). In a documentary about Cuban Americans entitled *Café con Leche: Voices of Exile's Children* (1997), one of the interviewees comments that "[o]ur country only lives here [inside our minds]," and continues, "[O]ur country, the one we left, no longer exists

[; It was] a wonderful country that a crazy, schizophrenic man destroyed because he hates Cubans" (my translation). In this rather reductive plotline, often recited in various forms by, especially, the first wave of Cuban exiles, Castro "caused" the diaspora. There seems to be no history in this communal story before Castro (other than perhaps the history of independence from Spain, useful for the rhetoric of nationalist heroes like José Martí)—no rehearsal of economic or even nationalistic factors (and certainly not racial or ethnic ones) leading up to the events culminating in Castro's revolution. In the recollections of Flavio Risech, a child of Cuban exiles, "the lament for a [...] mythical Cuba where everyone had wealth, health and high culture, where there was no racism, was the constant refrain at the dinner table. Always in counterpoint was the theme of the communist evil which had despoiled our island paradise" (531).

Roberto Fernández's novel *Raining Backwards* (1988) lampoons nostalgic reconstructions of a perfect, prelapsarian (that is, pre-Castro) Cuban origin in a hilarious episode entitled "Retrieving Varadero," referring to Cuba's famous Varadero Beach. In this vignette, an exiled Cuban woman uses her idealized nostalgic stories of her Cuban past to elicit increasingly intimate favors from a much younger Cuban exile hungry for stories of the homeland he does not remember:

> Eloy had been serving Mirta faithfully for the last two months in exchange for tidbits of the past. He was thirsty for learning about the golden-roofed cities of that enchanted island [...]. Very slowly, Mirta came to realize that her words had a narcotic effect upon the youth, and shrewdly opted to trade her remembrances of memories for practical favors that could ease the burden of living [...].
> 
> "Why don't you bathe me before you go? [...]" [...]
> 
> "Okay, Miss Mirta, but tell me more. Tell me more . [...]" [...]
> 
> "It was on Varadero Beach that I met my only fiancé. It was a week after the 1943 storm [...] and the breezes were warm [...] a little bit more to the right, lather me right down there [...] but the breezes were never hot and you didn't need suntan lotion and the white seals would play happily with the swimmers [...] and when it rained, it rained molasses and rice so you just needed to open your mouth and eat and if you wanted more to eat you just simply said: 'Sea creatures, I'm hungry,' and the fish and the mollusks would jump from the water to your pan and the sand had the texture of baby powder and the breezes were warm but [...]"
> 
> "What's the matter, Miss Mirta? You're sweating! Are you okay? Do you want me to call my aunt?"
> 
> "It's nothing. It's just that I get excited when I remember so many

beautiful memories. But please, please don't stop lathering me, but now a little bit toward the left [. . .] please." (41–45)

Fernández parodies Cuban exile nostalgia as an always-already idealized construction of the past that is driven by desire; Mirta's sexual desires, which produce elaborate (and transparently fictional) romanticized narratives of the homeland, can surely be read as a metaphor for other kinds of desires frustrated by Castro's socialist revolution. In Mirta's reminiscences, there are, needless to say, no class disparities (food literally rains down from the heavens, without any need of economic transactions), much less class or racial antagonisms. Castro is the only despoiler.

Achy Obejas, in her most recent novel (as of this writing), *Days of Awe*, ironically reverses the exile narrative of Eden despoiled: "Without Fidel, there would have been no golden age, no paradisiacal past" (129)—for it is, paradoxically, because of Fidel's revolution that exiles must retrospectively "invent" paradise in Cuba. As María de los Angeles Torres notes of such exile narratives, nostalgia and its "[m]yths about the past" are driven as much by "forgetting" as they are by "remembering" (*In the Land* 37); preexisting racial tensions and inequalities, class differences—all are swept under the rug for the sake of representing a singular and unproblematized point of origin violated by the 1959 revolution, which "dispersed" an otherwise united people.

If the image of Cuba as a white nation could not always be fully be sustained, especially after the Mariel boatlift, nevertheless, the dominant narrative in exile was that the country prior to 1959 was not divided by race. Thus, Aguirre explains, "Cuban white exiles charge that Castro 'created' the race problem in Cuba" (114); before Castro, the story goes, there was "an almost idyllic environment of race relations in the island" (Aguirre 121 n. 41).[14] In an editorial published in 1984 in *Diario Las Américas*, a Miami-based publication for Cuban immigrants, the author writes, "When we say Cubans we are including everyone, regardless of color, because that is how it was in Cuba [. . .]. Cubans do not have prejudices, nor do we consider differences" (Perna 1984, qtd. in Croucher 118). (The irony of such a statement, on the heels of first-wave exile prejudice toward the Mariel entrants, is rather stunning.)[15] Apparently, until Castro took over and divided Cubans, there was only the unproblematic category "Cuban."

Isabel Alvarez Borland's 1998 book, *Cuban-American Literature of Exile*, provides one of the more surprising manifestations of this narrative at work. The only book written in English, to date,[16] to comprehensively treat "Cuban diaspora" literature in the United States and spanning the gamut from writers like Reinaldo Arenas and Guillermo Cabrera Infante, who came to the United States as adults, to the children of exile such as Achy Obejas and Cristina García, *Cuban-American Literature of Exile* suggests (by its silences) the degree to which 1959 has been represented as the starting point on a one-way street to Cuban biculturalism. Alvarez Borland's expressed intent is to "tell the story of the reformulation of Cuban literature as it crossed cultures and changed languages [...] in the history of the post-1959 Cuban literature of diaspora" (1). Adopting Julia Kristeva's distinction (in *Nations without Nationalism*) between the *"organic* nation," which is "founded on origins and tradition" and "relates to its citizens by integration," and the *"contractual* nation," Alvarez Borland suggests that 1959 represents for exiles *"the moment of rupture* of the organic relationship of individual writer and nation" (12; emphasis added); before 1959, presumably, all Cubans were "integrated" into an "organic" whole. Thus—perhaps taking her cue from the body of writing she examines[17]—Alvarez Borland deals with the topics of hybridity and biculturation almost exclusively in the context of being "Cuban and American, both at the same time" (82). Virtually nothing is said about *Cuban* hybridity, biculturation, and *mestizaje*.[18] Though she briefly mentions the appearance of Santería in the works of a few Cuban American authors (132, 137, 140, 143), such textual signs of Cuban hybridity go utterly unexplored. Similarly, she mentions in passing the racism of the Cuban exiles toward the "Marielitos" in the 1980s but otherwise ignores the issue of Cuban racial divisions (5). Needless to say, Chinese Cubans are invisible.

The term "Cuban diaspora," which Alvarez Borland takes as her subject, it might be noted, is useful enough to refer to the displacement of Cuban peoples and their subsequent geographic dispersal, but it does nothing to disrupt the racial/ethnic singularity of Cuba; rather, it posits Cuba as the source, the origin, of a multiplicity of end points. Hybridity implicitly becomes the effect of the revolution and subsequent diaspora (as we have seen). In a personal anecdote, I remember being asked by an audience member after a presentation on Cuban diaspora writing, "Is there a Cuban *im*pora?" Though awkwardly worded, the question was pushing for a complication of representations (including, perhaps, my own at that time) in which Cuba is conceived *only* as origin, and perhaps relatedly, for a challenge to the perspective in which the 1959 revolution is understood implicitly as the singular cause of Cuban hybridity.

It is this challenge to which recent novels by Cuban Americans Cristina García and Achy Obejas respond. García's *Monkey Hunting* and Obejas's *Days of Awe* focus on the Chinese and Jewish diasporas, respectively, *in* Cuba; they force U.S. readers *backward* in Cuban history, to consider the forms of diaspora that saw Cuba as an end point (or perhaps midpoint) rather than a point of origin—as always and already *trans*national—and to appraise forms and functions of Cuban hybridity beyond life on the Cuban American hyphen.[19]

## Cristina García's *Monkey Hunting*

One might argue, with good cause, that, if the notion of *cubanidad* posited by exiled Cubans is a "construct," so too is Havana's Chinatown. The Barrio Chino as it currently exists is, in many ways, the product of globalization; the particular "shape"—the "Chineseness"—of Chinatown is significantly dictated by the international flow of capital. Chinatown was all but "abandoned" as Chinese merchants went into exile "rather than hand over their businesses to the Cuban government" after Castro's takeover (Arrington); but the need for tourist dollars during Cuba's "Special Period" of economic crisis after the fall of the Soviet Union drove the government to invest funds in refurbishing Chinatown; thus "[i]n 1993 the Chinatown Promotion Group was created by the Cuban government to stimulate businesses and restaurants in the heart of the Barrio Chino" (Bauzá). As part of this new effort, "[s]tate resources were channeled to help revive a Chinese 'look' for the neighborhood. Street names were posted on clean white signs showing a red dragon, and a huge cement arch, with a sign saying 'Barrio Chino' in Spanish as well as in Chinese characters, was built to decorate the neighborhood's entrance. [. . .] Chinese societies were permitted to operate restaurants collectively and charge customers for meals in US dollars as long as they paid taxes on the profits" (Arrington). In a striking example of how economic and political forces can shape the construction of an ethnic identity, Chinese ethnicity in Havana, spurred by the need for tourist dollars, was deliberately (re)constructed and performed anew—including a renewed emphasis on "teaching the children [Chinese traditions]" (Arrington)—despite the fact that "most of the ethnic Chinese have intermarried and moved away" (Bauzá), so that "actual Chinese [in Chinatown] are vastly outnumbered by tourists and Hispanics" (Arrington). As one observer reports, waiters in Chinatown "wear traditional scarlet robes and long, fake braids down their backs as though serving up a repackaged Orientalism for the few tourists on Chinatown's pedestrian main street" (Bauzá).

But this more contemporary manifestation of globalization is, of course, only a partial explanation for the existence of Havana's Chinatown. As Leela Gandhi points out, "colonialism was the historical harbinger of the fluid global circuits which now—so compellingly—characterise the discomfiting propinquities of modernity" (125). Havana's Chinatown is a remnant and tell-tale sign of that colonialism. Lourdes Casal, a Cuban-born writer whom Cristina García includes in her telling compilation of Cuban and Cuban diaspora literature, *¡Cubanísimo!* (2002), and who, as the biographical information in that collection pointedly notes, was "of mixed African, Spanish, and Chinese heritage" (368), writes,

The importation of coolies to Cuba began in July 1847 (Zulueta & Co. of London, a Spanish ship, the *Oquendo*, 206 Chinese) and progressed slowly at first, then with great vigor from 1853 onwards, continuing busily and, of course, profitably—there is no need to say for whom—until 1874, the year of the visit to Havana of the imperial envoy, the Mandarin Chin-Lan-Pin, investigator-into-the-fate-of-the-sons-of-the-great-empire-contracted-to-work-in-the-empire-of-New-Spain. Alerted by Eça de Queiroz, he decided to leave the deceptive capital and travel into the hinterland. As a result of his report, the trade contract was terminated. (In ¡*Cubanísimo!* 193–94)

Cuban exile narratives aside, it is by now a commonplace that the history of colonialism produces hybridity, not "purity"; as Bhabha puts it, "the effect of colonial power is [. . .] the *production* of hybridization" (*Location* 112; emphasis in original). (I will return shortly to the role of what Casal calls the "deceptive capital" in recent representations of hybridity.) Further, although the discourse on "hybridity" generally is centered on colonialist with colonized or "native" hybridizations (in Cuba's case, where the indigenous were virtually wiped out, the most prominent variant on hybridity is a Spanish-African mixture), a variety of other possible hybridities are also the products of colonialism and other nationalist aggressions.

It is notable that hybridity was no secret—indeed, was a prominent, if contested, part of national discourse—in prerevolutionary Cuba. Fernando Ortiz, inheriting a mode of national discourse that dated back to José Martí, wrote in 1940, "The real history of Cuba is the history of its intermeshed transculturations. [. . .] [I]n Cuba the cultures that have influenced the formation of its folk have been so many and so diverse in their spatial position and their structural composition that this vast blend of races and cultures overshadows in importance every other historical phenomenon" (*Cuban Counterpoint* 98–99). "Blends," however, do not necessarily pose a challenge to the illusion of national singularity (even if they might to a Cuban exile "whiteness"). Indeed, they can serve as a mode for suppressing dissenting voices in the national imaginary, as Amaryll Chanady has argued: "Many Latin American discourses of identity emphasizing the mestizo nature of the continent's culture merely subscribe to another form of monolithic ideology in which the problem of the marginalized Other can be solved by simple integration within dominant cultural, political, economic, and discursive practices, and not by a willingness to listen to the Other's 'voice' as truly oppositional and capable of modifying hegemonic concepts of the nation and strategies of nation building" (xvi). Ada Ferrer concurs, noting that, "[a]cross Latin America and the Caribbean, [. . .] intellectuals and non-intellectuals [have historically] fashioned national identities that ostensibly reconciled the tensions of heterogeneity and hybridity and smoothed over the violent history of conquest and slavery" (60).

As Ferrer's comments suggest, blends can stabilize, calcify, into a new construction, a new identity of their own (see G. Sánchez 52). Thus Chicanos celebrate their mestizo heritage, and Chicano/a literature frequently revisits, in various forms, the "origin" story of Hernán Cortés and La Malinche, the indigenous woman who was his mistress and the "interpreter" (and thus, in the traditional formulation, the traitor) of culture who facilitated his conquest.[20]

Doris Sommer, looking at nineteenth-century Latin American novels that at times posit origin stories much like this one, suggests that, in these texts, "a variety of novel national ideas" are realized (or imagined) "in the marriages that provided a figure for apparently nonviolent consolidation during internecine conflicts at midcentury" (6).[21] In these national novels, "[e]rotic passion was less the socially corrosive excess that was subject to discipline [. . .] and more the opportunity (rhetorical and otherwise) to bind together heterodox constituencies: competing regions, economic interests, races, religions.[ . . .] Miscegenation was the road to racial perdition in Europe, but it was the way of redemption in Latin America, a way of annihilating difference and constructing a deeply horizontal, fraternal dream of national identity" (14, 39). The plots do not always end happily, as Sommer points out—sometimes the projected, ideal national future is thwarted in the novel's present—but in all cases the imagined projection is "to build through reconciliations and amalgamations of national constituencies cast as lovers destined to desire each other" (24).

Cristina García's latest novel to date, *Monkey Hunting*, spanning several generations of an African/Chinese/Cuban family, stands as a fascinating contemporary twist to this sort of "national romance." In some ways, the novel gives us its own "founding" origin story, filtered through the perspective of Domingo Chen, one of its central characters: "His great-grandfather had left China more than a hundred years ago, penniless and alone. Then he'd fallen in love with a slave girl and created a whole new race—brown children with Chinese eyes who spoke Spanish and a smattering of Abakuá" (209). Chen Pan, Domingo's great-grandfather and the novel's main focus, signs a contract in 1857 for four pesos a month for eight years and leaves China to work in Cuba. When he arrives, however, he discovers that he is to be a slave in the sugarcane fields. Eventually he escapes to Havana, where he sets up a secondhand curiosities shop in what will become the Barrio Chino. He buys, and then frees, an African-descended slave woman, Lucrecia (actually a mulatta, as I will discuss shortly); she stays with him voluntarily, and eventually they have children.

The novel follows Chen Pan's life, interspersed with chapters that take up the lives of two of his descendants. Domingo Chen is the product of a union between Chen Pan's grandson and an Afro-Cuban woman. Domingo comes to

New York in the late 1960s with his father, who has always been well disposed toward the "Americans" but who promptly kills himself once here. Domingo ends up in Saigon during the Vietnam War, where he has an affair with a Vietnamese woman, Tham Thanh Lan, who, in the closing chapter of his narrative, is about to have his baby.

The other narrative thread follows Chen Fang, Chen Pan's granddaughter in China by his son, Lorenzo Chen, who made return trips to China and founded a family there, as well as another in Havana. (Domingo is the product of the Cuban line.) Chen Fang is educated as a boy but then given in an arranged marriage to a husband whose family takes her infant son and pays her to abandon him. Chen Fang then goes to Shanghai, where she is able to teach openly as a woman. There she has a brief but significant affair with a French woman, the single love of her life. Eventually, Chen Fang is imprisoned as a victim of Mao Zedong's Cultural Revolution.

As this tangle of genealogical transplantations suggests, the figure of hybridity—in its nineteenth-century sense of racial miscegenation as well as, though perhaps more prominently than, in its more recent meaning of cultural hybridity[22]—is of primary importance in García's novel. Certainly, such a figuration fundamentally challenges any singular representation of the untroubled, pre-1959 national Cuban body. But I would go even further, to argue that the novel is an imaginative attempt to pursue a line of inquiry ascribed to Homi Bhabha: it "aims to disclose the intricate ways in which power is at work and at stake under colonialism" (and, I would add, under subsequent forms of nationalist aggression such as the Vietnam War); the novel takes as its subject "the ways it [power] is both challenged by and implicated in hybridity" (Simon 418–19).

García's text, for example, sketches out the violence by which hybridity is produced: the importation of slave and coolie labor, the pursuit of American "interests" in the Vietnam War, and so on. Lucrecia remembers her origins as the rape of her black mother by her white, Spanish (or perhaps creole) owner, and her own subsequent, repeated rape by her father: "once, when Lucrecia dared to call him Papá, Don Joaquín choked her so hard she stopped breathing. She saw flashes of white, then nothing at all. He slapped her awake. 'Say that again and I'll grind up your bones and sell you as pig feed.' It didn't stop him from battering her harder that night" (134). Lucrecia's open recognition of her own "hybridity" (in which she fittingly sees "flashes of white") *seems* challenging, or at least is responded to as a challenge or threat to hegemonic authority by Don Joaquín. But the hybridity itself is clearly just a product of the violence of slavery, not a challenge to it.

This does not mean, however, that hybridity is permitted unrestrained by nationalist interests. For at the same time, the representations of transnational hybridity suggested by the subsequent relationships of Domingo and

Tham Than Lan (in Vietnam) and by Chen Fang and Dauphine de Moët, her French lover, (in China) suggest that state interests *sometimes* thwart such linkages, channeling and containing erotic desires so that they pose no ideological threat to the state. The novel points, precisely in the face of increasing "globalization," to the "policing" of desires that have been produced by such transnational movements; but it also intimates that the imaginative projection of any nationalist "consolidation" is no longer an ideal, since too many crimes have been conducted in the name of nationalism.

Further, *Monkey Hunting* portrays the urban centers (Havana, Shanghai, New York, and Saigon) as what Sheila Croucher has termed "spectacular crash sites" in her call for a more careful exploration of "the role of cities as the physical space in which social and political identities are being reconfigured" (21). It is notable that, in the novel, it is the cities that are the primary sites for the production as well as the containment of hybridity. (The "deceptive capital" is deceptive not only in that ethnic "others" seem to do relatively well there—as in Casal's account—but also in that the appearance of complete tolerance for hybridity is frequently illusory.) While Chen Pan starts out in Central Cuba on a sugarcane plantation, where Chinese coolies interact with African slaves, Havana becomes the focal point for their "cross-pollination" both genetically and culturally in García's novel. Similarly, while Domingo fights in the central highlands of Vietnam, the possibilities of hybridity figured in his relationship with Tham Thanh Lan are given an urban context (Saigon). García, then, seems to be interested in the role of the urban space in both putting different peoples and cultures in extremely close contact with one another and, at the same time, policing or containing their interaction.

In Havana's Chinatown, Lucrecia, having taken on her husband's cultural attributes, comes to claim not a Cuban identity but a Chinese one for herself: "She was a part of Chinatown now, at peace here, with the smells and sounds she'd once found so foreign. How could she think of baking chicken without plenty of ginger? Or deciding something important without offering persimmons to the Buddha? [. . .] Sometimes Lucrecia questioned the origin of her birth, but she didn't question who she'd become. Her name was Lucrecia Chen. She was thirty-six years old and the wife of Chen Pan, mother of his children. She was Chinese in her liver, Chinese in her heart" (137–38). Lucrecia, that is, has "constructed" for herself a Chinese ethnic identity in Cuba—a transculturation that is distinct from cultural assimilation in that the culture adapted to, assumed, is another "foreign" minority culture in Cuba rather than the dominant Spanish one. In the ethnic enclave of Chinatown, Lucrecia's Chineseness is tolerated and relatively untroubled. We might view this as an illustration of what Leela Gandhi has called "the insidious—and ostensibly multiculturalist—procedures whereby the convenient Othering and exoticisation of ethnicity merely confirms and stabilises the hegemonic notion of [national identity]. In these circumstances, ethnicity is always-already named as marginal or peripheral to the mainstream" (126).

However, Lucrecia's own cultural identity is more complicated (or perhaps simpler) than her understanding of it might suggest. Rather than simply becoming Chinese (which, if taken at face value, might raise all sorts of intriguing questions about cultural authenticity and authority), she has become the character who most exemplifies in her cultural practices a Spanish, African, *and* Chinese cultural hybridity. In the same chapter of the novel—the only one which follows Lucrecia from a limited third-person perspective—she first recalls her mother's religious practices, suggestive of African heritage: "Mamá had been devoted to Yemayá, goddess of the seas. She used to dress Lucrecia in blue and white and together they'd take offerings to the beach on Sundays" (127). Only a few pages later, we learn that, after her son Lorenzo went to China to learn medicine, "[e]very day, she prayed to the Buddha and to all the saints to keep Lorenzo safe" (132). Her spiritual practices reflect the intermeshing of (at least) three cultures—Chinese, Spanish, and Yoruba—since "saints" (given the earlier reference to Yemayá) can surely be read not exclusively as Catholic but as a reference to the already syncretic "*santos*" or orishas of Cuban Santería, in which deities of Yoruban origin are merged with Catholic saints (see Barnet, *Afro-Cuban* 18, 26–27).[23] (Two generations later, Domingo's mother, who is also Afro-Cuban, compares "the planets to the *santos*. Venus was Ochún. Mars was Changó" [44].) As Lucrecia contemplates her cultural syncretism, "[i]n her opinion it was better to mix a little of this and that, like when she prepared an *ajiaco* stew. She lit a candle here, made an offering there, said prayers to the gods of heaven and the ones here on earth. She didn't believe in just one thing. Why would she eat only ham croquettes[?]" (129).

Lucrecia's (and García's) reference to *ajiaco* here draws quite obviously on Fernando Ortiz's prominent use of the metaphor as an emblem of Cuban identity.[24] Gustavo Pérez Firmat, in *Life on the Hyphen* (1994), has likewise elaborated on Ortiz's metaphor in his more contemporary (and definitively Cuban American) discussion of the hybrid origins of the Cuban mambo (80).[25] *Ajiaco* has thus become a symbol for what is paradigmatically Cuban; for Ortiz—as, later, for García—"Cubanness" is not represented as Spanish-descended "whiteness" (the typical genealogical narrative offered by first-wave Cuban exiles) but as characterized precisely by its "vast blend of cultures."[26] This construct is, notably, still shared by contemporary thinkers on the island, who have inherited the influential thought of Martí and Ortiz. Hebert Pérez, writing as a scholar at the University of Oriente in Santiago de Cuba, has recalled the writings of José Martí yet again to frame current Cuban national identity: "A nation where diverse racial elements unite and merge, in terms of complete equality, and whose identity would not be determined by one race or the other, is Martí's paradigm for Cuba. In this conception his genius is revealed in his capacity to reflect with incomparable lucidity the unconscious mind of the secular process of Cuban culture" (21).[27] Famed Cuban poet Nancy Morejón strongly concurs, citing Martí's vision of "a new race, a new culture" and celebrating "that welcome common denominator in all our [Cuban] culture: miscegenation. It is impossible to perceive or conceive of Cuba's national identity ignoring or even downplaying its essentially miscegenous condition" (232).[28] (Indeed, Castro echoed this very notion of Cubanness in a 1959 speech in which he declared that, in Cuba, "nobody can consider himself as being of a pure, much less superior, race" [Marable 11].) In *this* sense, the hybridity that Lucrecia represents not only is no challenge to Cuban nationhood, but is entirely in keeping with a Cuban national narrative that has fully embraced—in word, if not always in deed—the notion of racial and cultural *mestizaje* for the Cuban people.[29]

The Cuban national mythology of *mestizaje*, of course, does not necessarily translate into a lack of prejudice (perhaps most especially in pre-1959 Cuba, but also even in a postrevolutionary Cuba that touts an official end to racism).[30] Although, unlike the United States, Cuba has historically celebrated its tangle of racial roots, Helen Safa asserts that *mestizaje*, no less than the racial binaries and segregation found in the United States, can be traced to inherently racist attitudes. In both Cuba and the United States, she points out, "whiteness was identified with progress and modernity, while blackness was associated with backwardness and inferiority. [The difference was that] Cuba turned to a process of *blanqueamiento*, or whitening, through which Afro-Cubans would be biologically and culturally assimilated by intermarriage with whites and the adoption of white European norms and values. [Thus there are] ideological elements of white superiority implicit in mestizaje" (88–89). Alejandro de la Fuente, reviewing recent scholarship on the history of science in Cuba, concurs: "Like scientists elsewhere in the North Atlantic world, Cuban biologists, physicians, and anthropologists were deeply concerned about the racial makeup of the island's population. They [. . .] opposed the immigration of groups considered nonwhite [and] consistently viewed mestizaje as a way to achieve racial 'improvement'—that is, whitening" (202–3). Celebrations of *mestizaje*, then, are no guarantor against racism.

In *Monkey Hunting*, Domingo recounts how, during his childhood in Guantánamo, another child "used to taunt him, saying his Chinese eyes tilted everything he saw" (107). Interestingly, the characteristics that singled Domingo out for ridicule during his childhood in Cuba are those which make him visibly *Chinese* rather than mulatto—it is his Chineseness that "marks" him in a population that is already largely mulatto (of mixed African and Spanish heritage).

What specific aspect of his racial origins "marks" him among the Americans during the Vietnam War is less clear: "His skin was too dark, his features not immediately identifiable as one of them" (209). This may be a continuing reference to his "Asian" characteristics, which the white Americans could easily read as reminding them of the "enemy" Vietnamese—but in the 1960s, of course, *any* racially-marked characteristics (including and perhaps even especially those indicative of his "blackness") would designate him as not "one of" the white Americans. The dominant construction of American nationhood in the 1960s—while vigorously contested—was still a white construct.

In contrast, Cuba had for some time (even before the revolution) been cultivating a national identity characterized by racial and cultural mixture (despite entrenched prejudice in practice).[31] Safa writes, "[E]specially since the 1920s, Afro-Cuban cultural and biological roots are assumed to be an essential part of *cubanía*, or Cubanness [. . .]. A popular Cuban slogan [. . . ] says: '*El que no tiene de Congo tiene de Carabalí*' (those who have no Congo blood have Carabalí), affirming the African roots of all Cubans" (87–88). As Castro said to Cubans in 1966, "The blood of Africa runs deep in our veins" (qtd. in Lusane 73).[32] In García's reflection, and commentary, on constructions of *cubanidad* in postrevolutionary Cuba, Domingo's uncle's conga drums are appropriated as a sign of national *mestizaje*: "The authorities in Guantánamo had decided that the drums were cultural artifacts because they'd once belonged to Domingo's great uncle, the legendary El Tumbador. Now the congas were on display at a folklore museum where *el pueblo* could admire them but never hear their *boom-tak-tak-a-tak* again" (56). At the same time that the conga drums are appropriated in the service of constructing Cuban "nation" (even if, paradoxically, relegated to the status of quaint folklore rather than living culture, as has often been the ironic case in celebrations of national *mestizaje*), Domingo's Afro-Cuban mother says "that drumming was for blacks who didn't work and drank too much, meaning, of course, her brothers and uncles" (56–57). The cultural signifiers that can be celebrated and elevated to a mythical past are, in the present, denigrated as a sign of lower social (and racial) status. As Robin Moore has noted in his study of *afrocubanismo*, African-derived cultural elements became an intrinsic part of Cuban national celebration, but this dynamic was filled with "ambivalence": "perceived Africanisms served as simultaneous sources of pride and embarrassment to the nation. They were both powerful icons to rally behind *and* [. . .] reminders of a cultural legacy most considered shameful" (220; emphasis in original).[33]

In yet another irony, Domingo recalls having "been arrested by a policeman in Guantánamo for practicing 'negritude'—all because he'd let his hair grow into an Afro" (209). The cultural referent for this particular scene is not Cuban racism, per se, but Cuban antagonism to racial *separatism*. Helen I. Safa writes that "[t]he term 'Afro-Cuban' [. . .] suggests a racial division of society that for Cubans is at best meaningless and at worst threatening to the unity of a society that has had to struggle against tremendous odds to achieve national sovereignty" (88). Both before and after the 1959 revolution, "[p]olitical mobilization by Afro-Cubans was always discouraged [. . .]. Afro-Cubans were accepted as part of the polity so long as they acknowledged the hegemony of Cuban national culture based on *mestizaje* and posed no challenge" to it (Safa 88).[34] Clarence Lusane adds, "One of the first declarations of the new [Castro] regime was to outlaw institutional racism. This move cut both ways, however. Under the new law, any effort at expressed racial group consciousness, from black as well as white Cubans, could and would be determined to be racist. Such groups were sure to find legal and political resistance from the state, whether or not their objectives were counterrevolutionary" (76).[35] African culture has become recognized as a part of Cuban heritage, but "marking" oneself in terms of a separatist racial politics goes against the postrevolutionary (and even prerevolutionary) national construction.[36]

Notably, it would seem that Domingo is the character in the novel least likely actually to practice a separatist ideology. Despite having left Cuba with his father for the United States, Domingo, more than any other character, has internalized an ideology of *stable* national identity. (It is no coincidence that it is Domingo who conceives of his family genealogy as an "origins" story in which hybridity hardens and congeals into a "whole new race " of people [209].) We are told, "Domingo wondered about these migrations [the transnational movements created by colonialism and subsequent neoimperialist imperatives], these cross-cultural lusts. Were people meant to travel such distances? Mix with others so different from themselves?" (209). Longingly, he wishes, "If only everything could stop, remain fixed and knowable for an hour. Instead everything raced forward, unrelentingly, like a river, never settled or certain" (212). Domingo wants to "fix" identity and its allegiances, rendering these "knowable." When Tham Thanh Lan first meets him and asks him, "Where are you from?" he "fixes" himself by answering "'Cuba [. . .] I'm from Cuba" (156), thereby reducing his complex cultural genealogy (Spanish, African, Chinese) and his "migrations" through New York to Saigon into a singular national identity that supposedly explains everything.

Domingo, that is to say, has been interpellated by the rhetoric of nation and of national identity. Thus, unlike in Sommer's account of the national novels of nineteenth-century Latin America, in which the "[t]ensions that [. . .] drive the story on are external to the couple" and consist of the "counter-productive social constraints that underline the naturalness and the inevitability of the lovers' transgressive desire" (17–18), for Domingo the external social constraints are *internalized*, so that he understands his love for Tham Thanh Lan as *un*natural and their separation as inevitable: "Domingo heard of GIs taking their Vietnamese fiancées or wives home after their tour of duty. The army frowned upon this, did everything possible to keep the couples apart, more so if children were involved. A few men had killed themselves for the love of these whores. Everyone said they'd been *gook hoodooed*" (208). In this limited third-person rumination, Domingo transforms "Vietnamese fiancées or wives" into "these whores," taking on the racist rhetoric that hypersexualizes and simultaneously delegitimizes the exotic Asian woman. The sexual desire marked by the term "whores" thus is in itself provoked and shaped by a discourse of "othering."

George J. Sánchez, writing of "the many ways in which desire is structured by our own historical moments," notes that, "[a]s recent work on 'orientalism' has shown us, desire [...] can produce as powerful an 'othering' process as that [process] which emphasizes separation and containment" (53). Here the production of desire for the exotic Other works simultaneously with the processes of containment that render this object illegitimate. The term "hoodooed," indeed, carries quite the cultural baggage. It is obviously meant to suggest that through arts akin to black magic the Vietnamese women have "bewitched" the GIs; but its cultural reference is to folk magic practiced by African-descended slaves in the Americas, and it is itself reflective of cultural hybridity (with European-derived folklore and with American Indian botanical knowledge) (Yronwode). Yet "hoodoo" is rendered by the GIs as a frightening, illegitimate, and, above all, exotic practice linked to the Asian other.

That Domingo reproduces the rhetorical maneuvers of othering here shows his extreme discomfort—despite his own heritage and history of migrations—with the possibilities of a Vietnamese Cuban or Vietnamese American hybridity. As he goes on to recall, "Stories drifted back to Vietnam of former bar girls waking up in Georgia, bleaching their hair, wearing blue jeans and cowboy hats, renaming themselves Delilah. Other stories were sadder still. Of underaged girls dressed up like China dolls at their husbands' insistence, paraded around small towns in Texas or Mississippi, shopping for trinkets at Woolworth's. Saddest of all were the suicides—the poisonings, the slit wrists. Anything to set their souls free to fly home" (208–9). Domingo's stories all suggest the *un*naturalness of the pairing of GIs with Vietnamese women, who really only long to be "home"; thus his scenarios for a possible future with Tham Thanh Lan in the United States only confirm the army's prohibition against such a union. Though readers are told that the army "did everything possible to keep the couples apart," it is striking that in Domingo's case it has to do nothing at all. No external force propels him away from Tham Thanh Lan and his unborn child; he has already internalized the prohibition against this particular manifestation of hybridity, destabilizing as it is for a notion of national identity in the period of the Vietnam War.

Like Domingo and Tham Thanh Lan, Chen Fang and her French lover are brought together by political and economic interests which spur the process of "globalization." Chen Fang (whose heritage, like Domingo's, is Chinese/African/Spanish) is brought to teach in Shanghai in a school for "foreigners": "My students are the children of diplomats and industrialists: French children, English children, children of wealthy Chinese families, too" (101). The woman who becomes her lover, Dauphine de Moët, is the mother of three of these children and the wife of a "French businessman and former diplomat [who had] speculated in the Shanghai stock market and invested in a leather factory that later made army boots for the Japanese invaders"; they "lived in a French Concession mansion" (140). The historical backdrop to the story Chen Fang recounts is indeed one of Western imperialism and the responding national consolidation in China:

> As a result of several wars and many treaties with China since 1842, foreign powers had acquired a variety of unusual privileges for their nationals. These were specified in the "unequal treaties," which patriotic Chinese bitterly opposed. [. . .] In most major cities there were concession areas, not governed by China, for the residence of foreigners. Nationals and subjects of the "treaty powers" were protected by extraterritoriality (*i.e.*, they were subject only to the civil and criminal laws of their own countries); this extended to foreign business enterprises in China, providing a great advantage in competition with Chinese firms, which was enhanced when foreign factories or banks were located in concession areas under foreign protection. ("China" 71811)

Once again, the "hybridity" suggested by cross-cultural currents of erotic desire, figured in this instance by the relationship between Dauphine and Chen Fang, are a by-product of imperialism, since it is "imperialist" economic interests that bring the de Moëts to Shanghai. Indeed, it is the same interests—opposed by the Chinese nationalists—that have brought Chen Fang to teach in Shanghai in the first place, in the "foreigners' school" (99).[37] That this is a lesbian coupling, however, limits their function for any hegemonic model of "national romance," hybrid or otherwise. For, as Sommer argues, such national narratives inevitably require figures of "productive unions" (24)—even if only imagined rather than fulfilled. (The "exhortation" of these national romances, Sommer insists, is "to be fruitful and multiply" [6].) We know in advance that no hegemonic narrative of national consolidation will have any use for Dauphine and Chen Fang.

In contrast, Chen Fang's son by an arranged marriage (prior to her coming to Shanghai) *can* be read as a sign of "productive union" in national terms—he becomes a Communist leader who "has made his reputation running an important southern province." But in García's representation this "productivity" is actually wholly destructive: his is "[a] reputation, no doubt, built on corpses" (230). Imprisoned as a target of Mao's Cultural Revolution, Chen Fang reveals, "I have thought of using my son's name to help me get out of prison. But what would become of him if it were known that his mother was a traitor? Would he have to shoot me to prove his allegiance to the Revolution?" (231). Though Chen Fang's union has "produced" a figure for the Communist Chinese nation, the union itself is untenable and unsustainable, and its product (the child as metaphor for the nation) seemingly cannot tolerate the existence of the mother who gave him birth. National identity, in this case, does not *integrate* "heterodox constituencies" but disposes of those it finds irreconcilable.

Further, though it can certainly be argued that Chen Fang's romance with the Frenchwoman Dauphine stands out from the narrative of rigid Chinese nationalism as highly suggestive of the possibilities of hybridity, such hybridity is not a celebrated alternative to xenophobia but is itself tainted by imperialist imperatives. Culturally, Dauphine is, ironically, more of a Cuban hybrid than is Chen Fang: she introduces her to Cuban music, shows her "how to dance like the Cubans," and explains to her about rice made with saffron (141). This is because Dauphine's husband had been "the French consul general in Havana during the Great War. It was the time of the Dance of the Millions, she explained, when Cubans made overnight fortunes in sugar" (141). García underscores, however, that it was not just Cubans who made those fortunes; the suggestion seems to be that Dauphine's enterprising husband's political function in Cuba is somehow tied to his profiting from sugar. Capital, that is, drives diplomacy. In Vietnam, Domingo (who has absolutely no knowledge of his Chinese aunt, or of the history of her French lover) recalls "the stories about the French families from Bordeaux and Nantes who'd come to Guantánamo to make their fortunes in sugar" (163).

But just as nationalist imperatives and the flow of capital bring Chen Fang and Dauphine together, they also drive them apart. Chen Fang tells how, "[t]hat autumn, Dauphine's husband took his family back to France. There was talk of markets failing, of their fortune in ruins. [...] They were returning to Paris, she told me, to tend to their ruins" (143). The year can be calculated to be 1929—two years after the Nationalist government had been established in Nanking and the Nationalist army had taken Shanghai.[38] It is surely significant that the de Moëts' economic woes abroad coincide almost exactly, historically, with intensifying hostility to foreign influence in China's economy.[39] In the ideology of the Kuomintang (KMT, the Nationalist Party), "the first and foremost goal of the revolution would be to free China from the grip of imperialism. [. . .] [T]he KMT saw China as standing in the same relation to imperialist nations as workers stood to capitalists within their own nations" (Fewsmith 93). Special opprobrium was reserved for "those people who [came to China] from the internationalist capitalist nations" (Wang Jingwei, qtd. in Fewsmith 93). In the program drafted by the KMT in 1924, "Western privileges were openly menaced" ("China" 71812). The metropolis of Shanghai was, probably more than any other city, the focal point for xenophobic nationalism, since the international and French settlements in that city were "in the hands of foreigners"; it was the "'foreign city' of Shanghai, which the Nationalists were determined to bring under their control" (Henriot 1, 36). The shooting death in Shanghai in 1925 by foreign police of twelve Chinese, including students and workers who were participating in an anti-imperialist demonstration, had served as "a vivid reminder of the privileged position held by foreigners on Chinese soil" (Fewsmith 88).[40] By the time the Nationalists formally took control, "[t]he country was in a nationalistic mood, determined to roll back foreign economic and political penetration," and "[s]everal [foreign] concession areas were returned to Chinese control" ("China" 71818).

The entire story of Chen Fang's doomed love affair with Dauphine is told retrospectively from 1939, when Japan has control over Shanghai. During this period, "fired by anti-Japanese patriotism," Nationalists and Communists cooperated in a "common fight under Nationalist leadership" against Japan (Eastman 2–3).[41] The next time we hear from Chen Fang, it is 1970, the Communists have defeated the Nationalists and governed China since 1949, and she is narrating from prison, having fallen victim to Mao Zedong's Cultural Revolution: "I do not think anybody expected me to last this long. Too genteel, they sneered. Too corrupted by Western ways. [. . .] My fellow literature teachers reported that I introduced students to contaminating foreign authors (Kipling, Dickens, Flaubert). [. . .] I was charged with being a Kuomintang spy, of working for French intelligence, of engaging in decadent behavior with the enemy (I wondered what they knew about Dauphine). I was denounced as a friend to foreigners" (224, 228–29). Notable in García's depiction of the ideological impetus of the Cultural Revolution is her emphasis on its nationalism.[42] Indeed, in this sense, although the Nationalist Party and the Chinese Communist Party were political rivals during the earlier period Chen Fang narrates (when she and Dauphine were lovers), in García's representation the victory of the Communist Party only continues the trends in Shanghai established by the opposing Nationalist Party's regime.[43] As Chen Fang describes it, "When the Communists took over, they threw out the foreign teachers in our school: Dieter Klocker, our choral director; Serendipity Beale, the British historian who taught me to play cribbage; the biologist Lina Ginsberg, who'd come to Shanghai to escape the Nazis and married a Chinese scholar. The new leaders claimed they did not want such teachers burdening the students with alien ideas" (227).[44]

As before, the interests of Western imperialism promote the conditions of hybridity in the urban centers, but nationalist interests (in this case, opposing ones) also control, regulate, and manage the possibilities for such hybridity. In García's depiction in *Monkey Hunting*, as in her earlier *Dreaming in Cuban*, individuals are the pawns of much larger economic and political forces, their geographic—as well as, in this novel, their erotic—movements largely dictated by the ebb and flow of such forces. Further, for Chen Fang it is hard to say which victory, Nationalist or Communist, has the more calamitous consequences. Her imprisonment and interrogation by the Communists is clearly more violent and physically devastating, but her emotional devastation and decline date to the departure of Dauphine from Shanghai in the wake of the Nationalist Party's ascendancy. Chen Fang, that is to say, is buffeted by both historical manifestations of nationalism.

Yet, ironically, although Chen Fang derides the anti-intellectual elements of the Cultural Revolution ("Is this what we have become? A country of blind mules? Where are the ideas that took a lifetime to comprehend?" [228]), she fails to recognize at some level the significance of nationalist sentiment in the ideas that have imprisoned her quite literally. In 1970 Chen Fang—noting that her father's status as a "foreigner" is one of the contributing factors in her imprisonment—fantasizes about her release: "This is my plan. If I survive, I will search for my family in Cuba. [. . .] And I must teach myself Spanish! When I arrive, [. . .] I will smoke a Cuban cigar" (232–33). Chen Fang's is a fantasy of national identity; she dreams of going to Cuba, where her "family" is and where, perhaps by implication, she will not be a "foreigner" (surely a naïve idea). But Chen Fang's end-of-life ruminations are juxtaposed to the story line of Domingo Chen, who finds himself in New York in 1968, recalling the pitfalls of nationalist fervor in the very Cuba that Chen Fang longs for, and which he has recently abandoned.

In Cuba, growing up, Domingo learned about the crimes committed in the name of national expansion in the United States: "Domingo had learned that the white settlers in North America had murdered most of the Indians, that they'd killed off their buffalo, millions of them roaming the Great Plains, that the Indians were partitioned off on reservations" (210). But in the next breath we learn that recitation of these "crimes" is part of a project of constructing a Cuban national identity in opposition to the United States: "Domingo's teachers had taught him this, teachers who'd spat when they said *yanquis*, teachers who'd made him do the same" (210). In a striking parallel to Chen Fang's situation in China, Domingo's father is excoriated by the socialist revolution in Cuba for his association with foreigners (he works as a "short order cook at the American naval base in Guantánamo"): "When revolutionary officials had ordered his father to give up his job with the Americans, Papi had refused. Working the grill had made him a traitor? No amount of haranguing from the Committee for the Defense of the Revolution could convince him of that" (54–55). Such passages gesture toward Castro's rhetorical use of the threat of the United States to position ideological divergence from the "revolution" as antinational, that is, as treason.

And yet the bulk of García's novel, as I have suggested, also pushes against the singular "national" identity projected backward by the conservative Cuban exile community in Miami, which has spurred its own forms of violence and intolerance. (It is not just Communist nationalisms that come under fire.) Ultimately, *Monkey Hunting* seems to testify to the "horrific violence justified in the name of nationalism" (Gandhi 108), whatever form that nationalism may take.[45] In Sommer's account of nineteenth-century national Latin American novels, if the "lovers' transgressive desire" is thwarted by "counter-productive social constraints," nevertheless, the text projects an ideal narrative alternative, in the form of an imagined society where such constraints would not exist and the desire would continue unimpeded. That projected alternative is, of course, the "nation" as positively imagined by the novel. But García's text, I would argue, presents us with no such positive alternative. Certainly the relationship between Chen Pan and Lucrecia is depicted as beautiful and as, in Sommer's terminology, a "productive union." But the hybridity engendered by the slave trade has, within a couple of generations, hardened into the singular national rhetoric that would prohibit expressions of "negritude." New York in the 1960s happily tolerates manifestations of cultural hybridity such as the Chinese-Cuban restaurant where Domingo works, the Havana Dragon, where they serve "fried rice, and *tostones*" (44, 46); but the United States is also fighting a war in Vietnam to protect "American interests" and encouraging its soldiers to refer to Vietnamese as "gooks." If, in Sommer's account, the representation of "satisfying marriage [...] reads like a wish-fulfilling projection of national consolidation" (6–7), in García's telling, *any* form of nationalist consolidation—whether formulated around whiteness, antiforeignness, or hybridity—is the potential foundation of violence. By extension, García seems to warn, we must approach any narrative of collective identity with the deepest skepticism.

## Achy Obejas's *Days of Awe*

The case of Jewish Cubans presents a different dynamic from that of Chinese Cubans, since Jewishness does not necessarily challenge the image of Cuban (exile) whiteness. Caroline Bettinger-López has, in fact, suggested that Cuba's ordinarily "welcoming" stance toward Jewish refugees might have been driven precisely by racism: "Was the friendly welcome extended to white Jewish refugees, and the unfriendly rejection handed to blacks from Haiti and Jamaica, a reflection of the Cuban government's attempts to whiten the island's population during the first half of the twentieth century?" (23).[46] Regardless of the whiteness of Cuban Jews, however, it remains true that the hegemonic representation of Cubanness, both on the island and in the United States, has utterly ignored Jewish Cubans. In Miami so fully is it assumed that Jews are *not* Cubans—and vice versa—that Jewish Cuban exiles have repeatedly noted the incomprehension their identity provokes in others. One Miami woman has related how "[p]eople are always amazed to find out that my background is both Cuban and Jewish, as though I couldn't be both at the same time" (Sanford L. Ziff Jewish Museum of Florida 1997, qtd. in Bettinger-López xxxix). A teenaged Cuban Jew interviewed by Bettinger-López echoed this representation: "When the people at my high school find out you're Jewish, they're like, 'Oh, but which parent is Cuban and which one is Jewish?' They just can't grasp it. . . . No, people in Miami definitely freak out when you say you're Cuban *and* Jewish. It's not even accepted here [in Miami]! [. . .] They just freak out [. . .] at the mix. You can say you're Jewish, that'll be okay, but Cuban *and* Jewish?" (234). Another interviewee, in his thirties, whose family settled in New York rather than in Miami, describes applying for his first job: "[T]he owners were Jewish. And when I applied, and told them I was Jewish, they said it was impossible to be bilingual and Jewish. They wouldn't believe me when I told them that I was a Cuban-Jew" (233).

This reaction is what Ruth Behar has termed the "shock effect" resulting from joining "terms that are not 'normally' joined together" ("Juban" 163).[47] As Bettinger-López has explained, "the issue [in such cases] did not surround a misrepresentation or derogatory characterization of 'Cuban-Jews' by people who were not Cuban-Jews; rather, the issue was the latter's very denial of—or at least disbelief in—the former's existence" (234). The denial stemmed not only from U.S. (non-Cuban) Jews, but from other Cuban immigrants: "The Jewish Cubans belonged nowhere in Miami. Among other Cuban exiles, they became 'Jews'" rather than being recognized primarily as fellow Cubans with an ethnic or national bond (34).[48]

In Achy Obejas's second novel, *Days of Awe*—the first full-length fictional treatment by a U.S. Latino/a to bring notable attention to the experience of Jews in Cuba,[49] just as García's *Monkey Hunting* is the first to focus attention on the Chinese presence there—the narrator's father, who is a "*converso*" (an outwardly "converted" Jew),[50] invokes the hegemonic model of Cubanness when, in answer to his daughter's probing questions about whether they are Jewish, he answers, "We're Spaniards, we're Catholic [. . .]. We're like everybody else in Cuba" (115). As we have already seen, however, this monolithic representation of Cubans as a singular "nation" of people is a narrative that works—in the words of Ada Ferrer—to smooth over a violent history of oppression and conflict; and it does so no less in the case of the Jewish experience in Cuba than in that of people of African or Chinese descent. (Indeed, the fact that Obejas has her narrator's Jewish father deny his origins to his daughter is a testament to the violence that has driven his Jewishness underground.) The repeated testimony of Cuban Jews, both exiled and in Cuba, that Cuba has never been particularly anti-Semitic,[51] similarly works toward the erasure of memory of a less rosy history. As Bettinger-López writes, "it is essential to recognize periods in Cuba's history when the island was not so accommodating to Jews" (23).

Obejas's novel is quite obviously committed to examining those periods of "less rosy history" forgotten in dominant narratives,[52] and the dynamic by which even Cuban Jews disclaim a history of Cuban anti-Semitism, while non-Jewish Cubans simply suppress or ignore the existence of Cuban Jews. When Obejas's narrator Alejandra—nicknamed Ale (pronounced AH-leh)—prods Moisés Menach, an old family friend and a Jew (as well as a dedicated revolutionary who never left Cuba), "[W]hat I've always heard is that Cuba has always been tolerant of Jews," Moisés responds, "[N]ot in the thirties, not when your father was in Havana as a boy. I'm certain you never heard him say Cuba was tolerant. I'd be shocked if you had" (347). In place of silencing by way of a rosy history of Cuban non-anti-Semitism, however, Ale's father has substituted complete silence about his Jewishness:

> Whenever my father was asked if he was a Jew, he would slowly lower then lift his eyes [. . .].
>
> "All people of Spanish descent have some Jewish blood in them, of course," he would say.
>
> If he was asked if he practiced Judaism, he would sigh, exasperated.
>
> "Who doesn't? Don't all the great religions owe something to Judaism?" (37–38).

As Ale, who works as an interpreter, reports, "There is a word in Spanish, olvido, which is usually interpreted as oblivion or forgetfulness. But this is one term on which my father and I agree: Olvido is not just a void; but, much like memory itself, it is a place, with dimensions and weight. Rather than holding all we want to remember, it's a repository for what we want to forget" (103). As with the narrative that racial problems in Cuba were "caused" by Castro, the story that Cuba "welcomed" the Jews involves an idealizing of prerevolutionary Cuba as a land of undivided national identity—and it carries with it some fairly purposive forms of forgetting.

Like García's *Monkey Hunting*, then, Obejas's *Days of Awe* is quite interested in the dynamics of nationalism and collective narratives, and in the complex modes of remembering and forgetting that they invoke—as well as in how these dynamics are affected by their intersection with Jewishness. Ruth Behar, commenting on the fact that her "American Jewish colleagues [. . .] cannot believe that I can think of myself as being Cuban," has written that, for Cuban Jews, "nationality is not conflicted in the same way [as for Jews of European descent] by anger and legacies of exclusion and hatred" (*Translated Woman* 366 n. 10). In perhaps a more complex representation of the interplay between nationalism and Jewishness, Caroline Bettinger-López notes that scholars of the Cuban Jewish population have tended to see "distinctions between [. . .] nationalism and discrimination; and between international propaganda influence and domestic ideology" (23).

On the one hand, these scholars suggest, anti-Semitism was not "intrinsic" to Cuban society but was an "impure" import; therefore, there was no "essential" contradiction between being Jewish and being Cuban that needed to be resolved or negotiated. Yet, on the other, "nationalism" was the guise under which anti-Jewish sentiment passed—not because Jews were Jews, but because they were not "Cubans" (often by reason of being recent immigrants to Cuba rather than "native" born).[53] In *Days of Awe*, while nationalism is not the inevitable foundation of violence that it is in *Monkey Hunting*, its relationship to a strong Jewish identity is certainly represented as highly conflicted. Cuban identity and Jewish identity exert claims and exact pressures that are not easily reconciled by the characters who must negotiate them. At the same time, the notion of Cuban diaspora is both echoed and significantly complicated by Jewish diaspora, which renders Cuba not a (national) point of origin but a complicated, transnational midpoint in a much longer history of diaspora and migration.

Bettinger-López has written that Cuban Jews see themselves as enduring a "double diaspora": "many Cuban-Jews emphasize that the Cuban diasporic experience which landed them in Miami was, in a way, a continuation of their Jewish Diasporic experience" (159). Obejas, too, wants to make this connection between the Cuban and Jewish diaspora experiences: "exile and diaspora are like genetic markers for Jews, as normal as hair or teeth" (35–36). For Obejas, however, the connections that make the Cuban exile experience only a logical "continuation" of the Jewish experience are deeply obscured by the dominant discourse of Cuban diaspora. At one point, Ale, in her more "historical" narrative voice, informs the reader that Cuban exiles are referred to as "the Jews of the Caribbean": "It's meant as an epithet, playing off negative stereotypes about Jews. It alludes to the Cuban transmutation of Miami and Miami Beach (which, ironically, displaced a good number of Jews), from little meaningless metropolises to world-class cities. [. . .] When we are called the Jews of the Caribbean, it's almost an accident that, like Jews, we are a people in diaspora" (103–104). Most tellingly, even when Cuban exiles are being called "Jews," the fundamental assumption (as Obejas reveals) is one of difference rather than of similarity. The epithet reveals the pervasive sense that Cubans cannot actually *be* Jews—the two groups can be, at most, analogous. Further, the nature of the analogy is not diaspora, according to Ale, but "greed and covetousness" (104). Ironically, then, even when the exiles are being compared to Jews, there is no recognition that the presence of Jewish Cubans challenges homogeneous representations of the Cuban exile community or the reductive plot line of Cuban diaspora (in which hybridity "begins" in 1959).

Jewish Cubans are no strangers to hybridity—or to historical upheavals that have forced all manner of migration. Indeed, Bettinger-López has proposed that being Jewish might have rendered the experience of post-Castro exile less traumatic for Cuban Jews: "the Jewish people's familiarity with uprootedness and movement permeates their views of nationality and homeland and so eases the migration experience for Jews" (159). Bettinger-López's focus, however, is on Jews from Eastern Europe and the Mediterranean who came to Cuba in the earlier twentieth century—many of them hoping eventually to reach the United States and seeing Cuba merely as a way station, "one 'stop' on their Diasporic journey" (148). Obejas inscribes a much longer view of the Jewish diaspora in Cuba into her novel; her Cuban Jews have been in Cuba since its origins. Thus while her characters certainly understand the historical echoes of their post-1959 exile, it is rendered not less but—if anything—more traumatic for having had precedent in their communal memory.[54]

The central subject of Obejas's novel is not the recently arrived Jews from Eastern Europe (although Moisés Menach's family comes from early-twentieth-century Turkish immigrants) but the "Anusim," or "marranos"[55]—those Jews in the Spanish empire who were forced to convert to Catholicism but continued to practice Judaism in secret. The history of Ale's father's family, told in the early chapters of the book (although Ale is not aware of her Jewishness until after her first trip to Cuba), is traced back to the arrival in Cuba of Columbus, whose crew included large numbers of Jews fleeing the Spanish Inquisition during Ferdinand and Isabella's reign and forced to profess and openly practice Christianity, since Jews had been officially expelled from Spain and its colonies (32–33).[56] Hybridity predates even this forced exile, however; Obejas takes pains to project diaspora and its resulting hybridities even further back in time, complicating any singular point of origin. Before her father's ancestors were expelled from Spain they were part of a "particularly vibrant

Hebraic community" in Seville, where they "spoke Ladino and judeo-español (a mix of Spanish and Hebrew that works out like a Sephardic version of Yiddish)" (35).

This hybridity layers with subsequent forms of *mestizaje* occasioned by the Inquisition. As with Santería, the covert Jews' practice of religious subterfuge and dissembling leads to hybridity and syncretism.[57] Ale describes how her father's family "made the torturous trek to church in Santiago de Cuba at Christmas every year but changed their linens and lit candles now and then on Friday nights" (116–17); but while these dual practices suggest a *conscious* subterfuge, in which Judaism and Catholicism are to some degree still distinguishable in the minds of their practitioners, in other ways Ale's history betrays how the Jewish and Cuban "creole" (i.e., Spanish-descended and Catholic) cultures have fused. Ale's more historical narrative voice tells us that her father's family "had been in Cuba so long, their worship hidden and passed on in such subterfuge [. . .] like the distortions inherent in a child's game of whispers," that they no longer knew that "common words and expressions in the hills of Oriente—such as bizcocho, chinelas, fache—were all transparently judeo-español" (116). And from Moisés Menach, Ale learns that "Saint Esterika is a purely marrano invention: They Christianized Purim by making Ester a saint" (190). He also relays that her grandparents, in a fusing of icons highly reminiscent of Santería, "had braided home-made candles and a brass menorah in plain sight, right next to a small icon of the Virgin of Charity" (117).

Indeed, Santería, another manifestation of religious syncretism resulting from the suppression by Catholicism of a different belief system, is frequently compared to "crypto-Judaism" in the novel. Ale's grandparents Luis and Sima, for example, "remained indistinguishable" in terms of their religious behaviors "from the rest of the peasantry in the provinces," including "a large black population that relied on its own forms of venerations" (117). Ale relates, in illustration, how

> in the days before Yom Kippur, [. . .] Luis would wake up before dawn and take two chickens—a white cock for him, usually a speckled hen for her—and swing them by their feet around his and her heads, the animals screeching and flapping, while the two of them chanted the necessary prayers of thanksgiving and atonement. To anyone who might have spied them performing the kaparot, it would have seemed like just another campesino family, infused by the fevers of santería, cleansing themselves of whatever evil had been afflicting them. (118)

In her informative glossary, Obejas explains that the "kaparot" (or kapparot) "in which live chickens are used as absorbents of sin and evil [. . . ,] parallels an Afro-Cuban ritual called a limpieza or despojo, in which chickens are used for the same reason." Obejas then goes on to comment further on the striking resemblance of rituals: "It is impossible to tell if the rituals occurred as a result of influence from one another, if it was brought to the Iberian peninsula from Africa, or brought to Cuba by Jews, hidden or otherwise, and adapted by the slaves" (362–63).

What is remarkable about this presentation of possibilities is that all of them highlight the possibilities of hybridity, of cross-cultural influence. Obejas is seemingly uninterested in the possibility that the resemblance is a coincidence; the nature of her text is, rather, to trace back as far as possible the ways in which cultures have migrated and cross-pollinated—have always, that is to say, been panethnic and transnational. In this epic trajectory, Cuba (or, for that matter, even Spain) can continue to stand for the point of (prediasporic) "origin" and national singularity only through powerfully reductive forms of forgetting.

Hybridity, however, is once again not necessarily a bulwark against historical forgetting, as we see in the history of Ale's mother's family line. Ale has traced the genealogy of her mother's family, the Abravanels, back to Jews in Seville as well; but she distinguishes between her mother's and her father's families because "[a]t some point Jews like these Abravanels were no longer anusim, but real converts" (45). The story of the Abravanels' (hypothetical) history suggests how easily "hybridity" may become accommodation or assimilation: "[A]t some point, these Abravanels not only took on Christian rites, they began to drop Jewish ceremony. They had to work Fridays, so the lighting of kabalat shabat candles went by the wayside. [. . .] If Pesaj was forbidden in its Jewish form, why not Christianize it? Surely, if they had to, thirty-six Jewish saints could fit snugly into one Christian archangel" (45). While cultural manifestations such as the Christianization of Pesaj continue to suggest that cultural influence travels both ways, the Abravanels' history nevertheless hints at some "point of no return" at which hybridity ceases to be recognizable as such—at which the degree of "forgetting" involved on one side suggests absorption, rather than a two-way "transculturation."

This is a debate that *Days of Awe* engages with overtly. As in *Monkey Hunting*, hybridity is by no means necessarily resistant in this novel; indeed, at times the practice of Judaism under cover of Catholicism is represented as quite accommodationist. Ale comments of her father's ancestors that, "[w]anting desperately to fit in and survive, the first New Christians in our family [. . .] baptized themselves with the most exaggerated Catholic names available, those of saints" (36). Of more recent history, she notes that she has "often thought Luis and Sima [her grandparents] were more secret assimilationists than clandestine Jews. They wanted their families, after more than four hundred years in Cuba, to take root, to blend into the vast garden of Cuba" (120).

This representation of the Anusim as wanting to blend in with the crowd, so to speak, is literalized in Ale's father's foreboding, recurring dream about an angel whose wings are damaged when it falls from the sky, but that then disappears into the safety of a Cuban crowd—one in which Sima's face is at times glimpsed (213–14). Ale's family debates the meaning of the dream, with her mother arguing that "[t]he angel is us, irreparably wounded because we left our country," and her father adding that "it disappears into the unruly crowd—which is the United States, that's clear—the way we are also becoming a part of the fabric here, in spite of our injuries." Even as a child, however, Ale senses that this interpretation does not fit with the details of the dream and asks, "But doesn't the angel disappear into Cuba, into a Cuban crowd?" (214). The idea that the crowd is Cuban is resisted by both parents; later, however, when they learn that Sima has died after—to their surprise—apparently claiming, to some extent, an openly Jewish identity (217), the child Ale brings up the dream again, asking if her original interpretation, that "[t]he angel was Abuela Sima disappearing into Cuba," was the correct one after all. Enrique, her father, begins to contradict her: "[T]hen he stopped himself and exchanged a quick, cautious glance with my mother. 'Yes,' he said, 'that's exactly what it was. You were right.' There were centuries of denial in that look" (218). Though Enrique's "denied" interpretation is never explicitly clarified, the imagery of disappearing into a crowd, specifically a Cuban crowd, is repeatedly associated in the novel with the Anusim, and with Luis and Sima in particular. While Sima actually seems, at the very end of her life, to have metaphorically pulled *away* from the Cuban crowd by asserting (to some, questionable degree) her Jewishness, it remains the case that Enrique has always associated his mother with the opposing impulse (hence he sees her face in the Cuban crowd in his dream).

Like Ale, who notes that her parents' discussion of the dream prompts "one of my first and last excursions into their realm of prophesies" (214), readers are clearly being encouraged to interpret the dream (as literary metaphor, if not as psychological phenomenon) at this point, since only by doing so can we make sense of Enrique's "denial" of the true interpretation. (What is he denying—or, to use a heavily loaded psychoanalytic term, repressing?) Given the history revealed elsewhere in the novel, and the language used to convey that history, the metaphorical import of the dream is surely that Enrique himself is the angel. Certainly, the imagery Obejas uses to describe him is at times reminiscent of an angel or wounded bird: "He had a kind of expectant halo about him, his thin frigate of bones tipped forward [. . .]. [H]e looked like an injured bird, a crow fallen from the skies" (265).

Many years later, after her father's death, Ale learns from Moisés the history of trauma that drove her father's Jewishness forever underground, into "denial." In the late '30s, as Cuba experienced a wave of anti-Semitism, the young man Enrique (who had already suffered from a Nazi beating) one day found himself "swallowed by the mob, realizing much too late that the gathering was a demonstration by Cubans and Spaniards snapping their hands in the air to the rhythm of a sharp Nazi beat." Seeking safety precisely by blending into the crowd, Enrique, "in a moment of complete desperation, threw his own arm toward the fiery tropical sun and joined in the chorus: 'Heil Hitler!'" (352–53). The historical moment of Cuban anti-Semitism is revealed, at the novel's end, to be a wound which plagued Enrique throughout the rest of his life. Indeed, the word "wound" is used repeatedly to describe how Enrique felt about Cuba (18, 351).[58] Metaphorically, it is this wound (Cuban anti-Semitism) which has injured the angel, rendering it unable to fly to the heavens (and to its God) and forcing it instead to seek safety in the most repugnant forms of accommodation. (It is also a wound of ethnic conflict utterly obscured by dominant narratives of Cuban exile, with their picture of a paradisiacal and nonprejudiced past.)

Against the view of the Anusim as accommodationists (if not assimilationists) who want above all else to blend in, Obejas (again via her narrator, Ale) posits an alternative interpretation, which views Anusim "as part of an intrepid resistance. Against all odds, these men and women persevered in their Jewishness" (333). The conflicting interpretations are the subtext of an actual "debate" inscribed in the novel, near its conclusion, between Moisés and his granddaughter Deborah. Ostensibly, they are debating theories about when the first Jews set foot in Cuba. Moisés ascribes to the theory that the first Cuban Jews were actually "the descendants of the Ten Lost Tribes of Israel" and that they "eventually lost their Jewish identity" and became what we think of today as Cuba's indigenous populations (332). In Moisés's mythology, this makes "each Cuban" an "unwitting Jew" (332), thus reconciling Cuban national identity with Jewishness (an issue I will return to shortly). Deborah, in contrast, "because she likes the idea of resistance, of subversion against the established order, of secret meetings and rituals," espouses the theory that the Anusim who came with Columbus were the first Cuban Jews (333). Moisés's version makes Jews the *first* peoples to inhabit Cuba but also implies the obliteration of meaningful Jewish identity through forgetting; Deborah's version makes no claim to Cuba as originally or properly Jewish but emphasizes the *resistance* involved in maintaining a covert Jewish identity. The subtext of the debate, then, is whether it is preferable to claim a collective national identity as properly one's own or to resist notions of national identity as always hegemonically constructed. Notably, despite the Menach family's assertion that the stories "cancel each other out" and that Ale has to "choose" which one she likes better, Ale clings to her ambivalence about the options, insisting that she "can live with both possibilities" (336).

Despite historical moments of assimilation or conversion, however, the primary operative force in the novel's history is centrifugal, not centripetal—pulling away from any solidified, monolithic notion of Cuban "culture" rather than toward one. In the genealogical plotline of her mother's family that Ale traces, the intermingling of cultures and of peoples continues, apace, in Cuba long after their arrival there. Absorption and assimilation for the Abravanels are, remarkably, not to a monolithic Roman Catholicism but to an already hybrid Santería: "Santería and voodoo thrived in secrecy, and shrines to the Virgin of Charity began sporting glasses of water, dead chickens, bottles of rum and firewater" (47). Ale's mother is an active practitioner of Santería "who pray[s] while arranging glasses of water" (47) and whose "preferred icon" (5) is the Virgin of Charity—who, Obejas is quick to inform readers, is "[a]lso known as Ochún, [. . .] the Yoruba goddess of love, patron saint of sweet water" (6).[59]

"Conversion" thus becomes, in the course of Ale's family history, a transformation from one manifestation of hybridity to another—one that in Cuba's strongly African-influenced culture is ultimately more acceptable and permissible than the more surreptitious hybrid practices of her paternal grandparents, Luis and Sima. The marriage of Ale's parents is a merger of already hybrid religious practices: "my parents would find mystical coexistence, [. . .] they'd help each other—my father fixing my mother's icon, my mother learning to prepare holiday foods, even if the feast days themselves went unnamed at our table (among my favorites: her black-eyed peas with roasted fish head for Rosh Hashanah)" (284).

As the parallels between covert Judaism and Santería underscore, the Jews who come to Cuba as Anusim not only have a long, preexisting history of cultural synthesis but find themselves in a remarkable landscape of hybridity. (Jews, as Obejas's textual tapestry reinforces, are not the only displaced peoples in Cuba, a land composed entirely of displaced people.) The strands of Ale's mother's family intersect and braid not just with non-Jewish Spaniards or Cuban creoles but with other displaced populations: there is her mother's "grandmother Marta, the youngest daughter of Haitian slaves," and "the American confederate veteran who fled to the island after the U.S. civil war [. . .] who entered our bloodstream in the mid-nineteenth century (through a strong-willed mulata ex-slave)" (44). There is also her mother's cousin Barbarita, who "had a passionate, lifelong relationship with a Chinese-Cuban man named Wang Francisco Le" (41). Though Wang Francisco never actually enters the family's "bloodstream," the cultural hybridity he engenders is made evident through his impact on Barbarita, who, long after her lover's death, is sought after as a translator of Chinese poetry and referred to by neighbors as "la china" (241). Like García's Lucrecia in *Monkey Hunting*, Barbarita has *become* in some sense Chinese in Cuba; when Ale finally meets Barbarita, she describes her as having "an elegant face, round, with high, fat cheeks and little gleaming almonds for eyes, someone not Chinese by birth but perhaps by osmosis" (243).

The various manifestations of hybridity that the novel presents, in many ways coerced (as in the forced combinations of African and Spanish cultures brought about by the slave trade, or of Spanish and Chinese cultures via the importation of coolies), are also in many ways controlled or suppressed by constructions of "nation." Though Wang Francisco is referred to by Ale as a "Chinese-Cuban man," Chinese Cubanness as a category of identity clearly holds a most precarious status in the Cuban imaginary. Wang Francisco's relationship with Barbarita is never legitimized by marriage, which "was inconceivable to them" because "neither's family would have approved" (41). For the sake of public "appearances," the cultural *mestizaje* suggested by their union is suppressed (41); while it exists and even thrives, it is apparently not assimilable with the same ease as the African-Spanish mixture to the story of the Cuban nation. The same, it would appear, is true of crypto-Judaism, which is perceived, by its own practitioners, as more "dangerous" to practice publicly than Santería. Ale reconstructs her great-grandfather Ytzak's perspective: "The same Cuban Catholics [Ytzak] saw in church on Sunday morning drank blood from the severed jugulars of live goats at toques de santos in the dead of night. [. . .] Everybody, it seemed to him, lived openly with their burdens and contradictions. Yet he and the handful of other crypto-Jews he knew in Santiago all went about their lives pretending, fearful" (121). Given the ways in which, in Cuba, African heritage and the notion of racial mixture were woven into the national history, it is striking that this form of hybridity can be assimilated into the Cuban "nation" while Jewish Cubanness—as Obejas insistently makes clear—has much more difficulty in doing so.

Repeatedly in the past and present chronologies of the novel, characters struggle with the uneasy fit between being Jewish and being Cuban. Luis and Sima's impulse to dissemble about their religious identity, for instance, comes from a strong belief that it is somehow incompatible with the essence of "Cubanness" as they understand it: "What Luis and Sima wanted was to be like everyone else; to be, in effect, Cuban [. . .] to speak only Spanish, forget their slangy judeo-español, and both Ladino and Hebrew [. . .]; to feel connected to the verses of José Martí, resting right there in the cemetery in Santiago, instead of Judah Halevi, who wrote about how his body was in Spain and his heart in Jerusalem" (120).

Despite the parallels in exile experience between Martí (who lived for years as an exile from Cuba) and Halevi, it turns out that the Cuban narrative does not accommodate all forms of exile equally, even prior to Castro. Martí is a national hero and symbol par excellence of Cuban peoplehood; Judah Halevi cannot be made to fit at all.

Other characters—most notably, Moisés Menach and Enrique's grandfather Ytzak—insist on the possible coexistence of Jewish and Cuban identity. When Orlando, Moisés's son-in-law, reinforces the exclusionary narrative of Cuban nationality by asserting, "I'm not a Jew obsessed with Jews, like you all [. . .] I'm a Cuban, obsessed with Cubans," Deborah challenges him: "[L]ike you can't be both?" Moisés concurs, declaring, "We *are* both" (335). Ale, watching him, notes, "I think of Ytzak so many years ago and his insistence that he, too, was both: Cuban and Jew" (335). This insistence, however, is frequently undermined in the novel. Ytzak, for example, is discovered in 1980 to have been crushed to death on the grounds of the Peruvian embassy, as Cubans rushed to exit the nation in the prelude to what became the Mariel boatlift. It is left forever unclear whether he was simply an old man caught in the press of a mob or whether, ultimately, he found that he could not fit within the revolutionary Cuban nation (225–26).

Orlando later serves as Ale's informant for the ways in which Jewishness has been incompatible with revolutionary Cubanness. He begins to tell her about Moisés's children—his son, Ernesto (who tries to escape Cuba by raft in 1994 but dies in the attempt)[60] and his daughter, Angela (Orlando's former wife, who later leaves Cuba by marrying a Spaniard), both of whom Moisés tried to raise like "Cuban super-Jews": "Ernesto and Angela were Jews in Cuba in their youth, with all that implies. Do you know what my father-in-law said to them when his own children were denied the benefits of his boundless loyalty? He said that that attitude would pass, that the revolution would recognize its mistakes and they'd get their opportunities later. [. . .] Ernesto's dead and Angela's in Spain, and the last thing you could call either one of them is a Jew or a revolutionary" (338–39). So fully, according to Orlando, are the two categories incompatible that trying to be both may well result in being neither.

But Jewishness has fully as problematic a relationship with prerevolutionary Cubanness, as Ytzak's history makes clear. Unlike his daughter, Sima's, Ytzak's dream is not secrecy and assimilation but openness, a full recognition and realization of all aspects of his identity: "He liked to say that he was more Cuban than the Indian chief Hatuey (apparently forgetting that Hatuey was born in Hispaniola, modern-day Haiti), but what he desired more than anything was to be openly Jewish. He thought it was possible to be both, and to be whole" (120). In the countryside of Oriente province, where he and his family live, Ytzak meets a traveling salesman from Havana who openly acknowledges his own Jewish identity—though the peasants in the countryside, not knowing what to make of his difference, call him "The Moor" (122). (His difference is racialized, and then, in a typical move, the supposed racial difference is read not through the recent history of slavery but through the more distant one of the Moorish conquest of Spain.) For Ytzak, thanks to the "Moor" from Havana, the capital becomes an imagined place of possibility where the splintered identity of Jewish exile can be healed: "Ytzak headed for Havana, where he now knew it was possible to be both Cuban and Jewish out in the open, to let the light glint off his own gold Star of David" (123). Havana, the cosmopolitan space where (so he envisions) "men were free—free to be themselves in every sense" (143), represents for Ytzak "return" to an origin, even if not a geographical one; it is "his city, his Zion, his place of salvation" (348). He kidnaps his grandson, Enrique, against Luis and Sima's wishes, in order to have him circumcised in the traditional manner in Havana and, years later, returns with him—now an eleven-year-old—to raise him as openly Jewish there.

As in García's *Monkey Hunting*, Havana is depicted historically in *Days of Awe*—even centuries before Ytzak shows up with Enrique—as fully metropolitan, a transnational space and "spectacular crash site" (to use Croucher's terms [21]). Obejas describes seventeenth-century Havana as a place where "English pirates, Dutch slave traders, African freemen, and [. . .] hidden Jews" intermingled (37). But the metropolitan center that seemingly tolerated a proliferation of hybridity and transculturation became, in the late 1930s, the lightning rod for anti-Semitic sentiment and the Nazi demonstrations that so scarred Enrique; and the diversity that flourished in Havana has now given rise to more openly expressed ethnic "hatred" (351).

During this period, conservative and anti-Semitic publications in Cuba printed articles and editorials that constructed a dichotomy between "the Jews" and "the Cuban people," thereby engaging in an active (re)definition of Cubanness as not only excluding but threatened by Jewishness (Levine, 113–14).[61] In *Days of Awe*, Moisés Menach educates Ale about this history: "In the thirties, just about every newspaper in town [. . .] was on an anti-Semitic campaign, [. . .] especially the *Diario de la Marina*. [. . .] [It] was constantly threatening that a Jewish presence in Cuba undermined national sovereignty and native culture" (347). (In a far different sense, Moisés, years later, uses similar nationalist rhetoric, writing that he wants "Cuba for Cubans" [187]. The "Other" of his nationalist definition, however, is not Jews but the United States.) In the 1930s Cuban narrative of "national sovereignty," there is no room, clearly, for an Ytzak—a hero who lost his leg fighting in the war of independence against Spain. (Indeed, the construction of anti-Semitic Cubanness harkens back to the Spanish motherland in its narrative genealogy, rather than suppressing these connections, as Obejas makes clear [347].) As Enrique wonders of Ytzak's metropolitan Zion, "Why had Ytzak brought him to Havana? [. . .] Maybe his parents, back in the blameless wilderness of Oriente, had had the better idea after all" (351). It turns out that practicing Judaism under cover in the countryside is safer than being openly Jewish in the diverse and supposedly tolerant metropolitan center. Years later, the adult Enrique embraces Havana as origin, not because of its tolerance for hybridity or difference, but because it reinforces his narrative of Spanish ancestry, which he uses as a cover for his Jewishness: "When forced to admit to his Cuban origins, my father always described himself as a habanero, perhaps because of the urban quality that, in his mind, linked Havana back to Seville, the Spain of his imagination" (101). As in *Monkey Hunting*, the urban center presents an appearance of tolerance that turns out to be largely illusory; hybridity and cultural difference flourish there but are also dramatically recontained.

Nonetheless, while national identity always tries to create the impression of being coherent and stable, a bulwark against threatening "others," in fact it is fluid and constantly being reformulated. Thus even Moisés and Ytzak, who are both committed to the idea that Cubanness can include Jewishness, in other ways are dramatically different in their conceptions of Cubanness. As Amaryll Chanady has argued of the Spanish American former colonies, "[t]he imaginary constitution of the nation with respect to an external Other [. . .] characterized the nation-building strategies at the end of the eighteenth and the beginning of the nineteenth centuries" (xvii): "Although the concept of cultural or national identity nearly always implies differentiation with respect to a collectivity considered as Other [. . .], and is never merely a construction of historical continuity uniting different elements in the nation's past, the Latin American construction of identity was based to a very large extent on its differentiation with respect to the colonizer, and subsequently with respect to neocolonial powers" (xxx). In *Days of Awe*, while *cubanidad* is always defined in opposition to what it is not, "what it is not"—that is, what it is being defined *against*—changes.[62] Ytzak, veteran of the war of independence, defines Cuba (as did most Cuban nationalists at the turn of the twentieth century) against the "motherland" from which it has only recently had to separate itself in order to come into national being: "'We are Cubans—that is why we had a war of independence from Spain—and we are Jews.' He refused to link up to the mother country, refused to claim any blood but that of Abraham and what he'd spilled on the island" (141). On the other hand, Ytzak is predisposed to like Americans (140)—perhaps because the first open Jews he ever encountered were American Jews (122, 139), or because he perceives American ways as a useful alternative to those of the Spanish motherland (139–40). As Louis A. Pérez writes, "The determination of Cubans to define themselves as different from Spaniards was, in fact, another way to advance the claim of separate nationality. Contact with the North [i.e., the United States] provided new ways to distinguish between Cuban and Spanish and contributed further to the formation of national identity" (*On Becoming Cuban* 54–55). A generation later, with the threat of Spanish control receding into the historical distance but the threat of anti-Semitic prejudice still tenacious, Luis and Sima inculcate their son Enrique with the defensive narrative that "[w]e are Spanish, descended from nobility" (141). As an adult, Enrique later uses the same narrative of Spanish descent as "his way of [. . .] explaining his otherness in the United States without the blatant trauma of racism" (91).

Moisés, as fervent a Cuban nationalist as Ytzak but within the historical context of Castro's revolution, defines the enemy as American imperialism (as does Castro). Yet Moisés, too, can be read as heir to a long-standing intellectual current in defining Cubanness, one given voice, much earlier, by the Moor who is Ytzak's inspiration. (Unlike Ytzak, the Moor, who argues with him about the nature of *cubanismo*, insists that the "only way out of the morass [. . .] was to free Cuba of all foreign influence, especially that of the United States" [139–40]). As Louis Pérez elaborates of the fraught relationship between Cuba and the United States, "Cuban self-definition early incorporated as a major formative element resentment of U.S. policy designs on Cuba and hence set into place the central tension of Cuban nationalism: emulation of North American ways, especially as those ways could materially improve life for Cubans, and resistance to the United States because it posed a threat to a separate nationality" (*On Becoming Cuban* 95). This tension (exacerbated, no doubt, in the Special Period, when the U.S. dollar became a national form of Cuban currency) is a particularly poignant one for Moisés. Criticizing Cubans who flee Cuba for the United States, Moisés writes to Ale, "I know life is hard here [. . .] but it is our country, after all. Who will defend it if not us? How can they want to go [to] the United States when it is the source of all our problems?" (185).

Part of the struggle over defining the Cuban "nation," of course, has to do with whether people like Ale herself—those who left Cuba, and even more dramatically those who left Cuba too young to recall it in any depth—will be included.[63] (After all, in Moisés's letter, "our country" clearly does not include Ale, however much he embraces her at other times; his rhetoric constructs, instead, a dichotomy between the Cuban island "us," who will patriotically "defend" the country, and "they," those who leave "our country" to go to the enemy.) Running alongside the historical narrative of the Jews in Cuba that is slowly revealed and reconstructed—in fragments—by Ale, and very much in its shadow, is Ale's own contemporary story of her sense of displacement and search for origins. Obejas emphasizes that during Ale's first return trip to Cuba, as an adult, she feels not a sense of return (as does Ytzak arriving in Havana, which was never his geographical home), but, rather, a complete lack of connection. Ale sees herself as a "blank space, unconnected to history, bloodless" (182). (It is worth recalling here yet again Stephen Cornell and Douglas Hartmann's pithy summary of the affective quality of ethnicity: "ethnic ties are blood ties" [16].)[64] Indeed, Ale describes how she intentionally acts in ways which will emphasize her "otherness," her non-Cubanness, to the Cubans.[65] She recalls how she "clung to every privilege and habit that separated me from the islanders"—taking taxis, which Cubans could not afford, waving U.S. dollars, and wearing black "because black is not a color anybody wears in the tropics." As Ale explains, "Even though I ignored the island Cubans, my message was for them: I have nothing in common with you" (75). When asked whether she still has family in Cuba, Ale replies, "No [. . .] I don't have anyone in Cuba" (66). And, working as an interpreter in Havana, she insists, "I have no words of my own here" (76). This early Ale, that is to say, rejects any notion of transnational identity; she might have been born in Cuba, but she is 100 percent made in the USA. As she puts it to another interpreter who argues that all those of Cuban birth are to some degree "cursed" by its burden, "Not me, [. . .] I'm free" (67). (Later, though, she modifies this pronouncement, describing herself instead as a "hairless native pretending to live free" [192].) Ale disavows any claim to Cubanness and, as far as her public presentation of herself is concerned, deliberately disassociates herself from her origins, claiming that they are literally meaningless (producing no meaning, hence her lack of "words" in Cuba) for her.

Ironically, this is the very mode by which her father, Enrique, dissembles about his Jewish origins, much to Ale's scorn. (She mocks his "historical denial" and claims of "Spanish nobility," noting that, "when the neo-Nazis come, he and I will both be tossed into the ovens," despite those claims [174].) Like her father, who longs to be "free" of a background too burdensome to bear openly, Ale hopes, on one level at least, to disconnect herself from her Cuban history and the Cuban present.

Yet, just as her father's denials are belied by his continued religious observances in secret (108, 193), Ale's own "historical denial" of the ways in which Cubanness shapes her identity is belied by her use of phrases like "island Cubans," which implies, of course, that there are other kinds of Cubans besides the ones who reside on the island: diaspora Cubans like herself. Ale's rehearsal of the story of Jewish exile is heavily colored by her perception of the Cuban exile experience and speaks directly of her sense of division and displacement:

> [W]hen the Jews were expelled from Zion by the Babylonian king, he took the best and the brightest of the Israelites back to his kingdom. The Jews lamented this forced separation from their land, family, and friends. Yet, nostalgia aside, the Jews flourished in exile [. . .]. In short, they built a community along the Babylonian shores. Seventy years or so after the Jewish exile began, Babylon was conquered by King Cyrus of Persia, who offered the Jews an opportunity to return to their own land. Perhaps not

surprisingly, most of the Jews decided to remain in Babylon, [. . .] continuing to lead the only life they really knew, sending monies and goods back to those who had stayed behind in now mythical Israel. (93)

The story of Cuban exile, of course, shines transparently through this narrative of Jewish exile; for the Cubans, like the Jews, flourish—nostalgia aside—in the "community" they have built along the "shores" of their new land. The subtext of this narrative of exile, which recognizes the permanence of separation from one's origins, is the continued and "nostalgic" longing to reconnect, to be not only transnational but "boundless," to not have ninety miles and an embargo separating "island Cubans" from their exile counterparts.

It is this longing that is encoded, however obliquely, in Ale's interpretive efforts. For as Ale later reveals, her work as an interpreter is far more a manifestation of her desire for connection to her Cuban origins than she initially admits. In yet another pseudohistorical narrative—this one quite wishful—Ale hypothesizes that "[t]here was a time perhaps when everyone spoke the same language" and "[e]verything was understood" (89). For Ale, this "primal language" (90) is represented by "a speech strictly of vowels: ooooh-aaaah-iiiiiii," a "kind of glossolalia: ecstatic and pure and boundless" (89). Significantly, she describes her work as an interpreter in the same terms: "I'm an empath. I slip my client's words through my mouth as if they were formed by the electrical impulses of my own brain. I don't think, I hook in, I mind-meld, I feel, and I articulate all the agony or joy or confusion the client is experiencing [. . .]. When I'm in my reverie, I have no clue about what I'm actually saying. It's all aaaah-uh-eeeeeeeeeeeeee" (92). As an interpreter, Ale experiences "boundless"-ness; the distinctions between her and "Other," which she takes such pains to magnify on her first trip to Cuba, disappear. The sounds Ale describes hearing while swimming—another manifestation of the primal sounds of glossolalia—provide the explicit link to her yearning for her Cuban origins: "When I'm submerged completely, [. . .] I am always aware of the water talking. It's a low, low sound, like a moan, a rolling tenor from somewhere deep, horrible and dazzling. [. . .] [I]t's the last sound we make with our mouths wide open—it's a longing to belong. When I emerge, slick like a newborn, my first sighting is always, always Cuba" (245).[66]

The trajectory of Ale's search for identity takes place from the time of her return from her first trip to Cuba in 1987—the point at which she first discovers her father's Jewish roots—to his death and her second trip to Cuba in 1997 to spread his ashes. Hints in the text reveal how far Ale has come from her original disclaimer of any connection to Cuba, and of the role her discovery of her Jewishness, with its parallel and overlapping issues of exile and transnational identity, has had in this change; but this trajectory is never entirely elaborated in the novel. The fragmented and nonchronological nature of the text—in which memories of her first and second trips, ten years apart, are juxtaposed and interspersed with "plot" events from the intervening years, letters from Moisés, historical explications, and the stories of her father's, grandparents', and great-grandparents' lives—disrupts the usual bildungsroman structure and forestalls any linear outline of progression.[67]

Nevertheless, the narrator's much more concrete sense of identity (as both a Cuban and a Jew), ten years after her original trip to Cuba, is quite evident. In a scene tellingly framed by her recollections of her father's death, Ale wards off the proselytizing efforts of evangelists at an airport by asserting, "I'm a Jew" (272)—and recognizes, at the same time, the much greater freedom she has to make such an assertion than her ancestors had when confronted by similar religious zealots.[68] (This is the point at which Ale begins to interpret crypto-Judaism in terms of tenaciousness and survival, instead of sheerly in terms of assimilation.)

Linked to Ale's growing awareness of her Jewishness, with all it means in terms of exile and enduring bonds, is her increased identification as "Cuban." Her sketchily developed affairs with various lovers, which take place primarily "behind the scenes," so to speak, of the real action in the novel (its burdensome historical past and the grim present of the Cuban Special Period), seem to be connected to her gradual construction of a Cuban identity for herself. Of her lover Leni, for example, Ale says, "I've never been more Cuban than when I was with her. Between the two of us, I was [. . .] the one who related the history of Columbus and the island's genocidal Indians; I was the one who translated Ricky Ricardo's benign curses [. . .]. With Leni I could be as free as I wanted to be about my cubanidad because she never challenged my authenticity. I could use any stereotype I wanted in any way I wanted [. . .]. Leni listened, deferred; her very distance from Havana confirmed my proximity" (179). Ale's Cubanness here is, of course, not particularly a matter of inborn or inherited cultural knowledge ("authenticity" in the way that Ale means); her use of "stereotypes" and "translation" of stock figures like Ricky Ricardo imply only the most cursory and superficial knowledge. Rather, as Werner Sollors has put it, "ethnicity is [. . .] based on a *contrast*" ("Ethnicity" 288; emphasis in original): Ale can feel "Cuban" because Leni, in contrast, is distinctively *not*—and therefore will not challenge her historical lessons or cultural analyses as "inauthentic." Nevertheless, secretly, Ale envies Leni because she perceives her as having a more natural or obvious connection to her own Jewish origins, whereas Ale can pass for a nondescript American: "what I can barely admit to myself—is how much I secretly envy the inevitability of her Jewishness" (182).

At one point in the novel, after a mysterious phone call from a Spanish-speaking source which Ale and Leni are never able to trace, Ale tells us, "I was convinced the call was from Cuba—Cuba calling, if not Estrella, Deborah, Yosemí, or Moisés, then the island itself" (204). The image is part haunting, part clichéd: of a missed connection to Cuba calling out to her, of an insistence on the part of Cuba itself that she recognize her origin as meaningful. Eventually, Ale lays claim to the "inevitability" of her own Cubanness: "My passports—both of them—say I am Cuban: an American citizen but not American, Cuban, cubana, born in Cuba. This is the part that never changes" (237).[69]

Though the sentiment Ale expresses in passages like these smacks of essentialism, suggesting somehow that her Cubanness is determined at birth and unchanging over time, that notion is challenged by Orlando, disappointed revolutionary and present-day opportunist, who repeatedly says things to Ale like, "If you lived here, then maybe you'd get it," while she retorts, "I was born here. . . that means something. I was born here—like Martí, like you" (329). This struggle over Cuban authenticity becomes quite a bone of contention between them. When Orlando attempts to fill Ale in on the recent hardships "in my country—your country too, since you're so eager to claim it," Ale acknowledges his tales: "I've heard that, yes. It was awful." But Orlando insists on distinguishing between what Ale has "heard" and what he and other island Cubans have *lived*: "'*You don't know*,' he says, gritting his teeth, fists at his side" (338; emphasis in original).[70] Elsewhere, as we have seen, Ale's relationship to her Cuban identity in many ways parallels her father's to his Jewish identity; we might surmise that the corresponding parallel here is between Orlando, who "knows" what it is like to be Cuban, and Ytzak, the exemplar and conduit of Jewish "knowledge."

But it turns out that Ale is the more accurate parallel to Ytzak here. For Ytzak, the character in the novel most strongly representative of the struggle to be true to the "authentic" self, is similarly "inauthentic."[71] After we have already learned of Ytzak's life history, including his participation in the war of independence, his exposure to the Moor, his travels to Havana, and his kidnapping of his grandson, Enrique—after all this, we learn that Ytzak grew up known as "Antonio." Only as an adult, when he decides to be openly Jewish, does Ytzak announce that "he wanted to be called Ytzak—the Spanish spelling deliberately jagged, the same way Hebrew letters might seem to the unknowing, so as to provoke questions" (148). The name that signals his Jewish identity is, in fact, a construct, a deliberate approximation so as to mimic "authenticity."

Much later, Ale wonders whether the Ladino songs once sung at the synagogue Chevet Ahim in Havana were "passed down" by Ytzak and marvels "at Ytzak's persistence, at the inheritance I might have lost." But Moisés corrects her: "Oh no. [. . .] To be honest, Alejandra, I'm not sure he knew for a fact he was Jewish growing up, just different somehow" (345). Ytzak's Jewishness, like Ale's Cubanness, is largely a deliberate reconstruction, as Moisés explains:

"[Y]ou see, after he found out . . . after he came to Havana, he went through everything. He read, he studied. He was voracious. He could have been a rabbi, he was so ardent about it all, but it was mostly new knowledge" (345).

Obejas's deliberate inclusion of such moments in the text signals her concern with the constructed nature of identity and of collective bonds, and the work that such bonds often require to maintain. Like Ytzak, Ale, too, must "reconstruct" for herself a sense of Cubanness, from "new knowledge" rather than from lived experience (or from what is "in the blood"). No matter how much she claims that her Cubanness is what "never changes," we see in the course of the novel how very much her sense of herself as Cuban—as having something in common with "island Cubans"—*does* change over time. She has traveled far, by novel's end, from the disclaimer that she has "no one in Cuba" and is "free" to the insistence that it is her "country too," that she was "born here," like José Martí, and that this fact "means something"; it counts.

While the idea that Ale, as an exile, might be included in the Cuban "nation" certainly poses no significant challenge to the conservative Cuban exile narrative—which often proposes in its various forms that the exiles are the "true" and disinherited Cubans—it significantly complicates that narrative by interweaving it with the history of Ale's Jewish family, and by making Ale's embrace of her Cubanness dependent on her recognition of her Jewishness. Only in her being Jewish can Ale understand herself as also being Cuban. Or perhaps a better way to say this would be that, only in reconstructing her Jewish history for herself, and understanding the meanings of exile, adaptation, and the dogged persistence of (imagined) ties to one's origins that are implied in it, can Ale begin on the project of constructing her Cuban identity.

\* \* \*

In *On Becoming Cuban*, Louis A. Pérez Jr. has written that, because Cuba as nation was predicated on disentanglement from Spain, the discourse on "identity and nationality" in the emerging Cuban nation was marked by a lack of "pastness": "[A] coherent approximation of history was conspicuous by its absence. [. . .] Cubans did not situate themselves in a past; in fact, they lacked a coherent notion of an instrumental past" (94). Pérez's analysis offers a provocative lens through which to reexamine the current construction of *cubanidad* by Cuban exiles, which might be said to be similarly lacking a real historical narrative. While a past is certainly evoked, the mythical and nostalgic narrative of that past seems to be remarkably untroubled, as we have seen, by actual historical events before the revolution of 1959. It is the *erasure* of this history that gives the picture of "Cuba," as a land untroubled by racism or anti-Semitism or economic disparity, its coherence.

In their different ways, the texts by Achy Obejas and Cristina García both challenge this construction of idealized and homogeneous nationhood as well as of the "island-nation" detached from other national and collective identities and existing in isolation. (No island is an island, apparently.) By stretching the historical narrative of Cuba backwards in time, both novels render Cuba not an Edenic point of origin but a much more complicated, and scarred, midpoint in a far longer history of diaspora. Both Obejas and García uncover the violence undertaken in the name of nationalism and the forms of hybridity and transculturation simultaneously evoked and dramatically recontained by imperatives intimately connected to understandings of the "nation" itself. For García, as we have seen, the violence is so great that any nationalist sentiment becomes suspect. For Obejas, the problem is the difficulty of reconciling any notion of "nation" with those in the national body that dominant constructions of nation inevitably exclude—although the national "minorities" continue hopefully to cling to a more expansive vision of nation.

What are the implications of such texts for a notion of *latinidad*? As the nation becomes an ever more unstable and problematic category, then the panethnic category "Latino/a," which enacts even more historical erasures in the name of peoplehood, comes to seem even more precarious. Nonetheless, although García's skeptical rendition of nationhood would seem to render any project of ethnic peoplehood equally dangerous, Obejas's vision is more hopeful. Ale's embrace of a Cuban and Jewish ethnicity for herself is after all portrayed as progress, rather than as regression into delusional mythology. It gives her a larger and historically richer understanding of, and sense of connection to, a collective group of disenfranchised others.[72] As I will discuss in Chapter 7, the rhetoric of ethnicity can be useful for the forming of coalitions—as long as it does not harden into a definitional construct whose very definition enacts violence.

# Part Three

# Difference and the Possibilities of Panethnicity

# 5

## "The Pleas of the Desperate"

### Magical Realism, *Latinidad*, and (or) Collective Agency in Ana Castillo's *So Far from God*

Ana Castillo's *So Far from God*, a romping and inventive account of four Mexican American sisters (Fe, Esperanza, Caridad, and La Loca, translated as Faith, Hope, Charity, and The Crazy One) and their mother, Sofi, has clearly established its credentials as a progressive, politically concerned novel, and thus its place in the U.S. Latina/o canon.[1] The novel's pressing and overt themes, including gender inequity, challenges to cultural hegemonies (such as Anglo-American dominant culture or the earlier Spanish cultural domination of indigenous culture in Mexico), and the environment, are all topics that place it squarely at the heart of a "resistant" Chicano/Latino tradition.

Also frequently commented on is the novel's "magical realist" style; the observation that Castillo writes in a magical realist tradition, along with comparisons to Gabriel García Márquez, predominates in her popular and critical reception. The *New York Times Book Review*, for example, called the novel a "magical realist account" (Sandlin 22); the *Los Angeles Times* review (penned by Barbara Kingsolver) noted that Castillo had moved her writing "a step further into the domain of North American magic realism, a tentative genre descended from the politically astute masterpieces of Gabriel García Márquez and Isabel Allende." Kingsolver recommended, "Give [Castillo's novel] to people who always wanted to read *One Hundred Years of Solitude* but couldn't quite get through it. This one has levitating children and birds dropping out of the sky, too." And, in a somewhat grumpier vein, James Polk complained in the *Washington Post*, "Have we had enough of the magical yet? Is there still room on the world's bookshelves for another Hispanic novel set in a dusty town where [...] the marvelous is commonplace?" (D6).[2] Later scholarship has repeatedly returned to this critical classification,[3] with good reason: at times Castillo's novel seems literally to scream magical realism from its pages.

Of course, such critical affirmations themselves work to write Castillo firmly into a U.S. Latino/Latin American canon often characterized wholesale (and erroneously) by its use of a magical realist form. In this critical and readerly propensity we can see another manifestation of the underlying assumption that a metaphorical umbilical cord connects U.S. Latinos to our Latin American countries of origin. After all, as Laura P. Alonso Gallo has observed, "Magic realism [...] happens to be the best—perhaps the only—known Latin American literary style among Anglo Americans" (244). U.S. Latinos and Latinas are so essentially tied to our Latin American roots, according to this thinking, that the single writing tradition of which Latino/a authors are assumed to be a part is Latin American; and that "tradition" itself is reduced to the magical realist fiction of the Latin American "Boom" of the 1960s and 1970s.

Even Latino/a writers can participate in the essentialist equation between a generalized "Latin American" identity, presumably passed on (by blood or culture) to Latinos, and magical realism. As Gustavo Pérez Firmat comments in *Tongue Ties* (2003):

> Perhaps more than other types of serious writing, Latino literature caters to the limitations of its audience, which expects that the author and her stand-ins will act as cultural tour guides [to/in the countries of origin]. [...] And what does Latino literature teach? For the most part, what its readers already know, or think they know, about Latinos, Latinas, and Latin Americans: That they are slightly wacky, somewhat mysterious, very sensuous, and definitively spiritual. Julia Alvarez illustrates her admiration for a "compañero writer" with this anecdote: "I remember discovering Gabriel García Márquez and giving the novel to my father. He just couldn't put it down, and I told him, Papi, this is called magical realism. He said, what do you mean—this is the way we think!" (Alvarez, "Interview" 140–41; qtd. in Pérez Firmat, *Tongue Ties* 140)

Pérez Firmat picks up on this interesting use of "we," and rightly so.[4] For Alvarez, here, participates in the construction of a panethnic identity that includes Colombians currently living in Mexico, like García Márquez, and Dominicans currently living in the United States, like Alvarez's father (not to mention Dominican Americans raised in the United States, like Alvarez herself), suggesting that "we" all think in magical realist terms.

Delia Poey has astutely observed that, "[t]hrough a conflating of magical realism, the Boom and the beginning of Latin American literature itself, magical realism became mistakenly established as paradigmatic of Latin America" (28–29). It is only a short step from there, Poey notes, for readers to "indiscriminately lump simplistic paradigms of magical realism together with moments of 'magic' or narratives of the unexpected in Latina/o fiction" (38).[5] Ellen McCracken seems to strongly concur, arguing that "comparison [...] to the work of Gabriel García Márquez and Latin American magical realism" in book reviews of Latino writing demonstrates one of "the most common reductive modes by which the U.S. cultural mainstream has appropriated Latin

American fiction of recent decades as a palatable Third World commodity" (22). Indeed, we may read this critical trend as a manifestation of a larger essentializing tendency, whereby Latino/a culture in general is romanticized and exoticized as part of its more general commodification within mainstream U.S. culture.[6] Those aspects of Latin American (and, by association, Latino/a) culture which seem, to a Western audience, to be magical, mystical, primitive, and superstitious become sellable commodities (just as, to use an analogy, the clamor for things "primitive" generated an eager audience in the United States for images of a primal African connection in the poetry of Langston Hughes during the 1920s.)[7] As McCracken writes, Latina writers, including Ana Castillo, "are valorized in the press and by publishers for their presentations of what many perceive to be the exotic Other. They are foregrounded as exotic and different from the mainstream [. . .] precisely because sameness is not as marketable in current conditions as is difference. [. . .] Indeed, a structure of reappropriation similar to that of Orientalism characterizes much of the mainstream incorporation of Latina writers" (5).[8] As a sign of the exotic, ethnic "Other" (especially in a U.S. context), magical realism sells; and the critical response (as well as, on occasion, authors like Alvarez) seems to have participated in that commodification process.

Indeed, part and parcel of this romanticizing involves the automatic ascription of resistance to magical realism. If U.S. Latino literature is assumed to be connected by, on the one hand, a tradition of resistance (more on this in Chapter 6), and, on the other, its magical realist form, then it is no great leap to assume a fairly intimate link between the two. Markus Heide, for instance, observes that, in *So Far from God*, the "narrative strategies generally associated with Latin American and Chicano/a magical realism [. . .] are interwoven into depictions of political conflicts in rural New Mexico" (173); Gail Pérez places *So Far from God* within "a long tradition of voicing struggle and oppositional consciousness in the language of miracle and popular religion" (54), which she associates with "magic" (60); and Karen Christian posits that magical realism is inherently resistant: "Superstition, magic, and spirits—the inexplicable—are incompatible with rational Western thought; consequently, such performances are a form of opposition to Anglo-European positivist paradigms" (137). (If the text departs from the "realism" of Western rationality, the logic seems to go, then it must be good.) In this way, any appearance of magic in a Latina/o text—which inevitably gestures toward its connections to an indigenous and Latin American origin—comes also to signal its resistant politics. By implication, Latino/Latin American identity is essentially resistant.

By way of telling introduction to the status of panethnicity and resistance in this novel, I would like to briefly consider Castillo's depiction of Francisco el Penitente, a fascinating secondary character, because he seems, at first glance, to be one of the very few positive male figures in *So Far from God*—until his character rapidly disintegrates into a stalker and attacker (possibly a rapist). Francisco's representation gestures toward indigenous roots as he practices a folk spirituality; he is a *santero* who carves wooden sculptures (*bultos*) of saints out of materials "gathered from earths and plants" and who "labored with the natural elements, sun, air, and earth" (101–2). (Such representations of folk or indigenous forms of spirituality have often been associated with magical realism, as Wendy Faris has noted.) Nomenclature here creates confusion: a Puerto Rican war buddy in Vietnam, on learning that Francisco is a *santero*, responds, "Hey, no kidding? [...] My uncle in Carolina, Puerto Rico, is a santero, too!" (95). Aldama comments as follows on the panethnic possibilities offered by this scene:

> Francisco also comes into a new faith system—indigenous Catholicism typified by the syncretic santería [. . .]. At first, Francisco's identification with santería is simply a way for him to survive as a soldier in the Vietnam war. It acts as the vehicle for a solidarity to form between the New Mexican Francisco and a fellow soldier who is Puerto Rican. Both are already marginalized by the group of soldiers because they are Latinos; when they discover a cultural common ground, this solidifies their bond. [. . .] At this point, the Francisco character functions to demonstrate the power of santería as a modern-day, pan-Latinidad survival strategy. (82)

Aldama here rather ironically duplicates the soldiers' initial confusion about the term "*santero*," which in the novel is revealed to mean very different things to the Puerto Rican than to Francisco (that is, there is no "cultural common ground" at all). As Castillo's narrator explains,

> But no, as Francisco discovered when they got into it more, that Little Chico's santero tío practiced a very distinct variation of the Catholic influence on the New World—a Yorubic adaptation of the names of European and Hebrew saints to African gods [. . .] in which the santero himself contained the power to answer prayers, perform miracles, and cast out demons from the possessed.
>
> No, Francisco explained, a santero in Nuevo Méjico was a simple man [who] had no divine powers except during the time he was preparing a bulto, a wooden sculpture of a saint. (96–97)

That is to say, Francisco does not practice Santería at all; he is a *santero* because he makes images of saints, in the same sense that a *panadero* makes bread. Indeed, the entire gist of this scene in Castillo's novel is to undercut the automatic assumption of "common cultural ground" that is made by the other soldiers, who call Francisco (who is of Mexican descent) "Chico" and his Puerto Rican friend "Little Chico" because "to the white and black soldiers all 'Spanish boys' were 'Chico'" (94).

The confusion over the meaning of *santero* unravels the immediate ascription of common culture to common (Spanish) language, since the same word has very different cultural meanings. In his strong desire to see a resistant, panethnic *latinidad* in Castillo's text, Aldama actually conflates Mexican/New Mexican and Caribbean versions of hybrid Catholicism and invents a whole new version of Santería —one that is indigenous (rather than Yoruban) in origin: "[S]antería [. . .] speaks of the syncretic strategies used by Amerindians during the Spanish conquest and colonization of the Americas. (Shangó becomes Santa Barbara, for example.)" (82).

As I have already suggested, a similar critical tendency to automatically "read" resistance can be detected in the response to the novel's magical realism, to which I now return. Critical commentary on *So Far from God* has tended to draw connections between the themes of collective agency (i.e., the ability of groups to empower themselves collectively and change their social/political/economic situation)—particularly evident in the latter part of the novel—and its "magical realist" style as an *exemplar* or *facilitator* of such agency. This line of reading to some degree dictates the scenes in *So Far from God* to which critics will point as emblematic of resistance—scenes which often contain "magical" elements, such as the resurrection from death of La Loca; the spontaneous healing, after a vicious assault and rape, of Caridad; the latter's "death"—along with a friend—in a Thelma and Louise–like plunge from a mesa during which they magically dematerialize and leave behind absolutely no physical remains; and the organization of "M.O.M.A.S.," or "Mothers of Martyrs and Saints," in which the dead and deified children of the organization's members make occasional appearances and work miracles.

I propose, however, that an alternative list, focusing first of all on the novel's most obviously political scenes, can lead us to a quite different reading. My list includes the novel's portrayal of Fe's death from working with toxic chemicals in her position with a company involved in the production of weapons for the military (in other words, a classic manifestation of what used to be called "the military-industrial complex"); the novel's representation of Los Ganados y Lana Cooperative (146), a grass-roots movement that is both environmentally sensitive and economically sustaining for the people of the New Mexican town of Tome; and the description of the Holy Friday procession near the novel's end, which serves as a sort of communal dirge in which the stations of the cross are linked to environmental hazards and disasters with direct impact on the lives of Tome. These three episodes, which have a more explicitly political tone and commentary than virtually any other in the novel (and which notably foreground environmental concerns), are at the same time strikingly *lacking* in magical realism. Though Castillo clearly posits collective agency as an ideal response to the challenges of environmental degradation and economic injustice, her novel is also concerned with distinguishing between effective, active forms of collective resistance based on specific and, in many cases, local problems and illusory forms of "agency" or group identity that substitute for real resistance. In Castillo's novel, I wish to argue, this threat is embodied primarily and precisely in many of those textual moments that are marked by their "magic" overtones; in such moments, passivity and reliance on external forces replace activism and solidarity. I propose that Castillo's relationship to this genre—and thus to an essentialized, panethnic "Latino"/Latin American body imagined as a wellspring of resistance—might be entirely more complex than generally acknowledged.

Wendy B. Faris has provided a clear, cogent definition of magical realism: in a magical realist work, "[t]he text contains an 'irreducible element' of magic, something we cannot explain according to the laws of the universe as we know them. In the terms of the text, magical things 'really' do happen" (167). However, the magic is described with the tools of realism: "Descriptions detail a strong presence of the phenomenal world—this is the realism in magical realism, distinguishing it from much fantasy and allegory [. . .]. Realistic descriptions create a fictional world that resembles the one we live in, in many instances by extensive use of detail" (169). Further, Faris notes (and for my purposes this is crucial), "wonders are recounted largely without comment, in a matter-of-fact way, accepted—presumably—as a child would accept them, without undue questioning or reflection" (177);[9] that is to say, in magical realist texts, "magical"-seeming events are treated by the characters as an ordinary, recognizable, acceptable part of life.

Consider, for example, little Clara's "magical" powers of clairvoyance and telekinesis in Allende's *The House of the Spirits*, which are described as follows:

> Until that day they had never given a name to the eccentricities of their youngest daughter, nor had it ever crossed their minds to ascribe them to satanic influence. Clara's strangeness was simply an attribute of their youngest daughter, like Luis's limp or Rosa's beauty. The child's mental powers bothered no one and produced no great disorder [. . .]. It was true there had been times, just as they were about to sit down to dinner [. . .] when the saltcellar would suddenly begin to shake and move among the plates and goblets without any visible source of energy or sign

of illusionist's trick. Nívea would pull Clara's braids and that would be enough to wake her daughter from her mad distraction and return the saltcellar to immobility. (7–8)

The emphasis in Allende's descriptive passage is notably on how normal Clara's powers seem to her family. They are regarded as a character trait like any other, or at most as a form of misbehavior that she needs to snap out of; the defiance of the physical laws of the universe passes virtually without commentary. Similarly, in García Márquez's *One Hundred Years of Solitude*, magical flying carpets provide entertainment and amusement for young children but provoke astonishment and disbelief from no one (38); the appearance of the ghost of a murdered man elicits the murderer's anger at his return, followed by guilt—but not shock, fear, or wonder (30).

Indeed, often it is the "realistic" events in a magical realist text, rather than the "magical" ones, that strike the characters as unbelievable. As Faris writes, "In the light of reversals of logic and irreducible elements of magic, the real as we know it may be made to seem amazing or even ridiculous" (168)—or even shocking and horrifying. In Toni Morrison's *Beloved* (a non–Latin American novel frequently cited by Faris and others as "magical realist"), Paul D enters the ghostly presence of Sethe's murdered daughter and notes offhandedly, "You got company?" (8); but Stamp Paid reacts with horror on having to contemplate "a red ribbon knotted around a curl of wet wooly hair, clinging still to its bit of scalp," which he finds on the shallow river-bottom. "What *are* these people? You tell me, Jesus. What *are* they?"(180), he thinks to himself, in disbelieving shock at what the white perpetrators of this violence have done. In Louise Erdrich's *Tracks*, about the Chippewa, the elder Nanapush's ability to psychically guide Eli's hunt of a moose is reported without commentary on its wondrous nature (101–4); but the characters regard a map that details their land loss as unfathomable and inconceivable (173–74). The characters' lack of amazement at the fantastic occurrences in a magical realist text serves as a stark contrast that sets in relief the true sources of astonishment, horror, and disbelief—sources often grounded in real-life social, economic, and historical circumstances.[10]

According to the definition I have outlined above, which has the advantage of clearly distinguishing magical realism from other generic forms in which "magic" or "supernatural" events happen, I would suggest that it is questionable whether Castillo's novel indeed fits the parameters of the form. Magic is often regarded *precisely* as such in *So Far from God*; despite the fact that magical events happen quite frequently, characters nevertheless repeatedly react with astonishment at, if not utter disbelief in, the magical and miraculous. Certainly, as I will discuss shortly, there is a contrast between the magic and the real—but the contrast is not one of degree of astonishment. When Sofi's youngest daughter dies at three and then returns to life at her funeral, sitting up in her coffin and then flying to the church roof, the two interpretations offered are that she is "the devil's messenger or a winged angel" (23). If the latter, then she is a "miracle, an answer to the prayers of a brokenhearted mother" (23). The characters themselves regard the resurrection of "La Loca Santa," as she is nicknamed after this point (it eventually becomes shortened to "La Loca") as a *miracle*—as magic intervening in their world. Indeed, to highlight the contrast between magic and realism, Castillo also includes the reaction of a boy (later Francisco el Penitente): "And when little Franky [. . .] saw the child fly up to the church roof, man! What he wouldn't have given to know the secret of that trick! To the boy it was a trick, the way all children view the magical, which to them falls within the realm of possibility" (192). To view the magical as *within the realm of possibility* is a small boy's (mistaken) reaction, not the response of characters in general in the novel—and even the boy's interpretation is that it is a "trick"—that is, it is within the realm of possibility only insofar as it is not *really* magic, but deception.

The same collective response holds true for another miracle as well. One of the three older sisters, Caridad, has been brutally attacked; when "what was left of her" (37) comes home to be cared for by her mother, she is miraculously "healed":

> Dogs, cats, and women, twenty-eight eyes in all, saw Caridad walking soundlessly, without seeming to be aware of them, across that room. [. . .] Furthermore, it wasn't the Caridad that had been brought back from the hospital, but a whole and once again beautiful Caridad [. . . .]
> 
> "Dios mío," Sofi gasped. "Caridad."
> 
> "Mom," La Loca whispered, still on the floor, "I prayed for Caridad."
> 
> "I know you did, 'jita, I know," Sofi said, trembling, afraid to pull herself up, to go to the room where she suspected Caridad's corpse was now waiting [to] be taken care of.
> 
> "I prayed real hard," La Loca added and started to cry.
> 
> The dogs and cats whimpered. (37–38; emphasis removed).

The response to Caridad's healing, as to La Loca's resurrection, is a response to what is miraculous and astounding, not to an ordinary aspect of life. By contrast, what we are told of the attack itself is that whatever shock the community may initially have felt eventually wears off (33); after all, vicious attacks are a "real world" phenomenon.[11]

Such episodes should be a signal that Castillo's relationship to magical realism as a genre is, at best, ambiguous. Indeed, she has distanced herself from the "magical realist" label, pointing out that the "magic" found within the pages of *So Far from God* is modeled on religious miracles depicted in the lives of Catholic saints rather than on the fiction of the Latin American Boom.[12] (Of course, a strongly Catholic tradition is often cited as another means by which U.S. Latinos are connected both to one another and to their Latin American origins.) In this regard, it is surely worth noting Castillo's comments that she "stopped following the Catholic Church" at the age of eighteen and that she has been strongly influenced by the Portuguese collection *The Three Marias* because of its "challenging of the church" (Saeta 135), suggesting her critical distance from her Catholic source material, as well. Nevertheless, critics continue to conflate the novel's representation of miracles with magical realism—and to connect both to its political thrust.[13] Kamala Platt is one of the few commentators to discern a possible disjunction between the novel's labeling as "magical realist" and its activist politics: "The descriptive category *magical realism* may stereotype the text by situating it in the historical tradition of Latin American literature; this may assimilate the historically specific experience of Chicana/os into the larger Latin American tradition of *realismo marveloso* that has too often been depoliticized in the United States" (146). Notably, for Platt the panethnic critical move is a depoliticizing one; historical specificity in terms of concrete concerns and issues is more helpful for activism. Platt's comments point to the necessity of examining more carefully what *sort* of relationship obtains between magic, faith, and agency in Castillo's novel. Does the magical (or the miraculous) have the power to affect the political? If not, what does?

I would suggest that, in fact, Castillo draws a sharp contrast between the seemingly magical moments in her text and the realist ones, and that the "driving force behind collective activism" is distinctly different, in terms of the possibilities for agency and empowerment, from the driving force of miracles. The cooperative established by the people of Tome in the novel's most literal scene of collective activism, geared "toward some form of economic self-sufficiency for their area[,]" is described in notably realist terms:

> It would take YEARS of diligence and determination [. . .] to meet their goals but Sofi's vecinos finally embarked on an ambitious project, which was to start a sheep-grazing wool-weaving enterprise, "Los Ganados y Lana Cooperative" [. . .]. Every single step of launching off the cooperative took a lot of effort, a lot of time [. . .]. [M]any began working in some way for the cooperative—by learning an aspect of the business of sheep grazing, wool scouring, weaving, administration, and selling the wool products. (146–47)

What is emphasized in this arguably prescriptive passage on how best to address communal ills is the years of painstaking effort and collective participation, rather than the "magic" of divine or saintly intervention. Anyone reading in isolation the pages describing the cooperative would have absolutely no sense of Castillo's "magical realism."

This vision of cooperative endeavor does not necessarily replace a collective group identity understood in some sense as ethnic. Though Castillo does not emphasize the use of rhetoric that calls specifically on ethnicity in the description of the cooperative's formation, it is clear that most of its members are Chicano/a.[14] But ethnic identity—even a narrowly specified one (e.g., Mexican American)—is not in and of itself enough to establish what Felix M. Padilla has called "ethnic mobilization" (8). For the community to mobilize *as* an ethnic community, it needs to feel that common interests and goals override or take precedence (even if only temporarily) over differences. As Kamala Platt points out, the prototype for the community organizing efforts in the novel—which Castillo's narrator gestures toward in her enigmatic comment that the "Ganados y Lana Cooperative" is "modeled after the one started by the group up north that had also saved its community from destitution" (146)—is an actual community in northern New Mexico: the Ganados del Valle community (151). Laura Pulido, who interviewed one of the founders of Ganados del Valle, describes its genesis as follows:

> Ganados was born when two neighbors, Gumercindo Salazar and Maria Varela, began discussing "Gumi's" problems with his flock and ways to make ranching more profitable [. . .]. As a school teacher, Salazar, like most Hispano ranchers in the area, could only devote part of his time to his flock. Another major problem he faced was protecting his sheep from predators. After considering various alternatives, they decided to implement a guard-dog program, which in due course dramatically reduced his losses. Soon another rancher [. . .] joined the group. By pooling their resources, they realized they could make ranching more productive. After the initial success of the guard-dog program, they began telemarketing their products, which enabled them to get a higher price for their lamb. In 1983, Ganados invited other locals to participate, and while many were hesitant, due to the failure of previous cooperatives, a few joined. [. . .] During the early 1980s, local women took weaving lessons at the Los Ojos convent. [. . .] Since the sheep cooperative had been expanding, Ganados soon identified new opportunities by using the coop's wool for weaving, thus providing new job possibilities for locals. (128–29)

What is fascinating about this description is how the process of recognizing mutual interests is depicted as gradual and cumulative. First the ranchers realize that "pooling their resources," rather than adopting a competitive model, can make ranching more profitable for *all*. Then the women's interest in weaving is "identified" as a further opportunity for both the weavers and the ranchers, if their resources, too, are joined. Although all are "Hispanos" (New Mexicans of Mexican descent), that identifier alone does not automatically translate into a sense of common interests—as the previous failed cooperatives would seem to suggest.

Castillo's depiction also bears a striking analogy to Felix Padilla's description of ethnic organization even further north, in Chicago in the 1960s, in which coalition was generated out of the divergent interests and needs of recently arrived Mexican immigrants (both legal and illegal), immigrants of longer residence, and second-generation Mexican Americans (36–37). As Padilla describes it, the Pilsen Neighbors Organization in Chicago "developed a buying cooperative, housing and community development committees and a credit union" (Año Nuevo de Kerr 195, qtd. in F. Padilla 37), as well as a "youth club coalition [which] focused on a wide variety of issues such as health care, improved school facilities, bilingual and bicultural programs, job training, and social services" (37).

Likewise, the cooperative that Castillo depicts extends itself to other, initially unrelated, issues. For instance, we are told that "others, inspired by the diligence, ingenuity, and communal spirit of Sofi's vecinos, began to work on the drug problem that had found its way into the local schools and into their immediate vicinities, by forming a kind of hard-nosed drug SWAT team. And while the problem was not completely obliterated it would not be a lie to say that some lives had been saved because of the SWAT team's own diligence, ingenuity, and communal spirit" (148). The effects of communal activism in Castillo's novel ripple outward, having the potential to address communal problems *beyond* those originally targeted. But, as with both the New Mexican community of Ganados del Valle and the Pilsen community, a widely shared Mexican American identity is not, in and of itself, enough to ensure an automatic recognition of common interests—that recognition must be cultivated and educated. Though Castillo's inclusion of code switching, traditional recipes (165–67), and magical realism all serve as powerful ethnic markers in *So Far from God*, her depiction of the sheep-grazing and wool-weaving cooperative, with its extension to other communal issues, shifts the emphasis from identity markers to a model of collective identity *construction*, based on solidarity and cooperation in the pursuit of common goals. It is the active work of solidarity, rather than the passive reliance on ethnic identity, that is Castillo's focus.

In a later scene, Castillo once again forcefully highlights the chasm between the magic and the real—this time in a more pessimistic sense—in describing the death of Fe from her work with toxic chemicals:

> The rest of this story is hard to relate.
> Because after Fe died, she did not resurrect as La Loca did at age three. She also did not return ectoplasmically like her tenacious earth-bound sister Esperanza. Very shortly after that first prognosis, Fe just died. And when someone dies that plain dead, it is hard to talk about. (186)

In pointedly drawing attention to the stark contrasts between magical resurrections and Fe's startlingly *terminal* death, Castillo is engaging in a form of metafiction which forces readers to reflect back on the previous magic as *fiction*, when compared to the glaringly harsh realism of this "true" death. Fe's death calls on us to *stop* suspending our disbelief and to consider the difference between magical solutions and real problems.

In this context, it is helpful to invoke Delia Poey's intriguing argument that some Latino/a writers are in fact *parodying* magical realism for the purpose of creating "a strict distinction between the here, the now, the 'real,' and the nostalgia of another place, another time, another reality" (39).[15] Poey focuses on the contrast that magical realist parody draws between *now* and *then*, between "real life" in the United States and a nostalgia for the country of origin; I would elaborate, further, that Castillo uses what we might read as magical realist parody to draw a distinction between the realm of real, lived conditions (with the possibility of real social agency to change them), and the realm of collective fictions (e.g., magic and miracles—and perhaps also, by extension, an amorphous *latinidad*) that might actually derail concrete efforts toward agency.[16]

The parody is easily missed, however, when magical realism is privileged as somehow an "authentically" Latino/a narrative style. One result is that commentators on *So Far from God* incongruously read La Loca, the novel's most "magical" character, as linked to the novel's political-activist sensibilities, instead of seeing the distinctions among these things. Theresa Delgadillo, a critic who expresses a particular interest in *So Far from God*'s political thrust, nevertheless falls prey to the romanticizing of those elements which seem most quaintly and authentically "ethnic"—in this case, a hybrid or "folk" spirituality—in her privileging of La Loca, the "folk" saint. Suggesting that "[t]he death of the child La Loca and her funeral are powerful opening images that indicate clearly and strongly the direction of the story" (893), Delgadillo argues that, "[f]or Loca [. . .] in particular, the hybrid spirituality [she] practice[s] becomes one with [her] political action. The link between [her] faith and [her] action parallels the practice of liberation theology" (889).[17] But it is worth asking seriously how La Loca's death, resurrection, and folk canonization as a "saint" by the community "constitutes 'resistance'" or "is capable of effecting social change." In other words, what kinds of "agency" to resolve their "real-life" problems do La Loca's resurrection and subsequent "sainthood"—connected by Delgadillo with her hybrid ethnic identity—provide?[18]

Castillo seems to take pains to point out that La Loca is, in fact, utterly *isolated* from her specific community and has only a minor concrete role in it. Her resurrection, the narrator tells us, marks "the beginning of the child's long life's phobia of people" (23); near the end of her life, we are told that "Loca had never left home and her mother was the sole person whom she ever let get near her" (221). That is to say, most of La Loca's existence (with two exceptions, which I will discuss shortly) is divorced from any conceivable concept of political action or of effecting social change, and is certainly no driving force behind the notions of collective agency that critics read as the novel's ethical heart. Indeed, when Loca ascends to the church rooftop at her resurrection, "everyone below was either genuflecting or paralyzed, and crossing themselves over and over as she spoke" (23). Surely we should not ignore the close links between the display of worship of La Loca here (represented as a sort of frenzied, compulsive repetition) and the notion of paralysis. Far from establishing links between La Loca and liberation theology—which is based on the premise that faith in the next world must be interconnected with the struggle to "effect social change" in this world (as I will discuss further), such scenes firmly distance La Loca herself, as well as the community's canonization of her, from the activism of liberation theology; worship of La Loca (hybrid or not) *paralyzes* the people of Tome.

After La Loca's death, although she continues to be regarded as a "saint" by M.O.M.A.S., it is admitted that "[s]he was not particularly noted for answering the pleas of the desperate and the hopeless [. . .]. In other words, people never really could figure out who La Loca protected and oversaw as a rule, or what she was good to pray about. In general, though, it was considered a good idea to have a little statue of La Loca in your kitchen and to give one as a good luck gift to new brides and progressive grooms" (248). In death, as in life, La Loca remains detached from interventions in "worldly" affairs, although the community chooses to overlook this in its worship of her. Further, the novel implies, praying to La Loca may well run the risk of forestalling *real* social agency, since "good luck" replaces collective activism.

What we see in Tome's response to La Loca is the *gap* between liberation theology and a traditional Christian religious outlook stressing acceptance of "God's will." Jeana DelRosso reminds us of the Catholic Church's history of preaching "passivity and acceptance of one's lot in life [by] focusing attention on the rewards of the hereafter in order to maintain the submissiveness of oppressed peoples" (193–94), especially women.[19] In contrast, as Roger Haight explains, within liberation theology, faith "is conceived in terms of commitment, [. . .] doing and action" (67). Leonardo and Clodovis Boff agree, suggesting that, in the face of "the socially and historically oppressed [. . . ,] what is needed is not so much contemplation as effective action for liberation" (*Introducing* 4). Haight acknowledges that "this identification of faith with action appears startling" from a traditional Christian context: "Is not faith faith and action action?" (67). But liberation theology tends to reject the notion of faith as pure belief detached from the practical matters of this world; it suggests that true Christian faith "is no longer effectuated merely by religious practice in the strict sense (in devotional or liturgical practice). It has become a matter of joining to religious practices ethical and social ones as well, practices concerned with the promotion and advancement of 'the whole human being and all human beings'" (Boff and Boff, *Salvation* 3–4).

Liberation theology "conceives of faith as a form of praxis, or as identical with praxis" (Haight 66), where praxis is to be understood as "a certain kind of practice, namely, one that is for liberation in the public and social sphere" (Haight 67). Haight elaborates that liberation theology "supposes the broad and general truth that history is in some degree in human hands, that it is moved neither by blind fate, nor by a closed set of laws, nor by a predetermined providence. History is open and in some measure can be directed by human beings. Moreover this history is meant to move in the direction away from human imprisonment, enslavement and oppression of human freedom toward greater liberty and personal and social freedom" (41).

In contrast to Haight's explanation of liberation theology, Castillo's description of the religious "worship" of La Loca emphasizes the degree to which the people of Tome regard human affairs as *not* in their hands but in the hands of "saints," who are themselves not represented in particularly agentive terms.[20] As Castillo has commented of "female saints [. . .] upheld as models": "What kind of convoluted message do we give young Catholic women when we teach them to be obedient and submissive?" ("La Macha" 33). Given that, as Karen Christian notes, Castillo's narrator in *So Far from God* is "particularly merciless with respect to cultural norms that associate femininity with passivity and submission" (145), it is worth paying particular attention to those places in the text where passivity and submission are the end results of cultural practices such as the veneration of "saints"—even if they are folk saints.

The emphasis in liberation theology is, further, not merely on action versus nonaction but on finding the most *effective* form of action to liberate the oppressed: "The principal interest of liberation theology is to generate activity [. . .] that will aid the poor *efficaciously*. [. . .] The real question is: What praxis will *actually*, and not just seemingly, be of help?" (Boff and Boff, *Salvation* 4; emphasis in original). Though saint worship, even of "home-spun" saints who serve as collective symbols of a hybrid, indigenously rooted ethnicity, may be read as a resistant "action" in its intent or desire to improve the collective situation, it is clearly problematic in terms of its direct connections to efficacious action.[21] As Leonardo and Clodovis Boff explain, "The poor can break out of their situation of oppression only by working out a strategy better able to change social conditions [. . .]. In liberation, the oppressed come together, come to understand their situation [. . .], discover the causes of their oppression, organize themselves into movements, and act in a coordinated fashion" (*Introducing* 5). If we, along with Delgadillo, are indeed to read *So Far from God* in terms of liberation theology (and the resonances are clear), we must also read for the ways in which particular collective narratives and behaviors are represented in the text as either efficacious or illusory—as contributing to a full understanding of the causes of oppression, or as distracting from such an understanding. Though markers signaling ethnic connectedness (whether to Latin America, via magic, or to specifically indigenous roots, via folk spiritual practices) abound in the novel, they are no automatic guarantee of effective activism.

To return to La Loca's purported link to collective activism, one notable exception to her own political apathy is her participation in a jeans boycott, which she describes to her mother as follows: "I saw on the T.V. that some people in a factory are boycotting the company that makes these jeans [. . .]. Una factory that is unfair to its workers, just like where le Fe worked at. [. . .] They said on the T.V. that if you already have a pair of those jeans, then tear off the label to protest. They said it would make people ask why" (222–23). Far from this boycott's being represented as part and parcel of La Loca's resistant character or hybrid spirituality, however, it is, rather, depicted as an *aberration* in her character—Sofi is struck by "Loca's *sudden* social consciousness" (222; emphasis added). Further, the success of Loca's participation in the boycott depends on her mother, Sofi, who *does* participate in collective agency. Sofi asks Loca, "But *who* ever sees your jeans?" and Loca responds, "You, Mom. You asked. You'll tell somebody, qué no?" And Sofi indeed goes on to tell the story "at a meeting she was attending at the local high school about the noise pollution coming from nearby Kirtland Air Force Base" (223). La Loca's gesture of political resistance, limited though it is, *can* have effects, because it is *distinctly* different from her general mode of detachment—as well as from the community's investment in her to do the work of effecting change *for* them (even though they know better). But it depends, for its effects, largely on Sofi's more direct and involved political agency.

The second exception is Loca's participation in the Holy Friday procession that I mentioned at the beginning of this chapter.[22] The procession is a form of collective protest and agency propelled by the novel's starkest moment of realism, rather than by its magic or miracles.[23] This is not to say that politics are *divorced* from faith. Rather, the form of "faith" represented by Castillo in this scene has strong ties with liberation theology,[24] concerned precisely with the links between the *spiritual* and the *material*:

> When Jesus was condemned to death, the spokesperson for the committee working to protest dumping radioactive waste in the sewer addressed the crowd. [...]
> Jesus fell,
> and people all over the land were dying from toxic exposure in factories.
> Jesus met his mother, and three Navajo women talked about uranium contamination on the reservation, and the babies they gave birth to with brain damage and cancer. [...]
> Veronica wiped the blood and sweat from Jesus' face. Livestock drank and swam in contaminated canals.
> Jesus fell for the second time.
> The women of Jerusalem consoled Jesus. Children also played in those open disease-ridden canals where the livestock swam and drank and died from it.
> Jesus fell a third time. The air was contaminated by the pollutants coming from the factories. (242–43)

What is notable about this description is the *insistent* attention to "real," lived situations with correspondences in the "real world" outside of the novel (which induces Platt to refer to such scenes as examples of "virtual realism"). The scene reads in a *strikingly* different manner from that earlier passage in which the people of Tome wonder what to pray to La Loca for. Here the community *knows* what to pray for, quite specifically, and prayer is not a matter of vague and generalized hopes for "good luck" but a public, political protest in the service of effecting concrete social change in the areas of poverty, environmental destruction, and disease. As Leonardo and Clodovis Boff write, "The first reaction of Christian faith in the face of this reality is protest. This cannot be! This is not pleasing to God!" (*Salvation* 3). In comparison to such protest, the elevation of La Loca to sainthood may simply come across as silly.

Just as the community of Tome "canonizes" La Loca for her magical resurrection, her sister Caridad experiences a folk canonization as a result of what is perceived as her close connection with nature.[25] Critics tend to pounce on evidence of a "natural" sensibility in *So Far from God*, perhaps once again privileging it as part of a romanticized "Chicano/a" essence that provides an alternative to Western civilization. Delgadillo suggests, for example, that a closeness to nature is true of many of the female characters in *So Far from God*: "The affinity with the natural world and natural order [...] that these Chicana characters embrace leads to a site of female strength and power in this novel"

(899). And Mayumi Toyosato argues that "[a]n attachment to the land seems crucial to a sense of collective self and political action" in *So Far from God* (295), and that "the land functions as a place for the formulation of consciousness and action" (305–6). Here, too, however, I believe it is important to note the difference between *activist* agency and collective narratives that distract from such agency in *So Far from God*, this time with regard to the intersections between the magical or mystical and environmental consciousness.

Caridad's retreat to a cave for a year is depicted in terms which, on one level, might suggest that she is particularly attuned to her natural environment and instinctively seeks it out:

> Caridad herself could not explain, even if she were inclined to try, what led her up those mountains that day. She could not say why [. . .] she pulled up in that secluded area, thinking it was as good a place as any to rest, and abandoning her pickup, curled up that first night at the mouth of a cave and slept undisturbed by the cold mountain winds.
> 
> The following dawn, when she woke to a delicate scar in the horizon that gradually bled into day and saw the sun then raise itself like a king from its throne over the distant peaks, Caridad only knew that she wanted to stay there and be the lone witness to that miracle every dawn. (89)

While the appreciation of nature seems attractive and even ennobling, the emphasis on the miraculous and its connection to isolation ("lone witness to that miracle") should by now sound warning bells. When she is discovered, Caridad comes to emblematize, for the people of Tome, a romanticized and miraculous existence. And, as we may by now expect, some critical assessments seem to replicate this romanticized view of Caridad as one with nature (and thus as resisting Anglo culture through an imagined, deep connection to indigenous roots). Ralph E. Rodriguez, for example, suggests that her later death, in which she plunges off a cliff (with Esmeralda, who has not returned her love) but leaves no body, is "not a tragedy [. . .] but a romantic connection to the earth and a rebirth. A deep feeling of spirituality fills the termination of Caridad's and Esmeralda's lives [. . .]. They have returned to what the Acoma myth of creation refers to as the earth's womb" (77). And Delgadillo seems to concur: "Caridad and Esmeralda's leap from the top of the mesa at Acoma poignantly illustrates the idea that humans are of nature, rather than above nature" (900).[26]

For her supposed oneness with nature, Caridad is nicknamed "la Santita Armitaña" (the hermit saint) (90) and, like La Loca, is venerated by the people of Tome. The view of Francisco el Penitente is representative here of that of the larger community: "In Francisco's eyes, Caridad had proven herself to be all that was chaste and humble with that year of self-imposed ascetic life in a cave" (192). Yet it is surely worth noting that Francisco's "worship" of Caridad devolves into violence; it is he who drives her to her death. If the worshipful attitudes of the rest of Tome are not given quite so sinister a cast, they are nevertheless highly problematic for notions of political activism and agency:

> So it was that during Holy Week, instead of going to Mass at their local parishes, hundreds of people made their way up the mountain to la Caridad's cave in hopes of obtaining her blessing and just as many with hopes of being cured of some ailment or another. [...] Some claimed to have been touched and blessed by her and still some others insisted that she had cured them! One man said that when he laid eyes on her, he saw a beautiful halo radiate around her whole body, like the Virgen de Guadalupe, and that she had relieved him of his drinking problem. (87, 90)

In retrospect, however, *this* Holy Week procession stands in stark contrast to the later one; here we have the hope of miracles passively received instead of political action actively undertaken.

Further, as with La Loca, the main thing that is emphasized about Caridad's year as a hermit is its *social isolation*, and even social apathy:

> Until those three men rode up on their horses she did not think of no one, not Doña Felicia, not her mom or the other members of her family, not even herself [...] . After so many months of tranquillity [...] the entire mountain was invaded up to the threshold of her very cave home by hundreds of people!
>
> What did they want? As the first dozens arrived [...] she went deep inside the cave to hide. But later she heard them call to her: "Oh Holy One! We beg you, please take pity on us!" "Your blessing, Little Hermit!" "I beg you, santita armitaña, help my mi'jito! or "Cure my dying padre!" or ... "a mi abuela!" or "a mi pierna coja que ya no sirve pa' nada!"
>
> Of course, all this was confusing to Caridad, who, having been away from society for so long, made no connections between those please [*sic*] and her recluse existence and she just went deeper into the cave until all the voices finally went away. (89, 90 )

Caridad's spiritual connection to the environment—to the land in a pristine, untouched form—translates not into any kind of social consciousness (as with the wool and sheep-grazing cooperative's environmentally sensitive production of "hormone-free meat"[147] and "pesticide-free food" [148]) but into an escapist romanticism: she ignores the pleas/"please" of the community. (The same can surely be said for her magical death, which—however evocative in terms of its indigenous resonance and revisionist feminism—constitutes the ultimate escapism.) In this respect, Caridad might be read as a fictional condemnation of the "assumption [. . .] of an 'innermost self' that is primordial nature's 'aboriginal correlate'" and of the "the illusion of an essential 'ecological self'" (Buell 701–2)[27]—that is, of the very assumptions which undergird critical celebrations of an intimate bond with nature as one aspect of an indigenous-based Chicano culture. As Aldama writes, "the narrator's parodic voice" in this scene "calls attention to the construction of an 'authentic' precolonial [. . .] space of emancipation" and to "formulaic uses of magicorealism that peddle the Other as preternaturally exotic [. . ., thus] destabilizing [. . .] the spectacle of primitivism" (85). Caridad might be elevated to the level of indigenous myth by her connectedness with nature, but it is highly questionable how such a connection, in and of itself, helps her—much less the larger community.

In the arena of religion, as we have seen, a helpless (if collective) faith in miracles and magic is ultimately deflated as a route to agency in favor of a sort of liberation theology which combines religious rites with political protest; likewise, in the arena of environmentalism, romantic essentialism is measured against a most politicized representation of human relationships with the environment, once again manifested in the Holy Friday procession:

> One of the women [. . .] told the crowd this: "We hear about what environmentalists care about out there. We live on dry land but we care about saving the whales and the rain forests, too. Of course we do. Our people have always known about the interconnectedness of things; and the responsibility we have to 'Our Mother,' and to seven generations after our own. But we, as a people, are being eliminated from the ecosystem, too . . . like the dolphins, like the eagle; and we are trying very hard now to save ourselves before it's too late. Don't anybody care about that? (242)[28]

The "interconnectedness of things" here refers not to an "'innermost self' that is primordial nature's 'aboriginal correlate'" but to the interrelationship between environmental degradation and human degradation.[29] This politicized rendering of "environmental consciousness" demands that such consciousness *not* romanticize the "natural" at the expense of the "human" (or, indeed, romanticize Chicana identity for mystical connections with nature) and calls instead for an understanding of how damage to the ecosystem has real, material, physical effects on human lives—and generally on the poorest and most disempowered first. About *this* conception of ecological "interconnectedness" Caridad's retreat from the human community to a supposedly "untouched" natural landscape has nothing to say.

As I have already noted, the organization Mothers of Martyrs and Saints at the end of *So Far from God* has also received substantial critical commentary, which—once again—often links it with the novel's political and feminist concerns. Ellen McCracken's comments are fairly representative of this line of reading; she suggests that "the feminist utopian gesture of this chapter positively attempts to reverse the patriarchal power of the Catholic church throughout history" and that it, like Castillo's description of the Holy Friday procession, is "designed to show women's power and autonomy" (38).[30] McCracken, interestingly, ends up being critical of this scene nonetheless, citing the chapter's "confusing pan-Latino version of multiculturalism," in which "Castillo merges culture, politics and history from throughout the Americas" by alluding, in this New Mexican Chicana context, to Argentina's Mothers of the Plaza de Mayo (38), a real-life Latin American organization of mothers of dead sons and daughters. I would argue, however, that by lampooning M.O.M.A.S. (including through the magic gone wild in this scene), Castillo is precisely rejecting a preexisting and essentialized panethnic Latino identity as somehow inherently resistant. The Mothers of the Disappeared are a far cry from M.O.M.A.S. in terms of their political goals; a structural similarity (groups of mothers of dead children) does not make for underlying identity.

Indeed, my argument suggests that there might be distinct differences between other textual examples of "women working on social and environmental injustice issues," such as the wool-weaving cooperative (which was founded by "a core group of twelve women" [147]) or the Holy Friday procession, and M.O.M.A.S. In the latter, for example, as I have already discussed, La Loca is prayed to without any sense of "what she was good to pray about" (248), whereas in the Holy Friday procession prayer is combined with active protest; and in the cooperative, active agency replaces prayer entirely. It is notable that the description of M.O.M.A.S. entails magical realism gone rampant, and thus reaching its most parodic form: "But what a beautiful sight it all became at those reunions: 'jitos from all over the world, some transparent, some looking incarnated but you knew they weren't if you tested them in some way, like getting them to take a bite out of a taquito or something when, of course, after going through all the motions like he was eating it, the taco would still be there. Although, it really wasn't such a respectable thing to do to test a santo, even if he had once been your own chiple child!" (251). The tone here suggests not the political activism and urgency of earlier scenes but tongue-in-cheek mockery of magical realism gone "over the top." The only allusion to the realm of political activism at this point is a passing mention of the fact that the advice of the dead spirits is not taken seriously by "relevant local or federal governments" (251); the pressing concerns of poverty, environmental degradation, and gendered violence that have affected (and in some cases destroyed) the novel's women have disappeared, swept off the radar screen by the apparent lightheartedness (if not frivolity) of the annual M.O.M.A.S. conferences.[31]

Instead, the main activity of M.O.M.A.S. members seems to be to quibble over "whether a 'jito' of a M.O.M.A.S. member would be designated as a saint or a martyr" (248). The contrast to the nature of debate in the incipient stages of Los Ganados y Lana Cooperative is jarring; in the latter, "[t]here were many community-based meetings [with] debates as to what ideas would lend themselves best toward some form of economic self-sufficiency for their area"; then, when the cooperative is decided on, "[discussions] involved a lot of not only changing everyone's minds about why not to do it but also changing their whole way of thinking so that they *could* do it"; and "finally it became a debate of either everyone doing it all together or nobody doing anything at all" (146). The latter debates center on solving specific local, communal problems collectively; the members see the cooperative as a plan "to rescue Tome" (146). The debates suggest both the entrenchment of ideology that encourages acceptance of the status quo ("changing their whole way of thinking")[32] and the imperative of active self-empowerment ("so that they *could* do it"). In contrast, what is striking is M.O.M.A.S.'s inability to even address, much less pose an effective challenge to, the problems faced in the novel.[33]

It is within this context (rather than a reading of M.O.M.A.S. as antihegemonic, culturally subversive, or radically feminist) that we can make sense of what one reviewer has called "the 'Disneyfication' of the Society of Martyrs and Saints" (Hellein 25):

> Every year the number of vendors of basically more useless products and souvenirs than what a tourist could find on a given day at Disney World grew. For example, there were your T-shirts with such predictable stenciled phrases as "The Twenty Third Annual Convention of M.O.M.A.S., Flushing, NY," or "Perros Bravos, Nuevo Leon," or "Las Islas Canarias," or "My Mother Is a Member of Mothers of Martyrs and Saints—Genuflect, Please!," the usual posters, stationery, forever-burning votive candles with your favorite saint's or martyr's picture stuck on (or an instant photo of your own kid, if you preferred), "automatic writing" pens, and then, of course, the all-time favorite—La Loca Santa and her Sisters Tarot Deck drawn by a lovely and talented artist in Sardinia, Italy. (Castillo, *So Far from God* 249–50)

Whereas the cooperative produces "hormone-free meat" (147) and "pesticide-free food" (148), the products that proliferate at M.O.M.A.S. conferences are "useless"; they certainly betray no signs of environmental sensitivity. (If anything, they seem to contribute to environmental degradation through wasteful overproduction.) Consumer society offers the illusion of choice to disguise the absence of real agency to change one's life; thus the power of collective agency degrades into "useless" consumerism that cannot cope with the problems faced by the women in the novel but can certainly distract from them. (We cannot fail, here, to be reminded of the commodification of *latinidad* itself, via book jackets that tout magical realism and the marketing of actresses such as Salma Hayek and Penélope Cruz as exotic Latinas of unspecific origin.) The comparison of the M.O.M.A.S. conferences to Disney World, a deliberately manufactured fantasy land where the world of politics and political struggle "magically" disappears, is striking.[34]

\* \* \*

In a 1997 interview, Ana Castillo spoke of the dangerous consequences "if we submit ourselves to apathy," offering her unabashedly prescriptive conviction: "[W]e have to do something. We have to have a vision. [. . .] We have to speak up locally and nationally" (Saeta 149). While these comments would surely come as no surprise to most literary critics familiar with Castillo's work, I would suggest that their particular application to, and implications for, *So Far from God* bear closer consideration. When do the characters in the novel "do something" to actively improve their collective situation? When is their "vision" for a better future—and their voice to express protest—clearest? It is remarkable that such moments generally occur in passages *devoid* of magical elements (although not necessarily devoid of religious faith, as the Holy Friday procession shows). When, in contrast, are characters most "apathetic" about their (or their community's) concrete circumstances? As I have suggested, apathy is found in perhaps surprising places in the novel—in "mystical"-seeming retreats from society, in the diversion of consumerism provided by the magical M.O.M.A.S., and so on. Unlike with typical magical realist texts, the magical and the real are *not* seamlessly interwoven in Castillo's novel; rather, they come to stand in increasingly stark contrast to each other.

While it is fairly easy to pick out the self-conscious echoes of magical realism and thus link Castillo with her Latin American counterparts, a more discriminating approach to the magical elements in the novel leads us not compulsively back to Gabriel García Márquez (where so many commentators seem to want to take us) but to a distinctly different relationship between the magical and the political, as well as between collective identity and resistance. Ultimately, I would suggest, Castillo's text challenges the almost omnipresent critical assumption that Latino/a ethnic identity—signaled by textual markers such as magical realism, hybridity, folklore, and so on—is in and of itself resistant and offers instead a much more context- (and cause- ) specific sense of collective activism. The resistant potential of ethnic identity lies in the particular forms of its deployment; merely signaling ethnicity does not guarantee progressive politics. It is not so much "who we are" but, ultimately, what we fight for that gives us a sense of collective identity.

# 6

# Dirty Girls, German Shepherds, and Puerto Rican *Independentistas*

## "The Latino Imaginary" and the Case of Cuba

As we have seen in the previous chapter, the implicit assumption that Latino/a identity as a whole is characterized by a resistant, oppositional stance has historically permeated much of Latino studies. The notion of *latinidad*, David Román and Alberto Sandoval have observed, often "circulates as a critical shorthand valorizing seemingly authentic cultural practices that challenge both colonial and imperialist U.S. ideologies in North and South America" (558). In 1990 Ramón Saldívar's groundbreaking *Chicano Narrative* took up just such an argument with regard to Chicano literature in particular;[1] Saldívar's contention that Chicano narratives are "resistant ideological forces in their own right" (7) has influenced a wave of subsequent criticism on Latino literature more generally, such that, if the assumption that Latino/a writing is always resistant is not always explicitly stated, nevertheless, critics show no interest in discussing texts which may not fit this paradigm.[2] For example, in *Postmodern Cross-Culturalism and Politicization in U.S. Latina Literature*, Mujčinović groups texts which "engage in oppositional forms of enunciation, contesting and deconstructing dominant social discourses in order to ensure a progressive transfiguration and emancipation of the individual and the communal" (4). In *Reading U.S. Latina Writers*, Quintana describes the emergence of "an alternative Latina vision, which in essence synthesized issues relevant to both civil rights and women's liberation," and offers her collection of essays as an effort "to help fulfill U.S. Latina writers' visions of telling stories that will help liberate those who have been left behind" (1–2). (Less-liberating stories need not apply.) In *Dance between Two Cultures* Luis writes that Latinos "articulate a differentiated discourse; that is, an antidiscourse to the discourse of power, similar to that of blacks and slaves" (285). In a call for papers, the journal *Works and Days* invited submissions for a special issue on "Asian American, African American, and Latino/a American Cultural Criticisms," which once again reveals the continuing presumption that Latino/a cultural production will inevitably be "counter-hegemonic," "challenge the mainstream," and engage in "criticisms of whiteness, racialization, American Empire, imperialism, neo-colonialism, global capitalism, and so forth" ("Call for Papers").

In a more sophisticated vein, Allatson, in *Latino Dreams*, rightly notes the continuing assumption within Latino studies that "all Latinos can be placed under the subaltern rubric" (42) and declares his intent "to avoid the tendency to regard Latino narratives as invariably oppositional to majoritarian imaginations [and to celebrate] cultural heterogeneity as cultural resistance or counter-hegemonic success" (45). Yet Allatson's main lines of inquiry continue to be centered on "the resistant capacities of cultural production": "What narrative tactics are mobilized against the U.S.A. and its dominant myths [. . . ?] What is at stake for Latino cultural politics in the narration of alternatives to (or mobilities against) the 'American' Dream?" (13). In Allatson's more nuanced approach, "Latino counter-discursive ambitions" (21) can be thwarted by "moments of hegemonic complicity" (53), but the *ambitions* are still more or less taken for granted.

Anthologies, which inevitably serve the function of presenting critical constructs of the field for a general audience, have on more than one occasion reified the paradigm of the oppositionality of Latino literature.[3] In his introduction to *Currents from the Dancing River*, for example, Ray Gonzalez asserts that, "[A]lthough cultural differences remain between Mexican Americans, Puerto Ricans in the United States, and Cuban Americans, Latino writers *are coming together in a cohesive* [. . .] *whole*" which is characterized by (among other things) a "timeless struggle for social justice" (xiii–xiv; emphasis added). And Nicolás Kanellos introduces *Hispanic American Literature* (1995) by affirming that writers such as Tomás Rivera and Rolando Hinojosa "led the way in creating a working-class identity and aesthetic for *all Hispanic writers in the United States*" (4; emphasis added).[4]

In his discussion of U.S. Latino literature in *From Bomba to Hip-Hop*, Juan Flores skirts the pitfalls of some of these critical commentaries because he insists that "[t]he adequacy of the embattled 'Latino' or Hispanic' concept hinges on its inclusiveness toward the *full range* of social experiences and identities" (164; emphasis added). Flores, instead, details two *different* trajectories of Latino literary canon formation:[5] "The difference, I would suggest, [. . .] lies in the differential positioning of the varied Latino groups in the prevailing structures of power and domination within the United States and internationally. Those whose collective identities in the United States were constituted by a longstanding history of conquest and colonization [i.e., Mexicans and Puerto Ricans] generate a literary expression which contrasts with that of comparatively recent arrivals from countries with less direct ties to U.S. imperial power [i.e., Cubans and Dominicans]" (*From Bomba* 176). Flores argues that Ilan Stavans and Gustavo Pérez Firmat have been the key players in the construction of a Latino "canon" which privileges texts with a more middle-class, assimilationist perspective. (He includes among these the novels of Oscar Hijuelos, Julia Alvarez, and Cristina García.) Flores particularly scorns what he sees as Stavans's celebration of the "demise of the idea of Latino culture as resistance" (*From Bomba* 173).[6] But rather than calling the more "assimilationist" texts not rightfully Latino, Flores simply makes clear his own preference for the more "resistant" tradition.

Yet Flores, who is more sensitive to the differences among the various Latino populations than many previous critics, nevertheless also falls under the magnetic influence of the resistant and oppositional (i.e., "Left") Latino model. The pitfalls that Flores avoids in his chapter on Latino literature resurface in the following chapter, "The Latino Imaginary." Flores is now concerned with the question of how the groups of different national origin imaginatively "negotiate their relation to some more embracing 'Latino' or 'Hispanic' composite" (*From Bomba* 197). But the model he reverts to in sketching out this "composite" is once again resistant, with a markedly leftist orientation: Latinos' mobilization efforts are "directed first of all toward recognition and justice in this society [. . .]. The Latino imaginary infuses the clamor for civil rights with a claim to sovereignty on an international scale; retribution involves reversing the history of conquest and subordination" (*From Bomba* 200).

The problem perhaps is Flores's use of the word "the," as though there is only *one* Latino imaginary, whereas in his earlier chapter on Latino literature, there is clearly *more* than one, and they are often competing and at odds with each other. "Hybridity" and hyphenation, for example, are certainly a part of the current constellation of Latino/a imaginaries, and yet as Flores points out, they are by no means necessarily resistant and oppositional—when posited, for example, as a hyphen that is an equals sign (as Pérez Firmat does). It is certainly possible, as we have seen in the Introduction, to *imagine* a relationship to a panethnic Latino identity based not on civil rights and "reversing the history of conquest" but on supposed primordial ties suggested by a "common culture" and language which are, presumably, the *products* of conquest (by the Spanish). The term "imaginary" bears the weight of a resistance paradigm better than "Latino" does, but ultimately it, too, suggests a singular model for being (or imagining being) Hispanic.

The Cuban exile community in the United States has, needless to say, posed an interesting problem for this construction of Latino ethnicity. This group cannot be easily made to fit with the "Latino imaginary" as Flores (and others) have delineated it; as is well known, Cuban American politics are substantially more conservative than those of Mexican Americans or Nuyoricans (who, as we have seen, have shaped the paradigm for subsequent Latino populations). The Pew Hispanic Center reports, for example, that, of Latinos of Mexican origin who were registered to vote in 2004, 47 percent identified as Democrats and only 18 percent as Republicans; 50 percent of registered Puerto Ricans identified as Democrats, 17 percent as Republicans. For registered Cuban Americans the numbers were reversed: 52 percent claimed Republican affiliation and only 17 percent identified as Democrats ("2004 National Survey" 3).[7]

As Felix Padilla notes in his early study of formations of Latino solidarity, instrumental understandings of Latino ethnicity are more likely to link Puerto Ricans and Mexican Americans while excluding Cuban Americans. Padilla cites one respondent who worried about the panethnic category being extended to Cubans: "[W]e need to be concerned with the term Latino or Hispanic because that includes everybody. It includes the Cubans, [. . .] and I have always felt that the struggle has been a Chicano-Boricua struggle" (76). Another respondent commented: "I think that Mexican Americans and Puerto Ricans are the two major groups encompassing the Hispanics in the United States. We are the targets of programs such as Affirmative Action because we are so severely disadvantaged. [. . .] The Cubans who came here have all the tools to make it. [. . .] So from that point of view the Cubans are not the target group, they are not disadvantaged, they are not discriminated against. The Hispanic is low income and severely disadvantaged" (77).

In these earlier formulations of "Hispanic" identity, as we can see, that identity was imagined strictly on a Puerto Rican and Mexican American paradigm, so that Cuban immigrants, marked by substantial economic and other demographic differences from the other "Hispanic" groups,[8] sometimes got left out of the collective group identity entirely—at least by Chicanos and Puerto Ricans themselves. (It is worth noting that such a construct implicitly challenges the notion that the Spanish language serves as an essential, underlying common denominator for Latinos, as discussed in the Introduction; in this construction Spanish is by no means sufficient—or perhaps even necessary—to create a sense of unity.) As Flores has more recently noted, the "legendary" Puerto Rican singer Pedro Ortiz Dávila ("Davilita"), who sang of the sisterhood of "las Antillas"—Cuba, Puerto Rico, and the Dominican Republic—"might have been more befuddled had he reflected on 'las islas hermanas' at a time closer to our own, after the Cuban Revolution [. . .]. His concern over the divergent historical destinies of his three related islands might have reached a crisis pitch had he pondered the three emigrant enclaves that had taken such divergent shapes in the United States at the century's end" ("Islands and Enclaves" 60–62).

The notion of the Cuban enclave as a population separate indeed from other Latinos has continued to pop up in various forms. Consider, for example, the commentary of prominent Chicano scholar Rodolfo F. Acuña, author of the seminal book *Occupied America: The Chicano's Struggle toward Liberation* (1972; reprinted as *Occupied America: A History of Chicanos*), during the controversy over Elián González. Noting "the growing differences between Cuban Americans and other Latino American groups," Acuña insists that "[m]any Latinos are indeed [. . .] questioning whether Cuban Americans as a group have suffered a history of discrimination in the United States similar to that of Mexicans or Puerto Ricans. Cuban Americans have become a minority through the stretch of the 'Hispanic label,' which has allowed them entitlements usually reserved for Americans who suffered a history of discrimination" ("Miami Myth Machine").

These efforts (both earlier and more recent) to draw a more circumscribed line around the "Hispanic" group illustrate De Genova and Ramos-Zayas's point that "one of the central conflicts over the constitution of [. . .] Latinidad ultimately involves the racialized stigma of an abject 'minority' status that is unevenly distributed among distinct Latino groups" (20). The significant disparities among the groups lead to "[a] politics of inclusion and exclusion [that generates] competing productions of who can be counted as 'authentic' or 'legitimate' Latinos" (20).

The reverse side in this struggle over identifying who might count as "Hispanic" is the role of the federal government:

> [T]he invention of "Hispanic" homogeneity [. . .] created an unprecedented opportunity for the numerically small but remarkably influential community of Cuban exiles (who were predominantly from elite or professional middle-class backgrounds, racially white-identified, politically conservative) to mobilize their newfound "Hispanic" identity as a platform [. . .]. Thus, against Chicano and Puerto Rican affirmations of indigenous and national identities that often embraced Third World anticolonial nationalist or Marxist theories of national self-determination, anti-Castro Cubans supplied a vociferous "Hispanic" expression of Cold War–era anticommunism that was resolute in its newfound allegiance to U.S. nationalism and capitalism. (De Genova and Ramos-Zayas 17–18)

Historically, as De Genova and Ramos-Zayas underscore, Cuban Americans have held more conservative positions than their other "Hispanic" counterparts (e.g., on issues such as U.S. intervention in Latin America, especially in support of brutal but "anti-Communist" regimes), complicating the "Latino imaginary" that Flores describes.[9]

Aware of this difficulty for his formulation, Flores suggests that "today even many Cuban Americans, recent arrivals and long-standing citizens alike, are finding the red carpets and gold-paved streets illusory at best" (*From Bomba* 199) and goes from there to assert, "For the Latino imaginary, even when the relatively 'privileged' Cuban Americans are reckoned in, rests on the recognition of ongoing oppression and discrimination, racism and exploitation, closed doors and patrolled borders" (*From Bomba* 199)[10]—surely a highly arguable claim, even about the Latino population as a whole, not to mention Cuban Americans. According to the Pew Hispanic Center, for instance, while 46 percent of registered Latino Democrats in 2004 said "that discrimination is a major problem for Latinos" (even this is not a majority), only 29 percent of Republicans did ("2004 National Survey" 3). In the wake of the heated policy debates over immigration in 2006, Latinos were more likely (58 percent) to see discrimination as a major problem. But while a majority of those who identified as Democrats felt that increased discrimination had stemmed from the immigration debates (57 percent), those who identified as Republicans were significantly less likely (44 percent) to feel this way (Suro and Escobar 4, 6). These findings suggest some substantial, and continuing, divergence within the Latino population on the issues of "oppression and discrimination, racism and exploitation," with Cuban American Republicans not nearly as likely to see a significant problem.[11]

What is ultimately most interesting about the "Latino imaginary" is that it reflects not so much what Latinos collectively imagine about issues as what various commentators—both Latino and non-Latino (and perhaps mainstream society as a whole)—*imagine* that Latinos imagine about those issues. Especially in the wake of the 2004 presidential elections (in which Latinos, including non-Cubans, shifted toward Republican candidate George W. Bush in substantial numbers),[12] we cannot make generalizing statements about what Latinos as a whole imagine.[13] But the pervasive *critical construct* of a Left "Latino imaginary"—especially in literary studies—lingers.

Given that most prominent Cuban American writers today are in the United States as a product—direct or indirect—of Castro's socialist revolution, it is worth noting that, in the imaginary of non-Cuban Latino writers, that revolution has often been represented sympathetically (even, it might be noted, by those authors whom Flores views as assimilationist rather than oppositional). For example, in Dominican American author Julia Alvarez's second novel *In the Time of the Butterflies*, about the resistance movement in the Dominican Republic against dictator Rafael Trujillo, Castro's revolution provides inspiration to the movement (150).[14]

In Alvarez's fourth novel, *In the Name of Salomé*, which again takes up the themes of national commitment, resistance to oppression, and the building of a homeland, Camila Ureña, a Dominican American professor and the daughter of famed Dominican national poet Salomé Ureña, retires from Vassar College and goes to live in Cuba in 1960 so that she can be part of "patria" building during Castro's revolution. Castro is treated somewhat more ambivalently in this novel, with one of Camila's nieces arguing, years later, "I don't think Castro is the answer," and Camila responding, "It was wrong to think there was an answer in the first place, dear." She goes on to say, "It's continuing to struggle to create the country we dream of that makes a patria out of the land under our feet" (350). Yet if Castro is not the "answer," his revolution is still seen as part of the historical "struggle" for homeland. While on a return trip to the Dominican Republic late in her life, Camila encounters an illiterate Dominican boy working in a graveyard and thinks to herself, "In Cuba, he would know how to read. He would not be picking weeds on a schoolday" (352). Thus Camila—and Alvarez herself—credits the educational reforms of Castro's regime while also acknowledging its failures.

In contrast, the most vocal and visible strain of the Cuban exile population (led ideologically by Jorge Mas Canosa until his death in 1997, and, at least until recently, by the Cuban American National Foundation, which he founded) is vehemently anti-Communist and politically conservative, taking a stance of non-negotiation with regard to the evils of Castro's regime that seems increasingly anachronistic in today's post–cold war, post–Soviet Union world. (As I discuss in Chapter 4, a dominant Cuban exile narrative depicts Castro as the Satanic despoiler of the previously untroubled Cuban paradise. As of this writing, possible changes in the Cuban regime resulting from Castro's prolonged illness, as well as corresponding changes in Cuban exile discourse about the Cuban homeland, remain to be seen.) While most of the prominent U.S. writers of Cuban descent today are hardly as conservative as this vocal contingent of the Miami Cuban population, it is nevertheless still surely the case that there are very few outright fans of Castro's revolution among them. Thus their writings frequently can be seen to tentatively negotiate a precarious relationship with a larger body of Latino literature that has become identified in much literary criticism with left-wing and third world politics. In this chapter, I examine the ways in which Cuban American writers of various political sensibilities, including Margarita Engle, Elías Miguel Muñoz, Cristina García, Achy Obejas, Alisa Valdes-Rodriguez, and Ana Menéndez, imagine the possibilities of a pan-ethnic Latino/a (or Latin American) identity that might conceivably include Cuban Americans.

## Margarita Engle's *Skywriting* and *Singing to Cuba*

I begin my discussion of Cuban American writers with Margarita Engle,[15] not because her works are the first published, but because of all the writers discussed in this chapter she comes closest to representing the "typical" Cuban exile viewpoint of violent opposition to and demonization of Castro. Engle's reactionary views regarding Castro's regime, however, *co-exist* with what seem to be deliberate efforts to identify her writing as allied with indigenous, working-class, and peasant interests, as well as with Chicano and Latin American history and mythology—as we shall see.[16] Thus she proves a remarkably interesting case for exploring the dynamics of Latino/a (literary) identity construction.

Engle's use of symbolism would immediately seem to align her with conservative exile sensibilities: in her second novel, *Skywriting*, Castro is repeatedly represented as a "bearded demon" (266)—a quite literal demonization—and Cuba as "an island of fanged cannibals and one-eyed titans" (71). Pitted against these forces of evil is Camilo Peregrín, who tries to escape Castro's Cuba on a raft and is caught and imprisoned. The narrator, Camilo's Cuban American half-sister, Carmen—who is visiting Cuba when he tries to make his escape—imagines Camilo as being everywhere accompanied by an angel and as "climb[ing] onto the outstretched hand of God and [being] lifted to His shoulder" (6), thus creating a mythological opposition between the demonic Castro and the saintly Camilo.

How can such a viewpoint be reconciled with the progressive, oppositional, and generally Left-identifying paradigm of Latino literature (and, indeed, of Latino culture more generally)? For Engle, unlike Alvarez, nowhere recognizes possible gains—even limited ones—under socialist Cuban society.[17] I would suggest that Engle's novels, fitting as they do so uneasily with much other Latino/a writing—including writing emerging from the Chicano movement, which initially served to define the field—actually work very hard to insert themselves into a Latino/a literary terrain. In the process, they contribute to the continuing construction of Latino/a ethnicity as defined by the interests of the marginalized and oppressed, here and abroad. Mary S. Vásquez notes that "the ideological thrust of Engle's narrative approximates it to the Latin American novels of dictatorship" ("Contrapuntal" 138); this "family resemblance" serves a strategic function, even if it is ultimately misleading. In a move which potentially works to authorize her texts as U.S. Latina, Engle reinscribes anti-Castro Cuban conservatism as a revolutionary movement against a repressive Latin American dictator, in this way aligning it (and herself) with revolutionary politics in Central and South American countries that traditionally have seen themselves as affiliated with and inspired by Castro's revolutionary regime.[18] For one thing, Engle strews her novel with "fabulous" images and metaphors (such as the "bearded demon" Castro and his island of cannibals, or the angel Camilo who opposes him), giving it in the process a quite palpable magical realist texture that readers almost invariably associate with, and expect from, both Latin American and U.S. Latino/a literature, as I discuss in Chapter 5. The back cover of *Singing to Cuba* (1993), Engle's first novel, capitalizes on this connection, describing the book as a "lyrical novel told in the Latin American style of magical realism. The magic, but all too real paradox, is a Cuba where the splendor of natural beauty coexists with moral evil." *Skywriting*, too, is described as a "a hauntingly beautiful, magical story" in its promotional material.[19] As Mary Vásquez notes, Engle "calls upon the Latin American narrative tradition of magic realism to evoke betrayal of the Cuban people" ("Contrapuntal" 137). In Engle's hand, images of angels and devils, magic and myth—in other words, the appearance of what many commentators call "magical realism," that stock-in-trade marker of "Latino" writing—are called into the service of Castro's demonization.

Meanwhile, *Skywriting* positions itself as concerned with the hardships of Cuba's peasants under Castro. Camilo's mother, Marisol, recants her former support of Castro's revolution: "I thought the revolution would put shoes on the peasants' feet, food in their mouths. I didn't know it would shred the design of our lives, toss our scraps onto distant shores" (263). (Notably, however, this is the only point in *Skywriting* at which the economic motivations behind the 1959 revolution are addressed or even acknowledged.) Though one may question the telling differentiation between "peasants" and the pronoun "our" (perhaps implying that Marisol's original support was motivated by the hardships of the peasants while her withdrawal of support was spurred by more self-interested factors), such a deconstructive reading is clearly "against the grain" of the passage. The second sentence is obviously *supposed* to contradict the first—what Marisol "thought" about the benefits for peasants has somehow, the text suggests, been proven wrong. The novel, in other words, works to conceal the split between "the peasants'" interests and the interests of dissident Cubans of the middle and upper classes (although that split creeps insidiously back in) by suggesting that, in fact, the interests of the peasants themselves were not helped but hurt by the revolution (despite initial impressions).[20] This strategy is reinforced by the "epilogue" of sorts in *Skywriting* (purporting to be written in the year 2033), in which we learn that Camilo eventually gave testimony in Geneva which "was instrumental in triggering the process of thought that gradually altered international opinion regarding the Commander, who, until that time, had still been viewed by so many Third-World nations as a 'savior and culture-hero of mythic proportions'" (281).

Further establishing third world credibility, at several places in both novels Engle engages in a construction of a part "real," part metaphorical indigenous identity for Cuban dissidents and exiles; indeed, we can read her invocation of indigenousness as operating to affiliate her writing not only with the Latin American third world but also with Chicano/as within the United States, whose self-construction as a people has been strongly tied to a rediscovery and celebration of indigenous roots in opposition to the Spanish colonizers.[21] In *Singing to Cuba*, the (unnamed) narrator's great-uncle Gabriel, who was arrested and imprisoned by Castro and whose story is told in flashbacks interwoven with the more contemporary story of his Cuban American great-niece, is represented as having "a sprinkling of Taíno-blood" (50) and as being a repository of the history of the Cuban indigenous—a history which is set up as a parallel to the current situation of the Cuban peasants under Castro: "In Cuba there seemed to be only three choices, tyranny, rebellion or escape. Nothing had changed since the days of the *Conquistadores*, the slaughtered Indians" (53). Rather unsubtly, Gabriel's grandson is called "Taíno."

In *Skywriting* Carmen says of herself and her half-brother, Camilo, that "[w]e're like different primitive tribes" (194), metaphorically conjuring up an entire collective identity of indigenous peoples for each of these individual characters. But *Skywriting* also posits a historical (not just metaphorical) indigenous ancestry for the characters; in this novel, Engle creates an entire mythology of an indigenous past for Cuba's dissidents—despite the fact that the native inhabitants of Cuba were virtually if not actually annihilated. Camilo Peregrín has entrusted to Carmen the task of smuggling out of Cuba a mysterious package; it turns out that this package, representing their father's life's work, combines documentation of human rights abuses under Castro with an ancient manuscript written by an ancestor of the Peregríns and painstakingly translated by Carmen's father. The manuscript is supposedly the factual chronicle of this ancestor, Vicente Peregrín, a Spaniard who came to Cuba in flight from the Spanish Inquisition, married an indigenous Cuban woman, and thus became the progenitor of the entire clan of Peregríns.

On the one hand, this aspect of the narrative sets up a clear parallel between the family of Cuban dissidents and exiles and Chicanos: both are people born of a *mestizaje*. As with Mexican and Mexican American stories which recount as myth the union of Spanish colonizer Hernán Cortés and the indigenous woman Malinche, pinpointing there the origins of the Mexican people, the chronicle similarly recounts the seemingly mythical origins of a Cuban *mestizaje*; the Peregrín ancestor asks, "¿Have the others not sired half-native children? ¿Have they not married the beautiful daughters of the native *caciques* chieftains of this land, producing handsome red-hued children [. . .]? [. . .] Did Cortés himself not sire the Cuban Indian Catalina?" (124). Thus Vicente Peregrín, one of the forefathers of a "new" mixed race of Cubans, is linked to Hernán Cortés, forefather of the Mexican people—except that Vicente Peregrín is cast in a more positive ideological light, since (unlike Cortés) he is not a colonizer; rather, he is running from the institutional Spanish powers that are also responsible for the conquest of Cuba and the murder of its indigenous inhabitants.

Further, in echoes of the mythical Chicano homeland Aztlán, which has become associated with the actual geographical location of the U.S. Southwest but is also sometimes suggestive of the ultimate triumph, yet to come, of Chicanos, Engle posits the mythical land, "Antilia," corresponding geographically to Cuba but taking on mythical proportions as a refuge from oppression which Cuba has yet to become (154). The family name Peregrín, meaning "pilgrim," echoes this theme of a wandering people in search of a promised land: "The island seemed full of pilgrims, people wandering through cities and jungles, longing to go home. They were all seeking a promised land, had been seeking it for centuries, imagining triumph as a dream called home. And I was one of them" (239), the narrator tells us. Cuba's people, wandering in search of a homeland that they already physically occupy yet that is not available to them in its mythical form, thus become analogous to the Chicano descendants of ancient, migrating Aztec peoples, seeking to return to a homeland no longer fully available to them, even when they occupy it physically.

In this reconstruction of Cuban history, Castro's regime is a direct descendant of the Spanish Empire, with its intersecting policies of inquisition and colonization that have resulted in the "hanging of Sirena's cousins" (who are of course indigenous) "in groups of thirteen" (128). Accompanying the chronicle of Vicente is Carmen's father's "detailed analysis of attempts to control thought, a track of censorship from the Inquisition to the Commander" (88). We are told that Camilo's imprisonment is "a direct outgrowth of their poisonous Inquisition. [. . .] There was no difference [. . .] between the Holy Brotherhood and State Security, between informers who whispered into ears hidden beneath hoods, and those who whispered to the Neighborhood Committees for Defense of the Revolution" (165–66). In these constructed historical trajectories, the dissidents are the ideological equivalent (as well as the direct descendants) of Sirena's massacred indigenous cousins; Engle disassociates Castro from his public stance of resistance to foreign control (whether Spanish or U.S.) and aligns him instead with the oppressive force of the foreign invaders against the indigenous peoples of Cuba.

It is worth noting that, in constructing her elaborate analogy between Cuba's dissidents and exiles and Latin America's oppressed indigenous, Engle utterly obscures the real, predominant *mestizaje* in Cuba—that of the Spanish colonizers with the African slaves. As Vásquez observes in her discussion of *Singing to Cuba*, "Engle, who [. . .] celebrates indigenous Taíno Cubanness, offers little narrative treatment of the island's black population, or of black and mulatto experience"—a fact which, Vásquez notes, is surprising, considering that Engle writes about a "country half of whose inhabitants traditionally have been black" ("Contrapuntal" 136). A bit of mythological/metaphorical indigenous blood is apparently acceptable, but not the (actually far more likely) mulatto mixture. While the extinguished indigenous peoples of Cuba are put in the service of a constructed Cuban "mestizo" identity which shares the same interests with conservative Cuban exiles, Afro-Cubans are afforded no place in Engle's construction of ethnicity—indeed, are rendered all but invisible.[22] The absence in the novel of any significant Afro-Cuban presence attests to Engle's ultimate discomfort with the inclusion of Afro-Cuban heritage in her Cuban mythology.

One place in both texts where we *can* discern the traces of an Afro-Cuban presence is in Engle's repeated references to Santería, the syncretic Catholic/Yoruban religion whose particular elements are testimony to a history of resistance to Spanish/Catholic colonizers by African slaves[23]—surely providing rich fodder for metaphorical connections to "resistant" Cuban dissidents and exiles. Santería (much like Haitian Vodou) resulted from "the repressive imposition of the Catholic Church, which acknowledged no other religion," onto African slaves, who resisted by "syncretiz[ing] their divinities with the Catholic saints," thus continuing to practice their own beliefs under the "cover" of Catholicism (Barnet, "La Regla" 87). Yet, in Engle's texts, the historical and cultural roots of Santería are utterly obscured. In *Skywriting*, Santería comes up with reference to Carmen's mother, who "had entertained herself by collecting *santería* figurines and talismans from cults in the scattered slums surrounding Havana. [. . .] My mother dabbled in the realm of spirits. It was her fatal error. She had been initiated into *santero* rites [. . .]. She sacrificed animals and fed fruits and flowers into the mouths of statues. Then she met my father and swiftly traded idolatry for ideology, switching her blood rituals and occult Yoruba phrases for the memorized promises of the revolution" (249–50). Far from being represented as a legitimate religious belief system, Santería is "idolatry" (presumably because it detracts from the Christian God) and, as a "fatal error," is on a par with the sort of "ideology" that resulted in Castro's revolution. (Presumably, Cuban exiles opposed to Castro are ideology-free.)[24] Further, Santería worshippers are members of "cults" in "scattered slums," the racial factors influencing their lower-class status severely repressed (as are the novel's suddenly erupting classist sentiments with regard to Afro-Cubans).

In *Singing to Cuba* Engle goes even further, equating Santería explicitly with Satan worship, as when the narrator tells her cousin that "there are some [. . .] who believe Fidel received power through a contract with Satan." He responds, "Well, here there used to be some who thought that. They believed he had some sort of power through *santería*" (82). The narrator's cousin Miguelito, a credible character who serves as her "informant" on the Cuban situation, dismisses Santería as "the Cuban form of voodoo" (82). In context, this comparison evokes not the common syncretic origins of both belief systems, but, rather, the popular associations in the United States of "voodoo" with a form of "black magic." (Thus the cultural/historical roots of Vodou are also obscured.) In another comparison of Santería to "voodoo," the narrator notices a brown paper package left on the sidewalk with a chicken's beak sticking out of it, and another cousin tells her, "*Santería* [...]. We are afraid" (111). The narrator tells us that she does not know "whether she was referring to the voodoo-style curse, the secret police, the failing Cuban economy or the tense political situation" (111). Engle is presenting us not with alternatives here, but with metonymic substitutions in which any one thing is equatable with another and all are linked back to Castro; the "black magic" of Santería stands in for and is commensurate with the entire web of sociopolitical effects stemming from Castro's reign.

Engle's stance on Santería is, of course, quite telling. I would argue that, in spite of claims to a mythological indigenous history (which begins to look quite a bit like Piri's brother's claim to Indian blood as a way of denying black blood in *Down These Mean Streets*), Engle really presents no challenge to constructions of Cubanness as whiteness, particularly by the first wave of Cuban exiles, consisting primarily of upper- and middle-class white Cubans. As I discuss in Chapter 4, Cuban exiles' assertions of whiteness (in opposition to blackness specifically, rather than to some sort of nebulous indigenousness) were intimately linked to an anti-Communist, anti-Castro stance. Apparently, it is far less threatening for Engle to associate anti-Castro Cuban exiles with an extinct Cuban indigenous population than with a thriving and influential Afro-Cuban population. But in rejecting Santería, Engle reveals just how wide is the gulf between her and writers such as Gloria Anzaldúa and Sandra Cisneros, who embrace the complex, cross-pollinated religious/spiritual structures that hybridity affords them.

Toward the conclusion of *Skywriting*, the narrator, Carmen, ruminates on the birth of her political consciousness: "I was nearsighted. I had a hard time seeing anyone who wasn't standing right in front of me. I wouldn't be the type to go digging up human rights violations for investigation, or fighting in a jungle because I hoped that someday the children of strangers might receive shoes. The violations and bare feet would have to slap me in the face and shake me before I would notice them" (246). This passage hints at the difficulties Engle faces in fitting a strident anti-Castro sensibility into the dominant critical construction of U.S. Latino/a ethnicity. Carmen seems here to acknowledge her relative indifference to the struggles in other Latin American countries and her inability to "identify" with their refugees. Yet the passage continues to work in the service of Engle's reconstruction of ethnicity by depicting human rights violations and "bare feet" as the same fight; thus there is really no difference between Engle's *Skywriting* and, say, Tomás Rivera's . . . *Y no se lo tragó la tierra*, which documents the poverty-stricken and economically exploitative conditions of Chicano migrant farmworkers. Such an equation obscures the complexity of Castro's regime, in which serious human rights abuses have existed *side by side* with the successful implementation of measures to ensure increased education, health care, affordable housing, and other opportunities for Cuba's poor. Ultimately, I would argue, Engle's reinscription of anti-Castro sentiment as an indigenously rooted, peasant-oriented movement, conveyed through a weave of references and analogies and a magical realist "flavor" that will remind us, presumably, of other Latin American and U.S. Latina/o texts, rings false precisely because it seems to quite actively suppress or elide significant histories of oppressed peoples in Cuba.[25] For solidarity claims to be effective and convincing, they must be grounded in an acknowledgment of the *specificity* of different histories (a point I will return to in my discussion of Ana Menéndez in this chapter, and in Chapter 7.)

### Elías Miguel Muñoz's *The Greatest Performance*

Given the problems with a constructed Latino imaginary that Engle's novels reveal, we may well view *The Greatest Performance* (1991), by Elías Miguel Muñoz, as the opposite extreme in terms of its negotiation with a collective identity. One of the very first U.S. "Latino" novels (the irony in my use of the term here is intentional) to address the notion of such an identity in any significant fashion, *The Greatest Performance* seems to undermine this concept at every level, suggesting that it is in fact a largely illusory product of a homogenizing American mainstream perspective in which "the diverse Latino cultures are interchangeable" (Poey and Suárez xvi). Ultimately, any notion of panethnic Latino identity is simply deflated as a stereotype of U.S. culture; the problematics of the Cuban American relationship to the Latino imaginary are thus skirted by a repudiation of the imaginary itself.

*The Greatest Performance* is told in the alternating voices of two gay Cuban Americans, a man and a woman, who come to the United States with their families in their teens. As Karen Christian has persuasively argued, this novel's central theme is the uneasy relationship between the protagonists' transgressive sexual identities and the traditional, conservative models of gender encoded in the transmission of Cuban culture. Nonetheless, the Cuban narrators' contacts and sometimes confrontations with Latinos of other national origins form a recurrent backdrop for the novel's most pressing concerns; in fact, it might be said that their encounters with a larger "Latino" population (not to say "community") are one of the most salient aspects of their lives in the United States. It is Rosa's U.S. context—and, specifically, a majority Anglo-American population ("the blonde-boy type with T-shirts and pestilent tennis shoes predominated")—that thrusts her into a panethnic "Latino" community in high school: "My GSH [Garden Shore High] gang: The Colombian Leticia [. . .] The Korean boy, Ramón (the name the Gauchos gave him) [. . .] Marco the

Ecuadorian [. . .] Luisita the Cuban [. . .] Of all of them, I miss Francisco the most. Francisco El Mexicano" (85). The passage gestures toward the specific conditions under which *this* particular, local community gets formed (that is, in opposition to a "blonde-boy" majority). The inclusion of a Korean in the "Latin clique" (86)—"Through a dirty trick of fate they had ended up first in Argentina and then in 'America,' so they spoke fluent Spanish with a Tango accent" (85)—destabilizes, if only momentarily, the illusion of a group somehow naturally or essentially connected. So does Rosa's recollection of "Francisco El Mexicano": "Since I couldn't speak English, the school authorities 'assigned' me to this Mexican guy, Francisco Valdés, from day one of my freshman year. [. . .] I was told that he would help me with my classes and serve as my guide, until I felt ready to fend for myself. Whatever grades Francisco got (all of them Bs), I'd get, they informed me" (85). The leap from the innocuous premise that one Spanish-speaking student might help another to acclimatize, to the ridiculous requirement that, in effect, a Mexican must share his identity with the Cuban, parodies the automatic equation of the two groups. Literally, here, they are rendered "all the same." In Harlem, Mario—the novel's other narrator—is mistaken for Puerto Rican because "I have a suntan and I'm wearing shorts" (another jab at the ascription of sameness); he responds, "No, I'm from another island" (97).

Even Rosa falls prey to the illusion of sameness, commenting of her high school years, "My only source of happiness was the trips Mami and I took to downtown Los Angeles on Sundays to see old movies from Mexico at the Million Dollar Theatre. In that theatre that reeked of urine, I rediscovered, in ecstasy, handfuls of Mexican melodramas that took me right back to Cuba. Incredible, huh, that those dime-store stories and slapsticks [. . .] would make me long for Cuba. But they did" (84). On the surface, the identification of movies from Mexico with her Cuban past would seem to support the homogenizing tendencies of the U.S. mainstream. How could Mexican movies transport Rosa back to Cuba? It is precisely such a skeptical posture that is self-consciously conveyed in her commentary that her reaction is "incredible." Rosa's correlation of Mexican movies with her Cuban past is something that happens only in her current U.S. context, where they become associated for her with a distant Cuban childhood. (The American-made films she must surely also have seen in her childhood cannot hold the same associative power in this context.)[26] In another context (in Cuba, for example), the easy equation of Mexico with Cuba would have been unthinkable. And even in the United States, Rosa does not mistake Mexican food for Cuban food; she recalls that she "tried my first burrito and my first taco with Francisco," the Mexican American high-school friend. As she recounts, "He used to tell me that Mexican cuisine was the most varied and flavorful in the whole world." But Rosa disagrees: "[C]orn tortillas smelled of bats. No, I had never seen a bat, but if I had, and if bats possessed a particular smell, it would definitely be the same smell as the tortillas" (86). Food is always a prominent and telling marker of ethnic identity (even if it is a *constructed* marker), so it is notable that Rosa feels no connection to Mexican food.

Allusion to the role that media and marketing have played in the creation of a sense of (pan-) Latino identity is made via Rosa's lover, Joan, who creates TV commercials to reach "the Hispanic consumer" (which suggests, of course, that this consumer is singular in tastes, attitudes, and culture) and whose "biggest client" is the "Spanish American Programming Network"(114–15). Silvio Torres-Saillant has written precisely about the reliance of Spanish-language media outlets such as Univisión and Telemundo on the generation of a singular "Hispanic" identity that erases national difference: "Media executives have a huge stake in ensuring that U.S. Hispanics see themselves as one, for these executives can use their power over the community's perceptions and opinions as a bargaining tool in their competition with their corporate counterparts" (447). (Indeed, roughly a decade after the publication of *The Greatest Performance*, according to Torres-Saillant, Univisión conducted a "well-orchestrated publicity campaign that sings the praises of our common *hispanidad*. [. . .] [The campaign] insistently dwells on the language, the culture, and the traditions that make us *una sola familia*" [444–45].) The notion of Hispanic ethnicity—if it is not exclusively an Anglo construction (and it is surely worth noting that Joan is a "Gringa" [116])—is certainly "made in the U.S.A.," with all the emphasis on commodification and consumerism that this label implies.

Belying the idea of a singular Hispanic ethnicity that is touted by "targeted" marketing, at one point Rosa expresses her antagonism toward her department chair at the university where she teaches by repeatedly slurring his Argentine origins: he is the "Gaucho oppressor" and the "Padrino Argentino" (91). In this case, personal and professional conflicts become translated into the terms of ethnic conflict; far from giving rise to a sense of "Latino" solidarity, the U.S. context in this instance actually magnifies a sense of difference and distance. Interestingly, the Argentine professor later becomes reconfigured, in a sort of parodic fantasy by Mario (the male narrator) and Rosa, as a generalized "Latin American Dictator" with a striking resemblance to Fidel Castro. In the narrative they collaboratively spin about him, he "was a self-proclaimed socialist-humanist who stood up for the underdogs" and "the only one valiant enough to challenge the powerful Gringo chairman at departmental meetings, denouncing his dictatorial ways, his lack of democratic decency" (109), surely a spin on Castro's challenge to U.S. domination and on the prior Cuban dictator, Fulgencio Batista, who did the bidding of U.S. corporations. (This narrative, it might be added, recognizes the power of Castro's appeal in a way that Engle's writings do not.) But "[b]ehind the humanitarian Gaucho stood a despot and a power-hungry monster" who took power when the "Gringo" chairman retired, and "[h]istory [repeated] itself" with a new oppressor (110). In this instance, the "Gaucho" is rewritten into a Cuban script with which Mario and Rosa are familiar. Unlike with Engle, however, the generalized Latin American dictator script is not to be taken seriously; the source of the humor is the *conflation* of contexts. The narrative insistently reminds us that Mario and Rosa are Cuban exiles, even while their own language repeatedly tags the Argentine with his different national background.

Elsewhere in the novel, the tensions between Puerto Ricans and Cubans within the U.S. context are raised in yet another debunking of a single, collective Latino identity. Of Mario's Nuyorican lover, whose friends are *"Independentistas,"* Mario wonders, "Does he really not mind the fact that I'm a Cuban worm, a traitor to the Revolution?" (99)—gesturing to the, at times, diametrically opposed political allegiances of various segments of the "Latino" population. Interestingly, however, this difference turns out not to be a particular source of conflict within the relationship: *"Cubano,* eh?" the Nuyorican asks Mario. "'Yes.' 'Good for you'" (100). At that point, the thorny issue of political differences is quickly dropped. If *The Greatest Performance* does not make any kind of a case for inclusion in a larger Latino whole—indeed, it actively undermines the notion of such a whole—it also does not choose to elaborate on the ideological differences which might distinguish Cubans, in particular, from a leftist Latino imaginary.

## Cristina García's *Dreaming in Cuban*

In García's novel *Dreaming in Cuban* (1992), perhaps the best-known work to date by a Cuban American who is the product of exile from Castro's regime, the Cuban family is itself riven by ideological cleavages. Because García's novel has received by far the most critical commentary of any of the works I discuss in this chapter[27]—and because that commentary so often focuses precisely on the political divisions that score through the novel's family—I will only briefly here suggest the ways in which the novel's politics position it quite comfortably within the "canon" of U.S. Latino/a literature. In Cuba the family matriarch, Celia, is a staunch defender of Castro while one of her daughters, Felicia, is at best apathetic about the revolution. In the United States, Celia's other daughter, Lourdes, has become the typical radically conservative Cuban exile while her daughter, Pilar, a fan of punk music and with obviously Left-leaning sympathies, longs to return to Cuba. Each of these four main characters (as well as a handful of others) takes turns narrating her own story. Though this multivocality gives *Dreaming in Cuban* the appearance of being politically "neutral"[28]—reportedly resulting in conflicts with the adamantly anti-Castro Miami Cuban contingent[29]—the novel actually, I would argue, is propelled by an underlying progressive vision against which the various positions on Castro are measured. García presents a nuanced portrayal of Castro's revolution as addressing certain problems (for example, those of extreme poverty) while remaining seriously flawed according to other liberal/progressive criteria (e.g., with regard to civil liberties).

Indeed, by far the most negative portrayal in the novel is not of Castro but of Lourdes, the rabidly anti-Castro exile who places absolute faith in the power of American capitalism. When she returns to Cuba with her daughter, Pilar, she shouts to Cubans on the street, "*Oye!* [. . .] You could have Cadillacs with leather interiors! Air conditioning! Automatic windows! You wouldn't have to move your arms in the heat!" (221). Lourdes is, notably, a compulsive overeater in the bakery that she owns, linking her capitalist entrepreneurship with a dysfunctional drive toward consumption (27). García makes a point of underscoring Lourdes's lack of third world sympathies; as Pilar tells us, "She hires the real down-and-outs, immigrants from Russia or Pakistan, people who don't speak any English, figuring she can get them cheap. Then she screams at them half the day because they don't understand what she's saying" (31–32). Lourdes fires a new Puerto Rican employee whom she catches pocketing fifty cents and afterwards thinks to herself, "No wonder her son is a delinquent" (129). And she justifies herself against Pilar's accusations of bigotry by noting, "'I don't make up the statistics. [. . .] I don't color the faces down at the precinct.' Black faces, Puerto Rican faces" (128). Clearly, Lourdes feels no group affinity with the "Puerto Rican" faces equated, in her mind, with crime statistics.

But the novel as a whole makes that perspective an object of criticism, thus potentially positioning it within the group identity that Lourdes rejects. Indeed, Raphael Dalleo has suggested, intriguingly, that certain aspects of the novel "position *Dreaming in Cuban* as intertextual descendent to Sandra Cisneros' *The House on Mango Street*, a canonical text in its own right for the Latina literary tradition in the United States" (11), and that its "textual strategies [therefore] offer a relational poetics that emphasizes Latina writing as 'pan-ethnic' [. . .]: not reliant on genealogy as bloodlines, but as part of the cultural creation that helps forge a common identity" (16).[30]

Lourdes's rebellious daughter, Pilar, is the heart of the novel and, arguably, articulates the closest thing to García's own viewpoint. (It is perhaps not a coincidence that García's own daughter is named Pilar.) Early in the novel, Pilar's perspective is characterized by her reaction against her Cuban exile mother's sensibility. (Thus, for example, she gives Lourdes "a book of essays on Cuba called *A Revolutionary Society*" in which "[t]he cover showed cheerful, clean-cut children gathered in front of a portrait of Che Guevara" [132].) But Pilar's narratives within the novel constitute a sort of mini-bildungsroman, in which her own views must be tempered as she matures. By the time she arrives in Cuba for a visit, she realizes that the island is incompatible with her own "revolutionary" affinities:

> I think about how I'm probably the only ex-punk on the island, how no one else has their ears pierced in three places. [. . .] I ask Abuela if I can paint whatever I want in Cuba and she says yes, as long as I don't attack the state. Cuba is still developing, she tells me, and can't afford the luxury of dissent. Then she quotes me something El Líder said in the early years, before they started arresting poets. "Within the revolution, everything; against the revolution, nothing." I wonder what El Líder would think of my paintings. Art, I'd tell him, is the ultimate revolution. (235)

Coming fewer than ten pages from the novel's close, and articulated by its most sympathetic character at her point of greatest maturity, this is perhaps the novel's strongest critique of Castro's regime. Yet it is notable that the criticism is put in terms of that regime's distance from a "truly" revolutionary, radical spirit. Thus García is able to critique Castro while positioning herself within the constructed boundaries of literary Latino/a ethnicity.

## Achy Obejas's *Memory Mambo* and "We Came All the Way from Cuba"

Achy Obejas adopts a similar strategy for negotiating the terrain between Castro's Cuba and Latino/a ethnic identity in her well-received and poignant short story "We Came All the Way from Cuba So You Could Dress Like This?" from the collection of the same name. Once again, the central character is a child of Cuban exiles who rebels against the conservative exile perspective (this time embodied in the father rather than the mother). When she returns home on a visit from college and her father barrages her with the title's question, she strikes back: "Look, you didn't come for me, you came for you; you came because all your rich clients were leaving, and you were going to wind up a cashier in your father's hardware store if you didn't leave, okay?" (121), thus poking a hole in the rhetoric of escape from Communist oppression to reveal the economic (rather than political) motivations that have, arguably, been the real basis of much Cuban emigration.

But this narrator, like Pilar, has something to learn. As she discovers and explores her lesbian sexuality, the question "What if we'd stayed? What if we'd never left Cuba?" (124) takes on new resonance, as the narrator must consider the question in light of Castro's repressive policies toward gays and lesbians. That is, although the short story does not unambiguously support Castro's revolution, it still obviously aligns itself with leftist politics in other ways.

Obejas's 1996 novel *Memory Mambo* extends this consideration of *alternative* understandings of "Left" Latino identities. In this novel radical queer politics are represented as coexisting uneasily with and at times even contradicting other forms of radical politics (e.g., those identifying with the third world), pointing to an exploration of the ways in which multiple subject positions contest the cohesiveness of an imagined Latino/a ethnicity. This tension is, arguably, present, if latent, in *The Greatest Performance* as well, although in that earlier novel the main chafing is between the Cuban gay and lesbian characters and their traditional Cuban culture (and its importation into the United States), rather than between different notions of "radical" or nonhegemonic ideologies. *Memory Mambo* also elaborates, at much greater length than *The Greatest Performance*, on the conflict between Cuban *gusanos* (or "worms") and Puerto Rican *independentistas*.

Obejas's first novel is notable for its striking self-reflexiveness about the constructed and tentative (rather than essential) nature of Latino/a ethnicity; *Memory Mambo* "presupposes that interactions between Latino sectors are inevitable" in a U.S. context (Allatson 191), if fraught with difficulty. The Cuban narrator, Juani's, Puerto Rican lover, Gina, represents, on the one hand, the effort to construct an apparently coherent Latino identity that is identifiably leftist. When Juani first enters her apartment she notes,

> Gina's apartment struck me as a museum dedicated to Puerto Rican independence and Latin American liberation movements. There were posters of Albizu Campos [. . .]. Over her desk in the dining room I noticed a picture of Harry Truman outlined in a bull's eye, a macabre allusion to the 1948 attempt on his life by Puerto Rican *independentistas*, martyred when most of them ended up spending the rest of their lives in jail.
> 
> There were, of course, lots of tributes to the Sandinistas in Nicaragua—a signed photograph of President Daniel Ortega as if he were a rock star [. . .]. Posters commemorated celebrations of the fifth and tenth anniversaries of the Sandinista triumph [. . .]. Scattered on different walls were photos or drawings of César Chávez, Angela Davis, Frida Kahlo [. . .] and Ché Guevara.
> 
> Eventually, I came upon the one hero I knew Gina's museum couldn't exist without: Fidel Castro. (86)

At the same time, Gina is, paradoxically, also the focal point for the tension surrounding the uneasy relationship of Cuban exiles to other U.S. Latino/a groups. She accuses Cubans of being "racists and classists and [says] that we only made fun of Puerto Ricans because most of them were darker and poorer than us" (122)—thereby dramatically highlighting the intersection of race and class with ethnic identity in a way that underscores the schisms within the (supposedly unified) Latino "body."[31]

Obejas turns an unflinching light on such antagonisms and their economic and racial base; Juani herself recalls (with disapproval) a joke told by one of her relatives: "What's the difference between a Cuban and a Puerto Rican? A Cuban's a Puerto Rican *with a job*" (122; emphasis in original).[32] The joke calls on the assumption of identity (a Cuban *is* a Puerto Rican, but with a difference), only to radically unsettle that assumption through a claim that calls attention to the potentially competing interests and economic status (within a U.S. context) of the two groups. At the same time, this broad-strokes picture of the relative demographics of Cuban versus Puerto Rican populations in the United States serves, for Gina at least, to obscure the actual demographics of Juani's family, which left Cuba in 1978 (well after the so-called first wave of relatively privileged Cubans who fled in the immediate aftermath of Castro's revolution); in the United States, rather than working in the "professions," Juani's family owns and runs a Laundromat.[33] These distinctions, however, are lost on Gina (as, indeed, they are willfully glossed over by Juani's relatives themselves), who "articulates one result of the ways that the United States has played Cubans against Puerto Ricans" (McCullough 593).[34]

While in some circumstances the U.S. context might make for panethnic alliances that might not otherwise exist, in others it might be precisely the relocation in the United States—enabling, for example, anti-Castro Cuban exiles to confront Puerto Rican *independentistas* in close quarters—that would exacerbate antagonisms. Obejas herself has commented, "I think that in the States the tension [between Puerto Ricans and Cubans] gets underscored because of racism here and a perception by both groups that the other group has it better. There is no question that Puerto Ricans in the United States have privileges that other Latinos do not have. They're US citizens at birth. There's also no question that Cubans have received extraordinary amounts of aid compared to other immigrant groups" (Kleindienst 14).[35] Although an oft-repeated line of argument regarding the U.S. formation of Latino identity suggests that the confrontation with a discriminatory Anglo culture can contribute to a sense of cohesiveness and solidarity among Latino immigrants and their descendants, Juani's explanation (during a particularly raw argument with Gina) that "[t]he gulf between us was wider than the ninety miles from Havana to Miami" (131–32) suggests the opposite: in this moment, the antagonistic relationship between these Latinas of differing national origin is actually *greater* than the Anglo-Hispanic "gulf" figured by the ninety miles between the United States and Cuba and, indeed, might be largely provoked (as Obejas's comments suggest) by their close proximity yet different treatment in a U.S. context. The point is made even more forceful because the illusion of sameness attaches even more strongly to those of Spanish-Caribbean origin than it does across the different Latino groups in general (see Flores, "Islands and Enclaves"). (Indeed, the fact that both Juani and Gina are women overlays still another category of identity, with its essentializing illusions of sameness, on their conflict—in order to radically undermine all such totalizing illusions.)

Perhaps the conflict is all the more striking because Juani, who was brought to the United States as a child by her parents, hardly shares their conservative politics. The older generation of Cuban exiles—those who immigrated to the United States as adults—is portrayed in particularly unflattering terms in the novel for its rejection of any affinity with other, more marginalized, Latino identities. Juani recalls of a family wedding that

> Mario Varona, a young fellow of Cuban and Puerto Rican heritage, was hired to play guitar and sing Cuban songs during the ceremony. My mother, however, was not pleased with Mario's hiring.
>
> "Now every picture of the wedding is going to have a Negro in it," she said, rolling her eyes. (69)

But while Juani (who is, like García's Pilar in *Dreaming in Cuban*, the second-generation product of exile) rejects the elitism, racism, and classism of her parents' generation, Juani is herself struggling with the possibility of any kind of group identity with non-Cuban Latino/as in the United States

Indeed, as Kate McCullough points out, Juani's narration can be read as an effort to elide the importance of distinctions between Cubans and Puerto Ricans in the service of her love affair with Gina. In Juani's "romantically self-serving vision" (McCullough 597), she imagines Gina as "hills in which I would roll around, happy and dirty, as if I were back in Cuba, or perhaps in Puerto Rico" (119); McCullough correctly observes that this construct "problematically collaps[es] Cuba and Puerto Rico" (597) and removes the love affair from the realm of politics where differences matter: "Juani obsessively turns to narration to [. . .] depoliticize love, desire, and sexuality [. . . ,] casting them as separate from, as an escape from, and even, at points, as an antidote to political conflicts" (577).

Since the notion of undifferentiated *latinidad* is conveyed in the novel through Juani's romantic narratives, both those narratives and *latinidad* itself are ultimately deflated as fantasy. For *Memory Mambo* as a whole undermines Juani's depoliticizing romantic project and unravels her hopeful narrative of oneness. Though Juani might indeed want to turn a blind eye to difference (at least where Gina is concerned), she is not permitted to do so.

This issue is highlighted in a confrontation between Juani and one of her lover's Puerto Rican nationalist *independentista* friends, who starts the exchange by asking if she's "a good Cuban or a bad Cuban" (127), calls her a "Gusana" (127), and mocks her for preferring to identify herself as *"Cuban-American"* (128; emphasis in original), which the friend sees as assimilationist. Though Allatson calls the Puerto Rican activists in the novel Juani's "constructed family" and treats them as overlapping with other, more explicitly familial, groupings—her cousins, her immediate relatives, and "the web of relations by marriage" (163)—there is, strikingly, *no filiative* language used with reference to the *independentistas*, who, in this scene as in others, clearly see Juani as having no relation to them. Later in the evening,

> Gina and her friends began reminiscing about their trips to Cuba, about helping on sugar-cane cutting brigades, and hearing Fidel speak at the Plaza of the Revolution for hours on end while they ate ice cream and leaned on each other. They found it all inspirational, a blue-print for what they envisioned for Puerto Rico. [. . .] At her first opportunity, [Hilda] started telling me about the importance of the Cuban revolution (as if I, a Cuban, didn't know), and what it meant to Puerto Rican independence, and how throwing off *yanqui* imperialism was the right thing to do. (129–30)

Even though Gina and her friends seem here to be making connections between the Cuban and the Puerto Rican situation, Juani is excluded—by politics—from the envisioned group identity. And although Juani does not identify with the conservative politics of the Cuban exiles, she is obviously skeptical of the sort of Castro glamorization undertaken by the Puerto Rican *independentistas*.

Latino collective identity, as I have discussed, has been imagined as leftist, progressive, and even radical by a plethora of scholars. Yet, although this novel utterly undermines the illusion of a cohesive, singular "Latino/a" identity, it is far from certain who has the greater claim to radical politics. For while Juani is certainly more cautious than her Puerto Rican counterparts about embracing Castro's socialist revolution, her affinity with queer politics gives her a different route for potentially claiming a progressive identity. In a later scene, Juani meets Bernie, her sister's boyfriend, who turns out to be the son of Amparo Maure, a famous (fictional) Puerto Rican *independentista* woman poet with whose work Juani is familiar. During the conversation it is revealed that Bernie's mother is also a lesbian—at which news Juani notes that, "much as Gina and her *independentista* pals yakked up Amparo Maure, they'd never mentioned a word to me about her sexuality." Bernie responds, "Yeah, well, the *independentista* movement doesn't do well with lesbian and gay issues. [. . .] They're in solidarity with everybody but gay people. [. . .] [T]hey're not *anti*-gay per se, they just think homosexuality's a product of capitalist society" (171; emphasis in original). As Bernie goes on to elaborate, the assumption within *independentista* culture is that once capitalism is corrected by "the revolution," homosexuality will end. The implication, then, is that both capitalism and queerness are problems that need to be corrected.

Gina (who is in the closet) dismisses issues of sexual identity as not of primary concern to her radical politics:

> "Look, I'm not interested in being a *lesbian*, in separating politically from my people [. . .]. What are we talking about? Issues of *sexual identity*? While Puerto Rico is a colony? While Puerto Rican apologists are trying to ram statehood down our throats with legislative tricks and sleights of hand? You think I'm going to sit around and discuss *sexual identity*? Nah, Juani, you can do that—you can have that navel-gazing discussion."
>
> And though she never quite said it, I felt the sting: I knew part of the reason why I was pinned with this topic [was] because I'm Cuban, and in Gina's eyes, automatically more privileged [. . .].
>
> "That's so white, this whole business of *sexual identity*," she'd say [. . .]. "But you Cubans, you think you're white. . ." (77–78; last ellipses in Obejas).

Gina's comments collapse sexual identity, race, and class under the category of national origin; being "out" as a lesbian is a white, privileged, and, above all (somehow), a "Cuban" thing to do. But the novel itself is foregrounding how competing claims to radical politics stem from different subject positions. Gina privileges national identity to the point that it subsumes all others; Juani, on the other hand, prioritizes her lesbianism. But while Gina (echoing a long trajectory of literary scholars) delineates Latino/a identity primarily in terms of third world politics, preeminent Chicana texts such as Gloria Anzaldúa's *Borderlands/La Frontera*, Cherríe Moraga's *Loving in the War Years*, and Carla Trujillo's anthology *Chicana Lesbians* have put queer identities and issues at the very center of Latina literary issues. The conflict between queer politics and *independentista* affinities in *Memory Mambo* thus dramatizes a struggle over the heart of "Latino/a" identity—over who or what will define its symbolic elements (or whether, indeed, any *singular* definition will hold). As Lourdes Torres has written,

> women of color are themselves theorizing their experience in radical and innovative terms. Their condition as women, as people of color, as working-class members, and in some cases as lesbians, has led them to reject [. . .] theories [. . .] which have failed to develop an integrated analysis sensitive to the simultaneous oppression that women of color

experience. Rather, third world women are making connections between the forces of domination which affect their lives daily and are actively participating in the creation of a movement committed to radical social and political transformation *at all levels*. (275; emphasis added)

The narrator, Juani, certainly seems excluded from the third world Latina identity of the *independentistas*, characterized by its solidarity with Latin American revolutionary movements; but any reader well versed in the body of Chicana writing since the 1980s will note how far the *independentista* characters are from the sort of third world women's solidarity imagined by writers like Anzaldúa and Moraga in their groundbreaking *This Bridge Called My Back* (1981)—a solidarity based in large part on a recognition of what Adrienne Rich once called "compulsory heterosexuality."[36]

As the foregoing discussion suggests, Obejas's novel reveals the tensions inherent in the construction of Latino/a ethnicity, which threaten to violently rend its constituent parts, always at best only tentatively connected, from each other. The potential violence of the moment at which the fissures cleaving "Latina" identity become chasms is conveyed suggestively in the abusive physical battle between Juani and Gina, which lies at the heart of the novel. The internal pressure of widely disparate histories and ideologies becomes focused in Juani and Gina's relationship, building to an unbearable pitch until the relationship explodes from the inside out.[37] After the hostile discussion between Juani and her lover, Gina's, *independentista* friends (discussed earlier), and after those friends have gone home, Juani and Gina have another conversation on the topic. Juani asks Gina if she shares her friends' condemnation of Cuban exiles for having left Cuba:

> "So I'm a *baaaaaaaad* Cuban?" I asked, trying to keep it light.
> Gina shrugged. "It's a bad joke," she admitted. "It's what a lot of people call Cuban exiles."
> "Do you agree with Hilda?" I asked. "Do you really think I'm a *gusana*?" (132)

For Juani, "*gusana*" is a pejorative term which makes clear the ideological fault lines that separate Cuban exiles—even second-generation Cuban exiles like Juani, critical of their parents' conservatism yet uncertain about Castro—from Puerto Rican *independentistas*. Gina understands and acknowledges Juani's emotional reaction to the term, yet she attempts to smooth things over by calling Juani her "*gusanita*" (little worm) (132, 134), using the term as one of endearment. The burden placed on the word "*gusana*" by Gina, in other words, is to represent the ideological differences which separate them and at the same time to bridge those differences using affection. As Allatson notes, Juani "is constantly decoding Gina's conversation for [just such] signs that ideological enmities will not [...] destroy their romance" (189).

But in this moment, Juani herself discovers that the term *"gusanita"* simply can no longer bear that heavy ideological burden; romance is always inflected by history.[38] Juani smashes her fist into Gina's face, resulting in a scene of horrifying physical abuse on both sides that shatters Juani's "vision of love as a merger that is outside time and that erases difference" (McCullough 596).[39] At this point Juani resorts to describing the scene in impressionistic and poetic terms: "All of the blood pours savagely from my limbs, all of my limbs are severed" (135).[40] What is particularly notable about this description is that it works *only* on a metaphorical level; it is not the literal case, of course, that Juani's "limbs" are severed, so limbs—conceived as extensions of her "self"—must stand for something else. If, as George J. Sánchez writes, the "multiracial body has been appropriated [in popular as well as academic discourse] for use as a symbol of multiethnic America, often representing the nation's hope for the future and its potential for overcoming racial strife" (as opposed, Sánchez notes, to the figure of the "tragic mulatto" overcome by an internal warfare of conflicting black and white blood) (50), then we may perhaps read Juani's severed limbs as conveying the failure of a Latina multiethnic (or panethnic) body to overcome ethnic "strife." The rending of any illusion of coherent Latino identity is graphically mirrored in the image of a body's brutal dismemberment. Even leftist politics, it turns out, cannot guarantee a collective identity; the ethnic "body" is left irreconcilably torn.

## Alisa Valdes-Rodriguez's *The Dirty Girls Social Club*

Once again, we can discern an almost diametrically opposite dynamic at work in *The Dirty Girls Social Club* (2003), by Alisa Valdes-Rodriguez, which begins with a dramatic exposé of the differences and even schisms which cleave the category "Latino" into utterly dissimilar parts—in spite of mainstream culture's homogenizing stereotypes—and ends with a reinscribed fantasy of underlying commonality. *The Dirty Girls Social Club* places itself firmly in the realm of "popular culture"—Whitney Otto (author of the critically acclaimed *How to Make an American Quilt*) is quoted on the book cover as calling the novel a "guilty pleasure" that "ranks somewhere between Valrhona chocolate and Jimmy Choo shoes"—but popular culture is also the target which the novel takes to task for its oversimplifications, stereotypes, and downright prejudices. The opening of the novel explicitly fractures the notion of Latino identity into its various and diverse constituent parts; the effect of this critique, however, is to elide the ways in which the Cuban difference might be a more significant obstacle to imagined collectivity than are other forms of difference. As in *The*

*Greatest Performance*, a by-product of the dismantling of the category "Latino" is that all differences are equalized; the lingering impression is that there is no more troubling relationship between, say, Cuban Americans and Chicanas than there is between Chicanas and Puerto Ricans.[41]

The critique of ethnic construction is undertaken by Lauren, one of the alternating narrators. Lauren (whose father is Cuban), opens the novel with an informal "lesson" on being Latino/a for her, presumably, uninitiated readers. She assumes that they probably share the same stereotyped, conglomerate construct of Latinoness as the editors who have hired her to write a column "to connect to the Latina people" (8). Lauren's editors, we are told—in a metafictional scolding of the reader, as well—"expect me to reach up and pick mangoes out of the fruit basket I must wear on my head whenever I'm not in the newsroom talking about, you know, Mexican *jumping* beans" (11). The target of Valdes-Rodriguez's humor here is not only the essentializing "spicy Carmen Miranda" (7) image that has become the stereotype of a Latina woman, "thanks to TV and Hollywood" (5), it is also the unthinking equation of mangoes (a Caribbean fruit) with Mexican jumping beans—of Cubans with Mexicans. As Lauren snidely comments after one of her editors—granting her automatic "authority" in the knowledge of all things Latino/a—asks her where she can buy Mexican jumping beans: "even if I *were* a Mexican-American [. . .] I wouldn't have known something that stupid" (5).

Amber, the member of the novel's group of friends who has apparently rediscovered her Aztec roots, is also the character who most participates in this cross-cultural homogenizing of Latino/a identity: "she thinks all Latinas are just like *her*" (10). Once again, ethnic difference is conveyed through differences in cuisine. It is revealing that Lauren has to explain to Amber what *tostones* are—in terms that Amber, as a Mexican American, will understand: "Refried plantains." As Lauren elaborates to her reader, Amber "thinks we all eat the same dishes *she* grew up eating [. . .]. She thinks all Latinas give a rat's rear about *menudo*, a soup they *voluntarily* make with tripe, a line of little Mexican ladies rinsing corpse poop out of the pig intestines in the kitchen sink. [. . .] She honestly thinks California-style Mexican food is universal among Latinas and so the only bananas she'd ever seen before coming to Boston were the ones her mom got at the Albertson's and chopped over her corn flakes" (10). That is to say, Amber is unfamiliar with plantains, just as Lauren is clearly aghast at the idea of menudo. If food is an ethnic marker, it is clear that these two "Latinas" come from different worlds.[42]

In *Dirty Girls*, Amber falls prey to the illusions of Latinoness—not only in terms of cultural "markers" such as food, but also in terms of race. As the skeptical narrator Lauren comments, Amber buys into all that "'brown and proud,' West Coast *Que viva la raza* jive"—a sentiment she connects with the "dated, 1970s Chicano movement" (10). Lauren's comment implies that, in racial terms, as well as political ones, Chicanos have become the paradigm for Latinoness. But this assumes, of course, that all Latinas (and, for that matter, all Chicanas) will be "brown." Though the Chicano paradigm invokes a celebration of mestizo heritage, the assumption that indigenous ancestry ties Latinas/os together (as José Martí suggests in "Nuestra América") collides with the fact that "the Spaniards wiped out all the Indians in the D.R. and Puerto Rico" (289), as Lauren points out to readers in *Dirty Girls*.

As a white Cuban American, Lauren fits uneasily with the racial presumptions surrounding Latino/a identity; she notes of the billboards advertising her column that "the promotions department had my face *darkened* in the picture so I looked more like what they probably think a Latina is *supposed* to look like. You know, *brown*. First day those ads popped up [. . .] the *sucias* started calling. 'Hey, Cubana, when did you get Chicana on us?'" (9). (The ways in which this racial difference might significantly affect socioeconomic status and treatment in a U.S. context, however, are completely glossed over.)

Elizabeth, the black Colombian member of the group, also does not fit the presumption of Latina brownness: "White American guys [. . .] have a hard time wrapping their minds around the fact that she's Latina and *looks like that*, too," and "non-Latino black guys don't understand her background. I can't tell you how many times a black American guy has accused me of lying when I told them my beautiful 'black' friend was a Latina. 'She doesn't *look* Latina,' they say. 'She looks like a sister'" (32). Just as in Thomas's *Mean Streets*, the "misunderstanding" betrays fundamental assumptions about how race is contingently constructed in U.S. dominant culture. "Black" and "Latino/a" are understood as mutually exclusive categories—simultaneously ethnic (as suggested by the "black American guy['s]" use of a metaphor for kinship, "sister") *and* racial in nature.[43] As Hernández-Truyol observes, "[F]ederal forms usually provide the following options: black (not of hispanic origin); white (not of hispanic origin); hispanic" (24). ("Hispanic" often appears with the disclaimer "may be of any race.") Although the wording "implicitly recogniz[es] that ethnic identity and racial identity are two separate, co-existing traits" (Hernández-Truyol 24), in practice, the category "Hispanic" is made parallel with other *racial* categories—it is "constructed" by dominant U.S. culture (and, indeed, by much Latino/a "culture") as its own *separate* race.[44] To both black and white Americans, Elizabeth "doesn't look Latina" because she is not *brown*.

When Amber (the self-identified indigenous Chicana) wants to help out Lauren's new Dominican boyfriend because he's "Raza" (that is, mestizo), Lauren engages in a form of strategic essentialism which will enlist Amber's solidarity through the myth of common descent:[45] "I figure this is a bad time to point out Amaury is probably not Indian [. . .]. Let her think of him as Raza.

What do I care?" (289). While racial commonality can, in Amber's case, be projected (even if erroneously) from ethnic identification (e.g., "We are both Latino so we must both be Raza"), Lauren points out that ethnicity does not always override race: in Miami "white Cubans still ban other shades of people from their social organizations" (26). (This is one of the few instances in the novel where more significant tensions between racial/ethnic groups are suggested.) And another Mexican American friend, Rebecca, apparently denies her indigenous heritage for the status of whiteness, claiming, "I'm Spanish" (in a dynamic that reminds us of Anaya's *Bless Me, Ultima*), and insisting that her "straight black hair" and "brown skin" come from "Moorish blood" (22).

In such examples the reader glimpses how politics—whether the politics of solidarity or of white privilege—constructs racial identity. And while a dominant U.S. culture constructs Latino/as as all being of the same race, the various Latina friends in the novel each imagine themselves differently, based on a different set of historical and social circumstances determining their understanding of their racial identities.

The novel does not merely dismantle ethnic construction in the form of panethnic Latino identity, however; it also suggests, provocatively, how even more nation-specific ethnic groups are still social constructs, often manufactured out of present needs and binding myths. Amber, the Chicana character, bears the brunt of this commentary; she not only falls prey to the dominant culture's homogenizing tendencies, but also "re-discovers" her roots in ways that markedly challenge the implications of *recovery* (of lost or misplaced origins) in such a project. Although Amber, Lauren tells us, was a *"pocha"* when they first met (Lauren explains that "'[p]ocha,' for the uninitiated, refers to the kind of Mexican-American who speaks no Spanish and breaks into a sweat if she eats anything hotter than Old El Paso mild salsa" [27]), she has a "Chicana awakening" and is transformed: "She came back having exchanged all 'ch's with 'x' and all 'x's with 'ch.' Like Chicana was now Xicana, 'just like the Aztecs spelled it,' she said. Don't ask me how the pre-Columbian Aztecs had access to the Roman alphabet [. . . ]. She began to collect eagle feathers, ankle bells, and gold shields, and spoke almost nothing but Spanish" (28). Amber is clearly fully engaged in the process of ethnicity construction—which, in this case, has very little to do with recovery, either of her personal ethnic identity (she never spoke Spanish to begin with) or of a historical "truth."

As various scholars have noted, ethnicity construction has at times consisted of identifying certain symbolic elements associated with "origins" and an original, untainted culture, but which in fact are much more recent cultural products.[46] Cornell and Hartmann elaborate on this phenomenon: "much of the power of ethnicity [. . .] comes not from anything genuinely primordial but from the rhetoric and symbolism of primordialism that are so often attached" to it (90). Valdes-Rodriguez's clever exposition of her characters underscores the point that Latino or Hispanic identity in the United States, even while it points rhetorically backward to its supposedly "common" primordial indigenous origins, is a recent cultural product—one that must, of necessity, elide the significant cultural, demographic, and racial differences among the various groups. (In this sense, too, Valdes-Rodriguez—who grew up in Albuquerque—significantly revises her New Mexican predecessor, Anaya. As I discuss in Chapter 1, Anaya points toward precisely such an indigenous origin as the history which Chicanos must recover in order to understand the true nature of their collective identity.)

Nevertheless, the troubling question that remains after such an exposition is, Why, then, are all these very different women such close friends? What is it that draws all these Latinas together into a tight-knit group (that includes no one except Latinas) if there is nothing in particular that draws Latinas together? The explanation given in the novel is that, as the only Latinas in an introductory communications class in college, they are bound by "their collective power of intimidation," which "was enough to make us instant and permanent best friends. Still is" (4). But this explanation seems weak, indeed, given so many cultural forces pulling the friends in disparate directions. The unnerving sense of an underlying essentialism is reinforced when Lauren (always the most analytical narrator in terms of culture) tells us that, although "we had no idea what a Latina was supposed to be, that we just let the moniker fall over us and fit in the best we could," nevertheless, the "important thing [. . .] is that *we* were *sucias*, and *sucias* stuck together. We studied together, shopped together, worked out together, complained together, laughed and cried together, grew up together" (35).

It would appear that, for these friends, the way that they "let the moniker" of Latinoness fall over them is by accepting, at a fundamental level, what that label connotes: they are connected by their *latinidad*. And it is worth noting that, just as Cuban differences were no more significant than others in the fracturing of Latino/a identity, so they are also no greater an obstacle to the underlying similarity; indeed, it is a pun on a Cuban popular culture reference (the band Buena Vista Social Club, which has been the subject of a noted documentary) that provides the friends with their group nickname (the "Dirty Girls Social Club" of the title). Cuban American identity, that is, can serve just as well as any other as a synecdoche for Latino identity, because (it is implied) Cuban American identity holds exactly the same relationship to the whole as every other national-origin "Latino" group.

It is apropos here to recall Cornell and Hartmann's observation that ethnic ties are understood metaphorically as family ties—"Ethnicity is family writ very large indeed" (20). In the description of the friendships of the Buena Su-cia Social Club, we get precisely a model of family relations that presents the friends as sisters, different in their individual ways and bickering with each other at times, but ultimately returning to the family base. Thus at the novel's conclusion, Lauren revisits her expository insights: Though she "used to lecture [Amber] about how different all us Latinas can actually be, as diverse as all the world [...] Now [...] I think she has a point, too. We may be really different in a lot of ways, but there's something to it, this whole being a Latina—perception becoming reality and all of us finding each other and helping each other" (307). Though this explanation still seems to be informed by a social-constructionist understanding of ethnicity—gesturing toward the notion that particular social and historical circumstances, including (what Cornell and Hartmann would call) the "assignation" of a group identity by the dominant culture, can *create* an ethnic group which eventually claims that assigned identity as its own—there is nothing at all in the novel which accounts for this sense of group cohesion. The dirty girls' histories are too diverse, their interests too disparate; there are no "symbols" or "collective fictions" of any kind which hold an explanatory power for all of them (though Amber, as we have seen, does embrace the symbols and narratives of the Chicano movement). And though Lauren goes to great lengths in the novel to elaborate on her observations of the heterogeneity of Latinas, she offers no further commentary at all on the idea of "perception becoming reality." Indeed, the immediately following phrase—"all of us finding each other"—seems to imply, simplistically, that there *was* some common denominator, hidden beneath all the surface diversity, to "find"—to unearth—rather than a sense of common identity that is constructed. (They did not *build* a group identity out of separate elements—they "found" each other.)

For all its wittiness in terms of ethnic identity, the novel ultimately is unsatisfying because, after the nuance and detail of its exposition of constructed cultural identity, it simply lapses back into an unexplained essentialism which suggests that, beneath all the articulated differences, there *is* something fundamental that ties Latinos (including Cubans) together in an inexplicable bond.

## Ana Menéndez's "In Cuba I Was a German Shepherd"

I wish to conclude this chapter on Cuban American negotiations of *latinidad* by turning to Ana Menéndez's beautifully nuanced short story "In Cuba I Was a German Shepherd." This story focuses on two Cubans and two Dominicans—old and lonely men who gather daily to play dominoes in a park in Little Havana (in Miami). Though the men are friends, an undercurrent of cultural tension permeates their relationship. As the story's title suggests, Menéndez suggestively alludes to the ways in which former class status contributes to that tension—even when, in their present circumstances, the men's socioeconomic circumstances are virtually indistinguishable.

Like *The Dirty Girls Social Club*, this story gestures smartly toward the external construction of Latino ethnicity by the dominant culture. The men playing in Domino Park are photographed and stared at by tourists, through the "iron slats" of the park fence, as a sort of exotic species displayed in a zoo. This bothers Máximo, the central character and a Cuban exile, who notes, "'You see how we're a spectacle?' He felt like an animal and wanted to growl and cast about behind the metal fence" (24). Interestingly, Máximo's recognition that he *is* a spectacle here makes him feel that he ought to perform in the role constructed by others for him—a dynamic that resonates suggestively with Karen Christian's thesis that ethnic identity, like gender identity in Judith Butler's formulation, is a cultural "performance—a spectacle requiring an audience for interpretation" (16). As Cornell and Hartmann explain of the complicated dynamics by which an ethnic identity is constructed, ethnicity can sometimes (though it does not always) "have its origins in the claims others make about us or we make about them" (29).

Yet, though in this instance Máximo clearly feels an ambivalent compulsion to represent himself in accordance with an assigned (negative) identity, at other times he violently resists the understandings of his "ethnicity" constructed by others—as when a tour guide describes the domino playing in terms of authentic (if not primordial) Cubanness: "Most of these men are Cuban and they're keeping alive the tradition of their homeland [...]. You see, in Cuba, it was very common to retire to a game of dominos after a good meal. It was a way to bond and build community. Folks, you here are seeing a slice of the past. A simpler time of good friendships and unhurried days" (25). Máximo's angry response is "Mierda! That's the biggest bullshit I've ever heard" (26). Though Menéndez does not make explicit exactly how the tour guide's story is "bullshit," it is clear that Máximo rejects the assertion of ethnic authenticity associated with domino playing.

In fact, Máximo's memories of his past in Cuba center almost exclusively on his role within his family. If exile, as Kate McCullough suggests, "presupposes a relationship to a lost physical place or land that *comes to embody* the temporal zone of the past" (580; emphasis added), then Máximo's nostalgia for Cuba can be read as a metonymic substitution for his longing for a past characterized by his more important function in his children's lives: "He remembered holding his daughters days after their birth [...]. For weeks, he carried them on pillows, like jeweled china. Then the blank spaces in his life lay before him. Now he stood with the gulf at his back, their ribbony youth aflutter in the past" (29). Cuba, then, geographically "embodies" this past fatherhood. Given the emphasis on such memories and the particular kind of loss they convey, it seems entirely logical to assume that, for Máximo, domino playing, rather than being a "Cuban" behavior, as the tour guide suggests, is an activity undertaken exclusively in the United States and in his lonely old age, with Dominicans as a (poor) substitute for his family. This also suggests that his current Dominican companions are *not* understood by him as "family writ large." The familial connection is what has been *lost*.

Notably, the tour guide's narration of Domino Park utterly elides the presence of the Dominicans among the Cubans. And indeed, in contrast to the fundamental and overpowering ties that inexplicably bond the "buena sucias" together, the bonds that hold these four men are portrayed as tentative and fragile, in large part a product of circumstances. They are all immigrants, thus sharing some similarities of experience within a U.S. context. Being from neighboring Caribbean, Spanish-speaking islands, they share *some* cultural elements that enable their friendship with each other in their new context: "they ate their same foods and played their same games" (9). They are each alone (without family in their old age), a condition which no doubt plays a factor in their impulse to construct an alternative community. Menéndez's exposition of the friendship never replaces tentative affiliation with a preexisting and essential group identity, however, but always emphasizes the ways in which the men are friends *despite* their ethnic differences.

Although the men are friends, they never see themselves collectively as "Latinos"—rather, the Dominicans "*were not Cuban*" (10; emphasis added), a redundant (non)identifier which serves to call attention to the differences between these two groups (even though, arguably, they are culturally closer than either is, for example, to Mexican Americans, being both of Caribbean background as well as having a historically more recent sizable presence in the United States).

The story places repeated emphasis not on commonality but on what the men do *not* share; we are told, for instance, that "[f]or many months they didn't know much about each other" (11). There is apparently no larger knowledge or common history that can be assumed (in contrast, for example, to Cuban exiles who can all assume some knowledge of Castro's government). Further, certain moments stress that the friendship between the men depends not on common experiences but on *silences*—on that which must remain unspoken in order for their "group," tentative as it is, to remain intact: "Máximo and Raúl liked these blessed Dominicans, appreciated the well-oiled moves of two old pros. And if the two Dominicans, afraid to be alone again, let them win now and then, who would know, who could ever admit to such a thing?" (11) It is not just a matter of not admitting (ignoring) what one knows; it is, instead, and more extremely, a matter of willed forgetting. What the men might "know" on some level becomes *unknown*, even by them: "who would know?"

The necessity of ignoring or even forgetting is highly suggestive in a story that so fundamentally undermines the image of a homogeneous collective "Latino" identity: the existence of that identity relies, in this story, not on "symbols" of peoplehood (Spanish language, the history of colonization, *mestizaje*, Catholicism, etc.) but on what is "forgotten" or (sometimes temporarily) unspoken—on what is, so to speak, swept under the rug. The potential allusion to differences in socioeconomic demographics, political affiliation, and even legal status in the United States can hardly be ignored. The words of Ernest Renan about national identity can be just as easily applied to ethnic (or, indeed, any collective) identity: "the essence of a nation is that all individuals have many things in common, and also that they have forgotten many things" (11).

The tensions between the four men are carefully managed but always threaten to erupt to the surface. Antonio, the Dominican, responds to assertions of Cuban superiority—exaggerated and even comical though they may be—with barely suppressed impatience, such as when, for example, Raúl responds to Máximo's question about who invented dominos with the assertion:

> "Who else could have invented this game of skill and intelligence but a Cuban?"
>
> "Coño," said Antonio without a smile. "Here we go again."
>
> "Ah, bueno," Raúl said with a smile stuck between joking and condescending. "You don't have to believe it if it hurts." [. . .]
>
> "You people are unbelievable," said Antonio. But there was something hard and tired behind the way he smiled. (17)

Though the Cuban nationalist pride implicit in this and other remarks by Raúl and Máximo seems generalized, it is possible to surmise that it also invokes prior *class* differences between Raúl and Máximo, on the one hand, and Carlos and Antonio, as Dominican immigrants, on the other. The punch line to the "German shepherd" joke that Máximo tells—in which an immigrant Cuban dog, which is hitting on an "elegant white poodle," tells her that, "[h]ere in America, I may be a short, insignificant mutt, but in Cuba I was a German shepherd" (28)—implies particular nostalgia for a former class privilege or status that is lost to those viewed as "immigrants" in the United States. Though we do not know what Carlos or Antonio's former lives were, we are told that in Cuba "Raúl had been a government accountant and Máximo a professor at the University" (5). (It is worth recalling once again that, especially prior to the Mariel boatlift, Cuban immigrants to the United States benefitted from a distinctly more middle- and upper-class demographic than other immigrant Latino groups.) It might well be a desire to distinguish themselves from other "immigrants" with a low status in the United States that drives the comments by Máximo or Raúl regarding a generalized Cuban superiority. In any case, when the Cuban exiles tell stories or make comments that imply a hierarchical distinction between them and the Dominicans, Antonio responds, "You people," clearly demarcating a difference between "you" and "us." Cubans are not Dominicans—they are not the *same* people.

At other points in the story, however, it is precisely the recognition that Cubans and Dominicans are not the same people that allows the fragile bonds between the men to remain in place. It is the men's underlying awareness that similarities are *not* sameness that allows them to continue their game playing, despite the conflicts which sometimes divide them: Máximo and Raúl appreciated that "Antonio and Carlos were not Cuban, but they knew when to dump their heavy pieces and when to hold back the eights for the final shocking stroke" (10). Antonio knows how to "hold back" in other senses as well: When Máximo tells jokes about Cuba with a hard edge—hinting at his own despair over displacement—Antonio is "careful not to laugh too hard [. . .]. He and Carlos were Dominican, not Cuban, and they ate their same foods and played their same games, but Antonio knew they still didn't understand all the layers of hurt in the Cubans' jokes" (9). Here, the bond among the men is protected by an acknowledgment of what, precisely, is *not* understood between them.

Menéndez's short story thus skirts an interesting line between writers such as Engle or Valdes-Rodriguez, who seem to fall back on essentialist notions of a panethnic Latino identity, and those such as Obejas or Muñoz, who undermine notions of panethnicity but leave little in its place. (As I discuss in Chapter 4, Obejas offers a somewhat more hopeful view of collective identity in her more recent *Days of Awe*.) Though Menéndez deals with the *politics* of panethnic divisions much more enigmatically and allusively than, for example, Obejas does, she also suggests—again allusively—how "Latino" communities (including Cubans) might provisionally be formed within a U.S. context. Without giving short shrift to the tensions that might threaten at any point to destabilize such communities, Menéndez hints at a vision in which acknowledgment of such tensions might go some way toward creating something like solidarity. This possibility is given much greater elaboration in Demetria Martínez's novel *Mother Tongue*, as I discuss in Chapter 7.

# 7

## Imagining Identity/Seeing Difference

### Demetria Martínez's *Mother Tongue*

The fundamental necessity of recognizing *difference*, as a prelude to the forging of "solidarity" or of coalitions, is at the heart of Demetria Martínez's novel *Mother Tongue*. This novel is primarily concerned with the debunking of idealized, romanticized conceptions of essential connectedness between peoples of vastly different experiences, and with the substitution in its place of a carefully forged solidarity based on learning, listening, and, ultimately, activism. The novel's implications for the concept of a natural panethnic "Latino" identity are significant—although almost never explicit. As Dalia Kandiyoti observes, *Mother Tongue* "speaks to our contemporary obsessions with globalized, transnational identities and to borderless, pan-Latino ideals" (426).[1]

Juan Gonzalez has pointed out that, by the time Salvadorans and other Central Americans began to arrive in the United States in massive numbers during the 1980s, as a result of civil wars, human rights abuses, and massacres (sometimes U.S. backed) in their own countries,[2] "the [U.S.] Latino immigrants of prior years had built stable ethnic enclaves, had perfected their English-speaking abilities, and even boasted an embryonic professional class with a basic grasp of its civil rights. The average Central American, on the other hand, spoke no English, was undocumented, unskilled, and desperate for any kind of work" (140). On a similar note, Suzanne Oboler has suggested that part of the problem with the term "Hispanic" is that it "lumps together recent political refugees from El Salvador with past political exiles like the first wave of Cubans who arrived in the early 1960s [whose] upper- and middle-class status and racial composition" resulted in some significant "differences between their entry process and experiences and those of" other immigrant "Hispanic" groups (1).

Martínez's novel testifies to the difficulty of obtaining legal residency for Salvadorans, not only because they were generally poorer and darker skinned than their first-wave Cuban counterparts, but (perhaps even more important) because the Salvadorans were escaping a U.S.-backed regime and were perceived by the U.S. government as aligned with communism, while the whiter and more well off Cubans were escaping communism itself.[3]

*Mother Tongue* is virtually silent on the subject of Cuban immigration and the relationship of Cuban immigrants to Salvadoran ones;[4] but Martínez is at pains to note the vastly different experiences of her Salvadoran political refugee and the novel's narrator, a U.S.-born Chicana. Mary, the narrator, falls in love with José Luis (the Salvadoran) before even meeting him, spinning romantic fantasies about the almost mystical connections between them. Though these connections are not at any point put specifically in terms of their common "Latino" heritage, it is clear that in Mary's mind this is part, at least, of their affinity. Mary comments retrospectively on their first meeting: "I don't know why I had expected Olmec" (4). As Debra Castillo astutely notes in *Border Women* (2002), "In her first impression upon seeing the Salvadoran refugee there is a curious superimposition of expectations and the frustration of these expectations. José Luis initially represents for Mary a particular cultural site associated for her with her own incompletely understood, romanticized Mexican past." Thus Mary projects her own imagined past onto José Luis, even though the Olmecs are "entirely unrelated to El Salvador" (Castillo and Tabuenca Córdoba 173).[5]

At another point, in dealing with tensions that arise in their later relationship, Mary refers to her "credentials, the fact that I am Mexican American" (124). The use of the word "credentials" is both peculiar and telling. In response to José Luis's insistence that "you don't know what it's like" (123) to be a political refugee (or, worse, to see your people being murdered), Mary seems to be making a claim to be able to understand via her *identity*, as opposed to her experience—she, like José Luis, is Hispanic.[6] At the same time, she notes that José Luis rejects her claim to an essential understanding. At certain key moments (such as when he learns of the murder of two nuns who worked with El Salvador's poor), he sees Mary more as *American* than as in any way "related" to him and his experience:[7] "He saw in me an image of a gringa whose pale skin and tax dollars are putting his compatriots to death. My credentials [. . .] don't count now; in fact, they make things worse. [. . .] Earlier in the morning, he had made love to a Chicana. But [now] I am transfigured. [. . .] I am a yanqui" (124).[8]

Most of Mary's early, retrospective narrative, however, is a deliberate glossing over, or obscuring, of the significant differences in their experiences or "subject positions." Mary constructs, instead, a romantic narrative in which she and José Luis are connected by destiny: "I swear to God the moment I laid eyes on him I knew he was The One" (20), she says, and at one point she lays their horoscopes side by side to see how the stars have aligned their fates (40).

She describes their first lovemaking in terms of instantaneous and complete understanding that immediately transcends cultural difference: "We opened each other up like sacred books, Spanish on one side, English on the other, truths simultaneously translated" (66).

Though one critic, at least, has wholeheartedly embraced Mary's romantic narrative, arguing that "love asserts itself in this novel as an alternative to patriarchal and state oppression" (Mujčinović 156) and that both Mary and José Luis "embrace love as an empowering source that counters the destructive forces of the sociopolitical order" (151), such a reading utterly ignores the ways in which Mary's romantic plot is *itself* destructive, precisely because it ignores politics and history. In a striking parallel to Juani in *Memory Mambo*, Mary, too, envisions "love as a merger that is outside time and that erases difference"; Mary, too, "consistently interpret[s] her own desire as either outside of or the solution to political pressures and determinants" (McCullough 596, 594).[9]

The main thrust of the narrative of *Mother Tongue*, however, is continually to destabilize the grounds for such a fantasy of connectedness by emphasizing the ways in which Mary's experience as a Mexican American and José Luis's experiences as a Salvadoran have created fundamentally different subjects.[10] As Debra Castillo writes, "For both Mary and José Luis, what they see, and how they see it, is embedded in their national and ethnic identities" (Castillo and Tabuenca Córdoba 175).[11] When Mary asks José Luis, "[D]id the airline serve you peanuts or a meal?" he responds, "[B]oth, but I couldn't eat. [. . .] [T]he movement of the plane made me nauseated, almost as sick to my stomach as the time I breathed tear gas at the funeral of a priest that death squads shot and killed as he lifted the communion host" (11). When they consult over possible pseudonyms for him in the United States, Mary's inclination is for exotic, romantic names: "[W]hy not Neftalí, or Octavio? I wondered, why not pan for gold, for something weightier than the silt of ordinary names like Robert and John. He said, in my country names turn up on lists. Or in the mouths of army officers at U.S. embassy parties. A few drinks later, someone, somewhere disappears. Pick an ordinary name" (13).

This scenario is repeated compulsively in the novel to underscore José Luis's observation that "we're not seeing or hearing the same things" (128)—that they read the world *differently*. The same signifier conveys distinct meanings to each of them: "Even church bells mean something different to us. She hears them and sets her watch. I hear them and remember the endless funerals in the villages outside the capital" (128). At another point, Mary tells José Luis, "Last night I dreamed I was [in El Salvador], I smelled bougainvillea"; he responds, "I dreamed I was there too, mi amor, but it was something about white phosphorus, napalm" (67). Mary romanticizes a country she has never been to, associating it with "exotic" flora; José Luis connects the country inextricably to the political situation which has led to the massacre of his people. Mary's fantasy is to "take a war out of [the] man" (4), not recognizing that the war has *made* the man.[12]

Mary's romantic fantasy regarding her natural connection to José Luis is accompanied, notably, by rhetoric invoking bridges, border crossings, and even borderlessness. In the novel's opening passage, she recounts first catching sight of José Luis as he disembarks from a plane to enter into an assumed identity in the United States as a refugee, and she describes his face as one "I'd seen in a dream. A face with no borders" (3). The use of the border as metaphor has become popularized—indeed, has exploded with the field of "border studies"—since the decades following the publication of Gloria Anzaldúa's *Borderlands/La Frontera* (1987). Anzaldúa herself uses the idea of borderlessness to suggest ("construct") the commonality of the Mexican and Mexican American people: "the skin of the earth is seamless" (25); thus borders are by implication artificial and unnatural. As certain critics have noted, however, the use of border as metaphor that is at times enabled by Anzaldúa's writing risks the loss of *material* specificity. Whereas Anzaldúa's "text painstakingly grounds [the border] in specific historical and cultural experiences," when "border crossings" become a more general metaphor, critics ask, "[W]hat is lost in terms of the erasure of difference and specificity?" (Yarbro-Bejarano 7–8).[13] In a similar vein, Castillo and Tabuenca Córdoba note that "the U.S. theoretically conceived border serves as an objective correlative for discussions of U.S. dominant culture and its resistant spaces [. . .]. From the Mexican side, however, the borderline itself retains a stronger materiality than is typical in U.S.-based commentary, a not-unexpected result of the differential in ability to simply cross to the other side" (3–4).

To return to Mary's use of the border metaphor in *Mother Tongue*: in this case the metaphor seems so vague and idealized as to be almost meaningless. What "borders" would a face usually have that are lacking in José Luis's? Despite this awkwardness, however, the metaphor clearly is meant to suggest Mary's affective response to José Luis—her sense of the *absence* of whatever barriers would divide them. (Thus she also expected him to be "Olmec." When she sees him, she revises her characterization to note his "Mayan cheekbones" [3], continuing in this way to place him within a romanticized heritage that she might also claim as her own.) Since one of the clearest possible differences between their experiences at the moment of meeting is their respective political and national identities—Mary as a U.S. citizen, José Luis as a Salvadoran fleeing his country (and the real risk of death) and coming to the United States as an "undocumented" refugee—"borders," referring to the territorial boundaries that mark states, might with some accuracy be said to be the *very* thing that divides them, that makes the experience of each "foreign" and not fully knowable to the other. As Jean Wyatt has written in her discussion of the dangers of identification for cross-cultural communities (and Mary's and José Luis's relationship must surely be understood as cross-cultural), "a respect for the other's otherness requires both a limit on our expectation of what we can know of another person and a conscious brake on identification" (*Risking Difference* 171). Mary, however, puts no such brakes on her identification with José Luis; it is striking, in this context, that she would see his face as one *without* borders.[14] Surely this is a telling projection that enables Mary's own romantic "plot," in which she is already, on some level, intimately connected to José Luis.

Elsewhere, Mary collapses the metaphors of border and of bridge, recounting of her relationship with José Luis, "It is difficult to recall the day-to-day exchanges that became bridges by which we transcended borders of culture, language, and history. We strolled back and forth into one another's worlds [...] as casually as if crossing from El Paso to Juárez" (48). We can see here how very little Mary limits her "expectation of what [she] can know" of José Luis; she imagines him, almost literally, as an open book. Again, the parallel to Juani in *Memory Mambo* is striking: like Juani, Mary, too, "consistently codes her relationship in the language of a romanticized, boundary-melting" communion of soul mates (McCullough 594). Mary's understanding of her romance utterly obscures the very real differences in experience created by distinct cultures and histories. The borders between her and José Luis are not even crossed but are "transcended," made irrelevant; and this is done "casually," without any real effort. Significantly, the metaphor applied to this easy, effortless movement across (or above) borders is the "crossing from El Paso to Juárez"; what Mary does not register is that crossing is notoriously more difficult and more dangerous for those crossing in the other direction. In other words, borders matter.

Mary's naïveté regarding the ease of border crossing is undermined repeatedly, however, by the novel as a whole. For one thing, her use of this rhetoric is laughably clichéd: the poem fragment she writes in one journal entry, for example, is a plagiarized Simon and Garfunkel lyric: "Let me be / the bridge, / those troubled waters, / his eyes" (20). The very excess of such sentiment marks it as parody; having encountered it first, the reader is much more likely to be cynically disposed to the subsequent passage in which borders are casually transcended. As Mary herself remarks repeatedly, much of her narrative is invented, concocted, imagined—to fill her particular needs—rather than transcribed from accurate memory (26–27, 59, 149–50); thus we can assume that her initial representation of José Luis as himself "without borders" is likewise a motivated concoction. (For the romance to flourish, she *needs* to believe that there are no substantial borders between them.)

The novel, in fact, makes a point of elaborating on the materiality of borders and the *differences* that they designate. Borders might be "artificial," "constructs"—but their effects are very real. Thus Mary's activist friend Soledad, who sends detailed instructions to Mary about what to do with José Luis once he arrives, describes tricks for getting past the Border Patrol: make him put on a Yale sweatshirt; "speak to him in English"; "[t]ell him all about how 'the relatives' are doing" (5–6),and so on. (Another "tip" Mary later learns is that "the Border Patrol did not stop cars with Reagan-Bush or Right-to-Life stickers on them. Nor did the Patrol stop and question white men" [58].) Soledad even notes in her letter to Mary that, if José Luis should be deported, it is vital that the INS believe he is *Mexican*, since "[i]t'll be easier to fetch him from there than from a Salvadoran graveyard" (6).

In direct opposition to Mary's fantasy of borderlessness, Soledad's instructions suggest attention to *multiple* borders and their significance, and to the markers of "difference" (whiteness, U.S.-made clothing, conservative politics) that get "read" as designating belonging versus not belonging. It is these signs of difference that Mary at times willfully refuses to read. When José Luis—commenting on the markers that might, in certain contexts, be read for his possible immigrant status—tells her "that in the darkness [. . .], no one can tell he's an illegal," Mary responds, "[N]o human being on earth is illegal." José Luis's response is a gentle, pragmatic corrective: "He accused me of being romantic again and said, go tell that to the authorities" (76–77). Borderlessness is a "romantic" idea—on a par with reading the "stars" to learn lovers' destinies, love at first sight, and bridges over troubled waters.

The necessity of forgetting—or, perhaps more to the point, of *not knowing*—for sustaining Mary's fragile construction of a connected "destiny" with José Luis is clearly suggested by Martínez. For the fact is that Mary *does not want to know* what José Luis knows. As she writes in her journal after she has met him, "I don't know anything about that awful war he fled. Maybe it's better. He needs a friend who can just make him *forget*" (21; emphasis added). Mary, that is, does not want to learn about his difference (at least at first) but to obliterate the difference in the act of "forgetting." When she senses the magnitude of the borders between them, she shies away: "I caught a word or two that I knew had to do with his past. Cell. Water. Cry. The words had a barbed wire feel to them. I didn't dare climb the fence to find out what was on the other side" (37–38). She relishes her ignorance, at times almost basking in it. Though she talks with José Luis about "la revolución in Nicaragua," she admits to the reader, "Don't ask me what I said. I couldn't have cared less about politics" (50).[15] While José Luis translates "Urgent Action Alerts," Mary reads the horoscopes (97). When Mary daydreams, José Luis teases her by calling, "Mary, can you hear me?" (49)—a question with more significance than Mary realizes, since at times she seems literally not to be listening. Martínez's emphasis on Mary's *willful* ignorance suggests the degree to which her fantasy of connectedness is not just an illusion but a potentially dangerous one (or at the very least morally and politically bankrupt), since it threatens to gloss over the very history that José Luis and his activist circle are trying to bring to light in an effort to arouse international protest. José Luis wants, not forgetting, but remembering.

Notwithstanding Mary's propensity toward willful forgetting, however, she becomes educated almost by accident, by overhearing the stories of Central American fugitives who narrate El Salvador's situation. She recounts the consequent evolution of a "movement of sorts" on the part of U.S. citizens to work for the cause of El Salvador's oppressed populations. The historical referent (although never explicitly named in *Mother Tongue*) is the Sanctuary movement, in which "several Christian church groups responded to these Central Americans by forming an underground movement which transported fugitives into the United States and offered them 'sanctuary' in their churches and homes" (Cunningham, "Sanctuary" 372). (Demetria Martínez, as is frequently noted, was indicted in 1987—but acquitted—of charges related to Sanctuary movement activities.)[16] Mary, in explaining the "movement," focuses on the political power of storytelling: "in those days, when a refugee told his or her story, [...] it was testimonio, [...] facts assembled to change not the self but the times" (32). The *telling* (not forgetting) of stories, in this context, is a political act with intended political consequences. In Mary's once-again retrospective historical narrative, "[a]round the time of José Luis's arrival, large numbers of U.S. citizens were beginning to make trips to El Salvador in groups called delegations. They met with sisters and priests, unionists, students, those who worked the land [...]. And when delegations returned to the States, members spoke to anyone who would listen, in parish halls, homes, and on campuses. José Luis and I were among those who attended these presentations" (70–71). Mary then goes on to explain the "conversions" of U.S. citizens to the movement: "These conversions could be traced to the stories of Salvadorans, stories about torture, dismemberment, hunger, sickness" (72).

In Mary herself, too, the reader detects a subtle "conversion," presumably as a result of her overhearing such stories—and thus being made a participant in an act of collective remembering. The retrospective Mary who tells the story is much more politically knowledgeable and informed than the young and romantic Mary who cares more about horoscopes than politics; and, since Mary is an unreliable narrator who is "good at filling in blanks" (11), sometimes the two collapse as the young Mary's "blanks" are filled in by the older one. Thus, before reading the newspaper account of José Luis's own *testimonio*, the young Mary warns him, "[T]he only thing they'll get right is that El Salvador is the size of Massachusetts.[...] [B]ecause your skin is brown, what you say will be followed by words like Romero claimed. Whereas if you were white, it would read, Romero said. That is how they disappear people here" (33). Yet, after "reproducing" for the reader the article in the *Albuquerque Herald* which proves her observations to be remarkably prescient, Mary writes, "Did I really say all that, about reporters? Was I not, in fact, the one who read only the horoscopes, who looked to the stars to tell me what God could not?" (36). Somewhere between then and now, Mary's hearing of the *testimonios* has enacted a conversion in her.[17]

Consequently, when José Luis, on the way to see a therapist, spots chalk drawings of bodies on the sidewalk and experiences a panic attack, he acknowledges, "Thank God María [Mary] did not think I was changing my mind about going to the counselor. She understood what was happening. She had read in some newsletter about how the Salvadoran police outline in chalk the bodies that they find, documenting the "mysterious" deaths they themselves plan and carry out. María understood, and she sat with me in the truck until I stopped shaking" (129).

In this instance, Mary is able to "read" the world as José Luis does—or at least to understand *his* reading of it—based on her own reading. The novel may thus be read as a bildungsroman, a novel of education in its truest sense. (This is the difference between Mary and *Memory Mambo*'s Juani, who has not yet embarked on her education process.) Learning the story of El Salvador, Mary learns enough of the different historical experiences that shape her and José Luis's perspectives to shatter the illusion of identity while allowing for the beginnings of a more informed solidarity. (Yet in Mary's eyes, it is, ironically, neither her growing knowledge about El Salvador nor her activism on behalf of Central American fugitives that she sees as constituting her "credentials" for understanding José Luis; rather, she falls back on her ethnic status as a "Mexican American," as we have seen.)

It is striking that Soledad, the character in the novel who most represents political activism on behalf of Salvadoran fugitives is, like Mary, Mexican American (in Soledad's case, Mexican by birth). That is to say, in *Mother Tongue*, the "movement" is represented within the United States primarily by Latinas, which suggestively evokes a sense of ethnic connectedness as one of its grounds. The historical Sanctuary movement, it is true, included a Mexican as well as a U.S. constituency—of necessity, since Mexican members were vital in helping to transport Central Americans from further south to the U.S. border.[18] But in general the basis of the organization was *religious* rather than "ethnic" in nature.[19] As Cunningham notes, in the urban centers of Sanctuary activity, "[t]he profile of Sanctuary churches [. . .] tended to reflect an educated, anglo majority [. . .]. Southside's Sanctuary group [in Tucson], for example, was a network of roughly 200 churchgoers, 90 percent of whom were anglo" ("Ethnography" 587).[20] The Rev. Philip Wheaton, working with the Sanctuary movement in Washington, D.C., puts the demographics in yet more absolute terms: "This is a middle class, white, Catholic-Protestant movement" (qtd. in Masud-Piloto 124).[21] While individual Latina/o participants might have drawn on their sense of ethnicity in thinking about their involvement, Latino/a identity does not seem to have been a significant factor in the U.S. Sanctuary movement.

Instead, the movement saw itself as directed by religious imperatives. As Cunningham notes in "Sanctuary and Sovereignty" (377), the Sanctuary movement was significantly influenced by the development of liberation theology in Latin America and its emphasis on a solidarity reflected in *action* on behalf of the poor. The rhetoric deployed to describe participants' motivations was notably religious in nature, as Susan Coutin has documented. For example, one member explained, "For me, by helping a refugee, it's my way of helping the church—the martyred church in Central America. . . . It's where I see the Lord crucified" ("Oppressed" 69). Another, explaining why he assumed the risks associated with traveling to threatened Central American communities, noted that he was trying to be true to the words "'We will be with you.' [. . .] Which is what Jesus did with the poor. Which is what the prophets did with the Oppressed." The terminology of "sin" was also invoked with regard to U.S. government military aid to El Salvador's repressive regime, the suggestion being that the "sin" could be redressed (or at least addressed) by participation in the movement (Coutin, "Oppressed" 70). And, as Félix Masud-Piloto has noted, the religious foundations of the movement shaped language that was offered in defense of indicted Sanctuary workers during trial: "The earth itself is to become a sanctuary. This convenant [sic] forms us into a people of many nations, cultures, and creeds—a people that the Christians among us sometimes call the church!" (Hollyday 10, qtd. in Masud-Piloto 123). The community from which the movement emerged, and which it reinforced, was the "church" rather than any community conceived in national or even ethnic terms.

Yet, while *Mother Tongue* makes mention of gatherings at Quaker meetinghouses, the religious underpinnings of the movement are seriously downplayed by Martínez—a fact which is all the more surprising considering her work covering religion for the *Albuquerque Journal* and her freelancing for the *National Catholic Reporter* during the time of the Sanctuary movement (Manolis 37). Indeed, Martínez has described the genesis of the novel in the context of an "ethnic" community rather than a religious one: she thought of the novel's opening line while listening to Sandra Cisneros read at a poetry festival to which she had been invited by Luis Rodriguez (Manolis 42). Rather than linking Mary's affair with José Luis, and her subsequent politicization, to religious imperatives, Martínez has Mary describe her romance as a "center so far away from God that I asked forgiveness in advance" (5). Further, Soledad writes one of her instructive letters to Mary in a way which suggests that the teachings of the church *resist* the actions of the movement rather than underpin it: "El Salvador's leaders may be butchers, but they're butchering on behalf of democracy so our government refuses to admit anything might be wrong. Now I know St. Paul says we're supposed to pray for our leaders" (8). While liberation theologians reinterpreted the Bible as a *grounding* for activist politics on behalf of the poor, in Soledad's letter the emphasis is on a church founder who is figured as, at best, a preserver of the political status quo.[22]

Instead, Soledad evokes in the service of her cause the metaphor of kinship, which, according to Cornell and Hartmann, so frequently signals *ethnic* identity: she writes letters to members of the U.S. Congress about the Salvadoran situation in which she protests, "My friends and *relatives* are being killed" (116; emphasis added). As Mary explains, Soledad (who is of Mexican origin) has made the Salvadoran cause her own through an information-gathering process: "Every day she scanned Mexican and U.S. newspapers for news of deaths, crops, army movements, culling moments in history" (115); as a result she lays claim to the kinship metaphor in an expression of solidarity and a recognition of its potential power. It is much more powerful to write that one's relatives are being killed than to write that strangers are; in presenting herself as a relative of the dead, Soledad writes herself metaphorically into the image of another of the Mothers of the Disappeared, a group that, in El Salvador as in Argentina, was notable for its highly symbolic power.[23]

Nevertheless, the text at the same time makes clear the kinship metaphor's affiliative (rather than filiative) nature: "Having no children of her own, she *adopted* El Salvador" (115; emphasis added). Martínez has staked a similar familial claim, writing of Salvadorans, Cubans, Puerto Ricans, and Chicanas, "Whatever our ethnic differences, we are family!" But she adds, "Nothing is fixed," and proclaims, "I'm a Latina to promote pan-American unity" (*Confessions* 49). The implication is that such unity needs to be promoted; it does not always or already exist. Remembering that ethnicity can be understood as the *imagining* of "family ties" where, biologically, none exist, we might say that the *recognition* of that imagining, even in the *act* of imagining, substitutes for an essential ethnic identity a more provisional, context-specific notion of solidarity in Martínez's writing.[24] (Soledad, as the character working most obviously for solidarity, displays a wonderfully intriguing mixture of ethnic essentialism and self-conscious "constructionism." Thus she tells Mary, in a biological/primordial mode, that "we've gotten too far away from the foods of our ancestors," which "our cells never forget" [110]; yet the list of "old remedios" she gives Mary to counteract this problem is culled "from my childhood and from my *guidebook*" [108; emphasis added]—suggesting the degree to which guidebooks and other decidedly contemporary media construct the "old" and the "authentic.")

Mary's eventual political activity is driven, like Soledad's, by a sense of forged ties rather than by primordial ones. José Luis's words "made me want to sell my belongings, smuggle refugees across borders, protest government policies by chaining myself to the White House gate—romantic dreams, yes, but the kind that dwell side by side with resistance" (69). Much later in the novel, when Mary is faced with the possible death of her prematurely born infant (the son of José Luis, named after his father), she is urged by Soledad, "Offer it up, mija. Offer up your pain for the mothers whose children are disappeared" (147). Mary then translates this apparently religious sentiment: "I offered up my helplessness, all that was small and weak and frightened inside me, on behalf of those who were worse off. And somehow, Soledad's mandate became an umbilical cord [. . .]. Since that time I have tried to interpret 'offering it up' for my friends. 'Empathy' does not quite embody its spirit. No, the word I think comes closest is 'solidarity'" (147–48). In rejecting empathy—with its sentimental implications of feeling the pain of others and with the underlying assumption that the experience of another *can* be fundamentally felt or shared—for solidarity, in which group identity is forged self-consciously for a cause, Mary continues to evoke the language of kinship, of biological connectedness; her tie to others becomes the "umbilical cord" that saves her. But unlike her earlier romantic assumptions that she was magically connected by destiny to the fate of José Luis, this umbilical cord requires effort to sustain: Mary eventually participates in a "Parents for Peace" project (148). The *language* of family ties is thus appropriated to bring its symbolic power to bear in the creation of a powerful emotive connection to a group of a different sort.

The same is true regarding the title of the novel, *Mother Tongue*, with its reference to language itself as the symbolic signifier of kinship. The rhetoric of kinship that suggests that a particular people are all somehow related, of "common descent," is implicit in the use of the term "mother tongue," which imagines Spanish as the "mother" of the Chicana Mary and the Salvadoran José Luis alike. Spanish is, of course, one of the primary symbols used in the construction of a Latino "community," and it is often invoked—using precisely the language of kinship—by anthology editors and even by some Latino/a writers. The editors of *Iguana Dreams: New Latino Fiction* (one of the earliest anthologies collecting panethnic U.S. Latino/a writing, published in 1992), for example, recognize the "distinct and separate cultures under the term *Latino*" but then go on to note, "Bringing all these cultures together in one volume may be comparable to the tension of sharing a meal with distant relatives—there is a separate history and experience, yet there exists a bond of recognition, a family camaraderie. The central point of our unity is language" (Poey and Suárez xvi). Julia Alvarez has echoed this notion: "I think that sharing a language connects us as a widespread Hispanic culture throughout the Americas, and it connects us also with people from Spain" ("Territory" 17). Such statements beg the question of how "culture" and even "connection" should be defined. (See, for example, my discussion of the premise of a common culture and a common language in the Introduction.)

But the complex and thorny nature of such questions (which at some point risk becoming sheerly *quantitative* in nature—how *much* "common culture" is enough to make a "common people") is, more often than not, simply elided by commentators, who turn, strikingly, to metaphors of biological consanguinity to do the work of making a convincing case for connection. Julia Alvarez, intriguingly, has suggested that "language [. . .] is a kind of embryo for who we can become as a people" ("Territory" 17). This metaphor seems to actively *resist* interpretation or translation: what does it mean for language to be an embryo "for" a group of people? Bryce Milligan, one of the editors of *¡Floricanto Sí!*, makes more explicit the primordial and maternal assumptions embedded in Alvarez's words, although he still relies on tangled figurations: "At the root of this common culture is the fact that Spanish, often the first language of U.S. Latinas or of their parents, constitutes a deeply cherished transnational/transhistorical linguistic umbilical cord" (xxix). Here language, symbolically the cultural "root" (the image is vertical, a sort of "family tree") is also a horizontal "umbilical cord," connecting people (metaphorical siblings) together. The "mother" figure drops out explicitly in this image and yet is still suggestively present behind the scenes. Logically, that "mother" would be the "mother countries," or perhaps even Spain; but the more powerful (if less tidy) implication is that Spanish is somehow *both* mother and umbilical cord—both the connector and the source being connected to. Further, Spanish connects these "siblings" in some presumably profound and meaningful way, despite differences of national origin or of history. The connection, that is, is timeless.

This is an important aspect of the figure of language here, since a significant factor in the demographics of U.S. Latinos is that, over time, Spanish is lost. Indeed, Martínez has self-identified, humorously, as a "Berlitz-tape Chicana": "I speak of the tongue-tied generation [of Mexican Americans], buyers of books with titles like *Master Spanish in Ten Minutes a Day While You Nap.* We're the Chicanas with cassettes in our glove compartments; commuting to work, we lip phrases for directing an Argentine cabbie to a hotel or ordering tapas at a bar in Spain. [. . .] We refer to our 'broken' Spanish as if it were a broken bone and speak of how, when we least expect it, the language 'comes back' as if it were a pre-existing condition" (*Confessions* 43–44). Martínez is obviously poking fun at the notion that Spanish is a biological, organic element (like a bone) or that it "exists" inside the Latina essentially, somehow, even if the Latina knows no Spanish.

As she provocatively implies, however, these collective fictions about Spanish and Latino/a identity are powerful indeed. To counter the notion that English-speaking (and -writing) Latinas might no longer be "kin" to each other, for example, Milligan extends the metaphor of language as "umbilical cord": "But this 'linguistic umbilical cord' is evident in much more than simply the usage of the Spanish language. [. . .] Latina literature appears to English-language readers 'to have been newly translated from Spanish'" (Milligan, Milligan, and de Hoyos xxix; Castillo-Speed 17–18, qtd. in Milligan, Milligan, and de Hoyos). Even in English, that is, the Spanish somehow magically makes itself felt, is not lost at all.[25] The biological charge of such images is palpable; ethnicity is transhistorical, transnational, essentially unchanging over time—"in the blood." Ethnicity will tell.

Significantly, however, even the most superficial incursion into the pages of *Mother Tongue* undercuts the implication that Mary and José Luis are connected—"related"—by Spanish. The young Mary, who is the subject of the first part of the novel, is clearly uncomfortable in Spanish; Soledad tells her to "use the experience [with José Luis] to shore up your Spanish" (40), and the young Mary notes in a journal entry that, as a result of their romantic relationship, "[n]ow I have reason to improve my Spanish" (63). Retrospectively, Mary recalls that José Luis "offered to help me with my Spanish" and that "[a]lmost every day we sat together at the kitchen table where we conjugated Spanish verbs with an old grammar" (49). As Silvio Torres-Saillant has noted, "Simply to assume Latino unity is to forgo the hard work, long time, and deep thought that bringing it about will take" (435). The novel's title, with its reference to the Spanish language, once again invokes the symbolism of kinship and ethnic unity—but in this case the *illusion* of kinship is undermined by an emphasis on the work required for Mary to have access to this particular ethnic "marker." If Spanish is Mary's mother tongue, it is an adoptive mother.

Nevertheless, here again the language of kinship opens onto a model for solidarity. As Mary tells us of her attendance with José Luis at the presentations of delegations of activists returning from El Salvador, "I got good at whispered translations, rapid-fire summaries. Sometimes, exhausted, I reverted to Spanglish" (71). Rather than being a manifestation of a preexisting relationship, Spanish is a tool with a certain amount of symbolic value but also with practical or strategic value that Mary and the other activists can employ in the building of solidarity for their cause. As Martínez has said about her own Spanish, "For me the process of forever attempting to improve my Spanish is a political decision to better my political work" (Manolis 45). Ultimately, the "family" that is suggested by this mother tongue can be understood, in Werner Sollors's terms, as "a case not of organic identity by descent and unbroken tradition but of constructed, symbolic ethnicity, built on consent [...] and defiance" (*Beyond Ethnicity* 206). This is, notably, the very notion of "family" advanced by Jorge J. E. Gracia in his argument for the relevance of a collective Hispanic identity: "[T]he metaphor of the family must be taken broadly to avoid any understanding of it as requiring genetic ties. [...] [T]he very foundation of a family, marriage, takes place between people who are added to a family through contract, not genesis" (50). Instead of genetics, we might think of family in terms of voluntary association of a profoundly committed sort, that is, of solidarity.

Later, Mary's son, José Luis, flatly rejects the unspoken assumption that he would feel innately or genetically compelled toward Spanish: "When José Luis was in high school [...] I told him that if he passed his Spanish class, I would send him to El Salvador for a summer, to volunteer in one of the new communities [...]. He thundered: Ma, I don't wanna go there, I don't wanna major in Spanish. How come you never say anything about how good I'm doing in science?" (143). José Luis feels no natural or instinctive connection to the Spanish tongue or to the "cause" of El Salvador; his own budding political interests lie with environmental issues, with "saving the planet" (142). José Luis eventually decides to take a college course in Spanish when he becomes interested in learning the history of his father—and its context, the larger history of the civil war in El Salvador (178, 182). In other words, his voluntary commitments, rather than his biology, lead him to his mother tongue.

Perhaps disappointingly, after such a careful exploration of the illusory primordialness of the mother tongue, Mary (and perhaps even Martínez) continues to be compelled to use essentialist images that interweave language with biology: "A new language," Mary tells us of her son's education in Spanish, "is a tincture, a drop of which forever changes the chemistry of the person who is learning it" (187). By this late point in the text, such a claim that language (even a "drop") somehow metaphorically enters the blood and transforms the person seems dangerously problematic. Mary relies repeatedly on such images of almost magical biological "knowledge," claiming of Salvadorans, for example, that, "even if they were too young to remember life without war, their bodies remembered; their very cells concealed the scent of a healed El Salvador" (108). And, retrospectively relating to her son a painful memory in which his father, suffering from a fit of traumatic shock, pummeled Mary with his fists, Mary uses the incident to explain her son's "angry streak" (180): "It's not your fault that anger sometimes splits you in pieces that crash like plates of earth. Those sounds penetrated my body the night we conceived you, and the blows figure into your destiny as surely as the positions of planets that ruled the night" (162). Such passages of biological or cellular "knowledge" seem to be in the tradition of magical realism: they suggest alternative forms of knowledge from those recognized by the laws of science.

But in this novel, which has worked so hard to demonstrate the perils of willed ignorance and the commitment to learning that is necessary for true knowledge of history to take place, passages regarding a magical, cellular "knowledge" of events ring very false indeed—on a par (as the above passage suggests) with Mary's reliance on astrology to produce the magical "destiny" that will connect her with her lover.[26] Unsatisfying as it may be to readers, Mary's continued reliance on primordial connectedness (to events as well as to people) suggests the quite compelling nature of such narratives; they are, in the words of Werner Sollors and Benedict Anderson, the "collective fictions" that form "imagined communities" (see Sollors, *Invention* xi).

That Martínez herself might ultimately not be immune to the attraction of such "fictions" is indicated, perhaps, by an even more troubling aspect of the novel's ending (at least for this reader): the surfacing of a suppressed memory that Mary was sexually molested as a child. This revelation, coming literally out of nowhere (both for Mary and, in its use of the convention of climactic revelation, for readers) is made to fit thematically with the novel's political themes through Mary's analysis that her abuse and the Salvadoran death squads are "all part of the same pattern. Of people loving power, or some such thing, more than life" (173). It is, in fact, the case that sexual abuse was a significant aspect of the human rights abuses occurring in El Salvador in the 1980s. Stephen writes, "Rape is a well-documented method of terrorizing and torturing women in the name of maintaining national security. [. . .] The Salvadoran army, National Police, National Guard, and Treasury Police have all been implicated in the use of rape as a systematic method of torture. [. . .] Rape as a routine part of torture has been a common experience not only for women in CO-MADRES [the Mothers of the Disappeared organization in El Salvador], but also for many Salvadoran women in the course of the civil war" (817). Strangely, however, rape is not emphasized as an aspect of the Salvadoran situation in *Mother Tongue*; even Martínez's recounting of the murder of two American nuns (an incident with a historical parallel, in which three American nuns and a lay missionary in El Salvador were raped and killed in 1980) leaves out mention of sexual abuse (118–23)—though José Luis does mention that his own torture included "electric wires on my genitals" (133), virtually the only reference to sexual abuse in the novel. The novel's relative silence on this issue makes Mary's connection of "death squads" to her memory of molestation all the stranger, and potentially less convincing. The abstractness of her hazy, generalized vision of "power," by which the politics of economic and political repression in El Salvador—in which acts of horrifying torture, abuse, and murder against supposed subversives were carried out on a massive scale and rape was systematically used, and sanctioned, as a method of torture—can be made metaphorically parallel to the vastly different dynamics by which a man in the United States abuses a seven-year-old girl in secret (an act which may well have causes rooted in a larger social structure but which bears a distinctly different relationship to that structure) is unsatisfying, I would suggest, in the context of a novel which has insisted on detailing *differences* of experience in the face of a potentially dangerous assumption of connection.[27] We may, of course, attribute this analysis once again to Mary's naïveté, but in this instance it is more difficult to do so, since the structural "revelation" of the abuse *only* at the end of the novel suggests that its purpose in the plot is to connect Mary's experience, at a fundamental level, to that of José Luis after all: she, like him, has known real and traumatic suffering. Critics tend to simply accept this equation at face value; Castillo, for instance, notes of the revelation that "Mary too is a *desaparecida*, a survivor of another and intimate gender war [. . .]. His scars are also, in a different register, hers" (Castillo and Tabuenca Córdoba 179).[28] In such a reading—encouraged by the novel—José Luis's scars are *her* scars; her molestation is another "war," like his. Finally, it seems, Mary and her blurring of difference have the last word: only pages from the novel's conclusion, she places a snapshot of José Luis (the now disappeared Salvadoran lover), along with a snapshot of herself at seven, in the corners of a framed poster of the Mothers of the Disappeared (186). The implication, as Castillo correctly discerns, is that both José Luis and Mary's seven-year-old self were made to "disappear." As with *The Dirty Girls Social Club*, the final, perhaps too easy, impulse is to assert overriding connections, or equations, in the face of difference.

But the substance of Martínez's text has offered us what the other texts discussed in this book have not: an alternative conception of a hard-earned solidarity—one which recognizes difference and, where necessary, works strategically to bridge it. As Juan Flores has written, "solidarity can only be posited when the lines of social differentiation are fully in view, but the goal, nevertheless, is solidarity" (*From Bomba* 198). This solidarity, it should be said, certainly need not take the form of "ethnicity"; it is worth underscoring that the Sanctuary movement in the United States, which helped to transport Central American refugees across the border, envisioned its group identity as being constituted by faith rather than "blood" or kinship—as a "Christian community."[29] Martínez, however, transcribes (we might even say "translates") the notion of a strategic solidarity organized around theological principles into one which invokes, instead, the rhetoric of kinship, family, and relatedness. (It is perhaps for this reason that the Sanctuary movement is never actually mentioned by name in the novel.) The result is that, in *Mother Tongue*, we can understand ethnicity as a strategic form of solidarity—one which employs the specific metaphors of biological and cultural kinship in its cause *while recognizing difference*, rather than enlisting the rhetoric of "God's kingdom" or "God's children." Hilary Cunningham has observed that, while Latino/as were in fact divided on the Sanctuary movement, Demetria Martínez "represent[ed] one end of the political spectrum" among Latinos.[30] It is interesting, then, that Martínez's novel can be read as inviting Latino/as (like Mary and Soledad) to draw on imagined ties of kinship or common descent in the service of solidarity with the oppressed. Ethnic "ties," Martínez's novel reminds us, are always deployed *in response* to a particular set of circumstances;[31] *Mother Tongue* thus allows us to think in terms of multiple *latinidades*, organized around various points of interest, rather than of a singular, fixed "Hispanic" identity with predefined borders of inclusion and exclusion.[32] Ethnicity, in this view, is certainly powerful (the rhetoric and conviction of ethnic connectedness can operate as a significant motivating force), but it is also fluid, strategic, and provisional—not "essential" at all. Indeed, Latino identity (in its multiple manifestations) is inevitably a fragile, tentative "alliance" that survives *if*—and even *because*—we recognize difference.

# Conclusion

## The Shifting Nature of *Latinidad*

Felix Padilla, whose 1985 work, *Latino Ethnic Consciousness*, is still arguably the defining optimistic statement on the possibilities for Latino coalitions across lines of national origin, elevates as his model the Spanish Coalition for Jobs in the Chicago of the 1970s. As Padilla explains, this coalition of both Mexican American and Puerto Rican community organizations was formulated in response to frustration over discriminatory hiring practices (89). The coalition was able to negotiate agreements with Illinois Bell Telephone Company and with Jewel Tea Company regarding promised hires of a certain number of Latino employees (96–97, 101). But, subsequently, the coalition "went on to become another community organization providing direct services to the residents of the Pilsen community. As a result, the efforts of the coalition were transferred from citywide Latino concerns to community-oriented ones, servicing primarily the Mexican American residents of that area" (115). (As Padilla points out, Pilsen was known as a Mexican American neighborhood, while Westtown was considered the Puerto Rican neighborhood.)

The end of the story would seem to provide a bleak view of the possibilities for panethnicity, suggesting that, perhaps inevitably, the interests of one or another national-origin group will take precedence over coalition. As David Rodriguez notes in *Latino National Political Coalitions* (2002), Latinos tend to "prefer organizations that are based on their own groups. This makes it very difficult for Latino coalitions to develop and maintain multi-group organizations since Latino identity and organizational experience is single-group oriented" (63). Martha Gimenez argues that this trend signals the failure of Latino politics: "as long as Latino politics remains local, situational, and at most regional in nature, it will remain weak, its success linked to some degree to its failure to be more than factional identity politics" ("Latino Politics" 178).

Let me present, however, an alternative understanding of *latinidad*—one which takes its cue from the story of a different coalition. Whatever happened to the Sanctuary movement? As Hilary Cunningham notes in "Sanctuary and Sovereignty," by the summer of 1993, this coalition too was "clearly on its 'last legs'" (384), thanks to recent developments in both the United States and El Salvador. The 1990 breakthroughs in court (the *American Baptist Churches v. Thornburgh* decision) and Congress (the TPS, or "temporary protected status," law) had made it easier for political refugees from Central America to stay in the United States; concurrently, the 1992 peace accords in El Salvador had to some degree stabilized the situation there (see Cunningham, "Ethnography" 594; J. Gonzalez 142–43; Stephen 808). That is to say, the group identity of the Sanctuary movement was strategic and provisional, organized (to use Sollors's term) in "defiance" of a particular set of policies. When those policies relaxed, the group identity weakened.

Yet, for some individual members involved in the movement, activism did not cease; it merely took new forms. For instance, Cunningham reports, many former Sanctuary participants now became involved in "Friendshipments to Cuba"—caravans which carried medical equipment and supplies, including computers, across the U.S.-Mexican border, where the shipments were then taken by truck to the Tijuana airport and loaded onto a Cuban plane.[1] The caravans, organized by the Inter-Religious Foundation for Community Organization/Pastors for Peace, were repeatedly confronted by U.S. Customs officials at the border in the 1990s over the terms of the Cuban embargo and the necessity of a license. As Cunningham reports, Pastors for Peace "took a critical posture toward U.S. policies in Mexico, Central America, and the Caribbean. [. . .] Significantly, the Cuba Caravans movement explicitly utilized the U.S. Mexican border as an important symbolic arena in which to challenge state authority" ("Sanctuary" 385). The border that had become such a contested site in the case of the Sanctuary movement—and that figures so prominently in Demetria Martínez's novel—was now deployed for its symbolic value in a case that would at first seem to have very little to do with the U.S.-Mexican land border, since Cuba and the United States are divided from each other by ninety miles of an ocean "border."

What emerges from this history of shifting activist concerns is the degree to which commonalities could be perceived by activists—despite significant differences—between Salvadoran refugees and Cuban nationals, between U.S. policies regarding El Salvador (as well as Salvadoran immigrants) and the U.S-Cuban embargo, and between all of these and the situation of "illegal" Mexican immigrants. Though the Sanctuary movement did not survive as a *group* in any coherent, recognizable form, it is possible to say that some of its transnational commitments survived in different forms.

As I discuss in Chapter 7, the Sanctuary movement was not an "ethnic" movement but primarily a religious one. Nevertheless, this model is instructive, because it allows us to conceive of how the shifting and fluid nature of various Latino alliances and coalitions does not need to signify the "failure" of *latinidad* but might instead suggest its flexibility, its adaptability to new and changing circumstances. David Rodriguez reports, in this vein, that ad hoc coalitions might ultimately be *more* effective than institutionalized, national Latino coalitions: "[A]d hoc coalitions tend to form on an issue by issue basis [. . .]. Issues like immigration, voting rights, and civil rights create a climate of urgency and a need for unity which ad hoc coalitions can fulfill easily. [. . .] When the issue comes to a resolution, the coalition disbands" (88–89). Thus, for example, one of Rodriguez's respondents noted that, "when we are faced with a common enemy like the immigration bill in the early 1980s, you know we had no choice but to work together" (89).[2] If we can imagine not a single, monolithic *Latinidad* which must continually make a case for overarching commonalities among all the groups—a case which inevitably fails—but, rather, multiple *latinidades*, which reach across national-origin lines but need not account in some comprehensive way for *all*, then the notion of panethnicity does indeed begin to make more sense, as one form of identity—among several—with which we can engage.

Consider the following divergent manifestations of a panethnic sensibility, as outlined by Nicholas De Genova and Ana Y. Ramos-Zayas in *Latino Crossings*. Significantly, they are decidedly less optimistic than Padilla about the long-term possibilities for a panethnic solidarity that takes concrete, institutionalized forms. Nevertheless, they report, for one, that their respondents sometimes formulated a notion of common "*latinidad*" around a "shared 'migrant' status, and especially that of undocumented migrants, which located many Latinos within the space of the U.S. nation-state as 'illegal' border-crossers, but which notably tended to exclude Puerto Ricans altogether—due to their U.S. citizenship" (209). Though De Genova and Ramos-Zayas do not say so explicitly, such a construction of *latinidad* would also exclude Cubans, since most Cubans who manage to arrive on U.S. soil are not "undocumented" but legally accepted, thanks to the "wet-foot/dry-foot" policy still in effect. That is to say, this version of commonality includes Mexican, Central American, and, to some degree, South American migrants.

Similarly, in a discussion among Mexican migrants, "it became conceivable to some that the children of Central American migrants might be included among those marked as 'Chicano,' but it was unthinkable to include Mainland-born Puerto Ricans in that group" (De Genova and Ramos-Zayas 207). However, "[a]nother important modality of Latinidad," according to De Genova and Ramos-Zayas's respondents, "articulated class-specific forms of solidarity between Mexicans and Puerto Ricans (and also, other Latinos)—as workers" (209). This is the form of solidarity that Felix Padilla recognized some two decades ago when he argued, also looking at Chicago, that "at the center of Latino ethnic affinity and mobilization are the structural and circumstantial conditions of working-class solidarity and action" (118). In this formulation—quite a common one, as we saw in Chapter 6—Mexicans and Puerto Ricans tend to be included together (along with the more recently arrived Central Americans), but Cuban exiles, especially of the first wave, are again absent.

On the other hand, the issue of bilingual education is one that Cubans, as well as Mexicans and Puerto Ricans, have historically embraced in substantial numbers.³ As Ronald J. Schmidt notes, "Bilingual education for language minority students was placed on the national political agenda in the mid-1960s, primarily by Latino activists" (49). Cuban exiles in Miami were at the forefront of bilingual education implementation: "In 1962, the Dade County School Board [. . .] approved the first contemporary experiment in bilingual education. [. . .] [T]he bilingual program distinguished Miami from many cities and towns in the southwest United States that had bilingual education funds available and still resisted implementing such programs" (Stepick et al., *This Land* 39). As Earl Shorris notes, when a bilingual program was first implemented at Coral Way Elementary in Miami in 1963, "the students were the children of middle- and upper middle-class Cuban exiles." Now the students at Coral Way are often children of immigrants from Nicaragua, Guatemala, and El Salvador, but the Spanish-speaking teachers are still largely Cuban (Shorris 183). The influence of Miami Cubans has kept bilingual education programs in effect in Miami–Dade County public schools, even as anti-immigrant and English-only sentiments have largely succeeded elsewhere,⁴ suggesting the possibility that on this issue Cubans and Central Americans of much more recent arrival see a common interest.

In the same way that bilingual education in Miami has expanded from a "Cuban" issue to one that must surely be understood as a "Latino" one, other organizations—both local and national—with their roots in a particular national origin have expanded to service the needs of larger "Latino" populations. The Mexican American Legal Defense and Education Fund (MALDEF), founded in 1968 to promote Mexican American civil rights, over time has "extended its litigation advocacy work to include Hispanics other than Mexican Americans. [. . .] MALDEF has increasingly advocated for the rights of Hispanic citizens and noncitizens, legal residents, and undocumented immigrants. Through litigation, MALDEF has [fought for] equitable treatment for Central American immigrants seeking political asylum in the United States" (Sierra 62–63). Similarly, the League of United Latin American Citizens—which, despite its name, was also originally primarily Mexican American in scope—"has grown both in numbers and in ethnic representation. Puerto Ricans and Cubans are now part of the predominantly Mexican-American membership. Most importantly, in its advocacy work on immigration, LULAC increasingly addresses the rights of all Hispanic residents in the United States" (Sierra 64). Clearly, it is not the case that advocacy on issues of citizenship will equally address all Latino groups (this will not be a central issue for Puerto Ricans); nor will advocacy on, for example, issues of political asylum equally affect all. Nonetheless, the advocacy issues addressed by these groups clearly span more than one national-origin population (depending on the issue, the populations primarily addressed might be different combinations), and thus can justifiably be called "panethnic."

At the local level, Milagros Ricourt and Ruby Danta point to Queens as a New York City neighborhood in which an instrumental, panethnic understanding of *latinidad* has at times been fostered, despite the primacy of national-origin organizations. Ricourt and Danta note that Ciudadanos Conscientes de Queens/Concerned Citizens of Queens (CCQ) was founded in 1980 to offer immigration counseling services; later, other services, including citizenship classes, housing advice, voter registration, entitlement counseling, and a hotline on legal rights for undocumented immigrants, were added (108–9).

Though CCQ's effectiveness seems to have dissipated in the 1990s—in another example of the "shifting" nature of panethnic alliances—other organizations, some of them ostensibly national origin–specific, took up the slack (112–13). Acción Latina, for example, was founded in 1994 by a Honduran immigrant to help Latinos apply for citizenship and register to vote. The Sociedad Dominico-Americana de Queens/Dominican-American Society of Queens, founded in 1993, "offered citizenship workshops" and "expanded its services, available to all Latinos, to include afterschool tutoring, English classes, computer training, and high school equivalency classes" (113). The Latin American Integration Center, founded by a Colombian immigrant who wanted to help Colombians in Queens take advantage of a new dual-citizenship law in Colombia, likewise extended its services—including naturalization classes, help with citizenship applications, voter and child health insurance registration, and so on—to non-Colombian Latinos (112). "Heritage schools" in Queens with specific national-origin constituencies, such as Escuela José Pedro Varela (with students of largely Uruguayan heritage), Escuela Argentina, and Escuela Simón Bolívar (with Colombian students), "welcomed children of diverse Latino nationalities" (114–15). As Jones-Correa writes in *Between Two Nations*, "while an organization may draw most of its members from a particular region or nationality, their interactions are rarely limited to members of that particular subgroup. Affiliations are 'nested,' one within another [. . .], so that each national group has a variety of linkages with other regional, national, and Latino associations" (133–34).

Perhaps the best argument that can be made for "Latino" as a valid panethnic category is that such linkages—shifting and nonconcordant though they may be—do in fact occur. As a singular "people" Latinos cannot be said to exist; but Latino identity might well be found in the multiple alliances, along sometimes quite different panethnic and transnational lines, that we make with each other. In this sense Latino identity might properly be understood as *always* an "in-between" or "hyphenated" identity, not just in the more common (and overused) sense of the hyphen between Latino and "American," but in the sense that "Latino" is found in the boundaries between one so-called Latino group and another. It is in the connections we forge with each other—in that "space" between us—that we become something more than Chicano/a, Cuban American, Puerto Rican, Guatemalan American, and so on. We become Latinos.

## Coda

I wish to close by saying a few words about my own use of the term "Latino"— in my professional work and even as a self-identifier. Felix Padilla has written that "the notion of Latino ethnic identity [. . .] should reflect a conceptual *commitment* to explore those conditions which encourage the expression of a multiethnic group form" (147–48; emphasis added). What if we saw *latinidad* as *commitment*—not just to an exploration of conditions that encourage panethnic collectivity but also to an exploration of those conditions (including differences) which potentially inhibit it?

Here is a question I have often asked both myself and my students: Why have a class in U.S. Latino literature if I disavow the notion of a single Latino culture or identity? One reason, of course, is strategic. Given the realities of enrollment pressures and body counts, I am more likely to be permitted to offer classes on this subject matter if the classes are well enrolled, and they are more likely to be well enrolled if I can appeal to more than one segment of the student populace (in terms of identity *or* interests) at once.

Another reason might be the complex of overlapping themes which can give the course a degree of coherency, as well as their production via structural similarities that can be detected in the groups' histories with relation to the United States (e.g., migration/immigration, hybridity and biculturalness, racism, poverty and exploitation, U.S. intervention in home countries). These structural similarities, needless to say, are noncongruent (i.e., not all groups, or even all individuals within a group, share all issues, or share them equally), even if they are overlapping from some groups to others.

And—this brings me to my third point—the "Latino" rubric allows me to *discuss* those differences, paying careful attention to the divergent histories and present circumstances of different groups and the reasons for these, in ways I could not do if I were offering a class on just one group (or, analogously, writing a book on just one group). Thus, ironically, strategically accepting the to-some-degree hegemonically constructed, homogenizing category of "Latino" allows me to undermine the category's homogenizing tendencies.

Having said all this, I must confess that, if I had been one of the respondents in the study examined by Jones-Correa and Leal ("Becoming 'Hispanic,'" discussed in the Introduction), I would have identified myself as "Latina" (as well as Cuban American)—even though, in such a context, that identification surely would have served no strategic or "instrumental" purpose of any kind. On one level, this identification would clearly seem to mark my internalization of the reified category in its most simplistic form. (I am Latina because I am Cuban American, and Cuban Americans are Latinas.) But I would like to think, perhaps optimistically, that there is more to it than that. At its best, identifying as Latina or Latino also allows us to express, to ourselves and to others, our *commitment* to attending to the historical and present differences among Latinos, as well as to the sometimes overlapping or analogous histories and current structural problems—which is another way of saying our commitment to solidarity.

# Notes

Introduction: Who Are We?

1. F. Padilla notes, for instance, that in the first half of the twentieth century in Chicago, people of Mexican descent were themselves divided by time of immigration, class, and so on. It was not until the mid-1960s that an ethnic identity bridging these differences began to be self-consciously cultivated in earnest (*Latino Ethnic Consciousness*, 34–35, 38). In other words, according to Padilla, even a strong sense of *Mexican* ethnic cohesiveness needed to be "constructed" in Chicago.

2. As Luis rightly comments, the presumption that Latin American immigrants begin to identify as "Latino" on entry to the United States is counter to common sense (283).

3. Both Flores (*From Bomba* 149) and Oboler (*Ethnic Labels* 3) make this point.

4. The 1970 census, by contrast, asked the question, "Is this person's origin or descent" and then provided the following options: "Mexican"; " Central or South American"; "Puerto Rican"; "Cuban"; "Other Spanish"; or "No, none of these." It did not group these choices under a "Hispanic" category.

5. Stavans is perhaps one of the most problematic recent commentators on "Hispanic" peoples in the United States. Though, in *The Hispanic Condition* (1995), he nods toward the social-constructionist insight that "Latino" is not one culture but many (*Hispanic* 11), in practice he participates in the most egregious forms of essentializing, for example, "the entire Hispanic cultural experience in the United States" (*Hispanic* 8); "the Latino metabolism" (*Hispanic* 14); "a different collective spirit" (*Hispanic* 16). For an extended critique of Stavans, see Flores, *From Bomba*, esp. 172–76. Trueba, author of *Latinos Unidos* (1999), ostensibly, like Stavans, recognizes Latino diversity, yet also displays the pervasive impulse to claim a preexisting common culture and essential Latino identity, stating that Latinos "share culture, language, history, values, worldview, and ideals" (31)—surely an overly encompassing claim. Morales's *Living in Spanglish* (2002) is in many ways a direct descendant of Stavans's *The Hispanic Condition*. Again making the by-this-point prerequisite nod toward difference, Morales acknowledges, "It is a big mistake to lump Latinos together, but there are important ways we feel like one people. They have to do with physicality (dancing, body language, suspension of reserve) and spirituality (that strange syncretism between Catholicism and African and indigenous religions that allows us to be sacred and profane at the same time)" (28). Less egregiously, Shorris—who also insists at the outset that there are no "Latinos," only a diversity of cultures and peoples that have come collectively to be identified as such—also falls back at times on essentialist characterizations, such as the notion that the "traditional Latino family" has its origins in rural life, and that the patterns of rural life have pervasively structured all Latino culture (218). For a critique of this stereotype,

see Gimenez, "Latino/'Hispanic'" 560–61; Gómez-Peña 48; Juan Gonzalez 200–201; and Oboler 64.

6. See, for example, Gimenez, "Latino/'Hispanic'"; Rivero, "Hispanic"; F. Padilla. Gimenez argues that public policy ought to distinguish between Mexican Americans and Puerto Ricans, on the one hand, and other so-called Latino groups. Padilla argues in his landmark 1985 study, *Latino Ethnic Consciousness*, that Puerto Ricans and Mexicans in Chicago were, at given crucial moments and under the right set of circumstances, forming panethnic coalitions. From a literary standpoint, Rivero bases the parameters of Hispanic literature on the "Third World stance of many Chicano and Nuyorican writers" ("Hispanic" 183) and, on this basis, excludes Cuban exile writing from her definition.

7. As Oboler notes, the latter two symbols were appropriated by César Chávez in organizing Mexican American farmworkers (61).

8. Gimenez also notes that, "[b]ecause the label is used in the context of affirmative action, it places professional and skilled [recent] immigrants in objective competition with members of the U.S. minority groups and forces them to pass, statistically, as members of an oppressed group" ("Latino/'Hispanic'" 557–58). Gimenez makes a compelling case for the idea that affirmative action should properly be reserved for groups that have *historically* been oppressed in the United States and that are still, as a group, feeling the effects of that institutionalized oppression.

9. Data are drawn from Joyce A. Martin et al., "Births: Final Data for 2003."

10. Rumbaut notes that, since people of Mexican descent still account for by far the largest percentage of U.S. Latinos (63.3 percent in the 2000 census), "it should be underscored that aggregate statistics for the total Hispanic population reflect the predominant weight of the characteristics of the Mexican-origin population" ("Making" 33).

11. The specific national-origin figures provided here are from 2000 rather than 2003, but the basic point remains valid. Data are drawn from U.S. Department of Health and Human Services, "2000 Natality Data Set."

12. For that matter, Gimenez cautions, statistics based on national origin alone can be equally misleading. Not only do we need to consider how and why various populations come to reside in the United States, and the ways in which those reasons might skew the representative sample in the United States, but we must also note the different receptions the populations have faced once here ("Latino/'Hispanic'" 562).

13. Flores, however, insists on the need to retain a panethnic category and concept, as I shall discuss shortly.

14. For statistics on income levels and poverty rates by national origin, see U.S. Dept. of Health and Human Services, *Mental Health* 132; for statistics on racial identification by national origin, see Pew Hispanic Center, "2002 National Survey" chart 8; Tafoya 7.

15. According to Jones-Correa, some Latinos in New York City report that Puerto Ricans can be insensitive to the obstacles presented to other Latino groups by lack of citizenship (*Between Two Nations* 115). Flores counters by pointing out the "second-class nature of that supposedly privileged status," which, he argues, outweighs in the long run any advantages Puerto Ricans may gain from it (*From Bomba* 162). See also De

Genova and Ramos-Zayas on Puerto Rican citizenship versus presumptions of Mexican "illegality" (esp. 7–16, 58–62).

16. As Rodriguez-Morazzani writes, "much of the literature of the 1960s and 1970s in the social sciences concerning Puerto Ricans compares and contrasts their situation with that of African Americans. The propensity for such linking could lead anyone unfamiliar with the existence of the two different groups to view them as one" (145). For a discussion of the perceived link between Puerto Ricans and African Americans *on the part of Mexican Americans*, see De Genova and Ramos-Zayas, 77–78.

17. In this book, I follow authors' own published usage of accent marks in their Spanish names. Thus, although in Spanish the surname Rodríguez would be accented, I do not use an accent mark for Richard Rodriguez; the same goes for Julia Alvarez, although Álvarez is usually accented. Cristina García has published her most recent novels with an accent mark in her last name; reissues of her first novel, *Dreaming in Cuban*, also show an accent mark, although the original edition did not. In an interview, García told me that she had intentionally reclaimed the accent mark; therefore, once again, I follow her preferred usage.

18. Sollors observed (in 1986) that ethnic "literature is often read and evaluated against an elusive concept of authenticity" (*Beyond Ethnicity* 11). Thus, for example, the revelation that "Danny Santiago," the author of *Famous All Over Town* (1983), a novel about Chicanos in East L.A., was actually Daniel Lewis James, an Anglo-American, was greeted with critical outrage. (See Stavans, *Hispanic* 28–29, for a detailed discussion.) The same sort of "outrage," however, never accompanies the publication of a book on Chicanos by a Chilean or Cuban American, or a book on Salvadorans or Peruvians by a Chicana.

19. An intriguing case in point is TuSmith's critical study *All My Relatives* (1993), chapters of which are devoted to "Asian American Writers" and to "Native American Writers"; yet there is no equivalent, panethnic "Latino" chapter, but, rather, a chapter specifically on "Chicano/a Writers"—suggesting the degree to which, in the early '90s, even scholarship which recognized other panethnic categories felt uncomfortable treating "Latinos" as a single ethnic "community."

20. Rivero, for example, wrote in 1985 that "the works by Cuban immigrants can never be considered" as ethnic minority U.S. literature ("Hispanic" 187) because they are not in line with the progressive ideology of Chicanos and Nuyoricans.

21. Consider, for example, critical efforts to salvage María Amparo Ruiz de Burton's late-nineteenth-century novel *Who Would Have Thought It* as somehow challenging racism (R. Sánchez and B. Pita, xvi–xxi). For a more sophisticated analysis of Ruiz de Burton's novel, including its racism, see Alemán.

22. Piedra locates the origins of the idea of Hispanic race even further back, in Spain's efforts at national and imperial consolidation (284–85).

23. Cornell and Hartmann do not claim that actual blood ties or common descent must exist in order for a people to understand itself as an ethnic group. Rather, following Max Weber, they are explaining the fundamental *beliefs* that bind ethnic groups: "The fact of common descent is less important than belief in common descent. What matters is not whether a blood relationship actually exists, but whether it is believed to exist" (16–17).

24. Sidestepping such problems, Ed Morales argues—explicitly invoking the "raza cósmica" of José Vasconcelos—that Latinos are united by a long history of racial miscegenation and cultural hybridity, of various forms. The unifying factor is apparently the process of miscegenation, rather than its specific manifestation or results.

25. Critics who continue to assert Spanish as a fundamental connection include John García; Shorris xvi; Stavans, *Hispanic* 32.

26. Cornell and Hartmann's conception of ethnicity as constructed around various symbols takes the burden of ethnic cohesiveness off of the actual speaking of Spanish and shifts it instead to the symbolic importance of Spanish to continued group cohesion, even among those who might not speak it. Thus, for example, second- or third-generation Latino children or grandchildren of immigrants (like me) might not be Spanish-dominant or even comfortably bilingual and yet might feel an "emotive aura" around Spanish—even being driven to learn the language as a manifestation of "symbolic identification" (F. Padilla 151). The Pew Hispanic Center report's findings would seem to support this emphasis on the symbolic importance of Spanish; the report notes that "nearly nine in ten (88%) Latinos say that it is very (63%) or somewhat (25%) important for future generations of Latinos living in the United States to speak Spanish" ("2004 National Survey" 26). A decade-long study of children of immigrants in San Diego found that, "among the Mexican-origin respondents, [the] ability to speak and read in Spanish did not atrophy but rather improved appreciably from their teens to their twenties," suggesting a commitment to improving Spanish (Rumbaut, "Severed" 67). See also Demetria Martínez's essay, "Confessions of a Berlitz-tape Chicana," in her book of the same name.

27. The National Immigration Forum, however, cites predictions by the research firm Hispanic Trends that, by 2010, 70 percent of Latinos in the United States will be foreign-born. One can only expect that, given the large numbers of Latin American immigrants currently entering the country, the significance of Spanish dominance as a common denominator will increase.

28. Chanady here cites the work of Antonio Cornejo Polar.

29. See, for instance, John García 25.

30. See, for example, Flores, *From Bomba* 199; Juan Gonzalez xiii–xiv; Gracia, esp. 48–51; Oboler 9; Suárez-Orozco and Páez 16–20; Torres-Saillant 438

31. For an excellent discussion of how free trade has affected Mexicans and increased immigration to the United States, see "Free Trade: The Final Conquest of Latin America," in Juan Gonzalez's *Harvest of Empire*, 228-45.

32. On U.S. capital in Cuba prior to 1959, see, for example, Louis Pérez, "Cuba" 87–88. See Oboler 9–10 on other comparisons of immigrant groups.

33. The authors found a "clear progression in the use of panethnic identification from the first to the third generation. Among those of Mexican origin, for example, 28.99% of the first generation chose some kind of panethnic identification, increasing to 45.83% in the second generation, [. . .] and to 60.46% in the third generation. The trends are similar for the other two national groups" (Jones-Correa and Leal 224).

34. Jorge Gracia, approaching the question of Hispanic identity from a philosophical perspective in *Hispanic/Latino Identity* (2000), takes precisely the opposite position, arguing that consciousness is irrelevant to identity: "It is not [. . .] necessary that the

members of the group name themselves in any particular way or have a consciousness of their identity. Some of them may in fact consider themselves Hispanic and even have a consciousness of their identity as a group, but it is not necessary that all of them do. Knowledge does not determine being" (49). Most scholars interested in the question of panethnic identity, however, would reject the notion that it is irrelevant whether Hispanics see themselves as a group or not: *self*-identification is precisely the question at issue.

35. Fox makes a compelling argument that one of the pivotal factors in the construction of a sense of Latino peoplehood was the growth of media that attempted to appeal to *all* Hispanic groups at once in an effort to increase audiences. Prior to the 1970s, Fox argues, U.S. newspapers for Spanish-speaking audiences catered to specific Latino ethnic groups that "had little contact with one another, separated by geography, dialect, and radically different social and political concerns" (41).

36. Note that the race question is a *separate* question from the one which asks about Hispanic/Latino origin. In the 2000 census the Hispanic "ethnicity" question was asked *first*, so respondents identifying as "Hispanic" in the race question which followed were, in essence, identifying as Hispanic twice. Logan calls this group "Hispanic Hispanics" as opposed to white Hispanics, black Hispanics, and so on.

37. In the Pew Hispanic Center's 2002 National Survey of Latinos, this percentage of respondents rose to 56. This figure does not include the 20 percent who "[p]refer another option" (chart 7).

38. These findings serve as a corrective to those of Dutwin et al., who—noting that "[i]ndividuals who self-identify as Latino/Hispanic [. . .] associate themselves with the Democratic Party at higher rates than with the Republican Party" (154)—came to the conclusion that "Democratic affiliation [for Latinos] is situated upon the cherishing of an overarching Latino heritage" (156). Such a conclusion presupposes that using a panethnic identifier is in itself a sign of belief and investment in "an overarching Latino heritage," whereas Jones-Correa and Leal's study suggests that this link is relatively weak.

39. The widest range between respondent groups here tended to be between those who did not use a panethnic label at all and those who identified primarily using such a label but also employed other terms (such as national-origin terms). Oddly, the group of respondents that identified *only* using a panethnic term did not represent the furthest extreme in their responses from those who did not use such a term at all. Jones-Correa and Leal hypothesize that, for those who identify *solely* as "Latino" or "Hispanic," the term might signal merely an acceptance of a category imposed from "outside" rather than a strong sense of ethnic group identity (239).

40. Sollors observes that "[t]he ethnic approach to writing" jumps from the ethnicity of the author (e.g., "the writer is an X, meaning, not a Y") to the ethnicity reflected in the text (e.g., "X writes like an X, not like a Y"). This approach, "circular and tautological [. . .] reveals first and foremost this very Xness, a quality which cumulatively achieves the status of a somewhat mystical, ahistorical, and even quasi-eternal essence" ("Ethnicity" 290).

41. Sollors gives the example of a "slur" which takes various forms, depending on its object: it labels certain "blacks as Oreos, Asians as bananas, Indians as apples, and

Chicanos as coconuts—all with the structurally identical criticism 'they're white inside!' The warning had no specific cultural content but served as an interchangeable exhortation to maintain boundaries" (*Beyond Ethnicity* 28).

42. Although Oscar Hijuelos is one of the best known of Cuban American authors, I have chosen not to include him in this book because his family's entry to the United States predates the 1959 revolution, and therefore his writing does not face the same set of issues as those explored by the products of exile from Castro's Cuba.

43. Sollors called on literary critics to ask, "How is the illusion of ethnic 'authenticity' stylistically created in a text?" (*Invention* xiv); but he did not seem to acknowledge the possibility that ethnic texts might, in fact, undermine this illusion.

## Chapter 1. "Jasón's Indian": Mexican Americans and the Denial of Indigenous Ethnicity in Rudolfo Anaya's *Bless Me, Ultima*

1. Articles on *Bless Me, Ultima* are quite often included in anthologies of literary criticism discussing U.S. ethnic and U.S. Latino/a literature, such as *Hispanic-American Writers* (ed. Bloom) or *Teaching American Ethnic Literatures* (eds. Maitino and Peck). Poey has noted that Anaya's *Bless Me, Ultima* and Sandra Cisneros's *The House on Mango Street* "have become 'representative' of Chicano and Latina/o literature[, . . .] often being the only Latina/o works assigned in [. . .] Multicultural Literature and Contemporary American Literature syllabi" (80, 82).

2. This is no minor matter, since the scholarship on ethnic literature generally not only expects but assumes that ethnic American novels will have something important to say about being ethnic or bicultural in a U.S. context, and ethnic texts are often taught with an eye to what they might reveal—especially to often largely monocultural students—about the specific cultural situation from which the texts emerge. See, for example, Dasenbrock; Jussawalla; Maitino and Peck.

3. Calderón, a prominent representative of this line of criticism, has interpreted *Bless Me, Ultima* as a "flight from history" to a nostalgic and innocent "Golden Age" ("*Bless Me, Ultima*" 86, 88) in which mythic concerns substitute for—and erase—historical ones. Saldívar extends this argument, positing that *Bless Me, Ultima* narrates a "nostalgic myth of an organic social structure" as a way of coping with "the incomprehensibility of history" (113) and with "the loss of control over the means and forces of production" (115).

4. Tonn is one of the few critics who disagrees with this assessment, claiming that, in fact, *Bless Me, Ultima* is centrally concerned with sociohistorical issues. But while Tonn reviews the specific historical events that form the backdrop for *Ultima*'s plot (WWII and the atomic bomb) as well as those that constitute the immediate context for its publication (the Civil Rights movement, the Chicano field-workers' strike, landownership claims in New Mexico, the Chicano Moratorium, etc.), he fails to elaborate on the connection between the novel's moment of production (or of representation) and its themes.

5. Some critics nevertheless elide these difficulties by simply *assuming* some connection between the familial struggle and the conflicting ethnic heritages that form Chicano identity. Thomas Vallejos, for example, moves seamlessly from the Márez/Luna clash to the "syncretic mestizo culture" of Chicanos (9). Enrique Lamadrid asserts

(on the grounds that the two families have different "cultures," e.g., agricultural vs. pastoral) that the family conflict is a "cultural" conflict and reads *Bless Me, Ultima* as a "dialectical exploration of the contradictions between lifestyles and cultures" (154), thus vaguely evoking the Chicano/Anglo (or perhaps Spanish/indigenous) context. Along the same lines, Paul Beekman Taylor asserts without textual explanation that the "blend of vaquero and farmer" in Anaya's *Heart of Aztlan* is "a matrix for an Anglo-Chicano mestizo culture" (26).

6. Robert Franklin Gish, for example, focuses on La Llorona and *curanderismo* to make his case that "Anaya's novels (especially *Ultima*) can be read as [. . .] affirming Anaya's belief in the poetic rendering of one's ethnic identity" (128). Willard Gingerich concentrates on Anaya's bilingual writing style as a key to the text's ethnic content (207–8).

7. See Bus; Lattin; Parr.

8. See, for example, Hada; Holton; Kanoza; Taylor. Jane Rogers's "The Function of the La Llorona Motif in Anaya's *Bless Me, Ultima*" would seem from its title to belong to the "indigenous influences" camp of scholars but is actually more properly placed in the "Western/universal" camp, as it uses an entirely Western frame of reference; La Llorona is read as another manifestation of the sirens in Homer's *The Odyssey*. Ramón Saldívar has argued that it is precisely the novel's combination of "the venerable traditions of Western European high culture" with "indigenous belief, folk legend, myth, and poetically crafted scenes of local color" that makes it "a uniquely palatable amalgamation of old and new world symbolic structures," thus accounting for its relative success as a Chicano text (104).

9. My use of the term "Indian" reflects the usage of both *Bless Me, Ultima* and Anzaldúa's *Borderlands/La Frontera*; I also wish to respect efforts by indigenous peoples to reappropriate this term. Thus I use "Indian" interchangeably with "Native American."

10. In a striking misreading of the novel that testifies to how easily a Native American component to Antonio's identity crisis is taken for granted without an actual textual basis, Newkirk writes that Tony "must synthesize his Hispanic roots with the 'magic' of the letters of the Anglo School and the legends told by his Indian friends, Cico, Samuel and Florence" (143). Newkirk simply assumes that any of Tony's friends who are atheist or worshippers of the golden carp—that is, non-Catholics—are "Indian," although the novel explicitly states that "Jasón's Indian [. . .] was the only Indian of the town" (10). Less egregiously, Jussawalla identifies *Bless Me, Ultima* as one of several bildungsromans in which the "main characters' essential knowledge" is "an awareness of their rootedness within their cultures"; Tony, for instance, learns "that the rituals of the Native Americans provide more comfort than Anglo-American Catholicism and its education" (222). Such a reading ignores Antonio's striking *lack* of awareness of any Native American component to his own culture.

11. Indeed, in many ways earlier Spanish policy regarding land grants was *more* flexible toward Indians than subsequent Mexican policy. An Indian settlement with "claims and documents to show that it had existed under orderly government, and [which] indicated that its people would be loyal subjects" to Spain, could be granted a "royal *merced*, the land title of that town" (Cline 13); stable Indian settlements were

distinguished from nomadic "hostile" Indians under Spanish policy (Cline 13–16). In contrast, when Mexico achieved independence, "[m]any of the distinctions among Indian groups which earlier underlay Spanish practices had been forgotten or were now generally disregarded" (Cline 17–18).

12. Roberto Cantú notes, significantly, that, although Jasón, his father, and the Indian all reappear as characters in Anaya's *Heart of Aztlan*, the father's disapproval of the Indian has vanished (17)—and, I would add, with it the theme of repression of "Indianness" as an aspect of Chicano identity.

13. Cantú's rather unsatisfactory conclusion is that Antonio is an "unreliable narrator" (16).

14. Amaryll Chanady, writing on the construction of a Latin American identity, observes, for example, that "in spite of widespread miscegenation [. . .] 'forgetting' the indigenous heritage was a widely adopted strategy on the part of the mestizos in their desire to leave behind their marginalized condition" (xxvi).

15. Ramón Saldívar, intriguingly, also mentions the construction of New Mexican Hispano whiteness in his neo-Marxist reading of *Bless Me, Ultima*. Saldívar is primarily concerned with the novel's evocation of a mythical history in which "New Mexicans willingly and peacefully joined the Anglo-American nation and worked with Anglos as racial brothers and friends to create a garden in the wilderness" (117). Saldívar writes that "Antonio's narrative would have us believe that in Las Pasturas and El Puerto de los Luna men once worked freely together toward one common goal and in control of the means of production" (112).

16. Lux and Vigil cite Weiss 471.

17. Although, as I have suggested, *Bless Me, Ultima* fits perfectly with Brogan's thesis, she herself refers to the novel only twice in passing, connecting it loosely with "La Llorona" (3) and with "ghosts who straddle boundaries" (16) and making no mention of the episode of the Comanche Indian spirits.

## Chapter 2. "Puerto Rican Negro": Defining Race in Piri Thomas's *Down These Mean Streets*

1. It is not necessarily the case, of course, that Puerto Ricans have generally accepted this identification, just as we saw in the last chapter that it was not the case that Mexican Americans (especially prior to the Chicano movement) automatically accepted an association with indigenousness. See De Genova and Ramos-Zayas for a discussion of this issue with regard to Puerto Ricans and African Americans in Chicago.

2. Sánchez, notably, also discusses this scene near the beginning of her chapter on *Down These Mean Streets*, although the thrust of her analysis is that the racially loaded nature of the conversation is dissipated by a segue to the essentializing language of *male* privilege: "*Pussy's the same in every color*" (Thomas 191, qtd. in M. Sánchez 41; emphasis in original).

3. As I have already suggested, however, the racial self-construction celebrated during the Chicano movement was somewhat different from the one ultimately offered by Thomas. "Cross-group" solidarity between Chicanos and African Americans was not based on *racial* identity, as it comes to be in Thomas's memoir, but on similar positions

of marginalization within U.S. society due (in part) to the analogous position of non-white races.

4. The use of the rhetoric of contamination ("tainted"), ironically, echoes the loaded language of biologically inflected understandings of race as "blood," whether "pure" or "tainted." Similarly, for scholars like Gilroy, the rhetoric of race contaminates or infects radical politics: "Raciology has saturated the discourses in which it circulates. It cannot be readily re-signified or de-signified, and to imagine that its dangerous meanings can be easily re-articulated into benign, democratic forms" would be misguided (15).

5. For example, in an internal dissenting voice to the organizing principle of *"Race," Writing, and Difference*, Todorov warns (echoing Gates's phrasing but not his underlying argument) of the "dangerous trope" of "race": "if 'racial differences' do not exist, how can they possibly influence literary texts?" (371). More recently, Michaels has engaged in an extended argument which aims to establish that, if "we do not believe in racial identity as an essence, we cannot believe in racial identity as a social construction and we ought to give up the idea of racial identity altogether—we should [. . .] deny that there are such things as Jews, or blacks, or whites" (142).

6. An editorial in the *New York Times* by Glenn C. Loury, a Boston University economics professor and director of its Institute on Race and Social Division, expresses a similar view in a discussion of the "Racial Privacy Initiative"(which was eventually defeated) in California's 2003 election. This initiative threatened to further erode affirmative action correctives in that state (following on the effects of the infamous Proposition 209) by weakening the power of state institutions to collect racial data:

> [D]espite its superficial appeal, race-blindness is an ideal at war with itself: Strict adherence to this principle would [. . .] inhibit addressing the harmful effects of its own past violation. Fair employment laws are most effectively policed when courts and government agents can compare the racial composition of a company's work force with the racial demography of qualified prospective workers in that company's local labor market. But doing so requires the collection of data that classify individuals by race. [. . .] The trouble is that race-blindness is a narrow, technical aspiration and not a genuinely moral end. (13)

7. This is not reducible to an argument in which the end justifies the means. Loury, like others, is quite aware of the dangers of racial thinking; his proposal involves a careful and sophisticated weighing of the moral risks of the means against the moral advantages of the ends (13).

8. As Hannaford explains, key to the developing concept of race was that "a new relationship had to be established among bodily structure, bodily endowment, and mind, and here the argument was advanced that all three had a bearing on something new called 'national character.'" Hannaford traces, from 1684 to 1815, the development and elaboration of an argument "that custom and law depended on natural history and that each nation had a hidden but noble natural past that could be legitimized by the new scientific and historical processes" (189).

9. Consider, for example, Gates's citation of Hume's essay "Of National Characters" (1748): "I am apt to suspect the negroes, and in general all the other *species* of men (for

there are four or five different kinds) to be naturally inferior to the whites. There never was a *civilized nation* of any other complection than white" (10; emphasis added).

10. In the relatively slight body of critical work on Thomas's *Down These Mean Streets*, there is little acknowledgement of Piri's *use* of racism and racial privilege in the early part of the text as an essential part of its bildungsroman structure. Marta Sánchez points out, accurately, that, "[b]ecause for many whites at this time 'Negro' was a racist category, those who used it on Piri perpetrated acts of mutilation on him by refusing him the possibility of self-representation" (44); but she overlooks how frequently the young Piri's "self-representation" involves the *deployment* of racist categories for a stake in racial privilege. In general, commentators such as Herms, Luis, and Rodríguez de Laguna prefer to focus on Piri's *experience* of racism rather than on his wielding of it. Others, such as Mohr and Lisa González, put the problem in terms of being caught *between* categories or groups.

11. Rodriguez-Morazzani is here taking issue with Clara E. Rodríguez's claim in a 1974 article, "Puerto Ricans: Between Black and White" (a claim which, as Rodriguez-Morazzani points out, was later reduplicated almost verbatim in her 1989 book *Puerto Ricans Born in the U.S.A.*), that, "in Puerto Rico, racial identification is subordinate to cultural identification, while in the U.S., racial identification, to a large extent, determines cultural identification. Thus when asked the divisive question, 'What are you?' Puerto Ricans of all colors and ancestry answer, 'Puerto Rican,' while most New Yorkers answer, Black, Jewish, or perhaps, 'of Italian descent.' This is not to say that Puerto Ricans feel no racial identification, but rather that cultural identification supersedes it" (qtd. in Rodriguez-Morazzani 150).

12. And yet—lynching aside—as various critics have noted, the social positioning of African Americans and Puerto Ricans in U.S. urban centers has not been dissimilar: "Both groups experienced unemployment, housing discrimination, police brutality, racial violence, and racial devaluation [. . .]. In this context it is very suggestive that much of the literature of the 1960s and 1970s in the social sciences concerning Puerto Ricans compares and contrasts their situation with that of African Americans" (Rodriguez-Morazzani 145). Flores argues that, in terms of such demographics, Puerto Ricans could be said to have more in common with African Americans than with Cuban Americans or Mexican Americans (*From Bomba* 163).

13. See Marta Sánchez (47) for a different reading of this scene.

14. In yet another wonderfully ironic twist of fate, DNA studies—which can serve the purpose of grounding group (and individual) identity claims in a certain sort of biological "essentialism"—have suggested that, in fact, a larger percentage of Puerto Ricans actually have some indigenous heritage than the percentage that shares some African heritage. In other words, the historical "lesson" that the indigenous inhabitants of Puerto Rico were killed off, leaving no genealogical trace, might be wrong (see Kearns).

15. Ian López notes that such scenes "suggest a spatial component to racial identities, an implication confirmed in Thomas's travel from Spanish Harlem, where he was Puerto Rican, to Long Island, where he was accused of trying to pass, to the South, where he was Black" (12).

16. For a fascinating discussion of some earlier "texts" (both fiction and film) that

dramatize white consolidation of power in the face of a perceived black threat, see Stokes.

17. Piri's father acknowledges having similarly used linguistic difference to signal racial difference from "Negroes," when a phenotype might have suggested otherwise: "I saw the look of white people on me when I was a young man, when I walked into a place where a dark skin isn't supposed to be. I noticed how a cold rejection turned into an indifferent acceptance when they heard my exaggerated accent. I can remember the time when I made my accent heavier, to make me more of a Puerto Rican than the most Puerto Rican there ever was" (153).

18. This scene is an excellent illustration of Ian López's argument that "[c]hoice composes a crucial ingredient in the construction of racial identities and the fabrication of races. Racial choices occur on mundane and epic levels [. . .] and the effects are often minor though sometimes profound, for instance, slightly altering a person's affiliation or radically remaking a community's identity. Nevertheless, in every circumstance choices are exercised not by free agents or autonomous actors, but by people who are compromised and constrained by the social context" (13–14). In the incident with the prostitute, Piri is not "seen" as black until he *chooses* to engage in a behavior—speaking English—which he knows will cause him to be read as black.

19. Mohr, for example, argues that West "proposes a theory of racial options which [. . .] is in an absolute sense more reasonable than the system of restraints and impositions that actually governs" U.S. society (49–50). See also M. Sánchez.

20. For an interesting discussion of the implications of the concept of "passing" for notions of race, see Michaels.

21. This lesson seems to contradict Piri's earlier understanding that language may modify racial identification. His travels, that is, reinforce the concept of race as biologically, rather than linguistically, determined. In the United States speaking a "foreign" language can, in certain contexts, exempt him from the severity of the racial dichotomy; but he discovers that countries which speak a language other than English still make distinctions between "black" and "white." In Spanish-speaking countries in South America, for example, speaking Spanish will not "save" Piri from being racially identified as black—thus "Hispanic" logically becomes less of an assertion of whiteness.

22. Although racial issues arise again in prison, especially with regard to religion, Piri is no longer struggling with how to identify himself racially; as Mohr has noted, "Piri seems less troubled by the identity question" while in prison (53).

23. Interestingly, Lisa González detects an increasing emphasis on pragmatics in the trajectory of Thomas's oeuvre overall: "The unresolved [. . .] crisis in *Down These Mean Streets* [i.e., Piri's "identity" crisis] gives way to an important set of thematics in Thomas's later works, thematics that focus on the importance of direct intervention in the lives of urban youths rather than identity per se" (118).

24. A common race is also cited by some Chicago Latinos as a primordial category that would allow Latinos to unite against inequalities (F. Padilla 105).

25. To arrive at this finding, Jones-Correa and Leal sorted data from respondents based on (1) whether they had identified themselves, either primarily or secondarily, using some sort of panethnic label such as "Latino" or "Hispanic" (the four categories were "No preference" for a panethnic label, "Some preference," "First preference among

others"—that is, the respondent identified with more than one label, such as a national-origin label *and* a panethnic label but with the panethnic label first—and "Only preference") and (2) whether respondents believed that the different Latino cultures were "Very Similar," "Somewhat Similar," or "Not Very Similar." For each of the categories of labeling preference, however, only a relatively small minority of respondents asserted a belief in "Very Similar" Latino cultures (18.45 percent of those who did not identify at all panethnically believed this, while 16.46 percent of those who identified *only* panethnically did so). A much larger percentage in each category, ranging from about half to 65.29 percent, believed that the different cultures were somewhat similar (231). It is worth noting here that even to say that Latin American cultures are "very similar" is not to say that they are the *same* (that is, a "common") culture.

## Chapter 3. Speaking for Others: Problems of Representation in the Writing of Julia Alvarez

1. In Alvarez's most recent novel to date, *Saving the World* (2006), she exacts hilarious revenge on González Echevarría by poking fun at a fictional "patrón of Latino critics," intriguingly named "Mario González-Echavarriga," for his over-the-top criticism of the novel's protagonist, a Dominican American writer like Alvarez herself (20).

2. The San Diego Children of Immigrants Longitudinal Study (CILS) sample, which Rumbaut discusses here, is composed of Mexicans, Filipinos, Vietnamese, Laotians, Cambodians, Chinese, and smaller groups of other national origin. Rumbaut qualifies the findings by noting that, despite the low levels of transnational attachment among the second generation (those displaying strong transnational behaviors were less than 10 percent of each ethnic group), there were differences among ethnic groups, with Mexicans and other Latin Americans "much more likely to maintain a level of fluent bilingualism [one of the 'objective' measures of transnationalism used in the study] into adulthood" than were other national-origin groups studied. He continues: [H]owever, "the fact that the Mexicans in this sample reside in a city that is situated right on the Mexican border [. . .] greatly facilitates their transnationality, especially the frequency of visits across the border [another 'objective' measure]. Perhaps the surprise is that despite that advantage of nearness and familiarity, the level of binational and bicultural engagement is as low as it is" ("Severed" 90).

3. The biographical note for *In the Name of Salomé* reports that Alvarez "lives in Vermont and in the Dominican Republic, where she and her husband run a coffee plantation."

4. I do not mean to suggest that empathy is an unproblematic category, however. For more on this, see Chapter 7.

5. Among those killed were apparently substantial numbers of ethnic Haitians who were born in the Dominican Republic (Suárez, *Tears* 14).

6. Sagás notes that "the myth of the Dominican indio was the most important ethnic fabrication developed in the late nineteenth century—and remains influential to this day. [. . .] In order to varnish their common African past, the Dominican people essentially dropped the words *black* and *mulatto* from their vocabulary and replaced them with the less traumatic and more socially desirable *indio*" (35). As in Piri Thomas's

*Down These Mean Streets*, "Indianness" became a way to avoid "blackness." Sagás also reports that in the early twentieth century—decades before Trujillo's rule—Dominican newspapers were "full of complaints about the immigration of black laborers," and that a law passed in 1912 limited immigration by black Haitians into the Dominican Republic (41).

7. Several scholars have discussed *In the Time of the Butterflies* in the context of Haitian American author Edwidge Danticat's *The Farming of Bones*, which represents the 1937 massacre from a Haitian woman's point of view. Kelli Johnson argues that both novels serve similar functions, commemorating a collective history otherwise "excluded from historical discourse" ("Both Sides" 76). In a slightly more critical vein, Lynn Ink argues that Alvarez's novel attempts to offer a vision of nationalism that can counter the "masculinized [form of] nationalism [which] relegates women to the private sphere, establishing a gendered divide between the domestic and the political" (793)—but that, in its representation of the Mirabal sisters and the tensions between their "political" resistance and their private lives, it ultimately reinscribes this gender divide. Most negatively, April Shemak—who mentions Alvarez's novel only briefly in a discussion of Danticat—contends that, "for all of [*Butterflies*'s] radicalism, it ends up reproducing a nationalistic history that ignores class and racial divisions within the nation" (84); Myriam Chancy adds that it is also silent on divisions symbolized by the Haitian-Dominican border (177). Lucía Suárez muses over whether Alvarez's representation of "Trujillo's despotism served to soften the extreme cruelty suffered under his reign" (21).

8. See Ink.

9. Zentella cites A. J. Toribio.

10. For a more positive reading of Alvarez's representation of Chucha, see Kelli Johnson, *Julia Alvarez*, 139–45.

11. In a climactic scene of racial violence which introduces the events of the massacre, Danticat's narrator describes how "[s]omeone threw a fist-sized rock, which bruised my lip and left cheek. My face hit the ground. Another rock was thrown at Yves. [. . .] The faces in the crowd were streaming in and out of my vision. A sharp blow to my side nearly stopped my breath. [. . .] Rolling myself into a ball, I tried to get away from the worst of the kicking horde. [. . .] The air vibrated with a twenty-one-gun salute. People applauded and stomped their feet and sang the Dominican national anthem" (194). In this scene, the emphasis is not on Trujillo but on the *collective* nature of the violence. Lucía Suárez reviews correspondence in which historian Bernardo Vega takes issue precisely with this aspect of Danticat's novel. According to Suárez, Vega "express[ed] consternation about her [Danticat's] representation of the Dominican people in her novel. He notes that one comes away from her story with the impression that civil society approved and participated in such a horrible genocide. He underlines the fact that it was a military order issued by Trujillo and executed by his army" (13). Danticat responded to Vega, in part, by pointing to the lingering manifestations of Dominican racial/national ideology which created the necessary condition for the killings (Suárez 13). This issue is also emphasized in *The Farming of Bones*. After the massacre, a survivor—a Haitian priest—parrots, in his own trauma-induced dementia, the Dominican

nationalist discourse: "Our motherland is Spain; theirs is darkest Africa, you understand? [...] Those of us who love our country are taking measures to keep it our own" (260).

12. Indeed, as Kelli Johnson points out, Alvarez returns to the Haitian massacre once again in her fourth novel, *In the Name of Salomé*. One of the central characters, Camila Henríquez, a Dominican who is now a professor in the United States, is horrified by the massacre and eventually—in 1950—speaks of it publicly in what is intended to be a talk honoring her mother, famed Dominican poet Salomé Ureña. Johnson suggests that such repeated mentions "form a thread across Alvarez's work" that "reveals her commitment to exploring Haitians' role in Dominican collective memory" (*Julia Alvarez* 146). In fact, Alvarez explicitly discusses the racial component of the Haitian massacre in "A White Woman of Color." If she has yet to fully "explore" this issue in her fiction, it is certainly the case that she continues to revisit this particular, haunting gap.

13. In *Saving the World*, the thorny ethical issues raised by well-intentioned Americans imposing their will on the "third world"—even with the best of philanthropic intentions (e.g., developing a vaccine for AIDS)—are once again a subject of Alvarez's attention.

## Chapter 4. Complicating *Cubanidad*: Novels of Achy Obejas and Cristina García

1. The use of "somehow" here is perhaps telling, suggesting Eire still participates to some degree in the dominant exile construction of Cubanness by making the appearance of Chinese in Havana a whimsical fluke, without historical explanation.

2. Ana Menéndez's short story, "In Cuba I Was a German Shepherd," for example, suggests that the aging and widowed central character's nostalgia for Cuba is actually a symptom of a more familial longing: for an intimate, lost past with his now-grown daughters and deceased wife.

3. The standard explanation for the whiteness of first-wave exiles is that it is linked to class; those who immediately fled Castro's Communist regime were those with the most to lose: the upper and middle classes, who, because of a history of pervasive racial stratification in Cuba, were predominantly white (Olson and Olson 84). Interestingly, Aguirre complicates this interpretation somewhat by pointing out that, within a few years of the revolution, the "occupational characteristics of the exiles" became more diverse, so that by 1971 they represented a fairly good cross section of what had been the Cuban population of the 1950s (that is, no longer just the professional classes at the top of the socioeconomic ladder). Yet during the same years, Aguirre observes, the percentage of the exile population identifying as white *increased* (104–5). Thus class status by itself cannot account, he argues, for the racial demographics of the population by the end of the 1960s. He places greater emphasis on the Cuban revolutionary government's representation of itself as eliminating racism, its concomitant portrayal of the United States as racist, and also the U.S. policy after 1965 of giving priority for entry to those with family members already in the United States, which would have the effect of privileging the white families of the very early, professional-class immigrants (112–13).

4. See, for example, *The Cuban American Family Album* (1996), by Dorothy and

Thomas Hoobler (with an introduction by Oscar Hijuelos). In this photograph-filled book, virtually all the people pictured are strikingly white-looking; the cover photograph, of a wedding, and the full-page photograph opposite the title page, of a *quinceañera*, are of "white" Cubans. Mulatto or black Cubans register visually only near the end of the book, in two small pictures related to music and dance. (One is of jazz artist Mario Bauzá and singer Celia Cruz; the other is of a woman performing a "Latin dance" [114–15]). As Max Castro argues, the whiteness of the Cuban American exile population is dramatically unrepresentative of the Cuban nation as a whole prior to the revolution (303–4).

5. It was perhaps not always completely convincing, however. María Torres notes that Cuban exiles' *self*-identification as white "does not change the fact that they were not considered 'white' in the context of Southern politics" (*In the Land* 222 n. 1).

6. For a good overview of articles that touted the Cuban "success story" during the 1960s, 1970s, and even 1980s, see Croucher 113–15.

7. Statistics cited by various scholars as evidence that the majority of Cuban immigrants in the 1960s were white often simply assume that race is a "fact" documentable by such statistics. "It is well established that Cubans in the United states are primarily white," Aguirre writes (104), citing U.S. census figures from 1960 and 1970. James and Judith Olson variously cite, as fact, contradictory statistics that "more than 82 percent" or "[m]ore than 98 percent of the Cuban immigrants during the 1960s were white" (61, 84), depending on the source. But, contradictions aside, such reviews of statistical data neglect to consider the fact that the census and other data-gathering mechanisms are based largely on *self*-reporting of racial information. As Lusane has argued, it is important "to understand why people choose to identify themselves as black, white, or mulatto" (75). Allatson's qualification that Cuban exiles are predominantly "white *identifying*" (188; emphasis added) and M. Torres's similar emphasis on how exiles "choose" to identify racially (*In the Land* 222 n. 1) seem to be more conscious of the social construction of race.

8. In an interesting figure, "among the native-born of Cuban origin in Florida, 91 percent identify as white, while [. . .] [a]mong native-born Cubans living outside of Florida, only 66 percent identify as white" (Tafoya 13). This might be a sign that Miami-Cuban culture exerts a greater pressure on Cubans to claim whiteness than does the culture of other geographical locations in the United States. The Pew Hispanic Center report suggests that the historical dynamic here could well be similar to the one in Texas, "where a large Latino population was caught up both in Southern-style segregation and then the civil rights struggle to undo it"—propelling a substantial number (63 percent) of Texan Mexican Americans to identify as white (Tafoya 12). Racial self-identification, as we have seen in the first two chapters of this book, is fluid and circumstantially contingent rather than self-evident; the Pew Center quotes a respondent from a Cuban American focus group who said, "The white always has the highest social prestige and the darker skin always have the lower social prestige [. . . ;] you have some very dark skinned people who earn a lot of money, and you tell them[,] you're dark skinned . . . [and they reply] oh, no, I'm white" (Tafoya 8).

9. By 1970 a *greater* percentage of Cuban immigrants in the United States were identifying themselves as white than in 1960 (Aguirre 104). If, as M. Torres argues,

Cubans, despite their self-representation, were indeed to some extent "perceived to be nonwhite" (*In the Land* 76) by the majority U.S. culture in which they found themselves, then it is certainly possible that the response of the community was an even more vigorous claim to whiteness. Torres comments that "[f]or years to talk about [...] discrimination against Cubans was heresy. Those of us raised outside the [Miami] enclave, and therefore more exposed to racism, were ostracized in Miami when we tried to discuss racism or raise our voices in support of the civil rights movement" (*In the Land* 197). Torres's recollection, tellingly, implies that racism toward Cubans was viewed by the Miami enclave as inconceivable because they *were already* the dominant race, and therefore had nothing to do with the minority struggles of the civil rights movement. As Croucher explains, Cuban exiles have tended to advance a narrative which, "on the one hand, distances them from other minority groups, specifically black Americans and, on the other hand, absolves them from any responsibility for this minority group's disadvantaged plight" (107).

10. Of course, a more prominently discussed reason for this "difference" in reception and coverage has to do with the news that Castro had released a number of prison and mental hospital inmates and allowed them to depart with the "Marielitos" (Olson and Olson 81; see also Masud-Piloto 100–103).

11. Even before the 1980 boatlift, a study of rent differentials by race/ethnicity in Miami "found that the discrimination against black Cubans was strongest in the city's Cuban areas, as compared with white, black, and mixed tracts" (Nicholas and Prohias, cited in Aguirre 114)

12. The characterization of Cuban immigrants as primarily white persists even after the Mariel boatlift brought significantly larger numbers of black Cubans to the United States. For example, as Masud-Piloto notes, when in 1984 the INS gave legal status to the 125,000 Cubans who had arrived in the United States in the 1980 boatlift—but not to the 30,000 Haitians who had also arrived in 1980—the decision was reviled by many, including the *Miami Herald*, as "racist" (119), presumably because Cubans, even the Mariel entrants, were by and large still perceived as white, while Haitians were predominantly black. Scholarship on Cuban exiles—even when it attends to the different waves of exiles and their different demographics—still often employs terms that suggest that Cubans are not (ever) black. See, for example, *Cuban Americans* by James and Judith Olson, in which the authors go through an extended discussion of the Mariel boatlift and the prejudices the entrants faced from resident Cuban exiles, but then go on to talk unproblematically about job competition and other resentments between "blacks and Cubans" (86–87). In a more ambiguous example, Croucher, in *Imagining Miami*, repeatedly uses the terms "blacks," "whites," and "Hispanic" as separate and nonoverlapping racial categories, even though she acknowledges at one point that "Hispanics" include both black Cubans and white Cubans (56).

13. Santería, for example, which after the Mariel boatlift became a lightning rod of sorts for Cuban exile prejudice against the Mariel entrants (Olson and Olson 86), has now become a fairly prominent (if contested) part of the Cuban American collective symbolization. Santería is now written about even by authors with no notable Afro-Cuban heritage, and, as María Teresa Marrero puts it, "is being rearticulated currently by white U.S. Cuban women writers [...] in order to express their *cultural identity*

[. . .]. The representation of Santería by Cuban American writers challenges notions of the hegemonic, predominantly white, politically conservative Cubans to define identity politics for all Cubans in the U.S." (141). Media coverage of the controversy surrounding the practice of Santería in the exile community, including the 1992–93 case that reached the U.S. Supreme Court (in which the court ruled that ordinances in Hialeah, Florida, against the practice of animal sacrifice in Santería were unconstitutional) also brought it to the larger public eye. (For text of the court ruling and commentary, see "The Supreme Court on Santeria"; for a review of some earlier media coverage on Miami reactions to Santería, see Croucher 78–79).

14. Aguirre cites a 1973 doctoral dissertation by James M. Stevenson, "Cuban Americans: New Urban Class," in which fifty Cuban businessmen were asked, "What was the situation (prior to Castro) between the blacks and the whites in Cuba?" As Aguirre reports, answers included "[n]o problems," "no differences or distinctions," "no discrimination," "no racism," "like brothers," "equals," and "magnificent." None of the answers suggested any problems of racial struggle or tension in Cuba's history (120).

15. The statement also, quite ironically, is entirely in line with postrevolutionary rhetoric on the racial situation in Cuba, as we shall shortly see. Indeed, it is also a logical continuation of a national history—since Cuban independence—of silence about racial problems and struggles. For a fascinating discussion of this silence, including its purposes as well as challenges to it, see Ferrer, "Rethinking Race and Nation in Cuba."

16. But see *Guayaba Sweet* (2003), edited by Murrieta and Alonso Gallo.

17. Yet Alvarez Borland does not seem interested in commenting on those textual moments in the works she examines which do invoke the issue of racial diversity—and racial struggles—in Cuba, such as the insurrection of 1912, in which Afro-Cubans were massacred by the Cuban army, referred to by Cristina García in *Dreaming in Cuban*.

18. The index to Alvarez Borland's book is revealing: while we can find entries on the subjects of "ethnic perspective [. . .] and heritage" and "first generation: anger of" (193), there are no entries for "race," "racism," "African heritage," "Afro-Cuban," "mulatto," or "*mestizaje.*" Subentries on "hybridism" and "biculturation" (or some other variant of "bicultural") almost inevitably refer to discussions of Cuban American hybridity. (Ruth Behar's discussion of Jewish Cuban identity is the exception.)

19. This development in Cuban American fiction seems to correspond to a development in scholarship on Cuba. If it is true, as Louis A. Pérez Jr. has suggested, that Cuban studies in the '60s, '70s, and '80s was characterized primarily by examinations of the 1959 Cuban revolution ("History" 53), by the 1990s this was no longer the case (Childs 286). The first novels of both García and Obejas, as well as Obejas's earlier short story "We Came All the Way from Cuba So You Could Dress Like This?" all could be said to give much greater attention to the 1959 revolution as the defining, disruptive moment than their most recent novels do.

20. As the Cortés/Malinche example suggests, sometimes narratives of national identity have *incorporated* the violent history of the past while "smoothing over" its legacy in the present. For a discussion of the Malinche figure as interpreter/traitor, see Norma Alarcón's well-known essay "Traddutora, Traditora." As I discuss in Chapter 6, Cuban American writer Margarita Engle constructs an analogous origins story (to the Malinche/Cortés union) for Cubans in *Skywriting*.

21. Spitta reads Ortiz's representation of Cuba in *Cuban Counterpoint* as just such a national romance, in which Cubanness is "the product of a happy marriage of differences" (163).

22. For a clear and interesting discussion of the dual meanings of "hybridity," see Simon 415. Simon takes some issue with Young's account of hybridity.

23. Interestingly, the novel identifies Lucrecia's family as being from the Congo region (169) rather than from (present-day) Nigeria, home of the Yoruba people and geographical point of origin of the form of orisha worship known in Cuba as Regla de Ocha, Lucumí, or more commonly as Santería. The African diasporic religion in Cuba that is identified with the Congo region, in contrast, is Palo Monte. In Cuba, as famed Cuban ethnographer and writer Miguel Barnet explains, there was cultural exchange among these two religious systems:

> Among the peoples from sub-Saharan West Africa, those of Yoruba origin had the greatest influence on the integrative processes of the island's cultural and religious system. Within a short time they managed to disseminate their forms of expression. In the process they visibly influenced other African cultures, including those that had become established in Cuba long before that of the Yoruba. [...] The predominant Yoruba influence has conditioned the [ . . .] Congo gods and semigods [who] have absorbed elements and characteristics from the Yoruba deities while retaining their own body of stories. (*Afro-Cuban* 17,82)

García's deliberate mention of Lucrecia's family origins as specifically Congolese rather than Yoruban thus further points to cultural syncretism, hybridity, and cross-pollination in Cuba.

24. As Duany notes, "Ortiz first introduced his well-known metaphor for Cuban culture as an *ajiaco* in a 1939 lecture at the University of Havana, which was subsequently cited and reproduced on many occasions," including in his essay "Los factores humanos de la cubanidad," in *Ensayos etnosociológicos* (Duany 22, 38 n. 13).

25. "[T]he mambo is indeed a jumble, a forum for foreignness and a haven for the heterogeneous. The great Cuban ethnologist Fernando Ortiz aptly described it as an 'estofado de sonoridades,' a stew of sounds. Since for Ortiz the essence of Cuban culture was also its nourishing combination of foreign ingredients, the mambo's impurities did not make it any less Cuban. If the mambo was a stew, Cuba was one also. And who's to say that an *estofado* is any less Cuban than an *ajiaco*?" (Pérez Firmat, *Life on the Hyphen* 80; Ortiz, *Los bailes* 80, qtd. in Pérez Firmat, *Life on the Hyphen*). For an argument that Pérez Firmat's version of *ajiaco* is singularly unrepresentative, ahistorical, and, indeed, white, see Castro 294–95.

26. In a fascinating discussion of the difference between racial construction in Cuba and in the United States, Safa explains that, in contrast to the one-drop rule in the United States, which "made race a fundamental division in society" (86), in Cuba, racial mixing on a large scale resulted in "a racial continuum based on phenotype that made it difficult to isolate a bounded, recognized Afro-American [. . .] group and inhibited the development of a separate cultural identity. Instead, the intermediate mulatto stratum produced by race mixture came to be not only recognized but glorified in Cuba as a national symbol" (89).

27. Pérez draws specifically on Martí's article "Para las escenas," which, as he notes, was "found in his papers and published for the first time by the Center for Martí Studies in 1978" (20).

28. Although Morejón—who is here writing on the cultural legacy of Afro-Cuban poet Nicolás Guillén—centers her attention on the Spanish and African elements of Cuban culture, she makes specific note of other cultures, such as the Chinese, which have also been "of considerable importance" (231).

29. Morejón's narrative of Cuban identity is particularly striking in the degree to which she presents *mestizaje* as stabilized: "The diverse formative elements of the Cuban nation are *fused in a single substance* [. . .]. Cubans are characterized for having sought to build a nation that is *homogeneous in its heterogeneity*" (232; emphasis added). She then goes on to recollect that, "[w]ith his typically creole humour, Don Fernando [Ortiz] wrote: 'There are Cubans so dark they seem black and there are Cubans so light they seem white.' [. . .] A Cuban, though racially he may look Yoruba or Catalan, responds to a national character. [. . .] The sense of nationhood presupposes a melting pot of races and a mixed culture" (233). In Morejón's national narrative, racial identifications are effaced by the notion of "looking" (deceptively) white or black—all Cubans, it is strongly implied by the qualifiers "look" and "seem," are in actuality "mixed," whatever their deceptive appearance.

30. In a special issue of *Souls: A Critical Journal of Black Politics, Culture, and Society*, several contributors echo Soyini Madison's assertion that "[d]iscrimination is against the law in Cuba, but racial prejudice survives" (54). Safa, for example, writes that "[t]he revolution succeeded in opening new avenues of social mobility for Afro-Cubans and in promoting Afro-Cuban culture in music and dance, but it did not eliminate the ideological notion of white superiority" (90). Lusane begins from the premise that, "[e]ven in Cuba, after all, race matters" (73)—and then examines various theoretical explanations for why this might be so. Madison observes that, during a visit to Cuba as part of a Columbia University delegation, it was notable that "the workers [at the hotel] were [. . .] marked by color: The dark-skinned Cubans did the cleaning while the light-skinned Cubans interacted with the public. White Cuban women in hotel uniforms greeted guests inside, Afro-Cuban women in Spandex and high heels hustled johns outside" (55). This representation is echoed by Achy Obejas in *Days of Awe*. During her first visit to Cuba, Obejas's narrator, Alejandra, who is working as an interpreter, describes a meeting between Cubans and Chicago-based activists, some of whom are discussing the racism in the United States: "Then I looked around the room, at the varied colors of the members of our foreign-based delegation, and at the white-skinned, hazel-eyed descendants of northern Spain wearing official Cuban government name tags. The only island Cubans without them were the two charcoal-toned women in the room" who provided the drinking water and the toilet paper to the delegation members (61).

31. Despite the construction of *cubanidad* as racial mixture, Lusane notes that, "[i]n the 1981 census, for instance, about 66 percent of those surveyed claimed to be white, whereas 12 percent said they were black. Any visitor to Cuba knows that this does not seem entirely accurate, given that Cuba appears to be primarily a black and mulatto nation." Lusane uses the apparent contradiction as a springboard to contemplate the

question of "why people choose to identify themselves as black, white, or mulatto" (75). In a similar vein, Safa notes "the continuing persistence of racial endogamy in Cuba, especially among whites, 93 percent of whom in 1981 chose other whites as marriage partners" (90; Reca cited).

32. Louis A. Pérez notes that, as far back as the struggle for Cuban independence against Spain in the late nineteenth century, the developing category of "nation" was increasingly used to erase lines of racial division (*On Becoming Cuban* 90–91). "Conversely," as Manning Marable puts it, "American nationalism was so intertwined with white supremacy that it is impossible to imagine an African-American Maceo assuming the role of George Washington or Ulysses S. Grant" (8). It is interesting to speculate on the degree to which the emancipation of slaves *prior* to the achievement of national independence in Cuba (as opposed to the situation in the United States, where slavery was legal for almost a full century after independence) played a factor in the shaping of Cuban nationhood as an ideal of racial mixture rather than of whiteness.

33. As Moore elaborates, "Mainstream Cuban audiences came to accept representations of blackness in popular culture for a time, but only a blackness presented from a certain perspective, using particular stereotypes, and limited to well-defined aesthetic conventions." Moore notes the tension that existed between "an emerging racially and culturally based nationalism incorporating mulatto imagery and a widespread belief in the inherent superiority of whites over those of black or mixed ancestry" (220).

34. In *On Becoming Cuban*, Louis A. Pérez Jr. notes that the antagonism to racial group identity for Afro-Cubans dates back to the struggle for independence against Spain and to that paradigmatic Cuban, José Martí, who said, "The black man who proclaims his race, even if mistakenly as a way to proclaim spiritual identity with all races, justifies and provokes white racism" (qtd. in Louis Pérez, *On Becoming Cuban* 91).

35. Interestingly, Lusane reads the lack of "race consciousness" in Cuba as at times a "conservative form" of "color-blindness," and as supported by the "black internalization of racial denial" (76–77). For Lusane, "white Cuban rejection of the term 'Afro-Cuban,' the refusal by the state to appropriate the term in its official language, and black Cuban denial of a diasporic linkage with Afro-Latinos or African Americans," all can be read as "expressions of individual, institutional, and internal racial dilemmas" (77).

36. Lusane speculates on the possibility that the Special Period in Cuba (the name given by Castro to the continuing period of economic hardship created by the dissolution of the Soviet Union) might provoke "a process of racialization [. . .]. A broad acceptance of the term 'Afro-Cuban,' for example, would indicate a mature race consciousness that has not existed in almost a century among black Cubans" (75). At the very least, the Special Period certainly seems to have resulted in increased attention to race; Alejandro de la Fuente has noted that "more has been written about race and racism in Cuba during the last ten years [i.e. the 1990s] than in the three previous decades combined" (199), and he hypothesizes that the Special Period might explain this flourishing interest: "Like other forms of social inequality, racial disparities and racially defined tensions actually increased during 'the special period'" (200).

37. "Christian missionaries operated many schools, hospitals, and other philanthropic enterprises in China, all protected by extraterritoriality. The separate school

system, outside of Chinese governmental control, was a sore point for nationalists, who regarded the education of Chinese youth as a Chinese prerogative" ("China" 71811). Though García makes no mention of Chen Fang's school being run by missionaries, the fact that the school caters to foreign diplomats' children would suggest that it would have been one of the schools protected by territoriality and thus opposed by the nationalists.

38. For discussion, see "China" 71817; Eastman 1; Henriot 1–2, 20.

39. Fewsmith dates the increasing anti-Western sentiment in China to World War I: "Prior to World War I, Chinese had generally looked on the West as representing all that was progressive and modern, and hence as a model to be emulated. The Treaty of Versailles, which turned Germany's rights in Shandong over to Japan [China's enemy], provoked outrage and disgust at the West's crass pursuit of Realpolitik. [. . .] With this rejection of the West came a new emphasis on defining a specifically 'Chinese' path of development" (88).

40. See also "China" 71814.

41. For an overview of Communist-Nationalist cooperation and the sense of a united front against Japan, see "China" 71820–24.

42. The Cultural Revolution was indeed characterized by a renewed "hostility towards [. . .] foreign cultural influences"; the Chinese press, at various times, condemned Shakespeare, Tolstoy, Balzac, and Beethoven—as well as classical music and classical ballet in general (*Cultural Revolution* 14). Nevertheless, antiforeign sentiment does not seem to have been nearly so prominent a part of the rhetoric surrounding the Cultural Revolution as it was during the earlier Nationalist revolution. Rather, the rhetoric employed seems to have been much more clearly class-oriented: "The aim was to replace, in the jargon of the hegemonic ideology in China, the feudal-capitalist values and norms of the precommunist period with proletarian ones" (Kwong xii). Educational "goals were couched in general ideological terms such as purging the educational system of its authoritarian, capitalistic traits and to bring it closer to communist ideals" (xvi); the educational imperatives were conveyed "in slogans like 'to create intellectuals of the working class,' and to unify 'theory and practice, mental and manual labor, city and countryside'" (xiv). The main enemy was seen as "bourgeois" sensibility, ideology, and traditions (65). García's choice of emphasis on the continued national and antiforeign aspect of the Cultural Revolution thus highlights her concern with the varying manifestations of nationalism and the common threads between the Nationalist regime and the later Communist one.

43. Joseph Fewsmith has noted certain "striking similarities" between KMT ideology and that of the Chinese Communist Party: "Both parties accepted the Marxist critique of capitalism, the Leninist thesis on imperialism, and the idea of China as a proletarian nation" (113).

44. It is arguable that García emphasizes the nationalism of the Chinese Communists *more* than she does that of the Nationalist government, which gets comparatively little elaboration in the novel. Since the nationalist imperatives of Castro's Cuban Communist regime are also emphasized, it would be possible to read García's novel as an indictment of a *particular* form of nationalist fervor under Communist states rather

than necessarily of nationalisms in general. I would argue, however, that the distinctly anti-Communist nationalism of the United States during the Vietnam conflict comes equally under fire.

45. Gandhi's discussion attempts to account for—and to rehabilitate—an ideal of (postcolonial) nationalism which would *not* simply serve to consolidate the interests of the state (120). This possibility is left unimagined by García, however, whose view of nationalism—or of any fixed notion of collective identity—seems, I would argue, wholly pessimistic.

46. Robert M. Levine has noted that, in 1939, when Cuba was briefly resisting further Jewish immigration, the Dominican Republic offered to receive Jewish settlers, also in part "to whiten the population." As Levine puts it, "Dominican race prejudice created a haven for victims of a different race prejudice in the Reich" (134).

47. Behar is actually speaking broadly about Latin American Jews here, but, as one of Bettinger-López's interviewees attests, there are perceived differences even among Latin American countries in this regard. Albert, a nineteen-year-old Miami Cuban Jew, has said, "It's funny, most Jews, when I tell them I'm Cuban [...] they're shocked, they're literally shocked. Argentina they know; they know there's Jews in Argentina. And South America, they're not so shocked about the Jews. But Cuban Jews?" (161).

48. Bettinger-López seems to suggest here that Gentile Cuban exiles started to differentiate between themselves and Jews only on arrival in the United States (34). But, of course, a relative lack of anti-Semitism in Cuba does not necessarily translate into a lack of distinction. As she notes only a page later, "in Cuba they had stood out *as Jews*" (35; emphasis in original). Jewish Cubans did not "become" Jews to other Cubans in Miami—they always had been perceived as such, as Ruth Behar anecdotally suggests by describing the street in Agramonte where the "store on one corner [was called] *la casa de los polacos nuevos*"—"*polacos*" is the term used in Cuba to refer to Ashkenazi Jews (from Eastern Europe)—"and the store on the other corner *la casa de los polacos viejos*. You see," Behar goes on to explain, "there were two Jewish families in Agramonte; but my family got there first, so they became 'los polacos viejos' [the old Jews], while the others were merely 'nuevos' [new]" ("Juban" 168). For an explanation of the terms "*polacos*" and "*turcos*," see Bettinger-López xxxiv and Levine 26.

49. Ruth Behar has, of course, written in a nonfictional vein about her experiences as a Cuban Jew. More recently, journalist Gigi Anders's memoir *Jubana!* (2005) treats her experiences as a Cuban Jew in the United States.

50. As Obejas explains in her glossary, "*converso*" is the word "for Christianized Jews who continued to privately practice their ancestral faith. Both anusim and conversos profess Catholicism but practice Judaism covertly; the anusim are forced, the conversos may or may not be forced" (361).

51. See, for example, Bettinger-López 22.

52. As Maya Socolovsky writes of Obejas's work in general, her writing "insists on articulating what the hegemonic discourse has silenced" ("Deconstructing" 244). It is worth noting, for instance, that Cubans are not the only culprits in the erasure of history in *Days of Awe*. When the narrator's family decides shortly after immigrating to relocate from Miami to Chicago, they look up their new city's history in an *Encyclopae-*

*dia Britannica*: "The encyclopedia did not say much about Jean Baptiste DuSable, the city's African-American founder, and nothing at all about the race riots of 1919" (96).

53. Bettinger-López cites, for example, the Cubanization Law of 1933, which "required all businesses to employ at least 50 percent native Cubans" (22). Such evidence has prompted Boris Sapir to argue that "the roots of anti-Semitic tendencies in Cuba lie not in discriminatory attitudes toward Jews from Europe, but 'in the oversensitive national self-consciousness'" (Bettinger-López 22; Sapir 55, qtd. in Bettinger-López).

54. In 1997 Ale's parents are horrified when a jazz musician from Cuba is denied U.S. citizenship, thanks to changing U.S. policies toward Cuban immigration, which resulted in closing doors to would-be exiles. This turn of events was a sensitive issue for Cuban exiles. Ale reacts with predictable surprise: "Cubans are always welcome here, always" (265). But for Ale's parents, in particular her father, the event connotes something beyond itself: "[T]heir traumatized reactions seemed out of proportion to me. [. . .] 'This always happens to me,' my father sighed, tears welling. [. . .] 'What? What always happens to you?' I asked, disconcerted" (266). The exclusion of a refugee from the haven of the United States, as readers learn only at the novel's end (350–51), reminds Ale's father of the S.S. *St. Louis* incident, in which an entire ship full of Jewish refugees from Europe was denied entrance to Cuba and, later, to the United States, in 1939. Three-quarters of the ship's Jewish passengers eventually perished in the Holocaust. For a discussion of this incident, see Levine 102–49. For a discussion of changing U.S. policy toward Cuban immigrants in the mid-1990s and the Cuban exile reaction, see Masud-Piloto, 128–29, 140–44. On Cuban exiles' sense of betrayal by the U.S. government after increased restrictions on Cuban immigration, see Castro 301.

55. The term *"marrano,"* "[l]iterally, pig," is, as Obejas explains, the "[p]ejorative term" for *conversos* (363–64).

56. See also Levine 1–2.

57. See also my discussion of this issue in Chapter 6.

58. This moment is marked as well by the S.S. *St. Louis* incident, which leaves an indelible mark on the young Enrique.

59. The iconography associated with the Virgin of Charity, Cuba's patron saint, points insistently to her cultural hybridity (just as the Virgin of Guadalupe's does to hers), as Obejas explains: "[S]he floats above a turbulent sea in which a boat with three men is being tossed about. One of the men is black and he is in the center of the boat, kneeling in prayer while the other two, who are white, row furiously and helplessly. (It's unspoken but understood that it's the entreaties of the black man, not the labor of the white rowers, that provides their deliverance)" (6).

60. Masud-Piloto explains the 1994 mini-exodus by Cuban *balseros*, noting that the economic crisis that year was "the worst in the revolution's history":

> [A]s the economic crisis worsened in 1994, the number of Cubans arriving in the coasts of Florida in home-made and extremely unsafe 'balsas' (rafts) reached alarming proportions. Thousands of Cubans concluded that the economy would not improve anytime soon, and decided to emigrate by whatever means possible. [. . .] Indeed, so many tried that August 1994 soon became a record-setting month in the history of the Cuban migration to the

United States [. . .]. It was estimated that at least 25,000 "balseros" (rafters), travelling on anything that floated, had headed north from the port town of Cojímar, Cuba, during the month. (138–39)

61. Levine writes that,

[o]n May 25, Reich diplomats in Havana dispatched a gleeful telegram to the Foreign Office in Berlin documenting what they described as a recent "intensification of the anti-Jewish campaign" in the local press. Excerpting examples of anti-Semitic articles in *Alerta, Avance,* and *Diario de la Marina,* the cable noted that the articles "state that that the Jews are forcing their way into local business, that they exploit the Cubans unscrupulously, and even begin to push them out of business; [. . .]." The articles predicted that "soon they will dominate all commerce in Cuba, and the Cuban people will have to suffer under capitalists of a new kind, who speak another language and believe in another God, and do not care about the problems of the country." The cable's authors added: "The newspaper [. . .] characterizes them as polyps who drain the blood of the Cuban people." [. . .] Dr. José Rivero wrote in a *Diario de la Marina* editorial reprinted in *Avance*: "Against this Jewish invasion we must react with the same energy as have other peoples of the globe. Otherwise we will be absorbed and the day will come when the blood of our martyrs and heroes shall have served solely to enable the Jews to enjoy a country conquered by our ancestors." (113–14)

62. In an intriguing deconstructive approach to *Days of Awe,* Socolovsky suggests that the novel's treatment of crypto-Judaism can be understood via the Derridean concept of "*différance*—the ghostly trace that cannot be presented, and that resides in the temporal and spatial moment of deferral or difference between signified concepts" ("Deconstructing" 229). Socolovsky argues that "the text is structured through a trace-like *différance*" ("Deconstructing" 242): "Judaism comes to mean Catholicism's absent presence [. . .]. Catholicism and Judaism are placed in opposition so that they become [. . .] meaningful only because of their opposition" (241). Thus Ale has "inherited a religious identity that traditionally depends on articulating itself through opposition" (243). To this analysis, I would add that the same is also true of the novel's representation of national identity, which is invariably defined in opposition, although the object of that opposition—and thus the "meaning" of Cuban national identity itself—changes.

63. In an interesting intertextual moment suggestive of the construction of a Cuban identity that would include diaspora Cubans, Obejas also writes Pilar Puente, the rebellious daughter and artist figure from Cristina García's *Dreaming in Cuban,* into her novel by having Deborah, a performance artist, talk about a collaborative project she has done with Pilar which involved "simultaneous actions in Havana and Miami" and in which "[t]hey each wrapped themselves in a Cuban flag" (322).

64. Cornell and Hartmann (drawing largely on the writings of German sociologist Max Weber) do not mean to suggest that ethnicity really is based in blood, but, rather, that it is imagined in this way—hence its power: "What matters is not whether a blood relationship actually exists, but whether it is believed to exist" (16–17).

65. In counterpoint to Ale's disclaimer of "blood" ties to Cubans, we might place

Ruth Behar's writing about her Cuban identity and the ways in which it has been challenged. Since Behar's family members were relatively recent (that is, twentieth-century) immigrants to Cuba, Behar notes that she has "often been questioned about the authenticity of my Cubanness. How could I, being Jewish, claim to be Cuban? Wasn't my Cuban identity nothing more than an accident of history, another stop in a Jewish diaspora? It wasn't deep, it wasn't in my blood, the Cubanness, so who was I fooling?" (*Bridges* 6). Behar, of course, chooses to claim a Cuban ethnicity for herself despite its not being in her "blood," giving rise to rather liberating new possibilities for the imagining of ethnicity itself—possibilities that, I would argue, Obejas also ends up evoking in her novel.

66. Ale's desire to connect to Cuba in the present, despite her disclaimers, helps explain one of the more troubling aspects of the novel—her sexual encounter with Orlando, who at first appears to be a highly unsavory character. During her first visit to Cuba, she witnesses him having oral sex with a fourteen-year-old girl; almost immediately thereafter, she herself is physically intimate with him (86–88). (This scene is juxtaposed to, and immediately precedes, Ale's mullings about glossolalia [89–90].) The fourteen-year-old girl, Celina, becomes an enigmatic sign of Cuba itself to Ale, who at first seems to want to partake of Cuba's exotic appeal in somewhat touristic fashion. (Later, in the United States, Ale imagines—incorrectly—that a *Playboy* photo of an almost-nude Cuban engineering student is the same girl. Her lover notes of the photo, "It's like they're officially advertising sex tourism" [205].) Eventually, however, through Orlando, Ale must come to terms with the sexual exploitation, and other forms of desperation, that mark Cuba's Special Period in the 1990s. Once a dedicated revolutionary, Orlando, by 1997, is a cynical chauffeur for a prostitute for foreign tourists, who also happens to be his son's girlfriend. When Ale demands an explanation, Orlando insists on the relative morality that marks the grasping improvisations of the Special Period: "I live in Cuba, Alejandra, I live in Cuba" (316). Notably, Ale's lovemaking with Orlando is described in terms strikingly similar to those of her fantasies of connectedness to Cuba. Like the latter, the former is depicted as a rebirth: "When I finally let go and air pops into my lungs again, I cry [. . .] just like a newborn covered with blood and brine" (331).

67. As Socolovsky notes of the formal structure of the novel, "In thus blending the personal, the familial, and the historic, the text resists generic boundaries and moves between different kinds of narrative" ("Deconstructing" 227). At another point, Socolovsky—who has been arguing that the novel is structured according to the "trace" of what is suppressed—notes that, "while the narrative insists on the secrecy of crypto-Judaism, and even tells us that the means for finding out the secret is closed (Enrique won't speak [about his history]), it lets us know that Alejandra knows the secret" ("Deconstructing" 242). The "secret," however, is laid out quite early in the novel, the exposition of which outlines the historical experience of Alejandra's crypto-Jewish ancestors in great detail. The surprise is not so much in the secret trace of Jewishness revealed (it is revealed up front) but in the fact that the secret *is* still a secret. Readers may well be disoriented, after reading Ale's careful exposition of her family history in the context of the Spanish inquisition, to come on the scene in which the adult Ale is questioned by a

stranger about her possible Jewish ancestry—and is obviously utterly ignorant of even the possibility. We are not prepared by the text for Ale's ignorance, which becomes in effect the first real revelation.

68. Socolovsky, correctly, I think, identifies this moment as "performative" ("Deconstructing" 244). What is crucial to note, however, is that *all* identity is implicitly "performative" for Obejas, rather than "in the blood" (to paraphrase Behar, *Bridges* 6). Ale denies the Jewishness of her mother's family, not because of their bloodlines, but because at some point, historically, they ceased to "perform" as Jews. This is the distinction between the crypto-Jews—who continue to "perform" Jewishness, even if in secret—and the true converts. Ale herself might be Cuban "in the blood," but nevertheless must begin to "perform" *cubanidad* (with her lover, Leni, in her exchange of letters with Moisés and Orlando, etc.) in order to feel Cuban.

69. Ale continues here: "I can be, of my own free will, a woman or a man, an engineer or a chef. [. . .] I can love anyone anytime in any way that I choose, and it changes nothing about that fixed moment in time: The first of January 1959, and my first gasp of air outside the womb, in Havana" (237). This passage sheds much light on the sexual fluidity of the narrator, Ale, who passes from a male lover to a female one without any commentary whatsoever on her sexual identity. That is to say, though Ale tells us about her individual lovers and about her sexual experiences with them, at no time does she comment on how those experiences might "categorize" her (as lesbian, straight, bisexual, queer, etc.). In contrast to Obejas's earlier *Memory Mambo*, in which lesbianism is a central category of identity and analysis for the narrator, Juani (who agonizes over her lover's refusal to identify similarly), sexual identity in *Days of Awe* is a nonissue. Ale, who discusses Jewish identity and Cuban identity at great length and in great historical depth, spends no time thinking about categories of sexual identity; she simply takes for granted that she can, indeed, love anyone she wants at any time she chooses. The novel is much more concerned with how we imagine our relationship to our origins then with relationships to present-day sexual mores.

70. "You don't know" is a repeated refrain in Orlando's conversations with Ale; see also 313.

71. Of course, the understanding of "authenticity" evoked here has to do with being *originally* ("from the beginning") knowledgeable about, immersed in, and faithful to a particular culture. But as Cornell and Hartmann persuasively argue, "all cultures and collective identities are constructions of one sort or another; they are changed and reformulated—continually reconstructed—over time. [. . .] At what point in that long process of exchange and adaptation have the cultures and identities involved been 'authentic,' and at what point did they lose their 'authenticity'? We would argue that authenticity has been present either at every point or at no point" (92, 94).

72. As Ale explains, "With Leni, I was closer than ever to all the dark peoples for whom I interpreted and to whom I represented a system and established order that I never felt a part of" (179). The fact that this sense of "closeness" only occurs as she contrasts herself with her non-Latina lover suggests just how constructed and tenuous it is; nevertheless, Ale clearly reads her emerging solidarity with other, "darker" Latinas and Latinos and her rejection of the oppressive "system," through the lens of her emerging Cuban sense of self.

Chapter 5. "The Pleas of the Desperate": Magical Realism, *Latinidad*, and (or) Collective Agency in Ana Castillo's *So Far from God*

1. Delgadillo, for instance, writes that the novel "expands our definitions of what constitutes 'resistance,' of what is 'political,' and of who is capable of effecting social change" (892); Platt, likewise, notes that it "portrays resistance [...] in the development of oppositional consciousness" (154); and Ralph E. Rodriguez argues that it exemplifies the mode of "contestatory literature" typical of recent Chicana/o writing, which "engages in social critique" and "continue[s] to struggle against antagonistic forces of oppression" (63, 67).

2. Polk's review, underscoring the perceived connections to Gabriel García Márquez and other Latin American writers, continues: "The trouble with *So Far from God* [...] is that it strikes too many familiar chords. From the opening, when Sofi's three-year-old daughter suffers a seizure and dies only to rise up at her own funeral and fly to the roof of the church [...], we can hear the echoes." Polk assumes that echoes of García Márquez can only be a sign of an insufficiently "original voice" (D6) and ignores the possibility that Castillo might be commenting on the magical realist tradition itself.

3. For instance, Porsche comments that Castillo draws "from the tradition of Latin American magical realism (Allende, Cortázar, Márquez)" (182); Walter observes her "magico-realist narrative texture" (89); Manríquez characterizes her "magical realism" as an aspect of the "absurd" in the novel (40); and Aldama argues that Castillo "engenders her magicorealism" in a challenge to the mode's prior masculinism (76; emphasis removed).

4. Pérez Firmat's commentary focuses on the way Alvarez's words bridge the boundary between Dominicans and Americans (rather than on the panethnic implications): "Since Alvarez includes herself in the 'we,' she partakes of magical-realist thinking. Yet, since she also can translate her father as saying, 'what do you mean—this is the way we think,' rather than whatever he originally said, Alvarez may think like a Dominican, but she thinks about thinking like a plain old American" (140).

5. Consider, for example, author Francisco Goldman's comment (as reported in Frase-Blunt 32) regarding publishers of U.S. Latino/a novels such as his own *The Long Night of White Chickens*: "They will paste the words 'García Márquez' onto every single book jacket—they even did it to me. I kept telling them 'I don't do magic realism.'" Karen Christian, despite recounting Goldman's comments in her work, also seems to fall into the same trap when she compares Esmeralda Santiago's childhood memoir *When I Was Puerto Rican* to García Márquez's *One Hundred Years of Solitude*; in both, she asserts, "invasions of 'progress' are surrounded by the same aura of irreality" (126). This connection seems like quite a reach, however, since Santiago's autobiographical text is the furthest thing imaginable from magical realism.

6. I thank Jean Wyatt for this insight.

7. For an excellent discussion of primitivism and its effect on African American cultural production, specifically with regard to Langston Hughes, in the 1920s, see Chinitz.

8. McCracken refers, of course, to the notion of "Orientalism" as defined by Edward Said: "Orientalism as a Western style for dominating, restructuring, and having authority over the Orient" (3), perceived and represented as the West's Other.

9. While Faris places the latter point under the heading of "secondary [...] specifications" in the definition of magical realism, I would argue that this is in fact one manifestation of a component *necessary* for the work to be magical realism (as opposed to a novel *about* the miraculous, regarded as such). As Polk suggests, we recognize that we are in the presence of magical realism when, within the text, "the marvelous is *commonplace*" rather than miraculous (emphasis added).

10. I include non–Latin American examples of magical realism in my discussion in order to move away from the sort of critical essentialism which finds the only, or primary, examples of magical realism in Latin American and Latina/o texts.

11. In one exception to my argument, Caridad's own response to the "magical" in her life seems to fit more closely with standard understandings of magical realism: "to Caridad such events as her Holy Restoration, her clairvoyance, the Screaming Sister [. . .] and such were just part of life. Falling in love . . . now *that* was something else altogether!" (80). Given the more general presentation of miracles as such, I would nonetheless argue that Castillo marks a certain distance from magical realism; in that light, the passage on Caridad's less-astonished reactions begins to look like a parody of magical realist passages such as Allende's.

12. "The women in *So Far from God* are modeled on the martyrs in the history of the Catholic Church. We are *made* to believe in these miracles. [. . .] [I]t's not magical fiction; it is faith" (Miller and Walsh, "So Far, So Good" 27; emphasis added).

13. Thus Walter, in discussing the novel's "magico-realist narrative texture," argues that faith in the miraculous is "revised and actualized through female agency, [and] is the driving force behind the collective activism" in the novel (89); Platt notes that an "examination of spirituality and miracles [is] brought into conjunction with social justice and material everyday existence" (146); and Christian suggests that "'magical realist' religious performances" and a "belief in miracles" in *So Far From God* constitute a "powerful" response to "insurmountable obstacles" (137).

14. The cooperative's Spanish name clearly suggests this. Further, not only is Sofi's campaign manager her "comadre" (145), but the cooperative's members are repeatedly referred to as "Sofi's vecinos" (146, 147), and their children as "'jitos" (147). Such offhand references suggest the *collective* use and familiarity of Spanish terminology among the community.

15. A few critical voices have begun to suggest that Castillo's version of magical realism may involve parody. Christian ventures the tentative hypothesis that *So Far from God*, in its very excesses, "may be to parody Boom fiction" (138); but this does not modify her reading of the novel's magical realism as connected to its cultural resistance. Similarly, Aldama argues that Castillo's "parodic technique [. . .] *engenders* her magicorealism to write within and against its primitivist and masculinist identifications" in other texts (76); it is these earlier identifications, rather than magical realism itself, that are being parodied. Thus Castillo's use of magical realism continues to be associated with the novel's political thrust: "she uses magicorealism as a form to convey a story wherein characters learn to oppose and subvert capitalist ideology" (Aldama 80).

16. It is worth noting that Faris, among others, has made a strong case for the politically committed nature of magical realist fiction itself. Nevertheless, some critics have argued that the Boom's magical realist novels "demonstrated the abandonment

in Latin America of the '*novela comprometida*' or politically committed novel, and the emergence of the '*novela metafísica*' or metaphysical novel" (Poey 33; Poey cites Shaw 322). This *perception* of magical realism as less than politically committed may possibly drive its parodying in Castillo's very political novel.

17. Gail Pérez links La Loca to the Mothers of the Plaza de Mayo in Argentina, who protested the disappearance of their children during the so-called Dirty War (1976–83) and were called "Las Locas" (74); thus Pérez, too, reads La Loca as emblematic of political activism.

18. Caridad's on-again, off-again boyfriend Rubén, who goes with her to peyote meetings and sweat lodges in his version of Native American spirituality, is portrayed in highly negative terms as being insufferably sexist. While we might attribute this portrayal (as well as that of Francisco el Penitente) to a critique of masculinist and misogynist gender norms, it is certainly telling that the hybrid and folk-based spiritual practices that to critics so often signal Latino ethnicity and "resistance" are assuredly no guarantor of progressive politics or of collective activism in Castillo's novel. Yet commentators who can easily discern the disparity between ethnic practices and progressive politics where the male characters are concerned seem to have much more trouble doing so with the women in the novel.

19. DelRosso is drawing on the arguments of Daly 30.

20. Even if the "saints" were depicted in the novel as actually helping the people of Tome, such help, read through the lens of liberation theology, might still be understood as depriving the community of its agency to help itself. As Leonardo and Clodovis Boff explain, "Aid increases the dependence of the poor, tying them to help from others [. . .], not enabling them to become their own liberators" (*Introducing* 4–5)

21. Gail Pérez insists that we can "view popular miracles" in the novel "not merely as the opium of the people" but as a form of what Norma Alarcón terms "effective political interventions" (67; Alarcón, "Chicana Feminism," 254, qtd. in Pérez); Pérez illustrates with an example (drawn from Fuentes and Ehrenreich 28–30) in which, in Malaysia, the sighting of an evil spirit by a worker in a factory may shut the factory down for several days. My question, however, is whether popular miracles are portrayed this way *by Castillo*; it is remarkable that the prominent instances of "popular miracles" I have cited in the novel are insistently represented in terms of their *lack* of productive intersection with the socioeconomic circumstances of the people of Tome.

22. See Delgadillo for a reading which interprets the Holy Friday procession as evidence of Loca's connection with political activism (911). I would argue, by contrast, that Loca's participation is again portrayed as an aberration. As the narrator opens the chapter, this "was the only occasion in Loca's life [. . .] that Loca went out into the world" (238).

23. Several critics have noted the importance of this scene for a reading of the novel's concern with political and collective activism (see, e.g., Delgadillo 911; Platt 153).

24. It is worth noting, of course, that liberation theology also emerged out of a Latin American context and is strongly associated with that context. That is to say, here Castillo strategically calls on a philosophy with panethnic, Latin American associations, because it is contextually useful to her.

25. La Loca, too, is associated with nature, through her "intuitive connection" to animals (Castillo, *So Far from God* 164), which she prefers over humans.

26. Pérez, similarly, reads this scene in a celebratory light, although focusing on its feminist rather than environmental ramifications (71).

27. These assumptions may be found within the body of "ecocritical" scholarship more generally and are not just limited to commentary on the environment in Castillo's novel. As Lawrence Buell has pointed out, ecocriticism is composed of many, often divergent, positions vis-à-vis the human relationship to the environment; this particular one has been challenged by the work of scholars such as Robert Pogue Harrison and William Cronon (Buell 700).

28. This insistence, which runs counter to much "green" thought, that human communities—especially poor, minority communities—must be taken into account in environmentalist discourse has its parallel in debates surrounding the real-life New Mexican cooperative Ganados del Valle. As Pulido reports, Ganados's requests to the New Mexico Department of Game and Fish (NMDGF) to allow limited grazing on Wildlife Management Areas were blocked by the NMDGF and opposed by environmental groups. Pulido argues that "[t]he situation presents, in microcosm, the conflict of philosophies espoused by mainstream environmentalists and advocates of sustainable development. More specifically, it shows how myopic is any view of nature that does not take into account the needs of low-income, minority communities" (132–33).

29. Platt is quite helpful in linking environmental concerns to human ones in the novel; she reads *So Far from God* through the lens of "environmental justice": "When environmental concerns and a concern for justice are combined, new issues are raised. The coined term *environmental justice* poses questions for environmentalism. Whose environment is protected? Whose environment is neglected?" (140).

30. Along the same lines, Heide proposes that the last chapter, detailing the organization and function of M.O.M.A.S., "appears as the narrator's vision of the empowerment of a community that stays traditional and spiritual but at the same time is globally connected" (176). And Toyosato reads both the Holy Friday procession and M.O.M.A.S. as examples of "women working on social and environmental injustice issues for their lives and communities" and argues that each scene "demands respect for women—for collective resistance—by pointing out how individuals' or a family's survival is related to the community's survival in a society" (307). Gail Pérez, likewise, starts out by linking Sofi's founding of M.O.M.A.S. to the weaving cooperative and the Holy Friday procession—all are ways in which Sofi "begin[s] to create a world where her children might be safe" (73). The obvious nature of "spoof" in the final chapter, which Pérez recognizes, thus seems to cause her a bit of confusion: "Why Castillo focuses on the religious society of the women of Tomé and not on social renewal is hard to say" (75).

31. Manríquez is one critic who sees the absurdity of M.O.M.A.S. (45).

32. Kavanagh presents a clear, accessible gloss on the term "ideology" (as derived through Marx, Louis Althusser, etc.):

> [In] a weak social regime, [. . .] a lot of people from the subordinate classes [races, genders, etc.] (as well as some from the dominant classes) perceive themselves as being in an unjust situation, and are trying to do something to change it. Much better [for the given social regime] is a situation in which

everyone—from dominant and subordinate class alike—understands and perceives the prevailing system of social relations as fundamentally fair on the whole (even if it hasn't done so well by them), and/or as better than any possible alternative, and/or as *impossible to change anyway*. (308; emphasis added).

Ideology, then, "encourages men and women to 'see' their specific place in a historically peculiar social formation as inevitable" (310).

33. Further, in place of the distinctly *communal* efforts of the wool and sheep-grazing cooperative, in which all members contribute on the same equal, nonhierarchical footing, M.O.M.A.S. substitutes a markedly individualistic concern with *status*; in this "very prestigious (if not a little elitist) organization" (Castillo, *So Far From God*, 247), it is *more* prestigious to be the mother of a saint than just the mother of a martyr (248).

34. Castillo's own comments on this scene would seem to pose some problems for my reading. She has noted in an interview that, originally, her story ended with Sofi crying on the graves of her daughters: "But my agent who was reading the manuscript commented that 'Well, this is very depressing. You know, you promised Norton a happy ending.' So I thought, 'what would she [Sofia] do to change that [. . .]?' She takes over. She doesn't submit to that point in history when patriarchy took over her authority" (Saeta 147). Earlier in the same interview, however, Castillo describes how the humor in her work "is pointing out the contradictions—always. That's being done more than anything in *So Far from God*. [. . .] It's the very careless reader that will see something and say 'Well, she really means that.' And of course, I'm always saying things with tongue in cheek. I believe that if we see the irony and the contradictions [. . .] that is part of our ability [. . .] to contribute to a change" (146). Though Sofi "doesn't submit" to patriarchal religious constructs and instead founds the decidedly matriarchal organization M.O.M.A.S., that organization is also marked by contradictions that undermine its challenge to patriarchal power, as I have argued—and Castillo depicts the organization with her usual brand of tongue-in-cheek humor.

## Chapter 6. Dirty Girls, German Shepherds, and Puerto Rican *Independentistas*: "The Latino Imaginary" and the Case of Cuba

1. "I argue that the narratives of Chicano men and women are predominantly critical and ideological. [. . .] [A]s oppositional ideological forms Chicano narratives signify [. . .] how the values, concepts, and ideas purveyed by the mainstream, hegemonic American culture that tie them to their social functions seek to prevent them from attaining a true knowledge of society as a whole. My study shows how Chicano narratives [. . .] confront and circumscribe the limiting ideologies imposed upon them" (Saldívar 6).

2. Indeed, the assumption—following a Chicano and Nuyorican paradigm—that Latino literature as a body is resistant dates earlier than Saldívar's *Chicano Narrative*. For example, in her 1985 field-defining article "Hispanic Literature in the United States," Eliana Rivero defines "ethnic minority art and literature in the United States as a form of cultural resistance and/or protest" ("Hispanic" 187) and notes that "Chicano literature [. . .] is by essence and definition a literature [. . .] of social protest" (178–79). Marc Zimmerman, in his 1992 *U.S. Latino Literature*, reproduces this line of argument: "Only those writers representing groups with several years of U.S. residence and having had

some working class as well as some *barrio* experience (including discrimination) are likely to write something which approaches community literary expression such as we find in U.S. Chicano and Puerto Rican literatures" (36).

3. Admittedly, some anthologies are also increasingly recognizing the tenuous nature of any construction of ethnicity as a coherent whole. Thus Augenbraum and Olmos, editors of *The Latino Reader* (1997), explicitly address "legitimate concerns that the compilers [of any anthology] are attempting to present [...] a cohesive literary tradition" (xviii). (Notably, *The Latino Reader* includes an excerpt from Richard Rodriguez's argument in *Hunger of Memory* against bilingual education. This text rarely finds its way into Latino/a anthologies because of its conservative bent.) Likewise, Milligen introduces *¡Floricanto Sí!* (1998) by raising the question of "why anthologies like this one gather a single group of writers—Latinas, in this case—if the result of the gathering is to emphasize diversity within the group" and begins by offering a very pragmatic response: "One answer is simple: for the most part, Latina poetry is simply not available at the average American bookstore" (xxi–xxii).

4. Ilan Stavans who is compiling the (as yet unpublished) "Norton Anthology of Latino Literature," suggests that "a sense of sameness has recently emerged among Latino writers" and elaborates that, "[e]ven though Julia Alvarez and Rudolfo Anaya, a Dominican-American and a Chicano, grew up worlds apart, they both see the universe through the lens of Hispanic civilization, with its own cadence and metabolism" ("Quest" B13). In his earlier *The Hispanic Condition* (1995), he elaborates on the nature of this purported "metabolism": "Latino art retains a belligerent tone," is "politically committed," and is "a vehicle for conflict and resistance" (85–86).

5. Commenting on constructs of Latino ethnicity more generally, Fox has offered a similar line of argument, suggesting that there are different versions of the "constructed" category of "Hispanics" as a singular people. One version—Fox associates it with the Right—has, as its goal, to gain access to power within existing social and political structures; but another, more "Left" (Fox's word), version is built around "solidarity for the other 'little guys'" and is directly antagonistic to the white "power structure" (11–12).

6. In doing so, Flores ignores the ways in which Stavans himself echoes the "resistance" model.

7. Note that these statistics, and those which follow from the Pew Hispanic Center, account only for registered Latinos, who themselves make up only 43 percent of Latinos and Latin Americans currently residing in the United States. Noncitizens make up 42 percent, while citizens who are not registered make up 14 percent ("2004 National Survey" chart 38).

8. According to the 2000 census, for example, Cuban American median family income is $39,530, versus $28,953 for Puerto Ricans and $27,883 for Mexican Americans; 14 percent of Cuban Americans are below the poverty line, compared to 27 percent of Mexican Americans and 31 percent of Puerto Ricans (U.S. Department of Health and Human Services *Mental Health* 132).

9. Consider these statistics. The Pew Hispanic Center reports that, of registered Latinos questioned about the 2001 tax cuts enacted by President Bush, 23 percent said that they had helped the economy, 21 percent disagreed, and the remainder (54

percent) said they had not made much difference or that they did not know. But when broken down by party affiliation, 44 percent of Republican Latinos felt the tax cuts were positive, while only 12 percent of Democrats did ("2004 National Survey" 9). Divisions among registered Latinos over the U.S. war in Iraq, similarly, strongly reflect partisan divisions (6). If substantially more Cuban Americans than Mexican Americans or Puerto Ricans are Republicans, it follows that there may indeed still be substantive differences on issues such as U.S. use of military force and—more ambiguously—taxes. (See "2004 National Survey" 14 for ambiguous findings regarding willingness to pay taxes to fund services.) For a commentary on Cuban American historical positions on civil rights, see Acuña, "Miami Myth Machine."

10. Rivero, facing (in 1985) the same difficulties in fitting Cubans into her imagined composite portrait of Hispanics, simply declared that "the works by Cuban immigrants can never be considered" as U.S. Hispanic literature (*Hispanic* 187), because Cuban exiles "oppose the socialist revolutionary process taking place in their homeland" (183) and embrace the "selfish, materialistic middle class values" (187) of U.S. dominant culture. (The works of the *children* of Cuban immigrants might count as U.S. Hispanic, on the other hand; "the closer [Cuban American writers] get to an appreciation of minority life in American society, and the more they empathize with Chicanos and Neoricans," the more they approximate what Rivero considers legitimate U.S. Hispanic writing ["Hispanic" 187]). Zimmerman concurs: "transplanted Cuban [. . .] novelists are not in any sense writing U.S. Latino literature, whether their characters twist and turn through Havana [. . .] or New York" (36).

11. On other issues Flores might be on firmer ground. The Pew Hispanic Center reports that "[t]he vast majority of registered Latinos say that they think the government should provide health insurance for those without it. Furthermore, most say that they would be willing to pay more in higher health insurance premiums or higher taxes to increase the number of Americans who have health insurance" ("2004 National Survey" 7). The report adds that "Latino views on these matters largely supersede partisan loyalties," with 89 percent of Democrats and 75 percent of Republicans supporting the above position ("2004 National Survey" 7).

Views on immigration policy also "superseded partisan identification," with a majority of both Democrats (73 percent) and Republicans (71 percent) "favoring a system that ensured future immigrants [from Latin America] permanent legal status and the opportunity to become citizens" ("2004 National Survey" 9). Democrats (83 percent) and Republicans (86 percent) also approved of a plan "that would allow undocumented Latino immigrants to gain permanent legal status and eventually citizenship" ("2004 National Survey" 8). In the 2006 National Survey, however, only 52 percent of total Latinos felt that *all* undocumented immigrants should have be permitted to stay permanently and have an opportunity for citizenship, although 66 percent of Latinos also opposed building more fences along the border and 70 percent opposed sending the National Guard to the border (Suro and Escobar 18, 20.) Furthermore, Latinos are increasingly ranking immigration as a top national priority, with only the war in Iraq ranking higher, although the weight given to this issue is much greater among the foreign-born than among native-born Latinos (Suro and Escobar).

The National Immigration Forum reports that, "[a]ccording to Hispanic Trends, a

Miami-based polling and research firm, [...] [b]y 2010, 70% [of Latino voters in the U.S.] will be foreign born. Naturalized Latino voters tend to vote at almost twice the rate of native-born Latinos. For these voters, immigration is a major concern." Thus immigration policy might increasingly be both an issue that cuts across party lines and one that matters significantly for Latinos who vote.

12. The exact percentage of support for George W. Bush among Latino voters in the 2004 presidential election has been widely debated, although most cited figures coincide to a close degree. The National Election Pool (NEP) exit poll cites a figure of 44 percent support for Bush and 53 percent for Kerry; the *New York Times* gives a figure of 43 percent for Bush and 56 percent for Kerry (National Council of La Raza 2; see also Fears; Kirk Johnson). Poll data from Gallup and Zogby roughly concur. The exit poll data of the William C. Velásquez Institute/Southwest Voter Registration Education Project, by contrast, give figures of 31 percent for Bush and 68 percent for Kerry (National Council of La Raza 2), explaining the discrepancy in terms of better methodology specifically for measuring Latinos (National Council of La Raza 2). The estimate of the National Council of La Raza (NCLR), which it claims "produces a result that can be reconciled with both the pre-election and exit polls' margins of error," is that the split was roughly 39 percent Bush, 59 percent Kerry (National Council of La Raza 7). Despite the debate over how many Latinos actually voted for Bush, however, the NCLR points out that *"the direction of the election-to-election changes* of the Hispanic vote in 2004 and 2000 is absolutely consistent across all polls," with most polls indicating a 7- to 9-point shift in favor of the Republican candidate in 2004 (over 2000), and all polls indicating a double-digit shift toward the Republican candidate in 2000 (over 1996) (National Council of La Raza 6; emphasis in original). For instance, the *Los Angeles Times* reported a 21 percent to 71 percent Latino split in the Dole/Clinton election of 1996, a 38 percent to 61 percent split in the Bush/Gore election of 2000, and a 45 percent to 54 percent split in the Bush/Kerry election of 2004 (National Council of La Raza 5). Further, the NEP polling data suggest that Mexican Americans in Texas, traditionally a Democratic-leaning population, actually may have voted for Bush in numbers roughly equivalent to or even exceeding the Cuban American population's (National Council of La Raza 3 n. 10). The conclusion? It is "'no longer sensible to think of Hispanic voters on a national basis as a core constituency of the Democratic Party,' said Roberto Suro, the director of the Pew Hispanic Center" (Kirk Johnson). To complicate matters further, however, the 2006 midterm elections suggest a new Democratic swing among the Latino population, with Latino voters preferring Democratic candidates for Congress and in gubernatorial races by margins of roughly 69 percent to 30 percent (Pew Hispanic Center, "Latinos" Fact Sheet). If Latinos cannot be counted on any longer to be a "core constituency of the Democratic Party," neither can they be counted on to continue a significant shift toward the Republican Party in large numbers over the long term.

13. For that matter, even blanket generalizations about Cuban American politics have become much shakier. As Jones-Correa notes, "Cuban Americans, who historically have voted Republican in overwhelming numbers, gave 40 percent of their vote in 1996 to President Clinton, the Democratic candidate" ("All Politics" 33). Observing that, in the following election, "Gore, like Clinton, took Miami-Dade and Broward Counties, the Cuban American strongholds in South Florida," Jones-Correa adds that

Gore "won these counties by 100,000 fewer votes than Clinton did in 1996. The shift back of the Cuban American electorate to the Republican Party arguably cost Vice-President Gore the election" (36). The point is that, with such a split Cuban American vote, the image of Cuban Americans as overwhelmingly Republican in their voting patterns is itself now more "imaginary" than real.

14. Ignoring these profound ideological differences, Ibis Gómez-Vega links Engle's *Singing to Cuba* to Julia Alvarez's *How the García Girls Lost Their Accents* and *In the Time of the Butterflies* through the thesis that authors such as Engle and Alvarez "bear witness to the chaos caused by the history of their respective countries" (232). Here the abstract concept of historical "chaos," under whose baggy umbrella Trujillo and Castro can be brought together, replaces and erases the concrete historical and political particulars of the two regimes. But Engle's texts, as I will argue, encourage precisely such a connection between repressive dictators.

15. As the biographical note to her novel *Skywriting* explains, Engle is the daughter of a "Cuban mother and American father."

16. By way of contrast, Richard Rodriguez, another Hispanic (in this case, Mexican American) writer whose work has been widely criticized for being conservative in its sensibilities, "[o]vertly assimilationist and opposed to bilingual education" (Zimmerman 98), actively disclaims the collective label "Chicano."

17. We can see the critical unease with Engle's position in such assessments as McCracken's that "Engle posits a single, master narrative about the [Cuban] revolution that turns the novel's strong principles into obsessions. In so doing, Engle enacts a kind of narrative violence [. . .]. *Skywriting* can see no good at all in leftist movements" (199).

18. For a critical discussion linking Castro unproblematically to another Latin American dictator, Dominican Rafael Trujillo, see Gómez-Vega. More nuanced discussions of the relationship between Castro and Trujillo—who was ideologically opposed to the rise of Castro and communism in Cuba—are found in López-Calvo and Sagás, as well as in the fictional representation of the last days of Trujillo's regime, *The Feast of the Goat* (2000), by Mario Vargas Llosa.

19. The inside cover quotes J. Joaquín Fraxedas, another Cuban American writer with a strong anti-Castro sensibility and the author of *The Lonely Crossing of Juan Cabrera* (1993).

20. Engle's first novel, *Singing to Cuba*, is even more blatant in this assertion, focusing its attention on the supposed "peasants" who are the real victims of Castro's rule: "[I]f people were really disappearing, if animals were really being slaughtered, houses destroyed, fields burned, what would become of the peasants, the people? [. . .] But no [. . .] the rumors could not be true. The bearded Comandante they'd fed and sheltered along with his rebels did not seem like a man so devious that he would turn against the very peasants who had supported him when he was weak [. . .]. Surely [. . .] that man Fidel would not reward his friends, the peasants, with such horrors" (24).

21. *Singing to Cuba* is, notably, published by Arte Público, still best known as an outlet for Chicano/a writing; and in Engle's acknowledgments she thanks "the late Dr. Tomás Rivera," whose novel . . . *Y no se lo tragó la tierra*, about the exploitative working conditions of migrant farmworkers, is a classic of Chicano/a literature. Gisele M.

Requena refers repeatedly to Rivera, as a point of comparison with Engle (148, 149, 151, 152).

22. Vásquez qualifies her observation by pointing out some fleeting references to "the myth of the escaped *cimarrón* slaves"; but she correctly notes that, despite this occasionally invoked remote past, "black experience [. . .] is entirely unheard in the present-day narrative" ("Contrapuntal" 136).

23. See Olmos and Paravisini-Gebert, *Sacred Possessions* 4–5.

24. Kavanagh reviews the popular understanding of ideology as a pejorative term labeling wrongheaded extremists. In this view, "there are a few people on the right and left (like Robert Bork or Fidel Castro) who 'have' an ideology, and who are *therefore* likely to mess things up, and there are the great majority of sensible people (and politicians) who [. . .] do not 'have' one" (306). Engle's use of ideology seems to contain within it this popular assumption. In contrast, the notion of ideology derived via Louis Althusser is that it is working most effectively *precisely* when we are unaware of its operations—when we consider ourselves to be free of ideology.

25. Prior to the socialist regime, the rural poor (the vast majority of Cuba's population, largely Afro-Cuban) suffered from illiteracy, lack of health care, and widespread unemployment.

26. In his memoir *Waiting for Snow in Havana*, Carlos Eire also mentions having watched both Mexican and American films in the movie theaters of his Cuban childhood (241–42).

27. See, for example, discussions of *Dreaming in Cuban* by Alvarez Borland, Brameshuber-Ziegler, Davis, Gómez-Vega, Herrera, Leonard, K. López, Luis, McCracken, Mitchell ("National Families"), Mujčinović, Payant, Machado Sáez, Socolovsky ("Unnatural"), Stefanko, Vásquez ("Cuba"), Viera ("Matriarchy"), and Zubiaurre.

28. See, for instance, McCracken's view that the novel's "refusal to invoke the closure of a single truth about the Cuban Revolution" leads to a "resultant unfinalizability" (23); or Luis's claim that the novel "presents both sides of the Cuban question without appearing to privilege one point of view over the other" (216).

29. See Viera, "Exile" 41.

30. Specifically, Dalleo argues, García signals her relationship to Cisneros's text with the chapter title "The House on Palmas Street" and with the "themes of female freedom and independence" (11) and the "image of the woman watching the outside world from behind a window" (13) that she revises from Cisneros's novel.

31. The racial identity of the Cubans is, of course, itself a construct, as Juani's narration about her mother's "white" aspirations reveals. Much like Piri Thomas's representation of his family's racial mythology—and, indeed, much like Margarita Engle's own construction of Cuban racial mythology—Juani's family's myth of origins "positions the question of race between white and Indian, consigning most of the issue of blackness to silence" (Obejas, *Memory Mambo* 33). See McCullough 584–85 for a discussion of this issue in *Memory Mambo*.

32. Similarly, Shorris recounts hearing an anti–Puerto Rican joke (or metajoke) among Cubans in Hialeah: "This guy comes to a friend and says, 'I have the latest Puerto Rican joke.' And there's a Puerto Rican standing right there, who says, 'Hey, listen, I'm a Puerto Rican.' And the first guy says, 'Okay, I'll tell you later. Slowly'" (161).

33. Intriguingly, McCullough suggests that Juani's anger at Gina and her *independentista* friends might be partially "class-based, since she has had to work in the laundromat while Gina and her friends traveled to Cuba" (606 n. 45), thus belying the assumption on both sides that Cuban immigrants to the U.S. necessarily occupy a more privileged position than their Puerto Rican counterparts.

34. Allatson correctly points out that "[s]uch antagonisms belie the romantic claim made by Ilan Stavans that shared experiences of U.S. residency enable the overcoming of the historical, cultural, and racialized divisions between Antillean-origin Latinos" (185).

35. The "extraordinary amounts of aid" refers, among other things, to the Cuban Refugee Program, "which spent nearly $1 billion between 1965 and 1976 [. . .]. Through this program, the federal government paid transportation costs from Cuba and offered financial assistance to needy refugees and to state and local public agencies that provided refugee services" (Stepick and Stepick, "Power and Identity" 76; Pedraza-Bailey cited in Stepick and Stepick). Alex and Carol Dutton Stepick note that Cuban immigrants also benefitted from more indirect forms of assistance, including Small Business Administration loans, as well as large-scale employment by the CIA and its "front businesses" ("Power and Identity" 76–77; Didion cited in Stepick).

36. I would argue that Gina rejects the multipronged "radicalism" of queers of color such as Anzaldúa and Moraga in favor of solidarity with her "people," conceived exclusively in terms of national identity rather than along the lines of Anzaldúa's shifting solidarities. For readings that argue, in contrast, for the resistant or even radical potential of Gina's refusal to self-identify as a lesbian, see Allatson 171 and McCullough 593.

37. McCullough argues persuasively that Juani's mode for interpreting her relationship with Gina is, from the very beginning, utterly shaped by her construction as a subject of exile. Thus she continually "reads" the relationship in terms of loss, even before she has lost anything (McCullough 591–92). In this way, too, then, the *differences* in Juani's and Gina's so-called ethnic identities (the ways their different national origins shape the way they differently see the world) contribute to the demise of their relationship.

38. In a baffled, but strikingly Conradian, reading of the scene of violence that follows, Linda J. Craft suggests that perhaps "Juani's incomprehensible aggression against her lover" is the product of "possession," a symptom of "darker currents in the novel" with "African" associations—for "How else can these outrageous acts be explained"? (382). In this way Craft, through recourse to notions of an African heart of darkness, explains Juani's anger. As with Conrad's novel, however, the explanation of the unspeakable horror lies in politics and history.

39. Somewhat implausibly, McCullough reads this scene of violence through the lens of "violence's constituent role in colonial conquest and its aftermath" (598), arguing that "Juani's vision of love" is "a response to the effects of colonialism and its legacy of exile" (596). I would suggest that such an argument "generalises and universalises the colonial encounter" (as Ania Loomba argues of Homi Bhabha, 178). While *some* types of "exile" and some manifestations of "diaspora" clearly have their roots in the colonial situation, it is only by a fairly long stretch that exile from Cuba due specifically to Castro's revolution can be read as a direct "legacy" of colonialism.

40. Suggesting the degree to which Juani continues to feel compelled to gloss over the differences that divide her and Gina, the story that is eventually concocted and told (with Juani's consent) about this incident—that Gina and she were both attacked by someone opposed to Gina's political work—positions her along with Gina on the same side of a political divide (139).

41. Such an impression glosses over the historical and demographic differences between Chicanos and Puerto Ricans in the continental United States, on the one hand, and Cuban immigrants, on the other—as I discuss in Chapter 4. It also ignores moments in which Chicanos and Puerto Ricans have historically come together in coalition to combat specific forms of oppression (such as discrimination in jobs or housing), as documented, for instance, by Felix Padilla.

42. In an essay on the thematics of food in Latina literature which, remarkably, ignores the cultural loadedness of food, Jacqueline Zeff writes about food primarily in terms of its mystical healing qualities: "One of the essential barriers in much of women's literature is that between the embodied self and the [. . .] spirit. For Latina writers, food seems to be a more available passageway through that barrier than, say, a bell jar, a room of one's own, or a mother's garden" (95). Leaving aside the essentialism that makes food somehow more important as a restorative agent to Latinas than to British, Anglo-American, or African American women (as well as the erroneous suggestion that the "bell jar" functioned as a restorative metaphor in Sylvia Plath's novel), Zeff's thesis works actively to flatten the political dimensions of texts. Thus she reads Demetria Martínez as suggesting that "the way to preserve the self from [. . .] insanity is to believe in a cause beyond the self. Even if that cause is posole" (96). The suggestion that food (posole is a traditional Mexican dish) is a suitable "cause" seems a rather dismaying emptying of the powerful content of Martínez's work, which I discuss in Chapter 7.

43. See Cornell and Hartmann 19–20 for a discussion of ethnicity's dependence on (sometimes metaphorical) claims of kinship.

44. The parenthetical exclusions are actually of very recent practice and obscure the fundamental point that the categories, for most of their existence, were meant to be *racial* (not ethnic) in nature. As Cornell and Hartmann note, in the 1990s, federal programs "required various public and private entities to report racial data using [. . .] five categories [. . .]: White, Black, Asian, Hispanic, and Indian" (22). That is, "Hispanic" was viewed as a separate race. See also my discussion of this issue in the Introduction.

45. See Cornell and Hartmann 16–17 for a discussion of the importance of "assumed common descent" to ethnicity.

46. See, for example, Werner Sollors's discussion of Hobsbawm and Ranger's *The Invention of Tradition*, which he calls a "model collection for applying the concept of 'invention'" (*Invention*, xii). He calls renewed attention to the implications for ethnicity in his own volume's focus "on the invention and diffusion of modern cultural symbols [. . .] in the name of supposedly ancient national and ethnic traditions," and to the emphasis on "the very recent (and highly inauthentic) emergence of such cultural features as the Scottish tartan and kilt or the Welsh love for music. Many traditions turn out to be 'neo-traditions' that are made up in order to [. . .] substantiate politically motivated feelings of peoplehood" (xii–xiii).

## Chapter 7. Imagining Identity/Seeing Difference: Demetria Martínez's *Mother Tongue*

1. Though Kandiyoti astutely comments on the ways in which the narrator Mary's assumption of seamless identity with her El Salvadoran lover José Luis actually threatens the project of solidarity, she nevertheless seems to fall prey to the assumption of *certain* kinds of panethnic identity on some level, which—she argues—José Luis fails to recognize, thus making the twin mistake of perceiving only "sharp difference," which equally threatens the possibilities for solidarity (429). Thus, for example, Kandiyoti notes that, although Mary is "a border woman, a Chicana," José Luis "denies her the ambiguity of her cultural mixture, which may have [. . .] brought her, a woman of Mexican origin and culture, closer to him as a Salvadoran" (437). As I will argue, however, the novel suggests that, ultimately, Mary's *education* about El Salvador and her resulting commitment to activism (long after José Luis's departure), rather than her Mexican American "cultural mixture" in and of itself, are a more efficacious basis for solidarity.

2. In El Salvador, the right-wing government ruthlessly suppressed protest by landless peasants, the urban poor, labor leaders, and students and violently persecuted those in the Catholic Church who practiced social action in behalf of the country's poor. According to estimates by human rights groups, "five hundred people a month were being massacred by the death squads. [. . .] 500,000 Salvadorans had arrived in the United States by 1984" (J. Gonzalez 138). Burns writes that, during the 1980s in El Salvador, "more than 60,000 people [were] killed in eight years—many of them civilian victims of right-wing death squads" (321). And Stephen reports that, "[a]s of late 1991, a total of 80,000 had died [in El Salvador] and 7,000 more had disappeared" (808).

3. Noting the discriminatory policy practiced by the U.S. government under the Reagan and Bush administrations regarding the granting of political asylum to Salvadorans, Juan Gonzalez writes that, "[b]etween 1983 and 1990, the INS granted only 2.6 percent of political asylum requests from Salvadorans [. . .], yet it granted 25.2 percent of those from Nicaraguans, whose Sandinista government Washington was seeking to overthrow. Even when the INS denied asylum to a Nicaraguan, the agency rarely sent that person home—of 31,000 denied between 1981 and 1989, only 750 were actually deported" (131).

4. Cuba is alluded to as part of a constructed panethnic Latino identity much like Gina's in *Memory Mambo*; one character in *Mother Tongue*, Soledad, has posters of "Zapata, Cuba, and Nicaragua libre" in her kitchen (12). How exactly Cuba—or the Cuban exiles fleeing Castro's regime—might fit into Soledad's larger political vision in the 1980s is never elaborated on.

5. Although *Border Women* is coauthored by Debra Castillo and María Socorro Tabuenca Córdoba, the chapter on *Mother Tongue* was originally published as a single-authored article by Castillo (in *Intertexts* 1.1, spring 1997). I therefore cite her singly as the author. Throughout this chapter I refer to her by her last name, though she is not to be confused with Ana Castillo, whom I discuss in Chapter 5.

6. Kandiyoti seems to take seriously Mary's sense that being Mexican American provides her with credentials for understanding José Luis's situation on some level, perhaps because of similarly marginalized positions—that is, because of similarities of experience, not just identity: Mary is coping with "her own unstable identity as a

Chicana in a country where, as she puts it, they 'disappear' people through misrepresentation" (432). Strikingly, however, there is scanty evidence in the novel suggesting a correlation between Mary's experience *as a Chicana* and José Luis's experience. (The passage Kandiyoti cites is actually a reference by Mary to U.S. newspaper reports of "testimonios" by Central Americans like José Luis.) Though critics of ethnic literature are perhaps predisposed to read for themes of ethnic marginalization, Martínez *resists* making a connection between Mary's situation as a U.S. Chicana and José Luis's as a Central American refugee. (A connection between their experiences is made, as I will discuss later, but it is not centered around Mary's position as a Mexican American.)

7. Martínez, like many others, uses the term "North American," common in Latin American countries, to designate U.S. citizens. The term protests the hubristic claim of the United States to own the name "America" despite the fact that the "Americas" actually refers to the North and South American continents. (This is, of course, the rhetorical point that is skillfully made in José Martí's famous essay "Nuestra América.") Nevertheless, I have chosen not to follow Martínez in her usage, since the term "North American" with regard to U.S. citizens seems inaccurate and unnecessarily confusing (at least in a U.S. context), as it also technically refers to Canada and Mexico. When the particular point being made has to do with the United States, or with the complicity of its citizens in certain forms of oppression, it seems more important to be accurate about meaning (that is, not invoke Mexicans or Canadians) than to continue to make the point about usurpation of the term "American."

8. Kandiyoti, arguing that José Luis fails to recognize the points of similarity, reads José Luis's response to Mary as problematic in that he "imagines her as an unalloyed American, one who is complicit with the forces helping to oppress his people" (437). According to Kandiyoti's line of argument, José Luis presumably errs when he ignores his "ethnoracial commonalities" (422) with Mary by seeing her as "complicit." In fact, however, participants in the Sanctuary movement, which is the novel's historical referent, often acknowledged that they were "morally accountable" for their government's role in the events of El Salvador, as a departure point for their activist solidarity (Coutin, "Oppressed" 70). Further, as I will discuss, Mary's willful and sustained ignorance of the political situation in Central America certainly can be said to add to her complicity.

9. McCullough refers, of course, to Juani, reading her narrative making through the framework of Sommer's argument about Latin American "foundational fictions [which] sought to overcome political and historical fragmentation through love" (Sommer 26, qtd. in McCullough 8).

10. Elizabeth Martínez, remarkably, completely obscures Demetria Martínez's emphasis on the important, even vital, differences between disparate "Latino" groups. The title of her article, "Nuevas voces salvadoreñas: Sandra Benítez y Demetria Martínez," suggests that Demetria Martínez, a Chicana, can unproblematically *be* a "Salvadoran voice." Indeed, within the article, Martínez's continual references to Dominican American Julia Alvarez's *In the Time of the Butterflies* suggest her investment in an overly simplistic panethnic vision of Latina writers.

11. Castillo focuses on the gendered aspect of these cultural differences. In the example she gives, for instance, "a complex historical process is reduced to the feminine projection of a masculinist bias" when Mary interprets José Luis's reaction to news

of the nuns' deaths in terms of a virgin/whore dichotomy in which she becomes the "gringa whore" (Castillo and Tabuenca Córdoba 175). By labeling herself a "whore" in José Luis's eyes (124), Mary implies that somehow "José Luis's country is being destroyed because in the United States women are seducing or being seduced" (Castillo and Tabuenca Córdoba 176). Intriguingly, Castillo's reading brings to mind yet another cultural overlay for this scene: the story of La Malinche, the indigenous woman who, in Mexican lore, aided Hernán Cortés's conquest of Mexico by serving as his mistress and "translating" the indigenous languages and cultures for him. La Malinche is thus the emblematic whore-as-cultural-traitor within this particular paradigm, which Mary imposes on the quite disparate circumstances of El Salvador by reading *herself* as whore/traitor in José Luis's eyes.

12. Martínez has commented of her novel that Mary "falls for the classic American romantic myth that if you love someone enough all will be well. [. . .] [Mary's misunderstanding] reflects my interest in the ways psychoanalysis has encouraged us, as a culture, to believe that we can individually become whole. We view the individual as a psychological entity, when in fact the root of much of our pain [. . .] has to do with inequality, with poverty, with health issues related to the environment" (Manolis 43–44).

13. See also Neill, Velasco for similar commentaries.

14. We might call this an example of what Neill terms "global intimacy." She expresses concern over an imagined "deterritorialized identity"(10)—that is, over the fantasy that white, middle-class U.S. citizens (for example) can engage in an "intimate identification [with an oppressed, 'third world' Other] that transcends national space." As Neill writes, this naïve "gesture at global solidarity eliminates the boundaries between the personal and the political at exactly the same time as it dissolves those between nations" (14). Such an illusory sense of "intimacy," she worries, problematically substitutes for critical attention to issues of "territorial sovereignty and political subjectivity" (10)—that is, to issues of borders, states, and citizens, and to the implications of one's own position within this larger field.

15. In an effort to dissemble the intensity of her romantic feelings, Mary later comments, "We're married, no?, to la revolución" (57). Castillo argues of this moment that Mary makes "a trivial cliché out of her partner's deep commitment, out of the deaths he has seen and the torture he still lives." José Luis resists "her too-facile identification with him" (Castillo and Tabuenca Córdoba 184).

16. See Coutin and Hirsch 11; D. Johnson 14; E. Martínez 110; McCracken 62. The author's biographical note in two editions of *Mother Tongue* also makes reference to this incident. For a discussion of Martínez's indictment and trial, see Manolis.

17. The authors of *Telling to Live* (2001) posit, in a similar vein, that *testimonio* has the power to both "disrupt the essentialized, homogenized understanding of Latina" (Latina Feminist Group 6) and to build a more reflective model of "pan-Latina/o solidarity, however fragile" (5). As the authors write of their group, through shared *testimonio*, "We learned how to construct a safer space that was not assumed a priori to be safe based simply on gender and national/ethnic affiliations. *Testimonio* was critical for breaking down essentialist categories, since it was through telling life stories and

reflecting upon them that we gained nuanced understandings of differences and connections among us" (11).

18. Cunningham notes that, "[a]t its height in 1986–1987, the movement spanned Mexico, the United States, and Canada" ("Ethnography" 587)—ironically giving new meaning to the usage of the term "North America." But as Susan Bibler Coutin has argued, the U.S. Sanctuary communities (Coutin specifically studied those in Tucson, Arizona, and the East Bay in California) "regarded the Sanctuary movement (excepting the Mexican and Central American segments of the underground railroad) as *North American* [i.e., as U.S. constituted]. Salvadoran and Guatemalan immigrants participated in the movement [but] neither they nor North American participants considered sanctuary *their* movement. Instead, Central Americans formed their own organizations" (*Culture of Protest* 11). Coutin's analysis suggests the degree to which ethnic connection was *not* a factor in the self-conception of the U.S. Sanctuary movement.

19. Indeed, as Coutin observes, participants often emphasized that their movement was religious rather than political in nature, as well. Indicted Sanctuary workers, for example, "deemphasized the political implications of their work in order to argue that sanctuary was a religious practice and therefore could not be curtailed by the federal government. [. . .] Participants who stressed the apolitical nature of the movement sometimes argued that [. . .] it would be a mistake for the sanctuary movement to replace a right-wing bias with a left-wing bias, and that it was important to aid refugees on the basis of need rather than politics. Defining the movement as religious rather than political refuted the government's suggestion that movement members were 'terrorists' who merited government surveillance" (Coutin and Hirsch, "Naming" 10–11)

20. In e-mail correspondence with me, Cunningham elaborates that "the impression I developed from my own research was that the Latino community in Arizona was pretty divided on this issue (as it continues to be on migration, border policy, etc.)." That is to say, ethnicity appears *not* to have been a substantive factor in the formulation of the Sanctuary movement—although, as I argue, Martínez reconfigures the rhetoric of kinship in the cause of solidarity with oppressed Central Americans.

21. Masud-Piloto quotes from an October 22, 1985, article in the *Miami Herald*, p. 8a.

22. This is not to say that Soledad sees her political activity as antithetical to her spirituality; clearly, just the opposite is true. As Martínez has commented in an interview, "Soledad embodies the wisdom that you can't sever spirituality from politics"; and Martínez has also noted her own fascination with liberation theology as a grounding for Soledad's character (Manolis 46–47). But in the novel, religious teachings are called much less explicitly into service as a basis for political activism than they are in, for example, Ana Castillo's *So Far from God* (see Chap. 5)—or than they were in the rhetoric of actual Sanctuary participants.

23. In El Salvador the Mothers of the Disappeared took the name CO-MADRES: "Founded in 1977 by a group of mothers, CO-MADRES was one of the first groups in El Salvador to denounce the atrocities of the Salvadoran government and military. [. . .] [T]hese women worked with priests and nuns to begin confronting the Salvadoran military and oligarchy and to demand an end to the gross inequalities that characterized El Salvador [. . .] Armed with a small list of missing relatives they demanded to know

who was in the jails, forced the excavation of clandestine cemeteries, and publicized the repressive tactics of the government in an international arena" (Stephen 813).

24. "In the name game," Martínez writes, "improvisation is the magic word" (*Confessions* 49). Thus she is a Latina in certain contexts, a Chicana in others, a Nueva Mejicana in yet others.

25. Poey and Suárez, the editors of *Iguana Dreams*, negotiate this difficulty by positing that the linguistic "unity" of U.S. Latinos lies in the fact that "we all share the experience of bilingualism"(xvi), which is, once again, statistically incorrect.

26. In this respect, the novel might be said to inhabit a relationship to magical realism similar to that of Ana Castillo's *So Far from God*; see Chapter 5. The potential tensions between the form of magical realism and content dealing with actual oppression is suggested by the reaction to the 2003 screening at the Venice Film Festival of the film adaptation of Lawrence Thornton's novel *Imagining Argentina* (1987). The film was reportedly booed and universally panned at the festival because of the incongruity of the scenes of "magical realism" within the context of the dirty war in Argentina, during which thirty thousand people disappeared or were killed (see "Actress Defends Comeback Film"; also Foley).

27. This is certainly not to say that José Luis's trauma ranks as greater or more important than Mary's; as she says, "the issue isn't who got hurt more"(172). It is, rather, to suggest that the specificities of these traumas are distinct enough that a vague analogy between them seems unhelpful, if not disturbing. They *each* deserve careful analysis and an exploration of the distinct forces that permitted them to occur. Kandiyoti makes a similarly problematic equation when she notes, of the molester, that, "after his act, the man turns on the television to watch the Vietnam War unfold, which is linked to the gender war that he has just waged on the body of the young girl" (439). It seems to me that the use of the term "war" here obscures a profound slippage of meaning indeed.

28. For other critical readings which accept at face value the comparison between Mary's abuse and the situation of Salvadorans, see Kandiyoti 438; E. Martínez 110, 117.

29. See Cunningham, "Sanctuary," esp. 377–78.

30. E-mail correspondence with me dated 2/11/2005.

31. Most interestingly, it would seem that, indeed, the metaphors of kinship were *also* invoked to construct an activist *religious* group identity enlisted in the service of the Sanctuary movement, as seen in the "Statement of Faith" put out by the Chicago Religious Task Force (which, Cunningham tells us, was "initially aligned with Tucson's Sanctuary group"):

> Authentic solidarity goes beyond remembering the suffering of our brothers and sisters. It embodies the biblical call to universal brotherhood and sisterhood. It lays upon us a new sense of kinship. We as North Americans are called to claim our family to the South.
>
> That means that Maria Elizabeth, the 55-year-old woman who goes every day to the San Salvador morgue carrying pictures of her disappeared son, is our mother. Cristina, the 17-year-old university student raped by the National Guard, is our sister. [ . . . ]
>
> When people ask what they can do to help the people of Central America,

our response is: What would you do if your sister were being raped, your brother killed, your father disappeared and your mother mourning daily? (Cunningham, "Ethnography" 592)

32. Consider Sandoval's explication of what she terms "differential consciousness," which "depends on the practitioner's ability to read the current situation of power and self-consciously choosing and adopting the ideological stand best suited to push against its configurations." Differential consciousness requires the "flexibility to self-consciously transform that identity according to the requirements of another oppositional ideological tactic if readings of power's formation require it" (59).

## Conclusion: The Shifting Nature of *Latinidad*

1. This is the explanation given me by David Wald, codirector of U.S.A.-Cuba-InfoMed, which has collaborated with Pastors for Peace on the Cuba Friendshipments, when I naïvely inquired what the U.S.-Mexican border had to do—logistically speaking—with shipments to Cuba.

2. Rodriguez quotes from an interview with Charles Kamasaki, who was vice-president of the Office of Research, Advocacy and Legislation for the NCLR.

3. In *Latino Voices* (1992), de la Garza et al. document that one finding of the Latino National Political Survey was that 79.6 percent of Mexican Americans, 87.2 percent of Puerto Ricans, and 88.4 percent of Cuban Americans either supported or strongly supported bilingual education (99) and indicated willingness to be taxed for it (69 percent, Mexicans; 70 percent, Puerto Ricans; and 54.1 percent, Cubans). Jones-Correa and Leal, reviewing the same set of data, note that support for bilingual education and for taxation in support of it was statistically correlated to some use of a panethnic identifier (233)—although, interestingly, sole identification with a panethnic term did not fit this trend (a finding that the authors interpret as indicating that people who identify exclusively as, say, "Latino" or "Hispanic" are actually signaling a "weaker sense of ethnicity overall" [239]).

4. "In contrast to the anti-bilingual policies instituted in California in 1998, MD-CPS [Miami/Dade County Public Schools] forcefully endorsed and advanced bilingual education. Every child is encouraged to become bilingual. Native English speakers are expected to take Spanish through elementary school" (Stepick et al., *This Land* 27).

# Works Cited

"1970 Census: Instructions to Respondents." <http://www.ipums.umn.edu/usa/voliii/inst1970.html#13b>. Accessed 17 Jan. 2006.

"1980 Census: Instructions to Respondents." <http://www.ipums.umn.edu/usa/voliii/inst1980.html#7>. Accessed 17 Jan. 2006.

"1990 Census: Instructions to Respondents." <http://www.ipums.umn.edu/usa/voliii/inst1990.html#7>. Accessed 17 Jan. 2006.

"Actress Defends Comeback Film." *Lawrence Journal World*, 3 Sept. 2003: 2A.

Acuña, Rodolfo. "The Miami Myth Machine." <www.aztlan.net/miami.htm>. [Undated but circa 2000]. Accessed 25 Jan. 2006.

———. *Occupied America: A History of Chicanos*. New York: Harper and Row, 1988.

Aguirre, Benigno E. "Differential Migration of Cuban Social Races: A Review and Interpretation of the Problem." *Latin American Research Review* 11.1 (1976): 103–24.

Alarcón, Norma. "Chicana Feminism: In the Tracks of the Native Woman." *Cultural Studies* 4.3 (1990): 248–56.

———. "Traddutora, Traditora: A Paradigmatic Figure of Chicana Feminism." *Cultural Critique* 13 (Fall 1989): 57–87. Reprinted in Inderpal Grewal and Caren Kaplan, eds., *Scattered Hegemonies: Postmodernity and Transnational Feminist Practices*. Minneapolis: University of Minnesota Press, 1994. 110–33.

Alcoff, Linda Martín. "The Problem of Speaking for Others." In Judith Roof and Robyn Wiegman, eds., *Who Can Speak? Authority and Critical Identity*. Urbana: University of Illinois Press, 1995. 97–119.

Aldama, Frederick Luis. *Postethnic Narrative Criticism: Magicorealism in Oscar "Zeta" Acosta, Ana Castillo, Julie Dash, Hanif Kureishi, and Salman Rushdie*. Austin: University of Texas Press, 2003.

Alderete, Manuel. "Forced and Politically-correct Labeling" [on-line rev. of *Living in Spanglish* by Ed Morales]. 21 Nov. 2004. <www.amazon.com>. Accessed 13 Jan. 2006.

Alemán, Jesse. "'Thank God, Lolita Is Away from Those Horrid Savages': The Politics of Whiteness in *Who Would Have Thought It?*" In Amelia María de la Luz Montes and Anne Elizabeth Goldman, eds., *María Amparo Ruiz de Burton: Critical and Pedagogical Perspectives*. Lincoln: University of Nebraska Press, 2004. 95–111.

Alexander, Tom. "Those Amazing Cuban Emigres." *Fortune*, Oct. 1996: 144–49.

Allatson, Paul. *Latino Dreams: Transcultural Traffic and the U.S. National Imaginary*. New York: Rodopi, 2002.

Allende, Isabel. *The House of the Spirits*. Trans. Magda Bogin. New York: Bantam Books, 1993.

Alonso Gallo, Laura P. "Latino Culture in the U.S.: Using, Reviewing, and Reconstructing *Latinidad* in Contemporary Latino/a Fiction." *KulturPoetik* 2.2 (2002): 236–48.

Alvarez, Julia. *How the García Girls Lost Their Accents*. 1991. New York: Plume/Penguin, 1992.
———. *In the Name of Salomé*. Chapel Hill, N.C.: Algonquin Books of Chapel Hill, 2000.
———. *In the Time of the Butterflies*. 1994. New York: Plume/Penguin, 1995.
———. *Saving the World*. Chapel Hill, N.C.: Algonquin Books of Chapel Hill, 2006.
———. "The Territory of the Storyteller." Interview with Marta Caminero-Santangelo. *Antípodas: Journal of Hispanic and Galician Studies of Australia and New Zealand*. 10 (1998): 15–24.
———. "A White Woman of Color." In Margaret L. Andersen and Patricia Hill Collins, eds., *Race, Class, and Gender: An Anthology*. 6th edition. Belmont, Calif.: Thomas Wadsworth, 2007. 166–71.
———. *¡Yo!* Chapel Hill, N.C.: Algonquin Books of Chapel Hill, 1997.
Alvarez Borland, Isabel. *Cuban-American Literature of Exile: From Person to Persona*. Charlottesville: University Press of Virginia, 1998.
Anaya, Rudolfo. *Bless Me, Ultima*. 1972. New York: Warner Books, 1994.
Anders, Gigi. *Jubana! The Awkwardly True and Dazzling Adventures of a Jewish Cubana Goddess*. New York: HarperCollins, 2005.
Anderson, Benedict. *Imagined Communities: Reflections on the Origin and Spread of Nationalism*. Rev. ed. New York: Verso, 1991.
Anderson, Gary Clayton. *The Indian Southwest, 1580–1830: Ethnogenesis and Reinvention*. Norman: University of Oklahoma Press, 1999.
Año Nuevo de Kerr, Louise. "The Chicano Experience in Chicago, 1920–1970." Unpublished Ph.D. dissertation: University of Illinois, 1976.
Anzaldúa, Gloria. *Borderlands/La Frontera: The New Mestiza*. San Francisco: Spinsters/Aunt Lute, 1987.
Anzaldúa, Gloria, and Cherríe Moraga, eds. *This Bridge Called My Back: Radical Writings by Women of Color*. Watertown, Mass.: Persephone Press, 1981.
Appiah, Anthony. "The Uncompleted Argument: Du Bois and the Illusion of Race." In Henry Louis Gates Jr., ed., *"Race," Writing, and Difference*. Chicago: University of Chicago Press, 1986. 21–37.
Arrington, Vanessa. "Havana's Chinatown Struggles." *Boston Globe* 26 Nov. 2004. Associated Press. *CubaNet*. Cuba News. <http://www.cubanet.org/CNews/y04/nov04/29e8.htm>. Accessed 12 Mar. 2005.
Augenbraum, Harold, and Margarite Fernández Olmos, eds. *The Latino Reader: From 1542 to the Present*. New York: Houghton Mifflin, 1997.
Baker, Houston A., Jr. "Caliban's Triple Play." In Henry Louis Gates Jr., ed., *"Race," Writing, and Difference*. Chicago: University of Chicago Press, 1986. 381–95.
Barnet, Miguel. *Afro-Cuban Religions*. Trans. Christine Renata Ayorinde. Princeton, N.J.: Markus Wiener Publishers, 2001.
———. "La Regla de Ocha: The Religious System of Santería." In Margarite Fernández Olmos and Lizabeth Paravisini-Gebert, eds., *Sacred Possessions: Vodou, Santería, Obeah, and the Caribbean*. New Brunswick, N.J.: Rutgers University Press, 1997. 79–100.
Barreto, Matt A. "National Origin (Mis)Identification among Latinos in the 2000 Cen-

sus: The Growth of the 'Other Hispanic or Latino' Category." *Harvard Journal of Hispanic Policy* 15 (2002): 39–63.

Bauzá, Vanessa. "Chinatown, Cuba: The Old Havana Neighborhood Clings Precariously to Its Chinese Ways." Fort Lauderdale (Fla.) *Sun-Sentinel*, 2 Sept. 2000 .

Begley, Sharon. "Three Is Not Enough." *Newsweek*, 13 Feb. 1995: 67–69.

Behar, Ruth, ed. *Bridges to Cuba/Puentes a Cuba*. Ann Arbor: University of Michigan Press, 1995.

———. "Juban América." *Poetics Today* 16.1 (Spring 1995): 151–70.

———. *Translated Woman: Crossing the Border with Esperanza's Story*. Boston: Beacon Press, 1993.

Bettinger-López, Caroline. *Cuban-Jewish Journeys: Searching for Identity, Home, and History in Miami*. Knoxville: University of Tennessee Press, 2000.

Bhabha, Homi K. *The Location of Culture*. London: Routledge, 1994.

———, ed. *Nation and Narration*. New York: Routledge, 1990.

Bloom, Harold, ed. *Hispanic-American Writers*. Philadelphia: Chelsea House, 1998.

Boff, Leonardo, and Clodovis Boff. *Introducing Liberation Theology*. Trans. Paul Burns. New York: Orbis Books, 1987.

———. *Salvation and Liberation: In Search of a Balance between Faith and Politics*. Trans. Robert R. Barr. New York: Orbis Books, 1984.

Brameshuber-Ziegler, Irène. "Cristina Garcia, *Dreaming in Cuban* (1992): Collapse of Communication and Kristeva's Semiotic as Possible Remedy." *Language and Literature* 24 (1999): 43–64.

Brogan, Kathleen. *Cultural Haunting: Ghosts and Ethnicity in Recent American Literature*. Charlottesville: University Press of Virginia, 1998.

Bruce-Novoa, Juan. "Learning to Read (and/in) Rudolfo Anaya's *Bless Me, Ultima*." In John R. Maitino and David R. Peck, eds., *Teaching American Ethnic Literatures: Nineteen Essays*. Albuquerque: University of New Mexico Press, 1996. 179–91.

Buell, Lawrence. "The Ecocritical Insurgency." *New Literary History*, 30.3 (1999): 699–712.

Burns, E. Bradford. *Latin America: A Concise Interpretive History*. Englewood Cliffs, N.J.: Prentice-Hall, 1994.

Bus, Heiner. "The Presence of Native Americans in Chicano Literature." *Revista Chicano-Riqueña* 13.3–4 (1985): 148–62.

*Café con Leche: Voices of Exile's Children*. (Documentary.) Dir. Joe Cardona. U.S., 1997.

Calderón, Héctor. "*Bless Me, Ultima*: A Chicano Romance of the Southwest." In César A. González-T, ed., *Rudolfo A. Anaya: Focus on Criticism*. La Jolla, Calif.: Lalo Press, 1990. 64–93.

"Call for Papers." *NewsNotes: E-Publication for the Society for the Study of the Multi-Ethnic Literature of the U.S.* Winter 2005. <http://www.marshall.edu/melus/news-notes/>. Accessed 10 Mar. 2006.

Cantú, Roberto. "Apocalypse as an Ideological Construct: The Storyteller's Art in *Bless Me, Ultima*." In César A. González-T., ed., *Rudolfo A. Anaya: Focus on Criticism*. La Jolla, Calif.: Lalo Press, 1990. 13–63.

Casal, Lourdes. "The Founders: Alfonso." Trans. Margaret Jull Costa. In Cristina García, ed., *¡Cubanísimo!: The Vintage Book of Contemporary Cuban Literature*. New York: Random House, 2002. 192–206.

Castillo, Ana. "La Macha: Toward a Beautiful Whole Self." In Carla Trujillo, ed., *Chicana Lesbians: The Girls Our Mothers Warned Us About*. Berkeley, Calif.: Third Woman Press, 1991. 24–48.

———. *So Far from God*. 1993. New York: Plume/Penguin, 1994.

Castillo, Debra A. *Redreaming America: Toward a Bilingual American Culture*. Albany: State University of New York Press, 2005.

———, and María Socorro Tabuenca Córdoba. *Border Women: Writing from la Frontera*. Minneapolis: University of Minnesota Press, 2002.

Castillo-Speed, Lillian, ed. *Latina: Women's Voices from the Borderlands*. New York: Simon and Schuster, 1995.

Castro, Max. "The Trouble with Collusion: Paradoxes of the Cuban-American Way." In Damián J. Fernández and Madeline Cámara Betancourt, eds., *Cuba, the Elusive Nation: Interpretations of National Identity*. Gainesville: University Press of Florida, 2000. 292–309.

Cavalli-Sforza, Luca; Paulo Menozzi; and Alberto Riazza. *The History and Geography of Human Genes*. Princeton, N.J.: Princeton University Press, 1994.

"Census 2000 Enumeration Form: Questions and Instructions to Respondents." <http://www.ipums.umn.edu/usa/voliii/inst2000.html#7>. Accessed 17 Jan. 2006.

Chanady, Amaryll, ed. *Latin American Identity and Constructions of Difference*. Minneapolis: University of Minnesota Press, 1994.

Chancy, Myriam J. A. "Diasporic Disconnections: Insurrection and Forgetfulness in Contemporary Haitian and Latin-Caribbean Women's Literature." In Deborah L. Madsen, ed., *Beyond the Borders: American Literature and Post-colonial Theory*. London: Pluto Press, 2003. 167–83.

Chasar, Mike, and Constance Pierce. "Interview with Mike Chasar and Constance Pierce." By Julia Alvarez. *Glimmer Train Stories* 25 (Winter 1998).

Childs, Matt D. "Expanding Perspectives on Race, Nation, and Culture in Cuban History." *Latin American Research Review* 39.1 (Feb. 2004): 285–301.

"China." *Encyclopaedia Britannica*. 2005. Encyclopaedia Britannica Online <http://www.search.eb.com>. 70958–71865. Accessed 17 Mar. 2005.

Chinitz, David. "Rejuvenation through Joy: Langston Hughes, Primitivism and Jazz." *American Literary History* 9.1 (1997): 60–78.

Christian, Karen. *Show and Tell: Identity as Performance in U.S. Latina/o Fiction*. Albuquerque: University of New Mexico Press, 1997.

Cline, Howard F. *Spanish and Mexican Land Grants in New Mexico, 1689–1848: A Technical Report*. New York: Clearwater, 1964.

Cornejo Polar, Antonio. "La literatura latinoamericana y sus literaturas regionales y nacionales como totalidades contradictorias." In Ana Pizarro, ed., *Hacia una historia de la literatura latinoamericana*. Mexico City: Colegio de México, 1987. 123–36.

Cornell, Stephen, and Douglas Hartmann. *Ethnicity and Race: Making Identities in a Changing World*. Thousand Oaks, Calif.: Pine Forge Press, 1998.

Coutin, Susan Bibler. *The Culture of Protest: Religious Activism and the U.S. Sanctuary Movement*. Boulder, Colo.: Westview Press, 1993.

———. "The Oppressed, the Suspect, and the Citizen: Subjectivity in Competing Accounts of Political Violence." *Law and Social Inquiry* 26.1 (Winter 2001): 63–94.
Coutin, Susan Bibler, and Susan F. Hirsch. "Naming Resistance: Ethnographers, Dissidents, and States." *Anthropological Quarterly* 71 (Jan. 1998): 1–17.
Craft, Linda J. "Truth or Consequences: Mambos, Memories, and Multiculturalism from Achy Obejas's Chicago." *Revista de Estudios Hispánicos* 35.2 (2001): 369–87.
Cresce, Arthur R., Audrey Dianne Schmidley, and Roberto R. Ramirez. "Identification of Hispanic Ethnicity in Census 2000: Analysis of Data Quality for the Question on Hispanic Origin." U.S. Census Bureau. <http://www.census.gov/population/www/documentation/twps0075/twps0075.html#tab02>. Accessed 17 Jan. 2006.
Croucher, Sheila L. *Imagining Miami: Ethnic Politics in a Postmodern World*. Charlottesville: University Press of Virginia, 1997.
"Cuba's New Refugees Get Jobs Fast." *Business Week*, 12 Mar. 1966: 69.
*The Cultural Revolution in China: Its Origins and Course*. Keesing's Research Report. New York: Charles Scribner's Sons, 1967.
Cunningham, Hilary. "The Ethnography of Transnational Social Activism: Understanding the Global as Local Practice." *American Ethnologist* 26.3 (Aug. 1999): 583–604.
———. "Sanctuary and Sovereignty: Church and State Along the U.S.-Mexico Border." *Journal of Church and State* 40.2 (Spring 1998): 370–86.
Daly, Mary. *Beyond God the Father: Toward a Philosophy of Women's Liberation*. Boston: Beacon Press, 1973.
Dalleo, Raphael. "How Cristina Garcia Lost Her Accent, and Other Latina Conversations." *Latino Studies* 3.1 (2005): 3–18.
Danticat, Edwidge. *The Farming of Bones*. New York: Penguin, 1998.
Darder, Antonia, and Rodolfo D. Torres. "Latinos and Society: Culture, Politics, and Class." In Antonia Darder and Rodolfo D. Torres, eds., *The Latino Studies Reader: Culture, Economy and Society*. Malden, Mass.: Blackwell, 1998. 3–26.
Dasenbrock, Reed Way. "Intelligibility and Meaningfulness in Multicultural Literature in English." *PMLA* 102.1 (Jan. 1987): 10–19.
Davis, Rocío G. "Back to the Future: Mothers, Languages, and Homes in Cristina García's *Dreaming in Cuban*." *World Literature Today* 74.1 (Winter 2000): 60–68.
De Genova, Nicholas, and Ana Y. Ramos-Zayas. *Latino Crossings: Mexicans, Puerto Ricans, and the Politics of Race and Citizenship*. New York: Routledge, 2003.
De la Fuente, Alejandro. "Race, Ideology, and Culture in Cuba: Recent Scholarship." *Latin American Research Review* 35.3 (2000): 199–210.
De la Garza, Rodolfo; Louis DeSipio; F. Chris Garcia; John Garcia; and Angelo Falcón. *Latino Voices: Mexican, Puerto Rican and Cuban Perspectives on American Politics*. Boulder, Colo.: Westview Press, 1992.
Delgadillo, Theresa. "Forms of Chicana Feminist Resistance: Hybrid Spirituality in Ana Castillo's *So Far from God*." *Modern Fiction Studies* 44.4 (1998): 888–916.
DelRosso, Jeana. "The Convent as Colonist: Catholicism in the Works of Contemporary Women Writers of the Americas." *MELUS* 26.3 (2001): 183–203.
Didion, Joan. *Miami*. New York: Simon and Schuster, 1987.
Duany, Jorge. "Reconstructing Cubanness: Changing Discourses of National Identity on the Island and in the Diaspora during the Twentieth Century." In Damián J.

Fernández and Madeline Cámara Betancourt, eds., *Cuba, the Elusive Nation: Interpretations of National Identity*. Gainesville: University Press of Florida, 2000. 17–42.

Dutwin, David; Mollyann Brodie; Melissa Herrmann; and Rebecca Levin. "Latinos and Political Party Affiliation." *Hispanic Journal of Behavioral Sciences* 27.2 (May 2005): 135–60.

Eastman, Lloyd E. *Seeds of Destruction: Nationalist China in War and Revolution, 1937–1949*. Stanford, Calif.: Stanford University Press, 1984.

Eichner, Bill. "Afterword." In Julia Alvarez, *A Cafecito Story*. White River Junction, Vt.: Chelsea Green, 2001. 39–45.

Eire, Carlos. *Waiting for Snow in Havana: Confessions of a Cuban Boy*. New York: Free Press, 2003.

Elam, Diane. "Speak for Yourself." In Judith Roof and Robyn Wiegman, eds., *Who Can Speak? Authority and Critical Identity*. Chicago: University of Illinois Press, 1995. 231–37.

Engle, Margarita. *Singing to Cuba*. Houston: Arte Público Press, 1993.

———. *Skywriting: A Novel of Cuba*. New York: Bantam, 1995.

Erdrich, Louise. *Tracks*. New York: Harper and Row, 1988.

Faris, Wendy B. "Scheherazade's Children: Magical Realism and Postmodern Fiction." In Lois Parkinson Zamora and Wendy B. Faris, eds., *Magical Realism: Theory, History, Community*. Durham, N.C.: Duke University Press, 1995. 163–90.

Fears, Darryl. "Pollsters Debate Hispanics' Presidential Voting." *Washington Post*, 26 Nov. 2004.

Fernández, Roberto G. *Raining Backwards*. Houston: Arte Público Press, 1988.

Ferrer, Ada. "Rethinking Race and Nation in Cuba." In Damián J. Fernández and Madeline Cámara Betancourt, eds., *Cuba, the Elusive Nation: Interpretations of National Identity*. Gainesville: University Press of Florida, 2000. 60–76.

Fewsmith, Joseph. *Party, State, and Local Elites in Republican China: Merchant Organizations and Politics in Shanghai, 1890–1930*. Honolulu: University of Hawaii Press, 1985.

Flores, Juan. *From Bomba to Hip-Hop: Puerto Rican Culture and Latino Identity*. New York: Columbia University Press, 2000.

———. "Islands and Enclaves: Caribbean Latinos in Historical Perspective." In Marcelo M. Suárez-Orozco and Mariela M. Páez, eds., *Latinos: Remaking America*. Berkeley and Los Angeles: University of California Press, 2002. 59–74.

Foley, Jack. "Thompson's Imagining Argentina Panned at Venice." IndieLondon. 2003 <http://www.indielondon.co.uk/film/imagining_argentina_venice.html>. Accessed 28 Feb. 2005.

Fox, Geoffrey. *Hispanic Nation: Culture, Politics, and the Constructing of Identity*. Secaucus, N.J.: Carol Publishing Group, 1996.

Frase-Blunt, Martha. "A New Chapter." *Hispanic*, Sept. 1992: 30–38.

Fuentes, Annette, and Barbara Ehrenreich. *Women in the Global Factory*. Boston: South End Press, 1984.

Gandhi, Leela. *Postcolonial Theory: A Critical Introduction*. New York: Columbia University Press, 1998.

García, Cristina. *Dreaming in Cuban*. New York: Ballantine, 1992.
———. *Monkey Hunting*. New York: Alfred A. Knopf, 2003.
———, ed. *¡Cubanísimo! The Vintage Book of Contemporary Cuban Literature*. New York: Vintage Books, 2002.
García, John A. *Latino Politics in America: Community, Culture, and Interests*. New York: Rowman and Littlefield Publishers, 2003.
García, María Cristina. *Havana U.S.A.: Cuban Exiles and Cuban Americans in South Florida, 1959–1994*. Berkeley and Los Angeles: University of California Press, 1996.
García Márquez, Gabriel. *One Hundred Years of Solitude*. Trans. Gregory Rabassa. New York: Avon, 1971. Trans. of *Cien años de soledad*. 1967.
Gates, Henry Louis, Jr., ed. *"Race," Writing, and Difference*. Chicago: University of Chicago Press, 1986.
Gilroy, Paul. *Against Race: Imagining Political Culture beyond the Color Line*. Cambridge, Mass.: Belknap Press of Harvard University Press, 2000.
Gimenez, Martha E. "Latino/'Hispanic'—Who Needs a Name? The Case against a Standardized Terminology." *International Journal of Health Services* 19.3 (1989): 557–71.
———. "Latino Politics—Class Struggles: Reflections on the Future of Latino Politics." In Rodolfo D. Torres and George Katsiaficas, eds., *Latino Social Movements: Historical and Theoretical Perspectives*. New York: Routledge, 1999. 165–80.
Gingerich, Willard. "Aspects of Prose Style in Three Chicano Novels: *Pocho*; *Bless Me, Ultima*; and *The Road to Tamazunchale*." In Jacob Ornstein-Galicia, ed., *Form and Function in Chicano English*. Rowley, Mass.: Newbury House, 1984. 206–28.
Gish, Robert Franklin. *Beyond Bounds: Cross-cultural Essays on Anglo, American Indian, and Chicano Literature*. Albuquerque: University of New Mexico Press, 1996.
Goldman, Francisco. *The Ordinary Seaman*. New York: Grove, 1997.
Gómez-Peña, Guillermo. *Warrior for Gringostroika: Essays, Performance Texts, and Poetry*. St. Paul: Graywolf Press, 1993.
Gómez-Vega, Ibis. "Metaphors of Entrapment: Caribbean Women Writers Face the Wreckage of History." *Journal of Political and Military Sociology* 25 (Winter 1997): 231–47.
Gonzalez, Juan. *Harvest of Empire: A History of Latinos in America*. New York: Penguin, 2000.
González, Lisa Sánchez. *Boricua Literature: A Literary History of the Puerto Rican Diaspora*. New York: New York University Press, 2001.
Gonzalez, Ray, ed. *Currents from the Dancing River: Contemporary Latino Fiction, Nonfiction, and Poetry*. New York: Harcourt Brace, 1994.
González Echevarría, Roberto. "Sisters in Death." Review of *In the Time of the Butterflies* by Julia Alvarez. *New York Times Book Review*, 18 Dec. 1994: 28.
Gracia, Jorge J. E. *Hispanic/Latino Identity: A Philosophical Perspective*. Malden, Mass.: Blackwell, 2000.
Hada, Ken. "Christ, Culture and Conscience: Rudolfo Anaya's *Bless Me, Ultima* and Carlos Fuentes' *The Good Conscience*." *Notes on Contemporary Literature* 29.4 (1999): 9–10.
Haight, Roger. *An Alternative Vision: An Interpretation of Liberation Theology*. New York: Paulist Press, 1985.

Hames-García, Michael. "Dr. Gonzo's Carnival: The Testimonial Satires of Oscar Zeta Acosta." *American Literature* 72.2 (2000): 463–93.

Hannaford, Ivan. *Race: The History of an Idea in the West*. Baltimore: Johns Hopkins University Press, 1996.

Heide, Markus. "The Postmodern 'We': Academia and Community in Ana Castillo's *So Far from God* and Denise Chávez's *Face of an Angel*." In Francisco A. Lomelí and Karin Ikas, eds., *U.S. Latino Literatures and Cultures: Transnational Perspectives*. Heidelberg: Carl Winter Universitatsverlag, 2000. 171–80.

Hellein, Tanya. "Simply a Question of Belief." Review of *So Far from God* by Ana Castillo. *Times Literary Supplement* no. 4774, 30 Sept. 1994: 25.

Henriot, Christian. *Shanghai, 1927–1937: Municipal Power, Locality, and Modernization*. Trans. Noël Castelino. Berkeley and Los Angeles: University of California Press, 1993.

Herms, Dieter. "Chicano and Nuyorican Literature—Elements of a Democratic and Socialist Culture in the U.S. of A.?" In Geneviève Fabre, ed., *European Perspectives on Hispanic Literature of the United States*. Houston: Arte Público Press, 1986. 118–29.

Hernández-Truyol, Berta Esperanza. "Building Bridges: Latinas and Latinos at the Crossroads." In Richard Delgado and Jean Stefancic, eds., *The Latino/a Condition: A Critical Reader*. New York: New York University Press, 1998. 24–31. Originally published in the *Columbia Human Rights Law Review* (1994).

Herrera, Andrea O'Reilly. "Cristina García, *Dreaming in Cuban*." In Alvina E. Quintana, ed., *Reading U.S. Latina Writers: Remapping American Literature*. New York: Palgrave Macmillan, 2003. 91–102.

Hijuelos, Oscar. 1989. *The Mambo Kings Play Songs of Love*. New York: HarperPerennial, 1992.

Hobsbawm, Eric, and Terence Ranger, eds. *The Invention of Tradition*. New York: Cambridge University Press, 1983.

Hollyday, Joyce. "A Spirit of Resolve." *Sojourners* 14.3 (Mar. 1985): 9–10.

Holton, Frederick S. "Chicano as *Bricoleur*: Christianity and Mythmaking in Rudolfo Anaya's *Bless Me, Ultima*." *Confluencia* 11.1 (1995): 22–41.

Hoobler, Dorothy, and Thomas Hoobler. *The Cuban American Family Album*. New York: Oxford University Press, 1996.

Horsman, Reginald. *Race and Manifest Destiny: The Origins of American Racial Anglo-Saxonism*. Cambridge, Mass.: Harvard University Press, 1981.

Ink, Lynn Chun. "Remaking Identity, Unmaking Nation: Historical Recovery and the Reconstruction of Community in *In the Time of the Butterflies* and *The Farming of Bones*." *Callaloo* 27.3 (2004): 788–807.

Johnson, David. Rev. of *Mother Tongue* by Demetria Martínez. *National Catholic Reporter* 31.7 (9 Dec. 1994): *Expanded Academic ASAP*. Infotrac. The University of Kansas Libraries. Lawrence, Kan. Accessed 11 Feb. 2005. <http://web6.infotrac.galegroup.com>.

Johnson, Kelli Lyon. "Both Sides of the Massacre: Collective Memory and Narrative on Hispaniola." *Mosaic* (Winnipeg) 36.2 (June 2003): 75–91.

———. *Julia Alvarez: Writing a New Place on the Map*. Albuquerque: University of New Mexico Press, 2005.

Johnson, Kirk. "The 2004 Election: The Electorate; Hispanic Voters Declared Their Independence." *New York Times*, 9 Nov. 2004: A1.

Jones-Correa, Michael. "All Politics Is Local: Latinos and the 2000 Elections." *Harvard Journal of Hispanic Policy* 13 (2000/2001): 25–44.

———. *Between Two Nations: The Political Predicament of Latinos in New York City*. Ithaca, N.Y.: Cornell University Press, 1998.

Jones-Correa, Michael, and David L. Leal. "Becoming 'Hispanic': Secondary Panethnic Identification among Latin American–Origin Populations in the United States." *Hispanic Journal of Behavioral Sciences* 18.2 (May 1996): 214–54.

Jussawalla, Feroza. "Teaching R. K. Narayan's *Swami and Friends*." *College Literature* 19.3 (Oct–Feb 1992): 219–24.

Kandiyoti, Dalia. "Host and Guest in the 'Latino Contact Zone': Narrating Solidarity and Hospitality in *Mother Tongue*." *Comparative America Studies* 2.4 (2004): 421–46.

Kanellos, Nicolás, ed. *Herencia: The Anthology of Hispanic Literature of the United States*. New York: Oxford University Press, 2002.

———. *Hispanic American Literature: A Brief Introduction and Anthology*. Berkeley, Calif.: HarperCollins, 1995.

Kanoza, Theresa M. "The Golden Carp and Moby Dick: Rudolfo Anaya's Multi-Culturalism." *MELUS* 24.2 (Summer 1999): 159–71.

Kavanagh, James H. "Ideology." In Frank Lentricchia and Thomas McLaughlin, eds., *Critical Terms for Literary Study*. 2nd edition. Chicago: University of Chicago Press, 1995. 306–20.

Kearns, Rick. "Indigenous Puerto Rico: DNA Evidence Upsets Established History." *Issues in Caribbean Amerindian Studies* 5.2 (June 2003–June 2004). Caribbean Amerindian Centrelink (on line). <http://www.centrelink.org/KearnsDNA.html>. Reprinted from *Indian Country Today*. Accessed 19 Aug. 2005.

Kingsolver, Barbara. "Lush Language: Desert Heat." Review of *So Far from God* by Ana Castillo. *Los Angeles Times Book Review* 16 May 1993. Reprinted in *Contemporary Literary Criticism—Select*. On line. Galenet. <http://galenet.galegroup.com.ww2.lib.ku.edu:2048/servlet/GLD/hits?r=d&origSearch=true&o=DataType&n=50&1=d&c=16&locID=ksstate_ukans&secondary=false&u=CA&u=CLC&u=DLB&t=KW&s=1&NA=ana+castillo&TI=so+far+from+god>. Accessed 24 June 2003.

Kleindienst, Kris. "The Clash of Cuban American Cultures." *GCN: Gay Community News* 23.1 (Summer 1997). 10–15.

Kristeva, Julia. *Nations without Nationalism*. New York: Columbia University Press, 1993.

Kwong, Julia. *Cultural Revolution in China's Schools, May 1966–April 1969*. Stanford, Calif.: Hoover Institution Press, 1988.

Lamadrid, Enrique. "The Dynamics of Myth in the Creative Vision of Rudolfo Anaya." In Harold Bloom, ed., *Hispanic American Writers*. Philadelphia: Chelsea House, 1998. 151–61.

Laó-Montes, Agustín. "Introduction: Mambo Montage: The Latinization of New York City." In Agustín Laó-Montes and Arlene Dávila, eds., *Mambo Montage: The Latinization of New York*. New York: Columbia University Press, 2001. 1–53.

Latina Feminist Group. *Telling to Live: Latina Feminist Testimonios*. Durham, N.C.: Duke University Press, 2001.

Lattin, Vernon E. "The Quest for Mythic Vision in Contemporary Native American and Chicano Fiction." *American Literature* 50 (1978): 625–40.

Leonard, Suzanne. "Dreaming as Cultural Work in *Donald Duk* and *Dreaming in Cuban*." *MELUS* 29.2 (Summer 2004): 181–204.

Levine, Robert M. *Tropical Diaspora: The Jewish Experience in Cuba*. Gainesville: University Press of Florida, 1993.

Logan, John R. "How Race Counts for Hispanic Americans." Albany, N.Y.: Lewis Mumford Center for Comparative Urban and Regional Research at State University of New York, 14 July, 2003. <http://mumford.albany.edu/census/BlackLatinoReport/BlackLatino01.htm>. Accessed 17 Jan. 2006.

Loomba, Ania. *Colonialism/Postcolonialism*. London: Routledge, 1998.

López, Ian F. Haney. "Chance, Context, and Choice in the Social Construction of Race." In Richard Delgado and Jean Stefancic, eds., *The Latino/a Condition: A Critical Reader*. New York: New York University Press, 1998. 9–16.

López, Kimberle S. "Women on the Verge of a Revolution: Madness and Resistance in Cristina García's *Dreaming in Cuban*." *Letras Femeninas* 22.1–2 (Spring 1996): 33–49.

López-Calvo, Ignacio. *"God and Trujillo": Literary and Cultural Representations of the Dominican Dictator*. Gainesville: University Press of Florida, 2005.

Loury, Glenn C. "When Color Should Count." *New York Times*, 28 July 2002: 13.

Luis, William. *Dance between Two Cultures: Latino Caribbean Literature Written in the United States*. Nashville: Vanderbilt University Press, 1997.

Lusane, Clarence. "From Black Cuban to Afro-Cuban: Researching Race in Cuba." *Souls: A Critical Journal of Black Politics, Culture, and Society*. Special issue: "Race and Revolution in Cuba" 1.2 (Spring 1999): 73–79.

Lux, Guillermo, and Maurilio E. Vigil. "Return to Aztlán: The Chicano Rediscovers His Indian Past." In Rudolfo A. Anaya and Francisco A. Lomelí, eds., *Aztlán: Essays on the Chicano Homeland*. Albuquerque: University of New Mexico Press, 1989. 93–110.

Machado Sáez, Elena. "The Global Baggage of Nostalgia in Cristina Garcia's *Dreaming in Cuban*." *MELUS* 30.4 (Winter 2005): 129–47.

Madison, D. Soyini. "Cuba: Great Contradiction, Even Greater Promise." *Souls: A Critical Journal of Black Politics, Culture, and Society*. Special issue: "Race and Revolution in Cuba" 1.2 (Spring 1999): 53–57.

Maitino, John R., and David R. Peck, eds. *Teaching American Ethnic Literatures: Nineteen Essays*. Albuquerque: University of New Mexico Press, 1996.

Manolis, Argie J. "The Writer as Witness: An Interview with Demetria Martínez." *Hayden's Ferry Review* 24 (1999): 37–51.

Manríquez, B. J. "Ana Castillo's *So Far from God*: Intimations of the Absurd." *College Literature* 29.2 (2002): 37–49.

Marable, Manning. "Race and Revolution in Cuba: African-American Perspectives." *Souls: A Critical Journal of Black Politics, Culture, and Society*. Special issue: "Race and Revolution in Cuba" 1.2 (Spring 1999): 6–17.
Marrero, María Teresa. "Historical and Literary *Santería*: Unveiling Gender and Identity in U.S. Cuban Literature." In Frances R. Aparicio and Susana Chávez-Silverman, eds., *Tropicalizations: Transcultural Representations of Latinidad*. Hanover, N.H.: University Press of New England, 1997. 139–59.
Martí, José. "Para las escenas." *Anuario del Centro de Estudios Martianos*, no. 1 (1978): 31–33.
Martin, Elizabeth. "The Effects of Questionnaire Design on Reporting of Detailed Hispanic Origin in Census 2000 Mail Questionnaires." *Public Opinion Quarterly* 66 (2002): 582–93.
Martin, Joyce A.; Brady E. Hamilton; Paul D. Sutton; Stephanie J. Ventura; Fay Menacker; and Martha L. Munson. "Births: Final Data for 2003." *National Vital Statistics Reports* 54.2 (8 Sept. 2005): 1–116.
Martínez, Demetria. *Confessions of a Berlitz-tape Chicana*. Norman: University of Oklahoma Press, 2005.
———. *Mother Tongue*. New York: Ballantine, 1994.
Martínez, Elizabeth Coonrod. "Nuevas voces salvadoreñas: Sandra Benítez y Demetria Martínez." In Priscilla Gac-Artigas, ed., *Reflexiones: Ensayos sobre escritoras hispanoamericanas contemporáneas*. Fair Haven, N.J.: Ediciones Nuevo Espacio, 2002. 109–19.
Masud-Piloto, Félix. *From Welcomed Exiles to Illegal Immigrants: Cuban Migration to the U.S., 1959–1995*. Lanham, Md.: Rowman and Littlefield, 1996.
McCracken, Ellen. *New Latina Narrative: The Feminine Space of Postmodern Ethnicity*. Tucson: University of Arizona Press, 1999.
McCullough, Kate. "'Marked by Genetics and Exile': Narrativizing Transcultural Sexualities in *Memory Mambo*." *GLQ: A Journal of Lesbian and Gay Studies* 6.4 (1 Sept. 2000): 577–607.
McKenna, Teresa. *Migrant Song: Politics and Process in Contemporary Chicano Literature*. Austin: University of Texas Press, 1997.
Menéndez, Ana. *In Cuba I Was a German Shepherd*. New York: Grove, 2001.
Michaels, Walter Benn. "Autobiography of an Ex-White Man: Why Race Is Not a Social Construction." *Transition*, no. 73 (1997): 122–43.
Miller, Kate, and Sean Patrick Walsh. "So Far, So Good: Ana Castillo, Novelist, Essayist, Poet, Painter." *io* 1.2 (1994): 24–27.
Milligan, Bryce; Mary Guerrero Milligan; and Angela de Hoyos, eds. *¡Floricanto Sí! A Collection of Latina Poetry*. New York: Penguin, 1998.
Mitchell, David. "Immigration and the Impossible Homeland in Julia Alvarez's *How the García Girls Lost Their Accents*." *Antípodas* 10 (1998): 25–40.
———. "National Families and Familial Nations: Communista Americans in Cristina Garcia's *Dreaming in Cuban*." *Tulsa Studies in Women's Literature* 15.1 (Spring 1996): 51–60.
Mohr, Eugene V. *The Nuyorican Experience: Literature of the Puerto Rican Minority*. Westport, Conn.: Greenwood, 1982.

Moore, Robin. *Nationalizing Blackness: AfroCubanismo and Artistic Revolution in Havana, 1920–1940*. Pittsburgh: University of Pittsburgh Press, 1997.
Moraga, Cherríe. *Loving in the War Years: Lo que nunca pasó por sus labios*. Boston: South End Press, 1983.
Morales, Ed. *Living in Spanglish: The Search for Latino Identity in America*. New York: St. Martin's, 2002.
Morejón, Nancy. "Race and Nation." In Pedro Pérez Sarduy and Jean Stubbs, eds., *AfroCuba: An Anthology of Cuban Writing on Race, Politics and Culture*. Melbourne, Australia: Ocean Press, 1993. 227–37.
Morrison, Toni. *Beloved*. 1987. New York: Plume/Penguin, 1988.
Mosher, W. D., et al. "Religion and Fertility in the United States: The Importance of Marriage Patterns and Hispanic Origin." *Demography* 23 (1986): 367–79.
Mujčinović, Fatima. *Postmodern Cross-Culturalism and Politicization in U.S. Latina Literature: From Ana Castillo to Julia Alvarez*. New York: Peter Lang, 2004.
Muñoz, Elías Miguel. *The Greatest Performance*. Houston: Arte Público Press, 1991.
Murrieta, Fabio, and Laura P. Alonso Gallo, eds. *Guayaba Sweet: La literatura cubana en Estados Unidos*. Cádiz, Spain: Ed. Aduana Vieja, 2003.
National Campaign to Prevent Teen Pregnancy. "Fact Sheet: Teen Sexual Activity, Pregnancy and Childbearing among Black Teens." Oct. 2005. <www.teenpregnancy.org/resources/reading/pdf/AfricanAmerican FactSheet.pdf>. Accessed 18 Jan. 2006. 1–5.
———. "Fact Sheet: Teen Sexual Activity, Pregnancy and Childbearing among Latinos in the United States." Nov. 2005. <www.teenpregnancy.org/resources/reading /pdf/latinofs.pdf>. Accessed 18 Jan. 2006. 1–5.
National Council of La Raza. "How Did Latinos *Really Vote* in 2004?" Memorandum posted on <www.nclr.org>, 16 Nov. 2004. 1–8. <www.immigrationforum.org/DesktopDefault.aspx?tabid=137>. Accessed 12 Jan. 2006.
National Immigration Forum. "Civic Participation: Undecided Latinos Swing Democratic in Final Weeks of Campaign." 17 Nov. 2000. <www.immigrationforum.org/PrintFriendly.aspx?tabid=168>. Accessed 12 Jan. 2006.
Neill, Anna. "Global Intimacies in the Cultural Studies Classroom." *Journal of Contemporary Thought* 8 (1998): 5–21.
Newkirk, Glen A. "Anaya's Archetypal Women in *Bless Me, Ultima*." *South Dakota Review* 31.1 (1993): 142–50.
Nicholas, J. D., and R. J. Prohias. *Rent Differentials among Racial and Ethnic Groups in Miami: A Report to the Florida Atlantic University*. Miami: Florida International University Joint Center for Environmental and Urban Problems, 1973.
Obejas, Achy. *Days of Awe*. New York: Ballantine Books, 2001.
———. *Memory Mambo*. Pittsburgh: Cleis Press, 1996.
———. *We Came All the Way from Cuba So You Could Dress Like This?* San Francisco: Cleis Press, 1994.
Oboler, Suzanne. *Ethnic Labels, Latino Lives: Identity and the Politics of (Re)Presentation in the United States*. Minneapolis: University of Minnesota Press, 1995.
Oclander, Jorge. "Latinos Split over Keeping Their House District." *Chicago Sun-Times*, 13 Dec. 1995.

Olmos, Margarite Fernández, and Lizabeth Paravisini-Gebert, eds. *Sacred Possessions: Vodou, Santería, Obeah, and the Caribbean*. New Brunswick, N.J.: Rutgers University Press, 1997.
Olson, James S., and Judith E. Olson. *Cuban Americans: From Trauma to Triumph*. New York: Twayne, 1995.
Ortega, Julio. *Crítica de la identidad: La pregunta por el Perú en su literatura*. Mexico City: Fondo de Cultura Económica, 1999.
Ortiz, Fernando. *Los bailes y el teatro de los negros en el folklore de Cuba*. Havana: Publicaciones del Ministerio de Educación, 1951.
———. *Cuban Counterpoint: Tobacco and Sugar*. 1940. Trans. Harriet de Onís. Durham, N.C.: Duke University Press, 1995.
———. *Ensayos etnosociológicos*. Havana: Editorial de Ciencias Sociales, 1991.
Ortiz Cofer, Judith. *The Latin Deli*. New York: W. W. Norton, 1993.
Padilla, Felix M. *Latino Ethnic Consciousness: The Case of Mexican Americans and Puerto Ricans in Chicago*. South Bend, Ind.: Notre Dame Press, 1985.
Padilla, Genaro M. "Myth and Comparative Cultural Nationalism: The Ideological Uses of Aztlán." In Rudolfo A. Anaya and Francisco A. Lomelí, eds., *Aztlán: Essays on the Chicano Homeland*. Albuquerque: University of New Mexico Press, 1989. 111–31.
Parr, Carmen Salazar. "Current Trends in Chicano Literary Criticism." In Francisco Jiménez, ed., *The Identification and Analysis of Chicano Literature*. New York: Bilingual Press, 1979. 134–42.
Payant, Katherine B. "From Alienation to Reconciliation in the Novels of Cristina García." *MELUS* 26.3 (Fall 2001): 163–83.
Pedraza-Bailey, Sylvia. *Political and Economic Migrants in America: Cubans and Mexicans*. Austin: University of Texas Press, 1985.
Pérez, Gail. "Ana Castillo as *Santera*: Reconstructing Popular Religious Praxis." In María Pilar Aquino, Daisy L. Machado, and Jeanette Rodríguez, eds., *A Reader in Latina Feminist Theology: Religion and Justice*. Austin: University of Texas Press, 2002. 53–79.
Pérez, Hebert. "Martí, Race, & Cuban Identity." *Monthly Review* 55.6 (Nov. 2003): 19–32.
Pérez, Lisandro. "Unique but Not Marginal: Cubans in Exile." In Damián J. Fernández, ed., *Cuban Studies Since the Revolution*. Gainesville: University Press of Florida, 1992. 258–68.
Pérez, Louis A., Jr. "Cuba, c.1930–1959." In Leslie Bethell, ed., *Cuba: A Short History*. Cambridge: Cambridge University Press, 1993. 57–93.
———. "History, Historiography, and Cuban Studies: Thirty Years Later." In Damián J. Fernández, ed., *Cuban Studies Since the Revolution*. Gainesville: University Press of Florida, 1992. 53–78.
———. *On Becoming Cuban: Identity, Nationality, and Culture*. Chapel Hill: University of North Carolina Press, 1999.
Pérez Firmat, Gustavo. *Cincuenta lecciones de exilio y desexilio*. Miami: Ediciones Universal, 2000.
———. *Life on the Hyphen: The Cuban-American Way*. Austin: University of Texas Press, 1994.

———. *Tongue Ties: Logo-Eroticism in Anglo-Hispanic Literature*. New York: Palgrave Macmillan, 2003.

Pérez Sarduy, Pedro, and Jean Stubbs, eds. *AfroCuba: An Anthology of Cuban Writing on Race, Politics and Culture*. Melbourne, Australia: Ocean Press, 1993.

Perna, Santiago Rey. "Cubanos y americanos negros." *Diario Las Américas*, 24 Apr. 1984.

Pew Hispanic Center/Kaiser Family Foundation. "2002 National Survey of Latinos." Chartpack. Dec. 2002. <http://pewhispanic.org/files/reports/15.4.pdf>. Accessed 24 Jan. 2006.

———. "The 2004 National Survey of Latinos: Politics and Civic Participation." Summary and chartpack. 22 July 2004. <http://www.immigrationforum.org/DesktopDefault.aspx?tabid=137>. Accessed 13 Jan. 2006.

———. "2006 National Survey of Latinos: The Immigration Debate." See Suro and Escobar.

———. "Latinos and the 2006 Mid-term Elections." Fact Sheet. 17 Nov. 2006. <http://pewhispanic.org/files/factsheets/26.pdf>. Accessed 7 Jan. 2007.

Piedra, José. "Literary Whiteness and the Afro-Hispanic Difference." In Dominick LaCapra, ed., *The Bounds of Race: Perspectives on Hegemony and Resistance*. Ithaca, N.Y.: Cornell University Press, 1991. 278–310.

Platt, Kamala. "Ecocritical Chicana Literature: Ana Castillo's 'Virtual Realism.'" In Greta Gaard and Patrick D. Murphy, eds., *Ecofeminist Literary Criticism: Theory, Interpretation, Pedagogy*. Urbana: University of Illinois Press, 1998. 139–57.

Poey, Delia. *Latino American Literature in the Classroom: The Politics of Transformation*. Gainesville: University Press of Florida, 2002.

Poey, Delia, and Virgil Suárez, eds. *Iguana Dreams: New Latino Fiction*. New York: HarperCollins, 1992.

Polk, James. "Battling with Magic." Review of *So Far from God* by Ana Castillo. *Washington Post*, 31 May 1993.

Porsche, Michael. "*So Far from God*: Ana Castillo's Telenovelistic Xicanista Reassessment of the Paulinian Triad." In Francisco A. Lomelí and Karin Ikas, eds., *U.S. Latino Literatures and Cultures: Transnational Perspectives*. Heidelberg: Carl Winter Universitatsverlag, 2000. 181–90.

Portes, Alejandro, and Alex Stepick. *City on the Edge: Miami and the Immigrants*. Berkeley and Los Angeles: University of California Press, 1993.

Pulido, Laura. "Sustainable Development at Ganados del Valle." In Robert D. Bullard, ed., *Confronting Environmental Racism: Voices from the Grassroots*. Boston: South End Press, 1993. 123–40.

Quintana, Alvina E., ed. *Reading U.S. Latina Writers: Remapping American Literature*. New York: Palgrave Macmillan, 2003.

Rebolledo, Tey Diana. *Panchita Villa and Other Guerrilleras: Essays on Chicana/Latina Literature and Criticism*. Austin: University of Texas Press, 2005.

Reca, Inés, et al. *Análisis de las investigaciones sobre la familia cubana 1970–1987*. Havana: Center for Psychological and Sociological Research, Cuban Academy of Sciences, 1990.

Renan, Ernest. "What Is a Nation?" Trans. Martin Thom. In Homi K. Bhabha, ed., *Nation and Narration*. New York: Routledge, 1990. 8–22.
Rendón, Armando B. *Chicano Manifesto*. New York: Macmillan, 1971.
Requena, Gisele M. "The Sounds of Silence: Remembering and Creating in Margarita Engle's *Singing to Cuba*." *MELUS* 23.1 (Spring 1998): 147–57.
Rich, Adrienne. "Compulsory Heterosexuality and Lesbian Existence." *Signs: Journal of Women in Culture and Society* 5.4 (1980): 631–60.
Ricourt, Milagros, and Ruby Danta. *Hispanas de Queens: Latino Panethnicity in a New York City Neighborhood*. Ithaca, N.Y.: Cornell University Press, 2003.
Risech, Flavio. "Political and Cultural Cross-dressing: Negotiating a Second-generation Cuban-American Identity." *Michigan Quarterly Review* 33.3 (Summer 1994): 526–40.
Rivero, Eliana. "Hispanic Literature in the United States: Self-Image and Conflict." *Revista Chicano-Riqueña* 13.3–4 (Fall–Winter 1985): 173–91.
Rodríguez, Clara E. *Changing Race: Latinos, the Census, and the History of Ethnicity in the United States*. New York: New York University Press, 2000.
———. "Puerto Ricans: Between Black and White." In Clara E. Rodríguez, Virginia Sanchez Korrol, and José Oscar Alers, eds., *The Puerto Rican Struggle: Essays on Survival in the U.S.* Maplewood, N.J.: Waterfront Press, 1980. 20–30.
———. *Puerto Ricans Born in the USA*. Boston: Unwin Hyman, 1989.
Rodriguez, David. *Latino National Political Coalitions: Struggles and Challenges*. New York: Routledge, 2002.
Rodriguez, Ralph E. "Chicana/o Fiction from Resistance to Contestation: The Role of Creation in Ana Castillo's *So Far from God*." *MELUS* 25.2 (2000): 63–82.
Rodriguez, Richard. *Hunger of Memory: The Education of Richard Rodriguez*. Boston: D. R. Godine, 1982.
Rodríguez de Laguna, Asela. "Piri Thomas' *Down These Mean Streets*: Writing as a Nuyorican/Puerto Rican Strategy for Survival." In Harold Augenbraum and Margarite Fernández Olmos, eds., *U.S. Latino Literature: A Critical Guide for Students and Teachers*. Westport, Conn.: Greenwood, 2000. 21–29.
Rodriguez-Morazzani, Roberto P. "Beyond the Rainbow: Mapping the Discourse on Puerto Ricans and 'Race.'" In Antonia Darder and Rodolfo D. Torres, eds., *The Latino Studies Reader: Culture, Economy & Society*. Malden, Mass.: Blackwell, 1998. 143–62.
Rogers, Jane. "The Function of the La Llorona Motif in Anaya's *Bless Me, Ultima*." In Harold Bloom, ed., *Hispanic American Writers*. Philadelphia: Chelsea House, 1998. 3–8.
Román, David, and Alberto Sandoval. "Caught in the Web: Latinidad, AIDS, and Allegory in *Kiss of the Spider Woman*, the Musical." *American Literature* 67.3: 553–85.
Roof, Judith, and Robyn Wiegman, eds. *Who Can Speak? Authority and Critical Identity*. Urbana: University of Illinois Press, 1995.
Rumbaut, Rubén G. "The Making of a People." In Marta Tienda and Faith Mitchell, eds., *Hispanics and the Future of America*. Washington, D.C.: National Academies Press, 2006. 16–65.

———. "Severed or Sustained Attachments? Language, Identity, and Imagined Communities in the Post-Immigrant Generation." In Peggy Levitt and Mary C. Waters, eds., *The Changing Face of Home: The Transnational Lives of the Second Generation*. New York: Russell Sage Foundation, 2002. 43–95.

Rushdie, Salman. "Imaginary Homelands." In *Imaginary Homelands: Essays and Criticism 1981–1991*. New York: Viking Penguin, 1991. 9–21.

Saeta, Elsa. "A *MELUS* Interview: Ana Castillo." *MELUS* 22.3 (1997): 133–49.

Safa, Helen I. "Commentary on Race and Revolution in Cuba." *Souls: A Critical Journal of Black Politics, Culture, and Society*. Special issue: "Race and Revolution in Cuba" 1.2 (Spring 1999): 86–91.

Sagás, Ernesto. *Race and Politics in the Dominican Republic*. Gainesville: University Press of Florida, 2000.

Said, Edward. *Orientalism: Western Conceptions of the Orient*. 1978. London: Penguin, 1991.

Saldívar, Ramón. *Chicano Narrative: The Dialectics of Difference*. Madison: University of Wisconsin Press, 1990.

Sánchez, George J. "'Y tú, ¿qué?' Latino History in the New Millennium." In Marcelo M. Suárez-Orozco and Mariela M. Páez, eds., *Latinos: Remaking America*. Berkeley and Los Angeles: University of California Press, 2002. 41–58.

Sánchez, Marta E. *"Shakin' Up" Race and Gender: Intercultural Connections in Puerto Rican, African American, and Chicano Narratives and Culture (1965–1995)*. Austin: University of Texas Press, 2005.

Sánchez, Rosaura, and Beatrice Pita. "Introduction." In María Amparo Ruiz de Burton, *Who Would Have Thought It?* Eds. Rosaura Sánchez and Beatrice Pita. Houston: Arte Público Press, 1995. vii–lxv.

Sandlin, Lisa. "La Loca Lives: A Novel in Which a 3-Year-Old Girl Dies and Then Has a Sudden Change of Heart." Review of *So Far from God* by Ana Castillo. *New York Times Book Review*, 3 Oct. 1993: 22–23.

Sandoval, Chela. *Methodology of the Oppressed*. Minneapolis: University of Minnesota Press, 2000.

Sarduy, Pedro Pérez, and Jean Stubbs. "Introduction: The Rite of Social Communion." In Pedro Pérez Sarduy and Jean Stubbs, eds., *AfroCuba: An Anthology of Cuban Writing on Race, Politics and Culture*. Melbourne, Australia: Ocean Press, 1993.

Schermerhorn, Richard A. *Comparative Ethnic Relations: A Framework for Theory and Research*. Chicago: University of Chicago Press, 1978.

Schmidt, Ronald J. "Language Education Policy and the Latino Quest for Empowerment: Exploring the Linkages." In Roberto E. Villarreal and Norma G. Hernández, eds., *Latinos and Political Coalitions: Political Empowerment for the 1990s*. New York: Greenwood Press, 1991. 47–60.

Scott, Janny. "In Simple Pronouns, Clues to Shifting Latino Identity." *New York Times*, 5 Dec. 2002: B1.

Shaw, Donald L. "Concerning the Interpretation of *Cien años de soledad*." *Ibero-Amerikanisches Archiv* 3 (1977): 318–29.

Shemak, April. "Re-membering Hispaniola: Edwidge Danticat's *The Farming of Bones*." *Modern Fiction Studies* 48.1 (Spring 2002): 83–112.

Shorris, Earl. *Latinos: A Biography of the People*. New York: W. W. Norton, 1992.
Sierra, Christine Marie. "Latino Organizational Strategies on Immigration Reform: Success and Limits in Public Policymaking." In Roberto E. Villarreal and Norma G. Hernandez, eds., *Latinos and Political Coalitions: Political Empowerment for the 1990s*. New York: Greenwood Press, 1991. 61–80.
Simon, Bruce. "Hybridity in the Americas: Reading Condé, Mukherjee, and Hawthorne." In Amritjit Singh and Peter Schmidt, eds., *Postcolonial Theory and the United States: Race, Ethnicity, and Literature*. Jackson: University Press of Mississippi, 2000. 412–43.
Socolovsky, Maya. "Deconstructing a Secret History: Trace, Translation, and Crypto-Judaism in Achy Obejas's *Days of Awe*." *Contemporary Literature* 44.2 (Summer 2003): 225–249.
———. "Unnatural Violences: Counter-Memory and Preservations in Cristina García's *Dreaming in Cuban* and *The Agüero Sisters*." *LIT: Literature Interpretation Theory* 11.2 (Aug. 2000): 143–67.
Sollors, Werner. *Beyond Ethnicity: Consent and Descent in American Culture*. New York: Oxford University Press, 1986.
———. "Ethnicity." In Frank Lentricchia and Thomas McLaughlin, eds., *Critical Terms for Literary Study*. Chicago: University of Chicago Press, 1995. 288–305.
———, ed. *The Invention of Ethnicity*. New York: Oxford University Press, 1989.
Sommer, Doris. *Foundational Fictions: The National Romances of Latin America*. Berkeley and Los Angeles: University of California Press, 1991.
Spitta, Silvia. "Transculturation, the Caribbean, and the Cuban-American Imaginary." In Frances R. Aparicio and Susana Chávez-Silverman, eds., *Tropicalizations: Transcultural Representations of Latinidad*. Hanover, N.H.: University Press of New England, 1997. 160–80.
Spivak, Gayatri. "Can the Subaltern Speak?" In Cary Nelson and Lawrence Grossberg, eds., *Marxism and the Interpretation of Culture*. Urbana: University of Illinois Press, 1988. 271–313.
Stavans, Ilan. *The Hispanic Condition: Reflections on Culture and Identity in America*. New York: HarperCollins, 1995.
———. "The Quest for a Latino Literary Tradition." *Chronicle of Higher Education*, 1 Dec. 2000.
Stefanko, Jacqueline. "New Ways of Telling: Latinas' Narratives of Exile and Return." *Frontiers: A Journal of Women Studies* 17.2 (1996): 50–69.
Stephen, Lynn. "Women's Rights Are Human Rights: The Merging of Feminine and Feminist Interests among El Salvador's Mothers of the Disappeared (CO-MADRES)." *American Ethnologist* 22.4 (1995): 807–27.
Stepick, Alex; Guillermo Grenier; Max Castro; and Marvin Dunn. *This Land Is Our Land: Immigrants and Power in Miami*. Berkeley and Los Angeles: University of California Press, 2003.
Stepick, Alex, and Carol Dutton Stepick. "Power and Identity: Miami Cubans." In Marcelo M. Suárez-Orozco and Mariela M. Páez, eds., *Latinos: Remaking America*. Berkeley and Los Angeles: University of California Press, 2002. 75–92.

Stevenson, James M. "Cuban Americans: New Urban Class." Unpublished Ph.D. dissertation, Wayne State University, 1973.
Stokes, Mason. *The Color of Sex: Whiteness, Heterosexuality, and the Fictions of White Supremacy*. Durham, N.C.: Duke University Press, 2001.
Suárez, Lucía M. *The Tears of Hispaniola: Haitian and Dominican Diaspora Memory*. Gainesville: University Press of Florida, 2006.
Suárez-Orozco, Marcelo M., and Mariela M. Páez, eds. *Latinos: Remaking America*. Berkeley and Los Angeles: University of California Press, 2002.
Subramanian, Sribala. "The Story in Our Genes." *Time*, 16 Jan. 1995: 54.
Sugg, Katherine. "Literatures of the Americas, *Latinidad*, and the Re-formation of Multi-Ethnic Literatures." *MELUS* 29. 3-4 (Fall-Winter 2004): 227-42.
"The Supreme Court on Santería." <http://userwww.sfsu.edu/~biella/santeria/dec1.html>. Accessed May 2005.
Suro, Roberto, and Gabriel Escobar. "2006 National Survey of Latinos: The Immigration Debate." Washington, DC: Pew Hispanic Center, July 2006. <http://www.ime.gob.mx/investigaciones/pew/2006/debate_migratorio.pdf>. Accessed 21 Jan 2007.
Tafoya, Sonya. "Shades of Belonging." Pew Hispanic Center. 6 Dec. 2004. <http://pewhispanic.org/files/reports/35.pdf>. Accessed 19 Jan. 2006.
Taylor, Paul Beekman. "The Chicano Translation of Troy: Epic *Topoi* in the Novels of Rudolfo A. Anaya." *MELUS* 19.3 (Fall 1994): 19–35.
Thomas, Piri. *Down These Mean Streets*. 1967. New York: Vintage/Random House, 1991.
Tobar, Héctor. *The Tattooed Soldier*. New York: Penguin, 1998.
Todorov, Tzvetan. "'Race,' Writing, and Culture." In Henry Louis Gates Jr., ed., *"Race," Writing, and Difference*. Chicago: University of Chicago Press, 1986. 370–80.
Tonn, Horst. "*Bless Me, Ultima*: Fictional Response to Times of Transition." In César A. González-T., ed., *Rudolfo A. Anaya: Focus on Criticism*. La Jolla, Calif.: Lalo Press, 1990. 1–12.
Toribio, A. J. "Language Variation and the Linguistic Enactment of Identity among Dominicans." *Linguistics* 38.6: 1133–1159.
Torres, Lourdes. "The Construction of the Self in U.S. Latina Autobiographies." In Chandra Talpade Mohanty, Ann Russo, and Lourdes Torres, eds., *Third World Women and the Politics of Feminism*. Bloomington: Indiana University Press, 1991. 271–87.
Torres, María de los Angeles. "Encuentros y Encontronazos: Homeland in the Politics and Identity of the Cuban Diaspora." *Diaspora* 4.2 (1995): 211–38.
———. *In the Land of Mirrors: Cuban Exile Politics in the United States*. Ann Arbor: University of Michigan Press, 1999.
Torres-Saillant, Silvio. "Epilogue: Problematic Paradigms: Racial Diversity and Corporate Identity in the Latino Community." In Marcelo M. Suárez-Orozco and Mariela M. Páez, eds., *Latinos: Remaking America*. Berkeley and Los Angeles: University of California Press, 2002. 435–55.
Toyosato, Mayumi. "Grounding Self and Action: Land, Community, and Survival in *I, Rigoberta Menchú, No Telephone to Heaven*, and *So Far from God*." *Hispanic Journal* 19.1 (Spring 1997): 295–311.

Trinh T. Minh-ha. "Not You/Like You: Post-colonial Women and the Interlocking Questions of Identity and Difference." In Gloria Anzaldúa, ed., *Making Face, Making Soul/Haciendo Caras: Creative and Critical Perspectives by Women of Color.* San Francisco: Aunt Lute, 1990. 371–75.

Trueba, Enrique (Henry) T. *Latinos Unidos: From Cultural Diversity to the Politics of Solidarity.* New York: Rowman and Littlefield, 1999.

Trujillo, Carla, ed. *Chicana Lesbians: The Girls Our Mothers Warned Us About.* Berkeley, Calif.: Third Woman Press, 1991.

TuSmith, Bonnie. *All My Relatives: Community in Contemporary Ethnic American Literatures.* Ann Arbor: University of Michigan Press, 1993.

U.S. Census Bureau. "Hispanic Heritage Month 2002: Sept. 15–Oct. 15." <http://www.census.gov/Press-Release/www/2002/ cb02ff15.html>. 3 Sept. 2002. Accessed 20 Jan. 2006.

U.S. Department of Health and Human Services. *Mental Health: Culture, Race, and Ethnicity—A Supplement to Mental Health: A Report of the Surgeon General.* Rockville, Md.: U.S. Department of Health and Human Services, 2001. <http://www.mentalhealth.samhsa.gov/media/ken/pdf/SMA-01–3613/sma-01–3613.pdf>. Accessed 25 Jan. 2006.

———. "2000 Natality Data Set" [CD-ROM]. CD-ROM Series 21.14 (2002).

Valdes-Rodriguez, Alisa. *The Dirty Girls Social Club.* New York: St. Martin's, 2003.

Vallejos, Thomas. "Ritual Process and the Family in the Chicano Novel." *MELUS* 10.4 (Winter 1983): 5–16.

Vargas Llosa, Mario. *The Feast of the Goat.* 2000. Trans. Edith Grossman. New York: Picador USA, 2002.

Vásquez, Mary S. "Contrapuntal Song: Celebration and Rage in Margarita Engle's *Singing to Cuba*." *Confluencia* 12.2 (Spring 1997): 128–41.

———. "Cuba as Text and Context in Cristina García's *Dreaming in Cuban*." *Bilingual Review/La Revista Bilingüe* 20.1 (Winter 1995): 22–27.

Velasco, Juan. "Automitografías: The Border Paradigm and Chicana/o Autobiography." *Biography* 27.2 (Spring 2004): 313–38.

Viera, Joseph M. "Exile among Exiles." *Poets & Writers Magazine.* 26.5 (Sept.–Oct. 1998): 40–45.

———. "Matriarchy and Mayhem: Awakenings in Cristina Garcia's *Dreaming in Cuban*." *Americas Review* 24.3–4 (Fall 1996): 231–42.

Vigil, James Diego. *From Indians to Chicanos: A Sociocultural History.* St. Louis: C. V. Mosby, 1980.

Wald, Gayle. *Crossing the Line: Racial Passing in Twentieth-century U.S. Literature and Culture.* Durham, N.C.: Duke University Press, 2000.

Walter, Roland. "The Cultural Politics of Dislocation and Relocation in the Novels of Ana Castillo." *MELUS* 23.1 (1998): 81–97.

Wang, Jinwei. "Zenyang cai neng shixing minsheng zhuyi" [How can the principle of the people's livelihood be realized]. *Wang Jingwei ji* [Collected writings of Wang Jingwei], *juan* 3. Shanghai: Guangming shuju, 1929. 29–49.

Weber, Max. *Economy and Society.* Eds. Guenther Roth and Claus Wittich. Berkeley and Los Angeles: University of California Press, 1968.

Weiss, Frederick A. "Self-Alienation: Dynamics and Therapy." In Eric and Mary Josephson, eds., *Man Alone: Alienation in Modern Society*. New York: Dell, 1962. 463–79.

Winn, Peter. *Americas: The Changing Face of Latin America and the Caribbean*. New York: Pantheon Books, 1992.

Wucker, Michele. *Why the Cocks Fight: Dominicans, Haitians, and the Struggle for Hispaniola*. New York: Hill and Wang, 1999.

Wyatt, Jean. *Risking Difference: Identification, Race, and Community in Contemporary Fiction and Feminism*. Albany: State University of New York Press, 2004.

———. "Toward Cross-race Dialogue: A Lacanian Approach to Identification, Misrecognition and Difference in Feminist Multicultural Community." *Signs* 29.3 (Spring 2004): 879–903.

Yarbro-Bejarano, Yvonne. "Gloria Anzaldúa's *Borderlands/La frontera*: Cultural Studies, 'Difference,' and the Non-Unitary Subject." *Cultural Critique* 28 (Fall 1994): 5–28.

Young Lords Party and Michael Abramson. *Palante: Young Lords Party*. New York: McGraw-Hill, 1971.

Young, Robert. *Colonial Desire: Hybridity in Theory, Culture and Race*. New York: Routledge, 1995.

Yronwode, Catherine. "Hoodoo Rootwork: Definition of Terms." In "Hoodoo: African American Magic." <http://www.luckymojo.com/hoodoohistory.html#hoodoo>. Accessed 17 Mar. 2005.

Zeff, Jacqueline. "'What Doesn't Kill You, Makes You Fat': The Language of Food in Latina Literature." *Journal of American & Comparative Cultures* (Spring/Summer 2002): 94–99.

Zentella, Ana Celia. "Latin@ Languages and Identities." In Marcelo M. Suárez-Orozco and Mariela M. Páez, eds., *Latinos: Remaking America*. Berkeley and Los Angeles: University of California Press, 2002. 321–38.

Zimmerman, Marc. *U.S. Latino Literature: An Essay and Annotated Bibliography*. Chicago: March/Abrazo Press, 1992.

Zubiaurre, Maite. "Hacia una nueva geografía feminista: Nación, identidad y construcción imaginaria en *Dreaming in Cuban* (Cristina García) y en *Memory Mambo* (Achy Obejas)." *Chasqui: Revista de Literatura Latinoamericana* 28.1 (May 1999): 3–15.

# Index

Acuña, Rodolfo F., 164
African Americans, 65; and Chicanos, 228n3; and Cubans, 96, 240n32, 240n35; and Dominican-Americans, 84; and Latinos 32, 33, 161; as minority 22; and Puerto Ricans, 9, 52–54, 57, 59–63, 67, 223n16, 228n1, 230n12; teen birth rates for, 7
African heritage, 237n18; in the Americas 110; Cubans and, 97, 101–104, 106–109, 111, 117, 124–25, 127, 171, 238n23, 239n28; Dominicans and, 33, 82, 232n6, 234n11; Haitians and, 81–82; and Conrad's *Heart of Darkness*, 257n38; in Latin America, 14; and poetry of Langston Hughes, 141; Puerto Ricans and 52, 57, 63, 230n14; and religion, 142, 221, 238n23. *See also* race; African Americans; Afro-Cubans
African peoples: and diaspora 63; and Haiti/Dominican Republic, 81; and hybridity 10, and racial mixing 52, 105; and religion, 172
Afro-Cubans, 237n18, 256n25; characters, 103, 106, 109; and Cuban national identity, 108–109, 239n30, 240n34, 240n35; and Nicolás Guillén, 239n28; immigrants to the U.S., 97; and insurrection of 1912, 237n17; and intermarriage, 107;and race consciousness, 240n36; and religion, 120, 172–73, 236n13
Aguirre, Benigno E., 96, 99, 234n3, 235n7, 235n9, 236n11, 237n14
Alarcón, Norma, 237n20, 249n21
Albizu Campos, Pedro, 6
Aldama, Frederick Luis, 142, 143, 157, 247n3, 248n15
Alemán, Jesse, 223n21
Algarín, Miguel, 52
Allatson, Paul, 10, 95, 162, 180, 183, 185, 235n7, 257n34, 257n36
Allende, Isabel, 139, 247n3, 248n11; *The House of the Spirits*, 144–455; *Infinite Plan*, 9
Alonso Gallo, Laura P., 140
Althusser, Louis, 250n32, 256n24
Alurista, 49

Alvarez Borland, Isabel, 10, 99, 100, 237n17, 237n18, 256n27
Alvarez, Julia, 9, 73, 140–41, 163, 168, 207, 223n17, 232n3, 247n4, 252n4; *A Cafecito Story*, 91; *How the García Girls Lost Their Accents*, 74, 81, 83–86, 92, 233n10, 255n14; *In the Name of Salomé*, 90, 166–67, 232n3, 234n12; *In the Time of the Butterflies*, 33, 74–83, 85, 90, 166, 233n7, 255n14, 260n10; *Saving the World*, 232n1, 234n13; *¡Yo!*, 33, 85–92
Anaya, Rudolfo, 9, 190, 252n4; *Bless Me, Ultima*, 33, 39–50, 52–53, 69, 189, 190, 226n1, 226n3, 226n4, 226n5, 227n6, 227n8, 227n9, 227n10, 228n15, 228n17; *Heart of Aztlan*, 227n5, 228n12
Anders, Gigi (*Jubana!*), 242n49
Anderson, Benedict, 3, 210
Anderson, Gary Clayton, 48
Anglo-Americans, 11, 47, 48, 203, 223n18, 227n10, 228n15, 258n42
Año Nuevo de Kerr, Louise, 149
Antihaitianismo, 81–83
Anti-Semitism, Cuban, 117–18, 122, 123, 127, 129, 242n48, 243n53, 244n61
Anzaldúa, Gloria, 173, 257n36; *Borderlands/La Frontera*, 9, 39, 54, 184, 199, 227n9; *This Bridge Called My Back*, 185
Appiah, Anthony, 55, 60
Arenas, Reinaldo, 99
Arrington, Vanessa, 101
Arte Público, 255n21
Aztecs, 5, 44, 48, 171, 187. *See also* indigenous peoples
Aztlán, 5, 46, 170

Baker, Houston, 56
*Balseros*, Cuban, 97, 126, 243n60, 244n60
Barnet, Miguel, 106, 172, 238n23
Barreto, Matt A., 4
Barth, Frederik, 30
Batista, Fulgencio, 176
Bauzá, Mario, 235n4

Bauzá, Vanessa, 93, 101
Begley, Sharon, 55
Behar, Ruth, 116, 118, 237n18, 242n47, 242n48, 242n49, 245n65, 246n68
Bettinger-López, Caroline, 115–19, 242n47, 242n48, 242n51, 243n53
Bhabha, Homi, 94, 102, 104, 257n39
Bilingual education, 22, 216, 252n3, 255n16, 264n3, 264n4
Bilingualism, Latinos and, 15, 116, 224n26, 232n2, 263n25; in *Bless Me, Ultima,* 40, 227n6; and bilingual programs, 149
Bloom, Harold, 226n1
Boff, Clodovis, 151–54
Boff, Leonardo, 151–54
Bolívar, Simón, 23, 217
Boom, Latin American, 34, 140, 147, 248n15
Border: Central American refugees and, 201, 203, 206, 211; Haitian/Dominican, 82, 233n7; as metaphor, 199–201; and positioning of U.S. citizens, 76, 261n14; U.S./Mexican, 166, 214, 215, 232n2, 253n11, 262n20, 264n1
Border Patrol. *See* United States Citizenship and Immigration Services
Borinquén, 5, 60
Boundaries, group: Chicano, 49, 53; Dominicans and, 247n4; ethnic, 30–31, 33, 41, 226n41; "Latino" 2, 30, 68, 179, 218; Puerto Rican, 6, 57, 59, 62, 67; racial binary and, 64
Brogan, Kathleen, 49
Bruce-Novoa, Juan, 40
Buell, Lawrence, 157, 250n27
Bus, Heiner, 227n7
Bush, George W., 166, 252n9, 254n12
Butler, Judith, 192

Cabrera Infante, Guillermo, 99
*Café con Leche: Voices of Exile's Children* (documentary), 97
Calderón, Héctor, 226n3
Cantú, Roberto, 43, 45, 228n12, 228n13
Caribbean peoples: Afro-Caribbeans, 67; Cubans as "Jews of the Caribbean," 118–19; cultural commonalities, 182, 193; differences among, 11; and panethnic category "Latino," 187; Spanish of, 16; syncretism of, 14, 17, 102, 143; tensions between, 11
Casal, Lourdes, 101, 102
Castillo, Ana, 6, 9; *So Far from God,* 139–160; 247n2, 247n3, 248n11, 248n15, 248n16, 248n18, 249n21, 249n24, 250n25, 250n27, 250n30, 251n33, 251n34, 262n22, 263n26
Castillo, Debra A., 6, 29–30, 197–199, 211, 259n5, 260n11, 261n15
Castillo-Speed, Lillian, 208
Castro, Fidel, 256n24: as cause of Cuban diaspora, 98–99; Communist government of, 234n3; and naming of "Special Period," 240n36; and race, 107–109, 117; and repressive policies toward gays and lesbians, 180; role in Mariel boatlift, 236n10; treatment in fiction, 166–73, 176–80, 183, 185, 241n44, 255n20; and Rafael Trujillo, 255n14, 255n18; and U.S. as threat, 115, 129. *See also* Cuban Revolution of 1959
Castro, Max, 235, 238n25, 243n54
Catholicism: in *Bless Me, Ultima,* 39, 41–43, 46, 227n10; as common denominator for Latinos, 17, 147, 194; and covert practice of Judaism, 120–21, 242n50, 244n62; in Cuba 33, 95; in *Days of Awe,* 116, 119–21, 124, 125, 244n62; in Dominican Republic, 81; in El Salvador, 259n2; and Sanctuary movement, 194; and Santería, 106, 120, 124, 172, 221n5; syncretism of, with indigenous beliefs, 31, 41–43, 142–43, 221n5; and women, 151–52, 148, 248n12
Cavalli-Sforza, Luca, 55
Census. *See* Central Americans; Cuban Americans; Dominican Americans; Mexican Americans; Puerto Ricans; South Americans; Spanish heritage; United States Census
Central Americans: and census, 221n4; and immigration to U.S., 12, 196, 211, 214, 260n6; and panethnic category "Latino," 2, 5–6, 12, 17, 25–26, 203, 215–16; and political oppression, 196, 202, 260n6, 260n8; and revolutionary politics, 168; and Sanctuary movement, 202–4, 211, 262n18, 262n20, 263n31; and U.S. asylum policy, 12
Chanady, Amaryll, 14, 15, 18, 19, 20, 102, 128, 224n28, 228n14
Chicago Religious Task Force, 263n31
*Chicanismo,* 31, 40
Chicano movement, 40, 188, 191; and indigenous heritage, 5, 39, 41, 45, 46, 49, 228n1; and literary production, 48, 49, 168
Chicano/a literature, 9–10, 13; and Arte Público, 255n21; and "authenticity," 223n18; connection to Latin American Boom, 34;

and conservative texts, 255n16; and success of *Bless Me, Ultima*, 226n1, 227n8; and magical realism, 34, 141, 147; and Malinche, 103; and migrant farmworkers, 255n21; and panethnic category, 222n6, 223n19, 223n20, 252n4, 253n10, 260n10, 260n24; portrayal of "La Migra," 8; presumptions about, 43; and queer identities, 184; representative works of, 39, 226n1, 255n21; as resistant, 139, 161, 251n1, 251n2, 247n1, 251n1, 252n2; and third world women, 185. *See also individual authors*

Childs, Matt D., 237n19

Chinatown: in Havana, 93, 101, 103, 105

Chinese Cubans, 93, 100–17, 124, 125, 234n1, 239 n28

Chinitz, David, 247n7

Christian, Karen, 10, 31, 141, 152, 174, 192, 247n5

Christianity, 31, 43, 119, 121, 151, 152, 154, 172, 202, 211, 240n37. *See also* Catholicism

Cisneros, Sandra, 9, 173, 204; *The House on Mango Street*, 178, 226n1

Class: Cuban exiles and, 8, 19, 94, 95, 169, 173, 180, 182, 184, 196, 216, 234n3, 253n10, 257n33; differences, among Latinos, 6–8, 11, 13, 165, 181, 191–92, 194, 221n1; differences, in work of Julia Alvarez, 33, 75, 81, 84, 86, 87, 90, 92, 233n7; disparities in Cuba, 99, 172; and elite New Mexicans, 46; and ideology, 250n32; middle-class perspective in Latino literature, 163; middle-class U.S. citizens, 261n14; and Sanctuary movement, 204; transclass identities, 32–33; working class, 12, 21–22, 25, 86, 92, 162, 168, 184, 215, 241n42, 252n2

Cline, Howard F., 44, 227n11, 228n11

Clinton administration, 8

Coalitions, 135, 196; across class differences, 81; Mexican and Puerto Rican, 33, 213, 258n41; Mexican, in Chicago, 149; pan-Latino, 20, 68, 213–15, 222n6

Collective fictions, 3, 5, 31, 150, 191, 208, 210

Colonialism, 20, 101, 102, 104, 109, 257n39; and Catholicism, 41–43; Mexican colonization of New Mexico, 44, 48; Spanish, 19, 48, 63, 81, 119, 128, 143, 161, 162, 169–72, 194; U.S. colonizing efforts in Latin America, 51; and whiteness, 46

Comanche, 48, 49. *See also* indigenous peoples

Common descent, 3, 14, 87, 188, 206, 212, 223n23, 258n45

Contact zones. *See* urban centers

Cornejo Polar, Antonio, 19, 224n28

Cornell, Stephen, 3–4, 6, 14, 21, 82, 86–87, 129, 189–192, 205, 223n23, 224n26, 244n64, 246n71, 258n43, 258n44, 258n45

Cortázar, Julio, 247n3

Cortés, Hernán, 103, 170, 261n11

Coutin, Susan, 204

Craft, Linda J., 257n38

Cronon, William, 250n27

Croucher, Sheila L., 96, 97, 99, 105, 235n6, 236n9, 236n12, 237n13

Cruz, Celia, 235n4

Cruz, Penélope, 160

Cuban American literature, 9–10, 25, 74, 99–100, 226n42; and *ajiaco* as metaphor, 106; and Cuban exile narratives, 95; *¡Cubanísimo!*, 101; and panethnic "Latino" construct, 34, 167, 253n10; and position on Castro, 166–67; and Santería, 237n13. *See also individual authors*

Cuban American National Foundation, 167

Cuban Americans: and Castro, 97–99, 165, 167, 168, 171, 173, 176–77, 178, 181, 185, 193, 255n17, 255n19, 259n4; and census, 221n4, 235n7; and change in U.S. policy, 243n54; and conservative politics, 115, 163–67, 168, 177, 179, 183, 185, 253n9, 254n12, 254n13; vs. Cuban nationals, 130–31, 133, 134, 244n63; and immigration waves, 33, 93, 181–82, 196–97, 216, 243n60; and Mariel boatlift, 97, 99, 100, 236n12, 236n13; and nostalgia, 94–95, 98, 124, 134; and panethnic category, 6–12, 16, 19, 21, 25–26, 28–32, 34, 162–67, 169–70, 174–75, 177, 178, 180–85, 186–88, 190–91, 193–95, 205, 215–16, 218, 219, 222n6, 223n18, 223n20, 230n12, 246n72, 252n8, 253n10, 256n32, 258n41, 259n4, 264n3; and parallels to Jewish exile, 118–19, 125, 130–31, 134; and preferential treatment in U.S., 8, 12, 215, 257n33, 257n35; and race, 31, 33, 95–100, 102, 106, 115, 134, 165, 169–73, 180–82, 184, 188–89, 196, 234n1, 234n3, 234n4, 235n5, 235n7, 235n8, 235n9, 236n11, 236n12, 236n13, 237n14, 237n18, 256n31; and transformation of Miami, 118–19. *See also* Cuban American literature; cubanidad; *individual authors*

Cuban Revolution of 1959: 93, 114–15, 129, 134, 164, 237n19, 257n39; as cause of diaspora, 97–100; in Cuban American literature, 167–69, 172, 177–81, 183, 184, 226n42, 255n17, 256n28; and Cuban exiles, 95; and Cuban "nation," construct of, 126; and economic crisis in 1994, 243n60; in non-Cuban Latino literature, 166; and race, 107–9, 234n3, 235n4, 237n15, 239n30

*Cubanidad*, 31; and Chinese Cubans, 125; in "In Cuba I Was a German Shepherd," 191–95; in Cuban exile narratives, 33, 93, 96–97, 101, 134, 234n1; and Jewish Cubans, 116, 125–28, 245n65; in *Days of Awe*, 128–30, 132–34, 246n68; in *Monkey Hunting*, 106, 108; in opposition to Spain, 128; in opposition to U.S., 129; as racial mixture, 107–8, 238n21, 239n31; in writing of Margarita Engle, 171, 173

Cubans: and attitudes toward U.S., 128–29; and Chinese, 93, 100, 101, 125; and Jewishness, 93, 115–18, 123, 125, 126–28, 242n47, 242n48, 242n49, 243n53, 244n61, 244n62, 245n65, 246n68, 246n69; and race, 33, 95, 100, 101–104, 106–9, 116, 117, 125, 170, 237n15, 237n17, 237n18, 238n21, 238n23, 238n24, 238n25, 238n26, 239n28, 239n29, 239n30, 239n31, 240n32, 240n33, 240n34, 240n35, 240n36, 256n25; and Special Period, 132–33, 240n36. *See also* cubanidad; hybridity: Cuban; mestizaje: Cuban; National identity

Cultural differences: African American vs. Puerto Rican, 62; among Latinos, 5, 7, 17, 28, 78

Cultural nationalism, 5–6, 50, 53, 183

Culture, common, 2, 13–17, 27–28, 68–69, 143, 163, 207, 221n5

Cunningham, Hilary, 202–4, 212–14, 262n18, 262n20, 263n29, 263n31, 264n31

Dalleo, Raphael, 178, 256n30
Daly, Mary, 249n19
Danta, Ruby, 217
Danticat, Edwidge (*The Farming of Bones*), 85, 233n7, 233n11
Darder, Antonia, 54
Dasenbrock, Reed Way, 226n2
Davis, Rocío G., 180, 256

De Genova, Nicholas, 2, 5, 8, 12, 15, 22, 27, 51–53, 59, 68, 69, 165, 215, 223n16, 228n1
De Hoyos, Angela, 208
De la Fuente, Alejandro, 107, 240n36
De la Garza, Rodolfo, 264n3
Delgadillo, Theresa, 150–51, 153–55, 247n1, 249n22, 249n23
DelRosso, Jeana, 151, 249n19
Derrida, Jacques, 76, 244n62
Diaspora, 135, 238n23, 257n39; Chinese, 100; Cuban, 97–101, 118–19, 130, 244n63; Jewish, 100, 118–19, 245n65
Díaz, Junot, 9
Didion, Joan, 257n35
Dominican American literature, 9, 74. *See also individual authors*
Dominican Americans: and African Americans, 84; and census, 4; class differences among, 86; compared to Cubans, 193–95; vs. Dominican nationals, 33, 74–78, 90, 246n4; organizations of, 217; and panethnic category, 6, 9, 26, 31, 74, 88, 140, 162, 164, 166, 188, 191, 193, 252n4, 260n10; and representations of Castro, 166–67; and transnational ties, 17, 90–91. *See also* Alvarez, Julia; Dominican American literature
Dominicans: compared to Cubans, 167; and Haitians, 20, 81–85, 232n5, 232n6, 233n7, 233n11, 234n12; and Jewish immigration, 242n46; lower class, 81, 90. *See also* Trujillo, Rafael Leónidas
Du Bois, W.E.B., 60–61
Duany, Jorge, 238n24
Dutwin, David, 225n38

Eastman, Lloyd E., 113, 241n38
Ehrenreich, Barbara, 249n21
Eichner, Bill, 91
Eire, Carlos (*Waiting for Snow in Havana*), 25, 93, 234n1, 256n26
Elam, Diane, 75, 76, 77, 91
El Salvador, 9, 14, 196–98, 202–205, 208–210, 213–14, 216, 259n1, 259n2, 260n8, 261n11, 262n23
Engle, Margarita, 34, 177, 195, 256n17; *Singing to Cuba*, 167, 168, 169, 171, 172, 255n14, 255n20, 255n21, 256n21; *Skywriting*, 167, 168, 169, 170, 172, 173, 237n20, 255n15
Environment, 74, 99, 139, 155, 156, 157, 250n26, 250n27, 250n28, 261n12; concerns about,

144, 155; consciousness of, 155, 157; degradation of, 144, 157, 158, 159; environmentalism, 157, 250
Erdrich, Louise *(Tracks)*, 145
Escobar, Gabriel, 5, 15, 20, 166, 253n11
Ethnicity, construction of: based on contrast, 132; in *Bless Me, Ultima,* 40–41, 50, 53; and Chinese Cuban ethnicity, 101; as coherent whole, 252n3; and common descent, 14, 223n23, 258n45; and common history 10, 21; common interests and, 148; and consent, 209; cultural content and, 31, 41; definition of, 2–3; in *Dirty Girls Social Club,* 187, 189; by dominant culture, 191–92; in *Down These Mean Streets,* 53, 59; and kinship, 6, 75, 86–87, 129–30, 188, 205–6, 208, 211–12, 258n43, 262n20, 263n31, 244n64, 258n43; and Latino literature, 179; by media, 176, 205–6; as marginalized, 106, 168, 252n5; and *Memory Mambo,* 180, 185; narratives in construction of, 21, 26, 30; New Mexicans and, 41, 46–47; and strategic solidarity, 211; symbolic elements of, 3, 5, 21, 152, 184, 189; 224n26, 258n46; in writings of Margarita Engle, 172–73. *See also* family, as metaphor
Exiles: and colonialism, 257n39; Jewish, 118–19, 125, 127, 130–32, 134; José Martí, 125; and nostalgia, 95, 98–99; political, 11; and relationship to past, 94; South American, 12. *See also* Cuban Americans

Family, as metaphor, 6; in "In Cuba I Was a German Shepherd," 193; in *Dirty Girls Social Club,* 188, 190–91; and Haitians vs. Dominicans, 82–83; and media, 176; in *Mother Tongue,* 205–6; in Sanctuary movement, 263n31; and solidarity, 208–9, 211–12; and Spanish, 14, 207–8; in *¡Yo!,* 86. *See also* ethnicity, construction of: kinship
Faris, Wendy B., 142, 144, 145, 248n9, 248n16
Faulkner, William, 64
Fears, Darryl, 254n12
Fernández, Roberto *(Raining Backwards),* 98–99
Ferrer, Ada, 102, 117, 237n15
Fewsmith, Joseph, 113, 241n39, 241n43
Flores, Juan, 8, 12–13, 18, 21, 23–24, 34, 162–66, 182, 211, 221n3, 221n5, 222n13, 222n15, 224n30, 230n12, 252n6, 252n11
Foley, Jack, 263n26

Food: and cultural differences, 2, 16, 175–76, 187; as ethnic marker, 258n42; as shared culture, 23, 193, 195
Fox, Geoffrey, 9, 225n35, 252n5
Frase-Blunt, Martha, 247n5
Fraxedas, J. Joaquín, 255n19
Fuentes, Annette, 249n21

Gallo, Alonso, 237n16
Gallo, Murietta, 237n16
Gandhi, Leela, 101, 105–6, 115
García, Cristina, 9, 34, 86, 163, 167, 223n17; *Dreaming in Cuban,* 25, 74, 94, 114, 177–79, 182, 223n17, 237n17, 237n19, 244n63, 256n27, 256n30; *Monkey Hunting,* 33, 95, 100, 101, 103–15, 116, 118, 121, 124, 127, 128, 135, 238n23, 241n37, 241n42, 241n44, 242n45
García, John A., 14, 21, 24, 224n25, 224n28
García, María Cristina, 12, 95
García Márquez, Gabriel, 140, 160; *One Hundred Years of Solitude,* 139, 145, 247n5
Gates, Henry Louis, 54, 55
Gays and lesbians, 111, 174, 179, 180, 183, 184, 246n69, 257n36. *See also* queer politics
Gilroy, Paul, 55, 56, 57, 68, 229n4
Gimenez, Martha, 7, 8, 23, 213, 222n5, 222n6, 222n8, 222n12
Gingerich, Willard, 227n6
Gish, Robert Franklin, 227n6
Globalization, 19, 101, 105, 111, 162, 196
Goldman, Francisco: *The Long Night of White Chickens,* 247n5; *The Ordinary Seaman,* 26
Gómez-Peña, Guillermo, 7, 12
Gómez-Vega, Ibis, 255n14, 255n18, 256n27; *Send My Roots Rain,* 9
González, Elián, 165
Gonzalez, Juan, 17, 23, 196, 214, 222n5, 224n30, 224n31, 259n2, 259n3
González, Lisa, 230n10, 231n23
Gonzalez, Ray, 12, 35, 162
González Echevarría, Roberto, 74–77, 86, 232n1
Gracia, Jorge J. E., 209, 224n30, 224n34
Guatemala, 6, 14, 216

Hada, Ken, 227n8
Haight, Roger, 151, 152
Haiti, 20, 81, 84, 116, 126
Haitian-Dominican conflict, 81; language differences, 84

Haitian massacre of 1937, 82, 83
Haitianness, 84, 85
Hames-García, Michael, 49, 50
Hannaford, Ivan, 58, 63, 229n8
Hartmann, Douglas, 3, 6, 14, 82–83, 86, 87, 129, 189, 191, 192, 205, 223n23, 224n26, 244n64, 246n71, 258n43, 258n44, 258n45
Hayek, Salma, 160
Heide, Markus, 141, 250n30
Hellein, Tanya, 159
Henriot, Christian, 113, 241n38
Herms, Dieter, 230n10
Hernández-Truyol, Berta Esperanza, 16, 188
Herrera, Andrea O'Reilly, 256n27
Hijuelos, Oscar, 9, 163, 226n42, 235n4; *The Mambo Kings Play Songs of Love*, 25
Hinojosa, Rolando, 162
Hirsch, Susan F., 261n16, 262n19
Hispanic." *See* "Latino" and "Hispanic"
Hobsbawm, Eric, 258n46
Hollyday, Joyce, 204
Holton, Frederick S., 227n8
Hoobler, Dorothy, 234n4
Hoobler, Thomas, 234n4
Horsman, Reginald, 52
Hughes, Langston, 141, 247n7
Hybridity, 95, 238n22; Chicano, 39, 43; in China, 111–12; Cuban, 33, 97, 101–09, 112, 115, 119–21, 124–25, 237n18, 238n23, 243n59; in *Down these Mean Streets*, 54; and "nation," 135; in Latin America, 14; and Latino identity, 10–11, 13, 218, 224n24; Puerto Rican, 52; and religion, 41–42, 124, 143, 150–53, 173, 243n59, 249n18; as resistant, 160, 163, 249n18; and slave trade, 115, 125; in Spain, 119–21; in urban centers, 114, 127–28; and Vietnam War, 110–11. *See also* mestizaje; syncretism

Imagined communities, 3, 53, 95, 210
Immigrants. *See specific national origins*
Immigration, 19, 20, 107, 166, 197, 215, 216, 217, 218, 221, 224, 233, 242, 243, 253, 254; marches in 2006, 5; policy debates, 5; U.S. immigration policy, 166, 215, 234n3, 243n54, 253n11, 262n20
*Independentistas*, Puerto Rican, 180, 181, 183, 185
Indians. *See* indigenous peoples
Indigenous peoples: and colonization, 47–48, 51–52; in Cuba, 123, 126, 170–171, 173; distinctions among, 48–49; forced conversion of, 42; and genocide, 102, 114, 132, 170, 171, 173, 188; lack of representation of, 6, 14; and land-grant policy, 43–44, 227n11; and racial categories, 258n44; and term "Indian," 227n9. *See also* Aztecs; Comanche; Mayas
Indigenous roots: and botanical knowledge, 110; and Chicano Movement, 39, 41, 49–50; claimed to mask blackness, 60–61, 173, 232n6, 256n31; and connection to nature, 155, 157; and magical realism, 141, 156, 174; La Malinche and, 103, 170, 261n11; "new mestiza" and, 39–40, 54; obscuring of, 40–47, 49–50, 53, 61, 189, 190, 228n12, 228n14, 228n1; as part of Latino hybridity, 10, 14, 31–33, 40, 139, 152, 188, 190, 227n5, 230n14; and spiritual beliefs, 17, 31, 40, 41–43, 44, 45, 47, 142–43, 152–53, 221n5, 227n8, 227n10, 249n18; as symbol of ethnicity 5, 165, 168, 169, 171, 173, 174, 227n8
Ink, Lynn Chun, 233n7, 233n8

James, Daniel Lewis, 223n18
Jewish Cubans, 93, 115–19, 121–22, 123–35, 237n18, 242n48, 245n65, 246n68, 246n69. *See also* Judaism
Jingwei, Wang Jingwei, 113
Johnson, David, 261n16
Johnson, Kelli Lyon, 233n7, 233n10, 234n12
Johnson, Kirk, 254n12
Jones-Correa, Michael, 8, 19, 20, 23, 26–29, 68, 69, 75, 76, 96–97, 217, 219, 222n15, 224n33, 224n33, 225n38, 225n39, 231n25, 254n13, 255n13, 264n3
Judaism, 117, 119, 120, 121, 124, 127, 242, 244; crypto-, 120, 125, 132, 244n62, 245n67, 246n68
Jussawalla, Feroza, 226n2, 227n10

Kandiyoti, Dalia, 75, 92, 196, 259n1, 259n6, 260n6, 260n8, 263n27, 263n28
Kanellos, Nicolás, 162
Kanoza, Theresa M., 40, 227n8
Kavanagh, James H., 250n32, 256n24
Kearns, Rick, 230n14
Kingsolver, Barbara, 139
Kleindienst, Kris, 181

Kristeva, Julia, 100
Kwong, Julia, 241n42

Lamadrid, Enrique, 226n5
Laó-Montes, Agustín, 18–19
Latin American identity, unified, 18–19, 76, 141, 228n14
Latin American migration. *See* immigration; *specific national origins*
Latina Feminist Group, 261n17
"Latino" and "Hispanic": as panethnic categories, 4, 7, 8–9, 20, 22, 27–28, 164–65, 196, 231n25, 264n3; structural inequalities and, 21, 29
Latino National Political Survey, 27, 264n3
Lattin, Vernon E., 227
League of United Latin American Citizens (LULAC), 4, 216
Leal, David L., 20, 23, 27–29, 68–69, 219, 224–25, 231, 264
Leonard, Suzanne, 256
Lesbianism. *See* gays and lesbians; queer politics
Levine, Robert M., 127, 242, 243, 244
Liberation theology, 150–54, 157, 204, 249, 262
Limón, Graciela *(In Search of Bernabé)*, 9
Llorona, 40, 227, 228
Logan, John R., 22, 225
Loomba, Ania, 257
López, Ian F. Haney, 63, 230n15, 231n18
López, Kimberle S., 256n27
López-Calvo, Ignacio, 82, 255n18
Loury, Glenn C., 229n6, 229n7
Luciano, Felipe, 52
Luis, William, 11–12, 52, 161, 221n2, 230n10, 256n27, 256n28
LULAC. *See* League of United Latin American Citizens
Lusane, Clarence, 108, 109, 235n7, 239n30, 239n31, 240n35, 240n36
Lux, Guillermo, 46, 47, 48, 228n16

Machado Sáez, Elena, 256n27
Madison, D. Soyini, 239n30
Masud-Piloto, Félix, 204, 236n10, 236n12, 243n54, 243n60, 262n21
Magical realism: and Julia Alvarez, 140, 247n4; attributed to Latino literature, 34, 140, 150, 247n5, 248n10; as commodity, 141, 157, 160; definition of, 144–45, 248n9; and environmental consciousness, 155, 156–57; and indigenous spirituality, 142, 156–57; and Latin American Boom, 140, 248n10, 248n16; and miracles, 146–47, 150, 153, 154, 157, 248n12, 248n13; in *Mother Tongue*, 210, 263n26; and resistance, 141, 143, 153; in *So Far From God*, 139, 144, 145–50, 153– 58, 160, 247n2, 247n3, 248n11, 248n13, 248n15; as threat to agency, 34; in writing of Margarita Engle, 168–69, 174
Maitino, John R., 226n1, 226n2
MALDEF. *See* Mexican American Legal Defense and Education Fund
Malinche, 103, 261n11
Manolis, Argie J., 204, 208, 261n12, 261n16, 262n22
Manríquez, B. J., 247n3, 250n31
Marable, Manning, 107, 240n32
Mariel boatlift of 1980, 96–100, 126, 194, 236n12, 236n13; Marielitos, 100, 236n10
Marrero, María Teresa, 236n13
Martí, José, 14, 18, 98, 102, 106, 125, 133, 134, 188, 239n27, 240n34, 260n7
Martin, Elizabeth, 4
Martínez, Demetria *(Mother Tongue)*, 34, 195–212, 261n16
Martínez, Elizabeth, 260n10
Marx, Karl, 250n32
Mas Canosa, Jorge, 167
Mayas, 44, 48, 199
McCracken, Ellen, 10, 140, 141, 158, 247n8, 255n17, 256n27, 256n28, 261n16
McCullough, Kate, 94, 181, 182, 186, 192, 198, 200, 256n31, 257n33, 257n36, 257n37, 257n39, 260n9
McKenna, Teresa, 49
Menéndez, Ana, 34, 167, 174, 191, 234n2; "In Cuba I Was a German Shepherd," 191–195
Menozzi, Paulo, 55
Mestizaje, 237n18; Cuban, 100, 103, 107–9, 125, 170, 171; in Latin America, 14, 18, 102, 228n14; Mexican and Chicano, 39, 41, 43–48, 103, 170, 188, 226n5, 239n29; and mulattoes, 84, 97, 103; and "new *mestiza*," 39–40, 54; and Spanish inquisition, 120; as symbol of Latino identity, 194. *See also* hybridity; syncretism
Mexican American Legal Defense and Education Fund (MALDEF), 216

Mexican Americans: and African Americans, 228n3; and assimilation, 40; and Aztlán, 5, 170–71; and census, 221n4, 222n10, 252n8; farmworkers, 31, 173, 222n7, 226n4; and indigenous roots, 14, 17, 31, 39, 41–50, 54, 103, 139, 143, 157, 169, 170, 188–90, 226n5, 228n12, 228n1, 261n11; and INS, 8; organizations of, 216; and panethnic category, 4, 6–10, 12–17, 19, 23, 25–26, 28, 30–32, 68, 142–43, 148–49, 158, 162–65, 168, 175–76, 187–88, 193, 197–99, 203, 205–6, 214–16, 218, 221n1, 224n33, 258n41, 259n1, 259n6, 264n3; politics of, 163–64, 253n9, 254n12, 255n16, 264n3; and Puerto Ricans, 5–6, 15–16, 33, 51–53, 68, 142–43, 162–65, 213, 215–16, 222n6, 223n15, 223n16, 230n12, 258n41; and romanticized image, 154, 157; and Spanish-speaking ability, 207, 224n26; in Texas, 235n8, 254n12; and transnational ties, 232n2. *See also individual authors; Chicano/a literature; Chicano Movement; New Mexicans*

Mexicans: and free trade, 224n31; and Sanctuary movement, 262n18; and term "North American," 260n7; and U.S. colonizing efforts, 51–52

Michaels, Walter Benn, 229n5, 231n20

Miller, Kate, 248n12

Milligan, Bryce, 207–08 252n3

Milligan, Mary Guerrero, 208

Mitchell, David, 81, 94, 256n27

Mohr, Eugene V., 230n10, 231n19, 231n22

Monroe Doctrine, 18

Moore, Robin, 108, 240n33

Moraga, Cherríe, 184; *Loving in the War Years*, 184; *This Bridge Called My Back*, 185

Morales, Ed, 221n5, 224n24

Morejón, Nancy, 107, 239n28, 239n29

Morrison, Toni: *Beloved*, 145; *Tar Baby*, 73

Mosher, W. D., 17

Mothers of the Disappeared, 158, 205, 210, 211, 249n17, 262n23

Mujčinović, Fatima, 11, 161, 198, 256n27

Muñoz, Elías Miguel, 34, 167; *The Greatest Performance*, 174, 176, 177, 180, 187

NAFTA. *See* North American Free Trade Agreement

National identity, 94, 102, 106, 128, 194, 135; Chinese, construction of, 111–12; Cuban, based on contrast, 128–29, 134, 244n62; Cuban, fantasies of, 114, 171; Cuban, as hybrid, 102, 106–9, 125, 239n29, 239n31, 240n32; Cuban, and Jewishness, 123, 126; Cuban, narration of by exiles, 34, 93, 95, 97, 99, 104, 134–35, 235n4; Cuban, as Spanish and Catholic, 117; Dominican, construction of, 33, 81–85, 233n11; in *Down these Mean Streets*, 59; of Latin American countries, 20, 103, 128; in *Memory Mambo*, 184, 257n36; and narratives of past, 237n20; U.S., 108, 111, 240n32

National Campaign to Prevent Teen Pregnancy (NCPTP), 7

National Council of La Raza, 4, 254n12

National Immigration Forum, 224n27, 253n11

National Survey of Latinos: 2002, 5, 27, 225n37; 2004, 5, 15, 96, 164, 166, 224n37, 252n7, 253n11

NCPTP. *See* National Campaign to Prevent Teen Pregnancy

Neill, Anna, 261n13, 261n14

Neocolonialism, 128

New Mexicans, 16, 31, 41–46, 141–43, 148–49, 158, 190, 226n4, 228n15, 250n28

Newkirk, Glen A., 227n10

Nicholas, J. D., 236n11

Nixon, Richard, 53

North American Free Trade Agreement (NAFTA), 19

Nostalgia, 94, 95, 97, 98, 99, 130, 131, 134, 150, 192, 194, 226n3, 234n2

Nuyorican literature. *See* Puerto Rican (mainland) literature

Nuyoricans. *See* Puerto Ricans

Obejas, Achy, 34, 93, 167; *Days of Awe*, 25, 33, 95, 99, 100, 115, 116–135, 195, 239n30, 242n50, 242n52, 243n55, 243n59, 244n62, 244n63, 245n65, 246n68, 246n69; *Memory Mambo*, 11, 25, 179, 180–86, 198, 200, 203, 237n19, 246n69, 256n31, 259n4; *We Came All The Way from Cuba So You Could Dress Like This?*, 25, 179–80

Oboler, Suzanne, 1, 2, 3, 5, 7, 13, 15, 18, 19, 46, 196, 221n3, 222n5, 222n7, 224n30, 224n32

Olmos, Margarite Fernández, 256n23

Olson, James, 97, 234n3, 235n7, 236n10, 236n12, 236n13

Olson, Judith, 97, 234n3, 235n7, 236n10, 236n12, 236n13

Ortiz Cofer, Judith, 9; *The Latin Deli*, 25

Ortiz, Fernando, 102, 106, 164, 238n21, 238n24, 238n25, 239n29
Otto, Whitney, 186

Padilla, Felix M., 4, 15, 21, 33, 68, 149, 164, 213, 215, 218, 221n1, 222n6, 224n26, 231n24, 258n41
Padilla, Genaro M., 39
Páez, Mariela M., 6, 13, 16, 17, 18, 19, 20, 21, 22, 91, 224n30
Panethnicity, instrumental argument for, 20–23, 27, 29, 50, 68, 134, 164, 169, 217, 219. *See also under* Cuban Americans; Dominican Americans; "Latino" and "Hispanic"; Mexican Americans; Puerto Ricans
Paravisini-Gebert, Lizabeth, 256n23
Parr, Carmen Salazar, 227n7
Payant, Katherine B., 256n27
Peck, David R., 226n1, 226n2
Pedraza-Bailey, Sylvia, 257n35
Pérez Firmat, Gustavo, 9–10, 106, 140, 162–63, 238n25, 247n4; *Cincuenta lecciones de exilio y desexilio*, 10; *Life on the Hyphen*, 106, 238; *Tongue Ties*, 140
Pérez, Gail, 141, 249, 250
Pérez, Hebert, 106–7, 140, 163, 238, 239, 240, 247, 249, 250
Pérez, Lisandro, 95
Pérez, Louis A., 128, 129, 134, 224, 237, 240
Perna, Santiago Rey, 99
Pew Hispanic Center, 5, 15, 27, 96, 163, 166, 222n14, 224n26, 225n37, 235n8, 252n7, 252n9, 253n11, 254n12
Piedra, José, 14, 223n22
Pineda, Cecile (*The Love Queen of the Amazon*), 9
Pita, Beatrice, 223n21
Platt, Kamala, 147–48, 154, 247n1, 248n13, 249n23, 250n29
Poey, Delia, 140, 150, 174, 207, 226n1, 249n16, 263n25
Policy debates, over immigration, 166
Polk, James, 139, 247n2, 248n9
Porsche, Michael, 247n3
Portes, Alejandro, 97
Prohias, R. J., 236n11
Puerto Rican (mainland) literature: and African roots, 52; and Chicano literature, 33, 53, 251n2; and panethnic category, 9, 10, 12, 25, 53, 222n6, 223n20, 251n2
Puerto Ricans: and African Americans, 9, 51, 53, 57, 59–63, 223n16, 228n1, 230n12, 231n17; and census, 221n4, 252n8; and citizenship, 8, 12, 51, 59, 88, 181, 215, 222n15; *independentistas*, 180, 183, 257n33; and Mexican Americans, 5–6, 15–17, 33, 51–53, 67–68, 142–43, 162, 164, 165, 213, 216, 222n6, 258n4; and national identity, 58–59, 184; and panethnic category, 3–4, 6–9, 11–12, 15–17, 23–27, 29, 31, 88, 142–43, 162–64, 165, 175, 177, 178, 180–85, 187, 188, 205, 215–18, 222n6, 222n15, 256n32, 257n33, 258n41, 264n3; politics of, 163–64, 183–84, 253n9, 264n3; and race, 9, 47, 52, 57, 59–67, 181, 182, 188, 228n1, 230n11, 230n14, 230n15, 231n17; and transnational ties, 17. *See also* Puerto Rican (mainland) literature; Thomas, Piri
Pulido, Laura, 148, 250n28

Queer politics, 180, 183, 184
Quintana, Alvina E., 10, 11, 161

Race: blackness and Haitians, 85; blackness and national identities, 58; blackness and Puerto Ricans in *Down These Mean Streets*, 53, 57–58, 61–62, 66–67, 233n6; claims of whiteness by Cubans and Cuban Americans, 97, 102, 106, 107, 115, 173, 234n3, 235n4, 235n8, 236n9; claims of whiteness by Dominicans, 83, 85; claims of whiteness by Puerto Ricans in *Down These Mean Streets*, 60, 231n21; claims of whiteness by Mexican Americans, 41, 189, 228n15; Cuban associations with blackness, 107, 173, 240n33, 256n31; differences in race among Latinos, 6–9, 13, 14, 31, 47, 52–53, 75, 188–90, 222n14, 228n3; essentialist understandings of race, 52, 54–55, 57, 58, 60, 61–64, 67, 69, 229n4, 229n5, 231n21; male privilege vs. race, 228n2; nationality and race, 58–59, 108, 184, 222n14, 229n8, 230n11, 239n29, 240n32, 240n33; one-drop rule in U.S., 238n26; perceived similarities of race among Latinos, 87, 187–89, 223n22, 224n24, 231n24, 260n8; race-blindness, 229n6, 229n7, 240n35; race as social construct, 14, 54–57, 60–65, 67, 188–90, 229n5, 231n18, 231n19, 231n20, 231n21; race in *Who Would Have Thought It?*, 223n21; racial categories, 22, 54–55, 64, 65, 188, 225n36, 229n6, 235n7, 236n12, 237n18, 258n44; racial

Race—continued
  consciousness, 65, 109, 240n35, 240n36; racial hybridity, 11, 13, 52, 54, 55, 97, 102–4, 106–9, 125, 170, 186, 224n24, 238n26, 239n29, 239n31, 240n32, 240n33; racialization, 8, 16, 22, 23, 51, 54, 57, 59, 126, 162, 165, 240n36, 257n34; racial privilege, 54, 59, 60, 61, 65–67, 230n10, 231n17; racial problems, 117, 186, 237n15, 240n36, 243n52; racial separatism, 108–9, 240n34; racism against Jews, 129; racism and Jewish immigration in Latin America, 116, 242n46; racism toward Latinos, 166, 218, 230n12; resolution of racial issues in *Down These Mean Streets*, 231n22; sexualization and race, 110; spatial component to race, 230n15; transracial identities, 32–34, 53, 228n3; U.S. associations with blackness, 107–8; whiteness and "American" national identity, 59, 201, 240n32. *See also* Cubans: and race; Dominicans: and Haitians; hybridity; indigenous roots; mestizaje; syncretism
Ramos-Zayas, Ana Y., 2, 5, 8, 12, 15, 22, 27, 51, 52, 53, 59, 68, 69, 165, 215, 223n15, 223n16, 228n1
Ranger, Terence, 258n46
Rebolledo, Tey Diana, 13
Reca, Inéz, 240
Religion: in *Bless Me, Ultima*, 41–43; in *Days of Awe*, 120, 124–25, 130, 132, 244n62; in *Down These Mean Streets*, 231n22; in *In the Time of the Butterflies*, 82; in *Monkey Hunting*, 106; in *Mother Tongue*, 204, 206, 262n22; in *So Far from God*, 147, 151–52, 157, 160, 248n13, 250n30, 251n34; in writings of Gloria Anzaldúa, 173; in writings of Margarita Engle, 172; in writings of Sandra Cisneros, 173. *See also* Catholicism; Christianity; Judaism; indigenous roots: and spiritual beliefs; Liberation theology; Sanctuary movement; Santería; Voudou
Renan, Ernest, 194
Rendón, Armando B., 46
Requena, Gisele, M., 255n21, 256n21
Riazza, Alberto, 55
Rich, Adrienne, 185
Ricourt, Milagros, 217
Risech, Flavio, 98
Rivera, Tomás *(Y no se lo tragó la tierra)*, 173, 255n21

Rivera-Valdés, Sonia *(The Forbidden Stories of Marta Veneranda)*, 25
Rivero, Eliana, 12, 13, 222n6, 223n20, 251n2, 253n10
Rivero, José, 244n61
Rodríguez, Clara E., 22, 230n11
Rodriguez, David, 213–15, 264n2
Rodriguez, Luis, 204
Rodriguez, Ralph E., 155, 247n1
Rodriguez, Richard, 223n17, 255n16; *Hunger of Memory*, 252n3
Rodríguez de Laguna, Asela, 230n10
Rodriguez-Morazzani, Roberto P., 59, 61, 223n16, 230n11, 230n12
Rogers, Jane, 227n8
Roosevelt Corollary, 18
Ruiz de Burton, María Amparo *(Who Would Have Thought It)*, 223n21
Rumbaut, Rubén G., 3, 75, 222n10, 224n26, 232n2
Rushdie, Salman, 94

Saeta, Elsa, 147, 160, 251
Safa, Helen I., 107–09, 238n26, 239n30, 240n31
Sagás, Ernesto, 81, 82, 232n6, 233n6, 255n18
Said, Edward, 247n8
Saldívar, Ramón, 161, 226n3, 227n8, 228n15, 251n1
Sánchez, George J., 10, 103, 110, 186, 228n2
Sánchez, Marta E., 54, 64, 66, 103, 186, 228n2, 230n10, 230n13, 231n19
Sánchez, Rosaura, 223n21
Sanctuary movement, 202, 203, 204, 211, 212, 213, 214, 260n8, 262n18, 262n20, 263n31
Sandoval, Alberto, 161
Sandoval, Chela, 264n32
Santería, 30, 100, 106, 120, 124, 125, 142, 143, 172, 173, 236n13, 237n13, 238n23
Santiago, Esmeralda, 9; *When I Was Puerto Rican*, 247n5
Sapir, Boris, 243n53
Sarduy, Pedro Pérez, 95
Schermerhorn, Richard A., 3, 21
Schmidt, Ronald J., 216
Scott, Janny, 24
Shaw, Donald L., 249n16
Shemak, April, 233n7
Shorris, Earl, 1, 6, 13, 46, 216
Sierra, Christine Marie, 216
Simon, Bruce, 104, 200, 238n22

Socolovsky, Maya, 242n52, 244n62, 245n67, 246n68, 256n27
Sollors, Werner, 3, 30, 31, 35, 132, 209, 210, 223n18, 225n40, 225n41, 226n43, 258n46
Sommer, Doris, 103, 111, 260n9
South Americans: and census, 221n4; and Jewishness, 242n47; and panethnic category "Latino," 2, 6, 12, 215; and politics, 168
Spanish, as common language, 9, 14–15, 24–25, 26, 34, 63, 75, 163–64, 194, 224n25, 224n27; differences among Latino groups, 2, 16–17, 143; as "foreign," 11, 29; and mobilization of Latinos, 68; in *Mother Tongue*, 206–9; and outsider perceptions, 3–4, 175; and Spanish-language media, 23; and symbolic value, 224n26
Spanish colonialism, 19, 42, 44, 46, 47, 48, 60, 63, 139, 143, 163, 169–72, 194
Spanish heritage: on census, 221n4; as common culture, 68–69; of Cubans, 97, 101, 102–7, 109, 111, 117, 120, 125, 127–30, 239n28; of Dominicans, 81; of Mexican Americans, 40–44, 46–48, 189, 227n5, 248n14; of Puerto Ricans, 57
Special Period, Cuban, 101, 129, 132, 240n36, 245n66
Spitta, Silvia, 238n21
Spivak, Gayatri, 54, 73
S.S. *St. Louis*, 243n54
Stavans, Ilan, 75, 162, 223n18, 224n25, 257n34; *The Hispanic Condition*, 221n5, 252n4, 252n6
Stefanko, Jacqueline, 256n27
Stepick, Alex, 97, 216, 257n35, 264n4
Stepick, Carol Dutton, 257n35
Stevenson, James M., 237n14
Stokes, Mason, 231n16
Strategic essentialism, 54, 67, 188
Stubbs, Jean, 95
Suárez, Lucía M., 16, 17, 18, 20, 21, 22, 91, 232n5, 233n7, 233n11
Suárez, Virgil, 174, 207, 263n25
Suárez-Orozco, Marcelo M., 6, 13, 16–18, 20–22, 91, 224n30
Subramanian, Sribala, 55
Sugg, Katherine, 24
Suro, Roberto, 5, 15, 20, 166, 253n11, 254n12
Symbolic elements of peoplehood, 3, 5, 21, 184, 189
Syncretism, 14, 17, 31, 42, 43, 97, 106, 120, 142, 143, 172, 221n5, 226n5, 238n23

Tabuenca Córdoba, María Socorro, 197, 198, 199, 211, 259n5, 261n11, 261n15
Tafoya, Sonya, 96, 222n14, 235n8
Taínos, 5, 170, 171. *See also* indigenous peoples
Taylor, Paul Beekman, 227n5, 227n8
Telemundo, 23, 176
Testimonio, 202, 203, 260n6, 261n17
Thomas, Piri, 9, 232n6, 256n31; *Down These Mean Streets*, 32, 33, 51, 52, 53, 54, 55, 57, 59, 61, 63, 65, 67, 69, 173, 228n2, 230n10, 231n23, 233n6
Thornton, Lawrence (*Imagining Argentina*), 263n26
Tobar, Héctor (*The Tattooed Soldier*), 25
Todorov, Tzvetan, 229n5
Tonn, Horst, 226n4
Toribio, A. J., 233n9
Torres, Lourdes, 184–85
Torres, María de los Angeles, 94, 96–97, 99, 235n5
Torres, Rodolfo D., 54
Torres-Saillant, Silvio, 6, 23, 76, 176, 208, 224n30
Toyosato, Mayumi, 155, 250n30
Transnationalism, 32, 34; in Cuba, 100, 118, 121; in *Days of Awe*, 130–31; and exile, 94; Haitian-Dominican, 81; in Havana, 127; and hybridity, 104; and migration, 105, 109, 121; in *Mother Tongue*, 196; and panethnic *latinidad*, 19, 218; and solidarity, 214, 218; and Spanish language, 207–8; and ties to country of origin, 33, 74–76, 81, 90, 91; and transnational behaviors, 17, 232n2
Tregian, Francis, 58
Trinh T. Minh-ha, 74, 77
Trueba, Enrique (Henry) T., 221n5
Trujillo, Carla, 184
Trujillo, Rafael Leónidas, 74, 78, 81, 82, 83, 166, 233n6, 233n7, 233n11, 255n14, 255n18

United States: dominant culture, 22, 139, 188, 189, 191, 192, 199, 253n10; domination of Latin America, 18, 19, 176; immigration policy, and Latino views, 166, 253n11, 262n20; immigration policy for Cubans, 215, 234n3, 243n54; imperialism, 129, 162; intervention, 19–20, 165; political asylum policy, 259n3
United States Census, 2–4, 8, 22, 29, 97, 221n4, 222n10, 225n36, 235n7, 239n31, 252n8

United States Citizenship and Immigration Services, 8, 201, 236n12, 259n3

United States Department of Health and Human Services, 8, 222n11, 222n14, 252n8

Umbilical cord, as metaphor, 75, 140, 206, 207, 208

Univisión, 23, 176

Urban centers, as cultural contact zones, 23–27, 105; Chicago, Cubans in, 25; Chicago, Mexicans in, 221n1; Chicago, Mexican, and Puerto Rican interaction in, 5–6, 15, 33, 51, 149, 213, 215, 222n6; Chicago, and pan-Latino solidarity, 23, 27, 231n24; Chicago, Puerto Ricans and African Americans in, 228n1; Havana, 105, 126–28, 234n1; and hybridity, 114, 115, 128; Los Angeles, 23–26; Miami, 23, 216; New York,16, 23–27, 105, 115, 217, 222n15; Shanghai, 105, 111, 113

Valdes-Rodriguez, Alisa, 34, 93, 167; *The Dirty Girls Social Club*, 93, 186–192, 211

Vallejos, Thomas, 226n5

Vargas Llosa, Mario (*The Feast of the Goat*), 255n18

Vásquez, Mary S., 168, 169, 171, 256n22, 256n27

Vega, Bernardo, 233n11

Velasco, Juan, 261n13

Verstegan, Richard, 58

Viera, Joseph M., 256n27, 256n29

Vietnam War, 104, 108, 111, 115, 142, 242n44, 263n27

Vigil, Maurilio E., 43, 46, 47, 48, 228n16

Villarreal, José Antonio, *Pocho*, 40

Virgen de Guadalupe, 5, 17, 31, 156, 243n59

Vodou, 172; "Voodoo," 81, 84–85, 124, 172–73

Wald, David, 264n1

Wald, Gayle, 56, 57

Walsh, Sean Patrick, 248n12

Walter, Roland, 247n3, 248n13

Weber, Max, 3, 223n23, 244n64

Weiss, Frederick A., 228n16

Winn, Peter, 81, 82

*Works and Days* (journal), 161

Wucker, Michele, 82, 83, 84

Wyatt, Jean, 24, 26–27, 76–77 200, 247n6

Yarbro-Bejarano, Yarbro, 199

Young Lords Party, 52, 53

Young, Robert, 52, 53

Zentella, Ana Celia, 16, 24, 84, 233n9

Zimmerman, Marc, 251n2

Zubiaurre, Maite, 256n28

Marta Caminero-Santangelo is an associate professor of English at the University of Kansas, where she teaches courses in U.S. Latina/o literature. She is the author of *The Madwoman Can't Speak: Or Why Insanity Is Not Subversive* (1998), as well as of several articles on U.S. Latina/o authors. She is also on the steering committee of Emergency Network of Cuban-American Scholars and Artists for a Change in U.S.-Cuba Policy.

www.ingramcontent.com/pod-product-compliance
Lightning Source LLC
Chambersburg PA
CBHW020943230426
43666CB00005B/137